D1247736

Charon
and the Crossing

Charon and the Crossing

Ancient, Medieval, and Renaissance Transformations of a Myth

Ronnie H. Terpening

Lewisburg
Bucknell University Press
London and Toronto: Associated University Presses

© 1985 by Associated University Presses, Inc.

Associated University Presses
440 Forsgate Drive
Cranbury, NJ 08512

Associated University Presses
25 Sicilian Avenue
London WC1A 2QH, England

Associated University Presses
2133 Royal Windsor Drive
Unit 1
Mississauga, Ontario
Canada L5J 1K5

Library of Congress Cataloging in Publication Data

Terpening, Ronnie H., 1946–
   Charon and the crossing.

   Bibliography: p.
   Includes index.
   1. Italian literature—History and criticism.
2. Classical literature—History and criticism.
3. Dante Alighieri, 1265–1321—Criticism and
interpretation. 4. Charon (Greek mythology) in
literature. I. Title.
PQ4053.C47T47 1984   850'.9'351   82-74492
ISBN 0-8387-5061-3

Printed in the United States of America

Contents

Preface

The initial impetus for this study was provided by Emmanuel Hatzantonis of the University of Oregon, at whose suggestion I began compiling a bibliography of Charon references while in Pavia, Italy in 1967. I am grateful to him for first bringing to my attention the possibility of studying the figure of the infernal boatman and for providing references I might otherwise have missed. I am also indebted to Louise George Clubb of the University of California at Berkeley for her critical comments, both in relation to the structure of the study and its style. In turn, Thomas G. Rosenmeyer provided bibliographical references and corrections of detail for the classical material, while Nicolas J. Perella offered suggestions and bibliography for the Italian material.

Others who have provided guidance, directly or indirectly over the years, include Perry J. Powers, Thomas R. Hart, Frederick M. Combellack, and Chandler B. Beall of the University of Oregon, Ruggero Stefanini, the late Arnolfo B. Ferruolo, Gustavo Costa, Gavriel Moses, and Donald J. Mastronarde of the University of California at Berkeley, John Tedeschi of the Newberry Library, Cecil Grayson of Oxford University, and Valeria Laube and Edwin P. Menes of Loyola University of Chicago. For stylistic improvements, thanks must also be extended to my copy editor, M. Buckingham.

Advanced research on this book was aided by two grants, one from the Renaissance Society of America to attend their Summer Workshop in Paleography and Methods of Archival and Manuscript Research in Florence, the other from the Mabelle McLeod Lewis Memorial Fund, Stanford. I am especially grateful to the trustees of the fund for their generosity.

Finally, let me thank my wife Vicki to whom this book is dedicated for her patience and support.

Acknowledgments

Selections from Euripides, *Alcestis* and *Herakles*, from *The Complete Greek Tragedies*, translated by David Grene and Richmond Lattimore, are reprinted by permission of The University of Chicago Press. Copyright 1955, 1956, by The University of Chicago.

Selections from *The Iliad of Homer*, translated by Richmond Lattimore, are reprinted by permission of The University of Chicago Press. Copyright 1951 by The University of Chicago.

Selections from *The Works of Lucian of Samosata*, translated by H. W. Fowler and F. G. Fowler, are reprinted by permission of Oxford University Press.

Selections from Dante Alighieri, *The Divine Comedy*, vol. 1 *Inferno* and vol. 2 *Purgatorio*, translated by Charles Singleton, are reprinted by permission of Princeton University Press. Copyright 1970 and 1973 by Princeton University Press.

Selections from "Petrarch's *Bucolicum Carmen* I: *Parthenias*," translated by Thomas G. Bergin, in *Petrarch to Pirandello: Studies in Italian Literature in Honor of Beatrice Corrigan*, edited by Julius A. Molinaro, are reprinted by permission of the University of Toronto Press. Copyright 1973 by the University of Toronto Press.

Selections from Petrarch's *Africa*, translated by Thomas G. Bergin and Alice S. Wilson, are reprinted by permission of Yale University Press.

All translations from Loeb Library editions—Homer, *The Odyssey*, translated by A. T. Murray; Aeschylus, translated by Herbert Weir Smyth; *The Greek Anthology*, translated by W. R. Paton; Lucian, translated by A. M. Harmon (vols. 1–6) and M. D. MacLeod (vols. 7–8); Lucan, translated by J. D. Duff; Seneca, *Tragedies*, translated by Frank Justus Miller; and Virgil, translated by H. Rushton Fairclough—have been determined by Harvard University Press to fall under the heading of "fair use." Grateful acknowledgment, nevertheless, is extended to the press for use of the texts cited.

Grateful acknowledgment is also extended to the following for use of illustrations: Fratelli Alinari; the Ashmolean Museum, Oxford; University of Chicago Department of Special Collections, Joseph Regenstein Library; Photographie Giraudon; Photo Marburg; The Metropolitan Museum of Art; the National Archaeological Museum, Athens; the Centre National de la Recherche Scientifique; and the Rhode Island School of Design, Museum of Art.

Introduction

My intention in the present study is to trace the development and analyze the transformations of the infernal boatman Charon from the earliest recorded references to him in classical antiquity to his later appearances in Italian literature from Dante through the mid-seventeenth century. The purpose is to provide not only a comprehensive history of a literary convention—in this instance the underworld crossing, a mythological episode of significance to writers from Homer to Marino and beyond—but also to examine the modifications undergone by the ferryman as his role is adapted to new forms or expanded in traditional stories.

Despite the fact that I deal with a variety of genres and use form as an organizational principle, this work is not a study in genre theory. Where appropriate, however, I have touched on the problem of literary form as it affects the depiction of Charon. As we might expect, the requirements of genre do result in transformation, but genre is only one of many forces at work on tradition.

My method of analysis is based on a limited structural view of texts. That is, I find aesthetic interest not so much in the structure of the descent myth itself as in variations in basic structure. The encounter with Charon is an aspect of many mythic descents, including those of Theseus, Peirithoos, Herakles, Dionysos, Alcestis, Orpheus, Persephone, Psyche, and Aeneas. From the standpoint of this study, my concern is less with an archetypal descent myth than with the aesthetic restructuring that shapes the original model into varied narrative forms.

To facilitate reference and analysis, let me point out a basic structure corresponding to the topos "the descent to the underworld." Its initial aspect, the descent and encounter with Charon, is most simply expressed through eight basic narrative units. These units, reconstructed from a variety of sources but most notably from Virgil's *Aeneid*, are by no means all employed by the majority of writers discussed in this study. Rather, from the units available in the basic myth, an author chooses and develops those items of interest. In my discussions, I will refer to the following units:

1. *The hero, heroine, or dead soul descends to the underworld proper.* The variables include not only the location of entrances to the lower world and the method of descent but also the motive of the descender. Among the reasons given are the desire to rescue a friend or liberate a spouse, the necessity of acquiring an infernal object, and the purpose of gaining knowledge from the deceased. The dead soul, of course, descends of necessity.

2. *The descender arrives at a barrier.* In medieval legend, this is often a bridge. For the purposes of this study, however, the only barrier of interest is an infernal river or swamp without a bridge, an obstacle varying in name and description. The obstacle's essential nature is limitation and confinement. It keeps some within and holds others outside the realm.

3. *The boatman appears.* Charon enters the scene, functioning most often as both a guardian and a ferryman of Hades. He may be depicted in action, either physical or verbal, or merely described in terms of his appearance and duties.

4. *The boatman addresses the descender.* The ferryman's discourse may entail interrogation and threats, vain blusterings, or benevolent offers of aid.

5. *The descender responds.* The person desiring to cross may explain timidly the purpose of his or her visit or may create a disturbance by threatening to use physical force. Often the descender displays a magical object or employs a supernatural power to aid his or her progress. The dead soul, on the other hand, may chatter inanely or reason with shrewdness and wit.

6. *The descender boards the ferry.* To obtain passage, one must often have fulfilled some prerequisite. For the dead, proper funeral rites are a necessity as is paying the fare. Lacking the prerequisite results in either a delay or a conflict with the ferryman.

7. *The barrier is crossed.* This unit occasionally entails a description of the ferry or the water barrier. A variety of physical means are employed to move the boat, from oars, to sails, to poles, or to magical means. The ferryman may require his passengers to aid in rowing. In certain forms, such as prose dialogues, this unit is of major importance, since it provides the opportunity for extended discourse.

8. *The passengers disembark at the far side.* Prior to landing, the ferryman often collects his fee. Following this, the descenders take leave of the boatman, who returns for a new load.

The subjects of units 4 and 5, I should note, may be reversed, since either figure, boatman or descender, may initiate the verbal encounter.

In examining these units and their variable features, I will analyze in what way different authors develop particular units. The factors affecting innovation are well known and many. In his study *The Ulysses Theme*, W. B. Stanford has referred to some of these factors, such as the question of individuality (following or rebelling against tradition), the desire for novelty, varied approaches to traditional material, the attempt to assimilate the past to the present, the author's technical intentions and personal reactions, and the requirements of genre (pp. 3–6).

The last factor, genre, is one of the more intersting ones, raising a variety of questions, some with answers more obvious than others. For example, we might ask if different genres require the development of particular units to the exclusion of others. When different genres treat the same unit, do they do so in a different fashion? If so, for what reasons? Or to change the focus, what are Charon's possibilities within the various genres? What are his comic features, for example? His functions in epic or lyric? In what ways do later poets transform tradition by borrowing features from unrelated forms? For example, in the Renaissance, how does the assimilation of Charon's comic traits affect the epic genre? These are some of the questions that arise, and, where possible, I have tried to discuss them; again let me repeat, I have not done so to develop a theory of genre.

An analysis of which units are treated and in what manner gives a general idea of the author's relationship to both previous material and his own time. It is these two forces, a synchronic one consisting of the writer's immediate environment (i.e., Lucian in a period of prevailing skepticism) and a diachronic one consisting of literary tradition (i.e., Lucian's use of myth), that determine in part variations from text to text. Since the basic units of the myth remain constant (whether or not all or a selected few appear), the subject of study becomes what has been called the local texture, features grouped around each unit as they vary from author to author and work to work.

Before approaching the representations of Charon in classical literature, I would like to refer briefly to the world-wide cultural significance of an afterlife boatman. The concept of a ferryman of the dead has been studied in a variety of cultures, both Eastern and Western. Comparative mythologists in the late nineteenth century found evidence of this concept throughout the world, in ancient and modern times. In the Far East, for example, there are stories of men visiting the realm of the dead where river barriers have to be faced.[1] And just as the ancient Vedic Yama, King of the Dead, crossed the rapid waters to the beyond, so, too, the modern Hindu hopes to be safely ferried over the dreadful Vaitaranî.[2] In the Near East, where Sumerian, Akhadian, Hittite, and Canaanite myths all narrate attempts to retrieve fertility deities from the underworld,[3] the ancient Babylonian legend of Gilgamesh, found on tablets from Ashurbanipal's library at Nineveh (seventh century B.C) and dating at least to the twentieth century and probably back to the Sumerian or pre-Semitic period of Babylonian myth, relates the voyage of Gilgamesh across the waters of death, guided by an ancient mariner Arad-ea.[4]

Such Babylonian harrowers of hell as Bel and Marduk, who descend to the abode of the dead beyond the setting sun in order to fight the sea monster Tiamat,[5] parallel such Assyrian descenders as the goddess Ishtar. In The Descent to the Underworld of Ishtar, a legend of Sumerian origin dating back to at least 2000 B.C. and preserved nearly complete in a Semitic version found on seventh-century tablets at Nineveh and Ashur, the goddess descends to the land of darkness, passing through several portals in order to find the waters of life.[6] Another Assyrian hero, Gisdubar, is conveyed to the regions of the dead by a ferry on his voyage to seek counsel from the shades of his ancestors.[7] In Egypt, equally ancient traditions tell of a celestial boatman who transports the souls of the dead across the sky-lake of Kha to the god Ra at the western side.[8] At the same time, primitive Aryan lore, according to one mythologist, tells of cloud-ships, one of which was supposed to be Charon's boat, crossing the sky.[9] A later Egyptian tale about Setme Khamuas, son of Rameses II (1292–1225 B.C.), relates how Setme and his son Si-Osiri descended to the underworld, a realm in the extreme west on the far side of the sea.[10] A Cyprian custom, borrowed from Egypt, entailed burying terra-cotta ships beside dead princes for the voyage to the beyond.[11]

The Charun of the Etruscans, a monster similar to demons in Chaldean civilization, or to Siva and Kali in India, is an Italic divinity, whose name appears to have come from Greeks who were in commercial contact with Etruria as early as the seventh century.[12] Initially quite distinct from the well-known Greek boatman, Charun is most often pictured as a winged demon with a hammer or mallet, although he occasionally acquires an oar despite the fact that it is extraneous to his Etruscan character and duties. More characteristically, Charun is an observer of violent death, a messenger of destiny as it were, or a demon who separates the

Charun and Ajax's slaughter of Trojan prisoners. Etruscan crater. Cabinet des Médailles 920, Bibliothèque Nationale, Paris. By permission of Photographie Giraudon (8150).

defunct from her/his family and leads the dead to the infernal regions. In general, Charun is an implacable monster, a cruel, sinister death-demon with a black beard, long hooked nose, big lips, snaky hair, and pointed animal ears. The Etruscan figure fulfills not only the duties of the Hellenistic psychopompos but is comparable as well to the Greek Thanatos, the Erinyes, and the Keres.[13] Charun's later Byzantine and modern Greek counterparts are equally versatile.

In other cultures, we find a bridge instead of a ferryman. The crossing in the Persian *Zend-Avesta* becomes the narrow Chinvat Bridge, where good and evil spirits struggle for souls;[14] Hebrew exiles introduced to the elaborate eschatology of the Zoroastrian religion passed on the idea through their apocryphal books to the chivalric romances and Christian visions of the Middle Ages.[15] In Irish visions, as guardians of bridges, dragons appear "with eyes like coals of fire," a feature reminiscent of Charon's inflamed eyes. One of these great beasts, found in the medieval vision of Tundal, is even called Acheron.[16]

But Irish literature does not restrict itself to the bridge crossing: One of the most famous voyages to the realm of the afterlife is the eighth-century *Voyage of Bran*, which takes place by sea.[17] For the Byzantine historian Procopius, Britain (Brittia) itself was an island of the dead, and the Celts ferried invisible but weighty souls in magic boats (*The Gothic War* 4. 20).[18] In the great Finnish epic *Kalewala*, the hero Wainamoinen is ferried to the island of Tuoni, the god of death, by the god's daughter Manala.[19] Disembodied souls pass the river Gjöll in the story of Balder in the *Prose Edda* (ca. A.D. 1230),[20] and Norse mythology also depicts a Charon-figure in Loki, the son of Farbanti.[21] The heroic legends of Denmark, furthermore, also present a death journey by ship.[22]

Other cultures, separate in time and space, have their Charon-figures and afterlife voyages; the voyages, whether containing a ferryman or a bridge, quite often depict some type of water barrier. Comparative anthropologists refer to an almost dismaying array of myths. For the Taïta, a tribe in eastern Africa, the final resting place of the dead is near a lake in one of their mountains; [23] for the Karens of Burma, the ghosts of the dead have to cross rivers to their graves. Instances of a river of death have also been noted among the New Guinea Negroes, the Khonds of Orissa, and the Dayaks of Borneo.[24] Several Australian aboriginal tribes, the Arunta, Warramunga, and Wotjobaluk, for example, believe that the dead live together in a place beyond the sea, on an island or the shores of a lake.[25] The Maori of New Zealand tell the tale of a woman, thought dead, who travels to the beyond; arriving at the sandy beach of a river barrier, she is borne to the other side by an old ferryman.[26]

In the Melanesian Hebrides of the South Pacific, the myth of Malekula relates not only a journey to the underworld but contains its own old ferryman.[27] A Polynesian myth describes a great gulf that souls must cross either in canoes or by swimming. In Patagonia (southern Argentina) canoe burial is common.[28] A ship for souls (Seelenschiff) has also been cited in northwestern America.[29] The North American Indians, in particular the Algonquin tribe, tell of dream voyages to the afterlife, with a river of the dead as a standard feature; the Sioux relate the same tale with the added touch that the soul of the dreamer swims across the river.[30] Other tribes who believe that the soul must cross a river, whether by bridge over rapid water or by ship, include the Minnetarees, the Choctaw, and the Ojibwas.[31]

This then is the situation that comparative mythologists of an earlier generation attempted to delineate; they were equally industrious concerning origins. However, universal aspects of the various phenomena concerning death (the barrier, crossing, and ferryman) make any attempt to discuss specific origins of the boatman and, in particular, Charon futile. Still, this has not hindered various mythological schools from making an attempt. Realistically, the feat is as difficult as picking an olive from the brine and trying to tell from which tree it fell. The nature mythologists have their solar theories, connecting Charon to Helios (deriving Χαρών from χαροπός and seeing the figure as an hypostasis of the celestial sun god).[32] The myth-and-ritual school finds refuge in Egyptian funeral rites and cites an illustrious predecessor in Diodorus Siculus.[33] Other anthropologists go further back, citing as sources neolithic rites (savage survivals à la Andrew Lang) and satyr-figures (Albizzati) or Pelasgian gods (Lawson, Maury), while according to others, an Asiatic influence is not to be denied.[34] Some anthropologists would attribute the figure to the early Greeks (Waser), denying that Charon could have become so firmly rooted in Greek mythology were he imported from outside (Decharme, Daremberg and Saglio, etc.).[35] We can imagine Freudian or Jungian theories where the descent reflects unconscious drives or universal archetypes; indeed, some have seen the underworld voyage as a descent into the unconscious mind with one becoming aware of its contents,[36] and the voyage might be interpreted as the descent into one's origins followed by rebirth. The possibilities are endless and sometimes absurd, especially if we consider the historical or euhemeristic approach, the natural or solar, the ritual, allegorical, symbolical, psychological, metalingual, social-anthropological or ethnological, structural, phenomenological, and so forth.

Walter Burkert, among others, has noted that myth is not identical with any given text, nor is it bound to pragmatic reality. A study of myth has to concentrate on its traditional aspect; that is, our fundamental concern should not be how the myth was created nor by whom but what happens to it in transmission. The real questions are first how myth can maintain its identity and then what are the basic features that endure or evolve around it. The attempts of scholars to find referents for myths, the search for origins, as G. S. Kirk has noted, is one of the few branches of classical scholarship where a great deal of learning has been applied with slight and often deceptive results (p. 172).

Thus while the phenomenon of an underworld boatman is undoubtedly wide-ranging and significant, the scope of this study is limited by time, space, and my own capabilities to literary representations of the ferryman Charon in classical Greek; classical and Renaissance Latin; and medieval, Renaissance, and baroque Italian. Concerning Byzantine literature, others have traced Charon's appearance and functions, though most often from an anthropological prospect, from early times to modern Greek society.[37] The depiction of the Etruscan Charun, who is rarely seen as a boatman, has also been thoroughly studied,[38] as has Charon in art;[39] the other world in medieval literature has also been delineated by scholars.[40] My interests lie in literary representations of the ferryman, and in this respect, regarding major representations of Charon within the fields mentioned, I have tried to be comprehensive. Without doubt, however, there are references to the figure that I have been unable to find and possibly extended portrayals of the boatman in medieval Latin or less-known epics and mythological poems from the periods treated. Despite these limitations, the volume and range of material is vast and ample for profitable analysis and comparison.

Notes

1. Orpheus's descent into Hades, for example, has been ascribed by Francesco Ribezzo [*Saggio di mitologia comparata. La discesa di Orfeo all'inferno e la liberazione di Euridice* (Naples: Giannini & Figli, 1901)] to an Indian myth, that of Ruru and Pramadvarâ as found in the *Mahâbhârata*. See Luigi Marrone, "Il mito d'Orfeo nella drammatica italiana," pp. 119–259. For more recent accounts of voyages to the beyond, see bibliographical items listed under Ernest J. Becker, C. S. Boswell, Marcus Dods, Howard R. Patch, and Thomas Wright.

2. Edward B. Tylor, *Researches into the Early History of Mankind and the Development of Civilization*, p. 361.

3. G. S. Kirk calls the pattern "an almost obsessive motif" (*Myth: Its Meaning and Functions in Ancient and Other Cultures*, p. 197). In discussing the myth of Enlil and Ninlil, he notes that Enlil in his disguise as the ferryman of the river of death is the Sumerian prototype of Charon (pp. 99–100).

4. See Dods, *Forerunners of Dante: An Account of Some of the More Important Visions of the Unseen World, from the Earliest Times*, pp. 8–10.

5. Robert Graves, *The Greek Myths*, 4.5 and 73.1,7. References here and later are to chapters and sections, which are numbered consecutively throughout the two volumes.

6. See S. G. F. Brandon, *Man and his Destiny in the Great Religions*, p. 79, and cf. Robert J. Brown, *The Myth of Kirkê*, p. 109.

7. Boswell, *An Irish Precursor of Dante: A Study on the Vision of Heaven and Hell ascribed to the Eighth-century Irish Saint Adamnân, with Translations of the Irish Text*, p. 69.

8. In ancient Egypt, the dead had to be transported by boat across the Nile to the western shore. G. Maspero has described the procession at length. While the body crosses the Nile, the soul passes over the "Western lake," which separates mankind from the gods. Inscriptions in the pyramids of the Pharoahs Teti and Pepi I, which date back to the thirtieth century B.C. or earlier, describe the crossing. Because of this ritual, almost all Egyptian tombs have boats painted in them. They were essential for the soul to cross to Osiris. Maspero also refers to a related Egyptian tradition in which the land of Osiris consisted of several islands, hidden in the marshes of the Delta. The dead, previously instructed by priests, went to a spot where a ferryboat waited to transport them. They had to be examined by the ferryman, and if their answers proved them to have been true followers of Osiris, they were allowed to cross over in order to confront the god and his judges. See Maspero, *Bibliothèque égyptologique* 1:283–324, 396, and *Life in Ancient Egypt and Assyria*, chap. 8, especially pp. 140–142. For inscriptions referring to crossing the lake, see Maspero, *Les Inscriptions des Pyramides de Saqqarah*, pp. 108–109.

9. H. A. Guerber, *Myths of Greece and Rome*, p. 397.

10. Dods, pp. 18–21; Becker, *A Contribution to the Comparative Study of the Medieval Visions of Heaven and Hell*, p. 16.

11. Graves, *The Greek Myths* 160.11.

12. Franz De Ruyt, *Charun: Dêmon étrusque de la mort*, p. 236; cf. Serafino Rocco, *Il mito di Caronte nell'arte e nella letteratura*, chap. 4.

13. De Ruyt, pp. 231–232 et pass. Can traces of the Etruscan death-demon Charun, with possible reminiscences of the Greek figure, be found in the Middle Ages? The medieval French *Eneas* contains

a demonic figure called Caro, and the boatman appears in the *Roman de Thèbes*. One might ask if there is any connection between Charon and such evil figures as the Green Knight or the guardian of the otherworld in the *Romance of Hunbaut*, the *grant vilain* who is a huge, black, ugly man with an ax (possibly related to the Etruscan Charon's mallet?) watching the castle of the King of the Isles. What about the grim King of the Wood near a volcanic lake with his sword? In the *Vulgate Lancelot*, the knight of the title meets a gatekeeper, a black-headed man with eyes and teeth like live coals and a flaming mouth. He, too, carries an ax. The resemblances to the Etruscan Charon are intriguing.

14. Patch, *The Other World According to Descriptions in Medieval Literature*, pp. 8–9.

15. Boswell, pp. 70–71. The Moslem hell also has its Bridge of the Dead, called Es-Sirat. See Tylor, *Researches*, p. 349.

16. "Ista enim bestia uocatur Acherons, que deuorat omnes auaros." *Visio Tnugdali*, chap. 7. See also Owen, *The Vision of Hell: Infernal Journeys in Medieval French Literature*, p. 63. Hades as a monster is a well-known motif in medieval literature. In the *Gospel of Nicodemus*, which narrates Christ's harrowing of hell, Hades complains that his belly is in pain. In later Italian literature, Anton Francesco Doni depicts a Charon within the body of Lucifer.

17. Patch, pp. 30–31.

18. See Procopius, *History of the Wars*, 8. 20. 47–58.

19. Tylor, *Religion in Primitive Culture*, pp. 132–133.

20. Tylor, *Researches*, p. 350; cf. Patch, pp. 60–61.

21. Charles Mills Gayley, *Classic Myths in English Literature*, p. 369. Patch cites the following two lines from the *Voluspá* (*Elder Edda*): "Sails a ship from the north / with shades from Hel; / o'er the ocean stream / steers it Loki . . ." (p. 62).

22. Axel Olrik, *The Heroic Legends of Denmark*, pp. 400 ff., cited in Patch, p. 61, note 9.

23. Alexander Le Roy, *The Religion of the Primitives*, p. 104.

24. Tylor, *Researches*, p. 350.

25. Emile Durkheim, *The Elementary Forms of the Religious Life*, p. 278.

26. Tylor, *Religion in Primitive Culture*, pp. 136–137.

27. The anthropologists Leo Frobenius and Adolf Jensen regard the tale as sharing an ultimate common source with Graeco-Roman tradition. See Michael Grant, *Myths of the Greeks and Romans*, p. 341.

28. Tylor, *Researches*, pp. 351–352.

29. Vladimir Propp, *Morphology of the Folktale*, p. 107.

30. Tylor, *Religion in Primitive Culture*, pp. 135–136, 138 note.

31. Tylor, *Researches*, pp. 350, 352.

32. Rocco considers Charon to be an old name for the sun god Helios embarking during the night for the East. "Sull'origine del mito di Caronte," pp. 73–81; cf. Rocco, *Il mito di Caronte*, chap. 1, especially p. 20.

33. Diodorus Siculus claimed that Orpheus studied the religion of the Pharoahs during his travels in Egypt and later employed some of their beliefs, including that of a ferryman of the dead, when he narrated his own descent songs (*Bibliotheke* 1.92, 96). Among Egyptologists, Beaurelait confirms Diodorus's statements (*Divinités égyptiennes*, quoted in Larousse, *Grand dictionnaire*, s.v. Caron), and Maspero supports it indirectly, calling the Egyptian celestial ferryman an "ancêtre éloigné de Charon." "Le livre des morts," in *Bibliothèque égyptologique*, 1:374.

34. For the influence of satyr-figures, see Carlo Albizzati, "Qualche nota su demoni etruschi," p. 235. Those supporting a Pelasgian source include John C. Lawson, *Modern Greek Folklore and Ancient Greek Religion: A Study in the Survivals*, p. 116, and Alfred Maury, "Inscriptions antiques de l'Italie" (*Journal des savants*, 1869, p. 563), cited in Panayota Kyriazopolou, *Le personnage de Charon de la grèce ancienne à la grèce moderne*, p. 38, and Rocco, *Il mito di Caronte nell'arte e nella letteratura*, p. 45. A. J. Van Windekens tries to establish a Pelasgian etymology for Charon in his article "Sur les noms de quelques figures divines ou mythiques grecques," p. 172. For the Asiatic source, see Kirk, p. 8, and De Ruyt, pp. 230–231.

35. Otto Waser, *Charon, Charun, Charos*, pp. 12 ff.; P. Decharme, *Mythologie de la Grèce antique*, p. 417, note 4; Charles Daremberg and Edmund Saglio, *Dictionnaire* 1. 2:1099; and cf. Rocco, pp. 13–14.

36. Such is the interpretation of Aeneas's adventures offered by W. F. Jackson Knight in *Elysion: On Ancient Greek and Roman Beliefs Concerning a Life After Death*, p. 134.

37. See, for example, the bibliographical items listed under Waser, Kyriazopoulou, D. C. Hesseling, Lawson, and Gyula Maravcsik.

38. See, for example, the works of Iulius Athanasius Ambrosch, Salvatore Rossi, De Ruyt, and Waser listed in the bibliography.

39. Among those to discuss Charon in art are the following authors whose works are listed in the bibliography: Ambrosch, De Ruyt, Friedrich K. von Duhn, Adolf Furtwängler, Edmond Pottier, and Rocco. The classical encyclopedias also contain relevant material. See Waser's article in Pauly-Wissowa's *Real-Encyclopädie* (3:2176-2180), Alfred Hermann's in the *Reallexikon für Antike und Christentum* (2:1040-1061), and the entries in Daremberg and Saglio's *Dictionnaire* (1. 2:1099-1101), and the *Lexikons* of Wilhelm H. Roscher and of Herbert Hungur (s.v.).

40. See the bibliographical references under Becker, Boswell, André Boutemy, H. W. L. Dana, Alessandro D'Ancona (no. 2), Dods, Hilda R. Ellis, Philippe de Félice, Victor Friedel and Kuno Meyer, Frederick Keener, Kaufman Kohler, Helen Laurie, John MacCulloch (nos. 1, 2), Kuno Meyer, Arnold van Os, Douglas Owen, Patch, St. John D. Seymour, Ralph Turner, Elizabeth Willson, and Thomas Wright.

Charon
and the Crossing

PART I

The Classical Background

1

Greek Epic: Homer and the *Minyas*

Then the boat on which embark the dead, that the old
Ferryman, Charon, used to steer, they found not within its moorings.

Minyas as cited in Pausanias

Despite the fact that the first extant reference to Charon in Greek epic is not
found until the late sixth century B.C. in the *Minyas*, it is more than a sign of
deference to begin a study of the underworld ferryman with Homer. For while it
is true, as Eustathius says, that "the ferryman Charon and his boat are mentioned
only after Homer,"[1] later representations of the descent with the boatman owe
much to the Homeric Nekyia (*Odyssey* 11) as well as to several other minor episodes in both the *Iliad* and the *Odyssey*.[2] Before analyzing the major descent
model, Odysseus's visit to the land of the dead, and the less developed Nekyia in
Odyssey 24, let me turn to two episodes in the *Iliad*, the speech of Patroklos's
spirit to Achilleus and Priam's visit to the same Greek hero, and to one from the
Odyssey, Kirke's preparatory description of the voyage to the dead.

While Homer often refers to burial rites, the most important reference for my
purpose is that concerning Patroklos. Up to this point in *Iliad* 23, the situation
has always been that immediately after the death of a warrior, his soul descends to
the house of Hades,with no apparent complications; most, in fact, seem to go un-
accompanied.[3] There is no mention in the *Iliad* of Hermes as psychopompos.
Whether the soul flies (as in iconography) or walks is unclear, although most
scholars seem to assume that the mode of transportation is flight. Once, however,
Poulydamas boasts mockingly that a spear thrown by him will be used by some
Argive "for a stick to lean on as he trudges down into Death's house" (*Iliad* 14.
456–457).[4] Turning to the episode of dead Patroklos, however, the descent is not
so easy. Now apparently one of the prerequisites for entrance into Hades is proper
funeral rites. But what exactly does the spirit of Patroklos say to his sleeping
friend?

> "εὕδεις, αὐτὰρ ἐμεῖο λελασμένος ἔπλευ, Ἀχιλλεῦ.
> οὐ μέν μευ ζώοντος ἀκήδεις, ἀλλὰ θανόντος·
> θάπτε με ὅττι τάχιστα, πύλας Ἀΐδαο περήσω.

25

τῆλέ με εἴργουσι ψυχαί, εἴδωλα καμόντων,
οὐδέ μέ πω μίσγεσθαι ὑπὲρ ποταμοῖο ἐῶσιν,
ἀλλ' αὔτως ἀλάλημαι ἀν' εὐρυπυλὲς "Ἀϊδος δῶ."

"You sleep, Achilleus; you have forgotten me; but you were not
careless of me when I lived, but only in death. Bury me
as quickly as may be, let me pass through the gates of Hades.
The souls, the images of dead men, hold me at a distance,
and will not let me cross the river and mingle among them,
but I wander as I am by Hades' house of the wide gates."

(RL, *Iliad* 23. 69–74)

Once his funeral rites are performed, adds Patroklos, he will not come back from
the underworld: "And I call upon you in sorrow, give me your hand; no
longer / shall I come back from death, once you give me my rite of burning"
(RL, 75–76).

In his translation, Richmond Lattimore has made the passage more consistent
than it actually is; in the Greek, the speech of Patroklos seems somewhat confused. The dead warrior first asks for his final rites, so that he may pass through
the gates of Hades; he also mentions a river (inside or outside the gates?) that he
is prohibited from crossing. Then he says that he is wandering, to use Murray's
translation, "*through* the wide-gated house of Hades" (my italics).[5] The preposi-
tion ἀνά, *up along* or *throughout* (Lattimore: *by*), gives rise to some confusion
(74). Is he actually in Hades' domain after all? Where Lattimore translates "no
longer / shall I come back *from death*" (my italics), the Greek reads *from* or *out
of Hades* (ἐξ Ἀΐδαο). Can it be that Patroklos is in the underworld realm (i.e., the
house of Hades)[6] but forbidden access to a particular area, perhaps through the
gates and beyond the river? Are the gates not at the outer limits of the realm?

Whatever the situation, the episode as a whole is important in regard to the
pattern of underworld descents. The speech of the dead Patroklos has far-reaching
effects on the motif of crossing to the beyond. The river as barrier is fundamental
to later treatments, and more importantly, there is, for the first time, a hindrance;
in Homer, this is a group of dead souls; for others, it will be Charon. That the Patroklos episode served as model, perhaps by way of lost intervening poems (or is
modeled on a folklore motif of later influence), is shown by a passage in the descent of Orpheus as related by both Virgil and Ovid. Since I discuss these Latin
poets later, let me merely quote in sequence the significant passages:

The souls, the images of dead men, hold me at a distance
and will not let me cross the river and mingle among them.

RL, *Iliad* 23. 72–73

Nor did the gatekeeper of Orcus suffer him again
to cross that barring pool.

Georgics 4. 502[7]

In vain the prayers of Orpheus and his longing
To cross the river once more; the boatman Charon
Drove him away.

Metamorphoses 10. 72–73[8]

Clearly, Charon prohibits the Thracian poet from crossing the infernal river much as the souls of the dead prohibit Patroklos.

Another parallel to later treatments of the descent of Orpheus is found in the following book, *Iliad* 24, prior to Hektor's funeral. The episode of Priam's visit to Achilleus in order to recover his son's body has caused at least one critic to postulate as model a folklore descent motif.[9] Let us see in what respects the episode is a structural imitation of a *katabasis*.

Twelve days after Hektor's death, Apollo reminds other immortals of the Trojan hero's many offerings to them. Lacking pity (24. 44), Achilleus, we might say, is as inexorable as Hades "the pitiless in heart" (*Theogony* 455–456). When the gods consider how to regain the dead man, Zeus dismisses stealing his body, counseling instead that Priam go with gifts to ransom it (71–76, 117–119). After sending Thetis to soften Achilleus's heart, Zeus orders Iris to tell Priam what he must do. He is to go himself with only one herald to manage the wagon and with no fear of death, since Zeus will send Hermes as escort (175–187).

Having received the message, Priam prepares for his journey, at one point saying that "before my eyes look / upon this city as it is destroyed and its people slaughtered, / my wish is to go sooner down to the house of the death god" (RL, 244–246). That he may, in fact, meet death on this journey is recognized by his kinsmen, who lament at his departure "as if he went to his death" (328). To double the image, Priam is figuratively going to the beyond just as Hektor, who lies in the Greek camp, is also, in one sense, in the land of the dead.

Zeus sends Hermes down, and the guide, who, we remember, is also psychopompos, encounters the two Trojans near a river (the Skamandros) and the tomb of Ilos (349–350), which we may consider, as Whitman says, "a sort of terminus between the two worlds" (p. 217). After a lengthy conversation, Hermes takes over as guide and leads the Trojans to the ditch and fortifications around the ships. Homer does not mention crossing the Skamandros on the downward journey, but as Whitman notes, it has to be crossed and thus "becomes the river of folk tale between the living and the dead" (p. 217). Hermes puts the guards to sleep with his wand, opens the gates, and brings Priam into the camp; interestingly, in this scheme, the river barrier is found outside the gates. Arriving at Achilleus's courtyard, they find it heavily barred, a fact not mentioned previously (452–456) but reminiscent, says Whitman, of the "forbidding triple walls of the city of the dead." On the return journey, Hermes again serves as guide, this time making his departure where he first met Priam—at the crossing of the river Xanthos (as the gods call Skamandros according to *Iliad* 20. 74).[10] If the episode as a whole is modeled on a folklore motif, it raises the questions of Charon's antiquity. We might assume that if the concept of infernal rivers existed, a boatman would be a likely addition.

The clarity of the underworld scene increases considerably in the *Odyssey*. Shipwrecked on the island of Skeria, home of the Phaiakians, Odysseus recounts his adventure at the court of Alkinoos. Among the episodes narrated is his sojourn with Kirke and descent into Hades. The first passage of interest to us, Kirke's description of the upcoming voyage to the land of the dead, is found near the end of Book 10. When Odysseus asks to leave Kirke, she informs him that he must first complete another journey, a voyage "to the house of Hades and dread Persephone" (ATM, 491). In despair, Odysseus weeps, having lost all desire to live. The immensity of the task, especially for a mortal, is evident in his response: "O Kirke, who will guide us on this journey? To Hades no man ever yet went in a black ship" (ATM, *Odyssey* 10. 501–502). We would expect divine assistance on this uncharted voyage, but Kirke tells Odysseus that no guide is needed. The North Wind itself will bear them across the stream of Okeanos to a level shore and the groves of Persephone.

Kirke instructs Odysseus to beach his ship there and then to continue to the dank house of Hades. The actual domain is characterized by the rivers flowing around it:

> "ἔνθα μὲν εἰς 'Αχέροντα Πυριφλεγέθων τε ῥέουσιν
> Κώκυτός θ', ὅς δὴ Στυγὸς ὕδατός ἐστιν ἀπορρώξ."

"There into Acheron flow Periphlegethon and Cocytus, which is
a branch of the water of the Styx."

(ATM 10. 513–514)[11]

Before flowing into Acheron, the two rivers meet near a rock (515);[12] it is at this juncture apparently that Odysseus is to dig a pit and pour a libation to the dead.[13] Following his libation and supplicating prayers,[14] Odysseus is to sacrifice a ram and a black ewe, turning their heads toward Erebos while he himself faces back toward the streams of the river. Apparently these ποταμοῖο ῥοάων refer to Okeanos; if they signified infernal streams, Odysseus would have to have crossed them. Having completed these rites, says Kirke, "Many ghosts of men that are dead will come forth" (ATM, 529–530). Apparently then, rather than a complete descent, we have the arrival at a river barrier and the evocation of dead souls at that point.

The actual voyage to the beyond takes place in Book 11. With the wind promised by Kirke, Odysseus and his crew sail throughout the day until the sun sets and all grows dark. The ship arrives at the furthest part of Okeanos, where Odysseus beaches his ship and goes with his men and sheep along the stream of Okeanos until he arrives at the place mentioned by Kirke, apparently at the juncture of several infernal rivers. As ordered, he digs the pit, pours the libation, promises the dead a sacrifice in Ithaka, offers prayers to them, and sacrifices the sheep.

The following description of the dead is impressive:

αἱ δ' ἀγέροντο
ψυχαὶ ὑπὲξ Ἐρέβευς νεκύων κατατεθνηώτων.
νύμφαι τ' ἠίθεοί τε πολύτλητοί τε γέροντες
παρθενικαί τ' ἀταλαὶ νεοπενθέα θυμὸν ἔχουσαι,
πολλοὶ δ' οὐτάμενοι χαλκήρεσιν ἐγχείῃσιν,
ἄνδρες ἀρηίφατοι βεβροτωμένα τεύχε' ἔχοντες·
οἳ πολλοὶ περὶ βόθρον ἐφοίτων ἄλλοθεν ἄλλος
θεσπεσίῃ ἰαχῇ· ἐμὲ δὲ χλωρὸν δέος ᾕρει.

(36–43)

And now the souls of the dead who have gone below came swarming up from
Erebus—fresh brides, unmarried youths, old men with life's long suffering behind them, tender young girls still nursing this first anguish in their hearts,
and a great throng of warriors killed in battle, their spear-wounds gaping yet
and all their armour stained with blood. From this multitude of souls, as they
fluttered to and fro by the trench, there came a moaning that was horrible to
hear. Panic drained the blood from my cheeks.[15]

The beauty of verses 38–41, especially the polysyndeton with τε and the assonance
of the repeated plurals αι and οι weave a rhythmic and phonic pattern of great enchantment.[16] The terrestrial appearance of the souls extends as in Achilleus's
dream of Patroklos to their apparel itself, including armor! These are no mere flitting shadows just as Patroklos was no normal whispy spirit gibbering faintly.[17]

Among the comments of the dead spirits, those of Odysseus's mother, Antiklea, are significant in regard to an underworld crossing. When she sees her son,
Antiklea marvels that although alive, he has come into the murky darkness.
"Hard is it for those that live to behold these realms," she says, adding, "for between are great rivers and dread streams; Oceanus first, which one may in no wise
cross on foot, but only if one have a well-built ship" (ATM, 11. 156–159). Antiklea thus assumes that her son has crossed not only Okeanos but other infernal
rivers as well; the barriers are many. After Antiklea has responded to various questions, Odysseus tries three times to embrace her (the action has a long and
felicitous literary fortune), but each time her spirit slips from his arms like a
shadow or a dream. As surprised as was Achilleus who tried to touch Patroklos's
image,[18] he wonders if she is but a phantom (εἴδωλον) sent by Persephone. His
mother states that this is the appointed way for the dead (218), noting that when
cremation destroys the sinews that hold the body together, the psyche then flies
away free (219–222). This image of a flying spirit would seem to deny the necessity of a boatman for all but the living; the iconography, however, proves otherwise.

Following his visits with the various souls of men and women who rise near the
pit, Odysseus apparently looks deeper into the underworld. It is possible that
Homer at this point has grafted on the features of a separate descent myth to an
episode of evocation. The visions that follow—Minos judging the dead, Orion,
Tityos, Tantalos, Sisyphos, and Herakles (568–626)—seem to take place deep

Charon and a winged spirit, by the Tymbos Painter. Greek lekythos. Courtesy of the Ashmolean Museum 547, Oxford.

within the realm itself. If two distinct episodes—an evocation and a descent—have been merged, in the process, earlier aspects of the descent episode (e.g., the initial crossing of rivers) have been cut. Whether or not a boatman of the dead existed in the folklore model of the descent is thus a matter of surmise. Among the figures seen by Odysseus, Herakles stands out for the parallels between his eyes and those of Charon, as described by later poets; the hero glares terribly—like dark night—his bow and arrow ready, while around him the dead clamor in terror.[19] On his wondrous belt are engraved equally fierce animals, they, too, with flashing eyes. Herakles, incidentally, mentions only one of his labors, appropriately that of his descent for the hound of Hades (11. 623).[20]

The underworld episode finally closes with Odysseus departing for his ship in fear that Persephone might send forth the Gorgon head. As the eleventh book draws to a close, we see the ship sailing down the stream Okeanos, aided first by rowing and then by the wind. In Book 12, the men return to Kirke's island, and the enchantress herself assumes that they "have gone down alive to the house of Hades to meet death twice" (21–22). Whether or not this implies entrance to the realm or crossing river barriers is not clear. The sixth-century poet Theognis possibly thought so, for he writes, "Remind me not of misfortunes, for sure, I have suffered even as Odysseus, who escaped up out of the great house of Hades. . . .''[21] Unfortunately, given Homer's method of fusing the latter half of what appears to be a true descent to the first part, which is merely an evocation, we are denied a clear glimpse of the early concept of how the living crossed the infernal rivers.[22]

The final underworld episode takes place after Odysseus has returned to Ithaka and slain the Suitors; I refer to Book 24, whose initial passage is often called the second Nekyia. Whereas previous spirits have apparently descended on their own, the souls of the dead Suitors are called forth by Kyllenian Hermes.[23] Rousing the spirits with his golden wand, he leads them on a strange journey to the beyond like gibbering bats:

> πὰρ δ' ἴσαν Ὠκεανοῦ τε ῥοὰς καὶ Λευκάδα πέτρην,
> ἠδὲ παρ' Ἠελίοιο πύλας καὶ δῆμον ὀνείρων
> ἤϊοσαν· αἶψα δ' ἵκοντο κατ' ἀσφοδελὸν λειμῶνα,
> ἔνθα τε ναίουσι ψυχαί, εἴδωλα καμόντων.

(24. 11–14)

Past the streams of Oceanus they went, past the rock Leucas, past the gates of the sun and the land of dreams, and quickly came to the mead of asphodel, where the spirits dwell, phantoms of men who have done with toils. (ATM)[24]

The rock Leukas or White Rock is unmentioned elsewhere in Homer. Other than the well-known geographical claims, such as the island of Leukas near Ithaka or the promontory of Epirus, the only analogy I can adduce is that this is the rock referred to be Kirke, where Kokytos and Pyriphlegethon join to fall into Acheron. Whatever the case, there is no apparent difficulty in crossing any of the streams and, of course, no mention of a boatman.

The story of Odysseus's journey to the outermost limits of Hades was followed by other depictions of the underworld. Pausanias mentions a Hesiodic poem that purportedly described the descent of Theseus and Peirithoos (9. 31, 5),[25] and other Nekyiai are found in the *Nostoi* and the *Minyas* (10. 28, 7). It is in a fragment of the latter work, in fact, that we find not only traces of a descent but, more importantly, an actual reference to Charon, which completes our picture of the descent and crossing in archaic and Classical Greek epic. Though the reference to the boatman is only two lines long and thus isolated and enigmatic in its brevity, we may surmise from other fragments that the *Minyas* as a whole was possibly a poem on Herakles.[26] Godofredus Kinkel, editor of the text,[27] claims that the poem narrated Herakles' victory over Minyas, the legendary founder of Orchomenus in Boeotia, and his storming of the city (p. 215).[28] Since the fragment containing Charon refers to Theseus and Peirithoos, the work may have contained as well a description of Herakles' descent to rescue them, accomplished as part of his task to steal Kerberos.[29] Other extant fragments from archaic epics on Herakles, however, contain no mention of Charon; Peisander and Panyassis, for example, have left us nothing pertinent.

Turning to the *Minyas* itself, the extant fragments of interest to this study are found in the *Description of Greece*, written by Pausanias, a second century A.D. native of Lydia.[30] In Book 10, Pausanias describes a painting by Polygnotus found in the Lesche, or Place of Talk of Delphi.[31] On the right wall, the taking of Troy and departure of the Greeks are depicted, while on the left, we find Odysseus's descent into Hades "to inquire of the soul of Teiresias about his safe return home" (10. 28); the scene is set forth as follows:

> There is water like a river, clearly intended for Acheron, with reeds growing in it; the forms of the fishes appear so dim that you will take them to be shadows rather than fish. On the river is a boat [ναῦς], with the ferryman at the oars [καὶ ὁ πορθμεὺς ἐπὶ ταῖς κώπαις]. Polygnotus followed, I think, the poem called the *Minyad*. For in this poem occur lines referring to Theseus and Peirithoüs:
>
>> Then the boat on which embark the dead, that the old Ferryman, Charon, used to steer, they found not within its moorings.
>
> For this reason then Polygnotus too painted Charon as a man well stricken in years. Those on board the boat are not altogether distinguished. Tellis appears as a youth in years and Cleoboea as still a maiden, holding on her knees a chest such as they are wont to make for Demeter. . . .

Pausanias emphasizes the contrast in the painting between Charon's old age and Tellis's youth through chiastic structure (γέροντα . . . τῇ ἡλικίᾳ as opposed to ἡλικίαν ἐφήβου). He continues:

Charon, by the Reed Painter. National Museum Στ 3, Athens. Photo of the Museum.

On the bank of Acheron, there is a notable group under the boat of Charon, consisting of a man who had been undutiful to his father and is now being throttled by him. For the men of old held their parents in the greatest respect. . . . Near to the man in Polygnotus' picture who maltreated his father and for this drinks his cup of woe in Hades is a man who paid the penalty for sacrilege. The woman who is punishing him is skilled in poisonous and other drugs. So it appears that in those days men laid the greatest stress on piety to the gods. . . .

Higher up than the figures I have enumerated comes Eurynomus, said by the Delphian guides to be one of the demons in Hades, who eats off all the flesh of the corpses, leaving only their bones. But, Homer's *Odyssey*, the poem called the *Minyad*, and the *Returns*, although they tell of Hades, and its horrors, know of no demon called Eurynomus. However, I will describe what he is like and his attitude in the painting. He is of a colour between blue and black, like that of meat flies; he is showing his teeth and is seated, and under him is spread a vulture's skin. (10. 28)

Polygnotus, then, integrates into an episode supposedly painted from the *Odyssey* a variety of creatures absent in the original but found in other epics, such as the *Minyas*. The most interesting figure for this study, of course, is Charon's, although the infernal boatman's representation lacks the pictorial display of Eurynomus. Perhaps the scantiness of details—in both the *Minyas* and Pausanias —reflects not lack of interest in, or knowledge of, the boatman but rather great familiarity with him. The lines in the *Minyas*, in fact, seem to presume an acquaintance with the ferryman; let us look closely at the verses devoted to Charon:

> ἔνθ' ἤτοι νέα μὲν νεκυάμβατον, ἣν ὁ γεραιός
> πορθμεὺς ἦγε Χάρων, οὐκ ἔλαβον ἔνδοθεν ὅρμου.

> Then the boat on which embark the dead, that the old
> Ferryman, Charon, used to steer, they found not within it moorings.

With these words, Charon first appears in Western epic as the boatman of the dead.[32] The description, though scanty, situates the figure both in appearance (he is physically old) and as concerns his duties (he is a ferryman of the dead). The adjective γεραιός lends itself to some comment. Many scholars have mentioned that the Greeks disliked old age;[33] is there any hint of this attitude in the *Minyas*? Possibly, but it is equally true that the Greeks were taught to venerate old age: "The immortals honor older men" (*Iliad* 23. 788).[34] The old are to be honored and pitied as Priam is by Achilleus.

When applied to a god, the adjective *old* most often means he/she belongs to the first generation;[35] does the use with Charon imply his antiquity in folk belief? Possibly. But again, Charon is not really a god in the sense of the great divinities. As an underworld servant (there is no mention of his divinity in the *Minyas*), perhaps Charon is merely old because he is associated with death; or as other commentators note, the connection may be with Kronos (Κρόνος), a god sent to rule in the world below when displaced by Zeus.[36] Or perhaps, as others maintain, the connection is with Chronos (χρόνος), or time.[37] Being an underworld denizen (and a minor divinity, as Virgil says) does imply immortality, and Chronos, the passing of time, does bring death. Finally, concerning the adjective *old*, I mention in passing that with this concept Virgil sums up his description of Charon (*Aeneid* 6. 298) and Dante opens his (*Inferno* 3. 82–83); each is discussed in a later section.

The other characteristic of Charon in the *Minyas* is that he is a πορθμεύς.[38] But he is not merely a ferryman on the Kopais Lake in Boeotia as some would have it (see note 28); clearly, his boat is used to transport the dead; it is νεκυάμβατος. That this refers to some earthly task—especially since Theseus and Peirithoos are involved—seems highly unlikely.

From the situation of the boatman, we pass to that of these two Greek heroes. Obviously, they have come to a water barrier and are unable to find the boat that is usually there. Because they expected to find a boat moored here leads us to believe that the legend of the ferryman was widely known and exact in its details. Most likely, the two heroes are descending, since their escape was not hindered by Charon but Hades, who imprisoned them in stone chairs to which they remained stuck.[39] Charon's absence can be explained by either the fact that he is busy transporting other souls across the barrier or he no longer performs his duties there. No known version of the myth supports any but the first conclusion.

Did Theseus and Peirithoos wait for Charon and were they ferried by him across the water? Perhaps not. In other versions of the descent, they avoid Charon's boat by descending at Laconian Taenarus, "a back way," according to Robert Graves,[40] that avoids the ferry passage. In this instance, perhaps they also took a different route. Whatever the case, in the text as it stands, there is no confrontation between the descenders and ferryman; whether he would have been helpful or obstructive must be left to the imagination.

In concluding this section on descents in Greek epic, let me state that the fact that Homer does not mention Charon does not imply the late addition of the boatman to the pantheon of minor Greek gods. Critics, of course, have claimed that neither Homer nor Hesiod knew the boatman. Instead they claim that the Greeks initially believed in a winged Thanatos who, along with Hypnos, guided the soul from the living to the dead (as in the *Iliad*)[41] and only later adopted Hermes as guide (as in the *Odyssey*)[42] and finally the boatman Charon, who was introduced late.[43] It should be noted, however, that there are many ancient mythological figures and stories that find no place in either the *Iliad* or the *Odyssey*.[44] Concerning the twelve labors of Herakles, which Nilsson says were "clearly . . . well-known,"[45] Homer refers only to the descent for Kerberos, an episode mentioned in both the *Iliad* (8. 368) and the *Odyssey* (11. 623); additional features of this and other myths, such as the Argonauts, referred to briefly in *Odyssey* 12. 69–72, lie outside the poet's story. Since the poet's model is an episode from a Nekyia in which Odysseus stands outside the realm, there is no need for a boatman to aid in penetrating Hades' domain; when the poet grafts a view of the deep underworld onto the middle of the descent, the place for the boatman (whether in the original or not) is long past. Neither Charon nor Kerberos appear in the Nekyia, since both belong to the outer limits of the realm and are connected to the motif of a barrier, which Homer chooses to ignore. Also, as part of folklore, Charon, like the ancient chthonian goddess Hecate, may have been avoided as too common.[46] Several scholars, among them Andrew Lang, have noted that Homer is a poet of ''comparative purity''; his pantheon of gods, for example, is noble and lofty.

Whatever the answer, Charon in time became established as part of the underworld. Still, in analyzing the structural units of the descent as narrated in Greek epic, we are severely restricted by both the brevity of the portrayals and the absence of more extended epic descents in which Charon may have appeared. The conclusions to be drawn thus center on the earlier and later units. The few descents examined are of two types—those that are undertaken by necessity (i.e., by all the dead souls from Patroklos to the Suitors) and those with a motive (i.e., by Herakles for Kerberos or by Odysseus). What is Odysseus's aim? As stated by Kirke and repeated by Odysseus, it is to gain knowledge of the future from Teiresias.[47] The descent is thus heightened by prophecy; it can be used to relate future events, even those outside the strict economy of the poem.[48] The practical reasons behind Herakles' descent lend themselves to little elaboration, and, in fact, they do not interest the poet. Priam's voyage for Hektor is developed because it is integral to the story. If it is modeled on the descent to the dead to regain a loved one, it continues a pattern that later poets will employ at length, because the situation lends itself to pathos and is, at the same time, an epic feat.

The second unit is well developed in Homer. The voyage to the underworld is prepared by advance descriptions and then detailed by the poet, especially in the *Odyssey*. In both poems, the arrival at a barrier is an important feature: In the *Iliad*, it stresses the necessity of proper funeral rites; in the *Odyssey*, the barrier is also not to be crossed. That is, while an initial water barrier, the stream Okeanos, is crossed through the hero's own effort (god-aided, however), the other infernal rivers are not traversed. Rather, the barrier stops the hero and facilitates a lengthy description of the rite needed to evoke the dead. Later poets will integrate Charon into the conjuration episode as well as the descent. The episode with Elpenor, incidentally, though conforming to the same type as that of Patroklos, does not mention the barrier. Like the other souls, he seems to come from the house of Hades and merely requests to be remembered with a burial mound.

The units of confrontation with the boatman are lacking even in the *Minyas*, at least as we have it today. Theseus and Peirithoos obviously need transportation and expect to be given, or to gain, passage in Charon's boat. In the two-line fragment, no mention is made of a fee or the fact that both are living, nor do we know if they eventually used the boat of the dead. A confrontation, however, is implied in Homer: Patroklos tells of the spirits of the dead who forbid him to cross the river and join them. Presumably, Charon will be equally demanding.

Unit 6, the description of the ferry, is the briefest. In the *Minyas*, the *naus* is merely *nekroambatos* and has an accustomed moorage. That the dead need a boat is first implied here, since in the Homeric poems, souls descend directly to Hades, possibly by flying and sometimes guided by Hermes. When the dead begin to acquire more solidity—*Odyssey* 11 helps to establish this—and are no longer thought of as flitting shades or winged souls but as having the needs of the living, then the boatman with his ferry becomes plausible if not indispensable.

In passing, I should mention that when Odysseus responds to Kirke's directive with the statement that "to Hades no man ever yet went in a black ship," he is both right and wrong. That is, though possibly the first to go by ship, he is wrong to assume that he is the first living man to travel to the house of Hades; as we soon learn, Herakles has made this same voyage.[49] Of the three descents by living men, those by Theseus, Peirithoos, and Herakles precede the voyage of Odysseus. Later poets will establish varied sequences, with the descent of Orphesus vying for primacy with the early Greek heroes.

Notes

1. "ὁ γὰρ πορθμεὺς Χάρων καὶ το κατ' αὐτὸν πλοιάριον μεθ' Ὅμηρον μεμύθευται." *Eustathii commentarii ad Homeri Odysseam*, p. 391 (= 1666.36–37). The twelfth-century Byzantine scholar's use of the diminutive *ploiarion* brings to mind Aristophanes, who is the first to use the lexis "ἐν πλοιαρίῳ τυννουτῳι" (*Frogs* 139).

2. I do not intend to enter into any of the controversies concerning the authorship of these two poems. A convenient summary of the polemic between "analysts" and "unitarians" can be found in Platnauer, *Fifty Years (And Twelve) of Classical Scholarship*, chap. 1, parts i and ii by E. R. Dodds. Let me merely mention two representative works: first, Denys Page, *The Homeric Odyssey* (cf. his "Multiple Authorship in the *Iliad*") and second, a study concentrating on the unity of the two poems, Cedric H. Whitman, *Homer and the Heroic Tradition*.

3. A possible exception is found in *Iliad* 2. 302,where the Keres seem to accompany their victims. Compare *Odyssey* 24. 207–208, where the Keres clearly do this and *Odyssey* 24. 1–10 for Hermes. In the latter passage, the dead Suitors descend so rapidly with Hermes that, as Amphimedon tells Agamemnon, "even now our bodies still lie uncared for in the halls of Odysseus" (186–187, trans. A. T. Murray). Page claims that this descent is a late addition, basing the standard Homeric practice in part on the Patroklos incident (*The Homeric Odyssey*, pp. 117–118).

4. Richmond Lattimore, *The Iliad of Homer*. Hereafter, all references to this translation will appear in the text followed by the initials RL.

5. Homer, *The Iliad*, trans. A. T. Murray, hereafter referred to in the text with the initials ATM.

6. Even Achilleus has assumed earlier that Patroklos is in Hades. In *Iliad* 23. 19, Achilleus addresses his dead friend as follows: " 'Good-bye, Patroklos, I hail you even in the house of the death god.' " But a few lines later, Achilleus tells Agamemnon to have his men "bring in timber and lay it by, with all that is fitting / for the dead man to have *when he goes down* under the gloom and darkness" (RL, 50–51, my emphasis).

7. *Virgil's Works*, trans. J. W. MacKail, p. 351.

8. Ovid, *Metamorphoses*, trans. Rolfe Humphries, p. 236.

9. Whitman, p. 217. The analysis that follows is based on Whitman's exposition.

10. For a discussion of these two names, see C. M. Bowra, *Tradition and Design in the Iliad*, p. 153.

11. For some interesting accounts of Homer's infernal rivers and geography, see Pausanias, *Description of Greece* 1. 17. 5 and 8. 18. 1–3, and Strabo, *Geography* 1. 2. 18, 5. 4. 5, 6. 1. 5, 7. 7. 5, and 8. 3. 15.

12. Pausanias (1. 17) thinks Homer is here imitating wild and gloomy Thesprotia in north west Greece with its rivers Acheron and Kokytos. But as W. B. Stanford notes, it is possible that these rivers took their name from Homer (*The Odyssey of Homer*, p. 379). It is also possible to take Acheron as a lake into which the other two rivers flow. Homer's description is vague and caused uncertainty in his imitators.

13. By the first century A.D., people are pouring libations to Charon himself! Josephus in his *Jewish Antiquities* claims that after the death of Agrippa, the people of Caesarea and Sebaste rejoiced as follows: "They poured libations to Charon, and exchanged toasts in celebration of the king's death" (19. 358). I quote from the translation of Louis H. Feldman.

14. For a much later example of this type of prayer, see Origenes, *Contra haereses* 4. 32 in Emma J. and Ludwig Edelstein, *Asclepius: A Collection and Interpretation of the Testimonies*, 1:167 and cf. Aristides, *Oratio* 49. 4 (ibid., 1:332–333).

15. Homer, *The Odyssey*, trans. E. V. Rieu, hereafter indicated by EVR.

16. The appeal of the description is evident in poets from Virgil on, including Dante and Milton (see *Paradise Lost* 1. 302 ff.). Virgil imitates it twice (*Georgics* 4. 475 ff., *Aeneid* 6. 306 ff.).

17. In *Iliad* 23. 65–67, we read: "there appeared to him the ghost of unhappy Patroklos / all in his likeness for stature, and the lovely eyes, and voice, / and wore such clothing as Patroklos had worn on his body." (RL)

18. When Achilleus reaches to embrace Patroklos, he "could not / take him, but the spirit went underground, like vapour, / with a thin cry" (*Iliad* 23. 100–101). Achilleus marvels that even in Hades there is a soul (ψυχὴ) and an image (εἴδωλον [103–104]).

19. In the *Argonautica* of Apollonius of Rhodes, one of the Hesperides, Aegle, describes Herakles as "a savage brute, hideous to look at; a cruel man, with glaring eyes and scowling face" (4. 1436, trans. E. V. Reiu, *The Voyage of Argo*, p. 186).

20. Kerberos is mentioned in both epics (see also *Iliad* 8. 367–368) but is nameless, as Pausanias notes (3. 25. 4–6), and lacks the picturesque detail of Hesiod's depiction. Hesiod says that Kerberos is "a monster not to be overcome and that may not be described . . . who eats raw flesh, the brazen-voiced hound of Hades, fifty-headed, relentless, and strong" (*Theogony* 310–313, trans. Hugh G. Evelyn-White). The Boeotian poet notes that the fearful hound has a cruel trick: "On those who go in he fawns with his tail and both his ears, but suffers them not to go out back again, but keeps watch and devours whomsoever he catches going out of the gates of strong Hades and awful Persephone" (770–774). As opposed to Hesiod's fifty-headed monster, the canonical three-headed figure was established only in late archaic and classical literature (see, for example, Euripides, *Hercules furens* 611). For a later epic depiction, see Quintus of Smyrna's description of Kerberos as he appears on the shield of the Trojan Euryplus, a shield bearing the deeds of Herakles (*The War at Troy*, trans. Frederick M. Combellack, Book 6, p. 131). Servius, incidentally, perhaps influenced by Hesiod, says that "Cerberus terra est et consumptrix omnium corporum" (*ad Aen.* 6. 395).

21. Edmonds, *Elegy and Iambus*, 1:365.

22. I might note that Welcker published what J. A. K. Thomson calls a "fascinating speculation" regarding Odysseus's hosts—the Phaiakians. Welcher observed that the word Φαίαξ is derived from φαιός (gray, dusky) and thus was led to the conclusion that the Phaiakians were in reality the dark ferrymen of the dead! (see Thomson, *Studies in the Odyssey*, p. 96). The fact that Odysseus relates his descent to the Phaiakians—among many other adventures—seems a poor foundation for this idea. Thomson says the ferrymen of the dead were "familiar personages in folklore," but to my knowledge there was but one Greek ferryman of the dead. To support his theory, Welcker notes that Odysseus falls into a deep sleep, scarcely distinguishable from death, and that the ship moves through the water like a hawk. Both images are entirely natural. Thomson's imaginative reader, however, feels "something mysterious or allegorical" in this sleep and finds the movement of the ship to be perhaps magical. It is true, of course, that the Phaiakians's ships are an element of marvel—they require neither pilots nor steering oars but understand the minds of men. The ships cross the sea swiftly never fearing harm, and they know all places (*Odyssey* 8. 557–563). But this is assuredly not characteristic of the ferryman of the dead, who is never situated on Okeanos and has no magical ship. Thomson would like, it seems, to accept Erwin Rohde's authority that this is all groundless fancy, but Thomson's idea that Odysseus represents the Eniautos-Daimon leads him to feel that it is appropriate that Odysseus "should be ferried between the shores of Life and Death [which he is not!] by mysterious Grey Men." Thomson concludes that Welcker is right (p. 97). For Welcker's hypothesis, see *Kleine Schriften*, 2:1–79. For Rohde see *Psyche* 1:63: "There is no reason to see in the Phaeacians a sort of ferry-people of the dead . . . ."

23. Diodorus Siculus, I might note, gives a euhemeristic reading of the Second Nekyia, basing the episode on Egyptian customs supposedly brought to Greece by Orpheus and imitated by Homer. See *Bibliotheke* 1. 96. 5–7; Charon is discussed in 1. 92 ff.

24. I might note that the gates of the sun are possibly a metalepsis of Hades' gates, arising from the fact that the sun sets in the West, where the other-world realm is located. Diodorus Siculus, incidentally, claims that the portals of the sun (Heliopylai) refer to the Egyptian city of Heliopolis (1. 96. 7).

25. Rohde, *Psyche: The Cult of Souls and Belief in Immortality among the Greeks*, 1: 236; cf. *Hesiod, The Homeric Hymns and Homerica*, trans. Evelyn-White p. xxiii. Though to my knowledge no one identifies this with the *Minyas*, fragments of this epic do contain such a descent.

26. The author of the *Minyas* has been variously identified; for details, see Rohde, *Psyche*, 1:237 ff.

27. *Epicorum graecorum fragmenta*, 1:215–216.

28. Herakles also blocked up the two large tunnels built by the ancient Bronze Age Minyans to carry the river Cephissus to the sea. As a result, the rich Kopaic plain was flooded. See Robert Graves, *The Greek Myths*, 121a–d. Perhaps the similarity of the marshy Kopaic plain to the Stygian swamp is what led Radermacher (quoted by Alfred Hermann in the *Reallexikon für Antike und Christentum*, s.v. Charon) to claim that the boatman Charon in the *Minyas* is just a local ferryman of the Kopaissee: "In der Minyas war Ch. zunächst nur ein lokaler Fährmann des Kopaissees (Radermacher, *Jens*. 31 ff.)" (p. 1042). To maintain this assumption from the brevity of the fragment in Pausanias seems especially hazardous, but typical of a modern euhemerist.

29. The episode of Theseus and Peirithoos, incidentally, was reinterpreted by the euhemerist Diodorus Siculus, who claims that the two never raided the underworld at all, but only a Thesprotian or Molossian city ruled over by a King Aidoneus. Theseus was confined to a dungeon, from which Herakles eventually rescued him (4. 63, cited in Graves, 103e). For the identification of Charon with a Molossian king in Italian commentators of Dante, see the Bibliography, Primary Sources, Part 2, A80.

30. Trans. W. H. S. Jones.

31. According to the *Oxford Classical Dictionary*, Polygnotus flourished around 475–447 B.C. and painted the Nekyia probably between 458 and 447.

32. The exact date of the *Minyas* is, of course, unknown; scholars vary in their estimation from the sixth to the early fifth century B.C.

33. In the *Theogony*, the Hesiodic poet associates baneful old age with strife and makes both of them children of Night, along with such figures as Doom, Fate, Death, and Woe (225). Later mythographers add Charon to the list of Night's offspring. One of the characteristics of the Golden Age in Hesiod is that while man died, it was as though subdued by sleep, and vile age was not imposed on them (*Works and Days*, 113–114). In the *Argonautica* of Apollonius of Rhodes, Phineus is punished by "lingering old age" (2. 179 ff.).

34. The reference in this instance is to Odysseus, who as the oldest competitor has won the prize for the footrace in the games following Patroklos's funeral. Odysseus's old age is significantly modified by a phrase (791) that Virgil will apply to Charon: "jam senior, sed *cruda* deo *viridis*que senectus" (*Aeneid* 6. 304). The noun ὠμογέρων—a fresh old man—is composed of ὠμός, meaning raw (with respect to flesh) or unripe (with respect to fruit) thus green, and γέρων, meaning old man. I might add that among the four worst crimes in the *Works and Days* was that of the person "who abuses his old father at the cheerless threshold of old age" (327 ff.).

35. G. S. Kirk points out that Greek myths often emphasize that a god is ageless, not merely immortal (*Myth: Its Meaning and Functions in Ancient and Other Cultures*, p. 198). Those who are referred to as old often belong to the ancient hierarchy—old Kronos or Saturn, for example. In discussing the replacement of elder gods by the younger, Kirk refers to the process as a reflection of the "frustrated resentment of old age itself" (p. 199).

36. See *Iliad* 15. 225 where we read of "the gods that are in the world below with Cronos" (cf. *Iliad* 14. 274). Zeus "thrust Cronos down to dwell beneath the earth and the unresting sea" (*Iliad* 14. 203–204). In Hesiod, Kronos rules over the heroes in "an abode apart from men . . . at the ends of the earth" (*Works and Days*, 167–169). In the Hesiodic *Theogony*, Kronos is with the Titans under Tartaros (851).

37. I am referring to commentators of Virgil and Dante who deal with Charon. See Part 2, chap. 12, under the heading Commentators of Dante.

38. Virgil begins his depiction of Charon (*Aeneid* 6. 298) with this very word (*portitor* in Latin). Strictly speaking, of course, Virgil varies his translation from ferryman to harbor-master, although the word in time also came to represent a ferryman.

39. Also, since the two are still together, it is unlikely that they are attempting to leave the underworld. In most versions of the story, Theseus alone is rescued from imprisonment by Herakles, but Peirithoos remains below. If the *Minyas* included any of the Argive deeds of Herakles, it might very well have represented this rescue. Concerning other versions, Theseus is also permanently detained by Hades in Virgil (*Aen.* 6. 617–618, perhaps already in *Odyssey* 11. 631), while in Hyginus, both men are rescued (*Fabula* 79).

40. Graves cites Hyginus, *Fabula* 79; Diodorus Siculus 4. 63; Horace, *Odes* 4. 7. 27; and Apollodorus, *Epitome* 1. 24; but says the ferry passage is across Lethe (103c). For more sources of this myth, see Apollodorus, ed. Frazer, 1. 234–235, note 3.

41. For a lengthy exposition on Thanatos, see Panayota Kyriazopoulous, *Le personnage de Charon de la Grèce ancienne à la Grèce moderne*, pp. 1 ff.

42. I might note that in his story of Alkmene, based as he says on the fifth-century Athenian mythographer Pherecydes, Antonius Liberalis writes that Zeus sends Hermes for the body of the dead woman, instructing him to carry it to the Isles of the Blessed where she is to be the spouse of Rhadamanthys: "Ζεὺς, δε Ἑρμῆν πέμπει κελεύων Ἀλκμήνην ἐκκλέψαι καὶ ἀπενεγκεῖν εἰς Μακάρων νήσους καὶ δοῦναι Ῥαδαμάνθοι γυναῖκα." *Les Métamorphoses*, ed. Papathomopoulos, section 33 (p. 56).

43. Rocco, *Il mito di Caronte*, pp. 11, 20.

44. As Kirk says, many archaic or mythopoeic episodes are heard of for the first time in Stesichorus or Hecataeus—or even Apollodorus in the first or second century A.D. (p. 174).

45. *The Mycenaean Origin of Greek Mythology*, p. 197.

46. Hecate, possibly of Carian origin (Nilsson), comes into sudden prominence in a disputed passage in the *Theogony* (411 ff.); see OCD.

47. Although some critics have questioned the *poet's* reason for introducing a descent, claiming that he wishes rather to initiate a dialogue between Odysseus and those dear to him or important to his past history, such motivation lies outside the first unit. Heraclitus takes knowledge as a point of departure for his allegorization of the descent. He says: "Ἡ δὲ φρόνησις ἕως Ἀιδου καταβέβηκεν, ἵνα μηδὲ τῶν νέρθεν ἀδιερεύντον ᾖ," translated by Félix Buffière as "La sagesse descend jusque chez Hadès, pour ne pas laisser de secteur inexploré, même dans les enfers" (*Allégorie d'Homère* 70. 8). Unfortunately, there is a missing section in Heraclitus's text where he discusses Odysseus's visit to the nether world.

48. Other features of the topos that lend themselves to imitation are found in the episodes following the crossing—such things as the catalogs, encounters between the living and dead, dialogues of dead heroes, and colorful depiction of the underworld tableau and its inhabitants. The descent can be heightened not only by prophecy, then, but by memory of the past.

49. Eustathius says that Odysseus is the first to go *in a black ship*: "εἰ γὰρ καί τινες εἰς Ἄιδος ἀφίχοντο οἷον καὶ Ἡρακλῆς καὶ Θησεὺς καὶ Περίθους, ἀλλα νηῖ μελαίνῃ οὐδείς" (p. 391 = 1666. 35–36).

2

Greek Lyric and Tragedy

Greek lyricists from the earliest archaic poets to those of Byzantine times and later —a period of well over a millenium—have referred, if not always directly to Charon, at least to infernal rivers and the necessity of crossing these rivers on the soul's voyage to the underworld. In doing so, the poets enriched the literary patrimony of the West with a variety of themes and images influencing later poets, both Latin and Italian. Among the prominent motifs that later poets integrate into the descent topos are those of passion and death, immortalized by Sappho;[1] love's power even in the underworld;[2] the life of man as a leaf;[3] and the impossibility of returning from Hades.[4] Descents by such men as Herakles, Sisyphos, and Adonis are also mentioned by early lyric poets, although Charon himself does not appear.[5]

The first to hint at the existence of a boatman is Pindar (518–438 B.C.), who talks of a ferry-crossing over the Acheron. Before citing the relevant poem, let me point out the gloomy tones that describe the underworld rivers. In Dirge 130, following a description of Elysium, the poet writes:

> ἔνθεν τὸν ἄπειρον ἐρεύγονται σκότον
> βληχροὶ δνοφερᾶς νυκτὸς ποταμοί. . . .

From the other side sluggish streams of darksome night belch
forth a boundless gloom.[6]

"Endless darkness" (*skotos* in Homer often refers to the darkness of death) is seen as being spewed out by the sluggish underworld rivers. Elsewhere, Pindar writes that with death, the soul is sped to the "shadowy shore of Acheron" (Pythian 11. 21), besides whose banks it dwells (Nemean 4. 85). The inevitability of death is also expressed through a metaphorical use of the underworld rivers. As Pindar says in Nemean 7, "The billow of Hades rolleth over all alike; that billow breaketh on the dimly known and on the famous" (30–31).[7] But while mankind is tormented by death, the gods are happily freed from sickness, old age, toil, and death. The contrast is aptly expressed by the first clear reference to Charon's ferry or the ferry place in extant Greek lyric. In Fragment 143 on "The Felicity of the Gods," Pindar writes:

40

κεῖνοι γάρ τ' ἄνοσοι καὶ ἀγήραοι
πόνων τ' ἄπειροι, βαρυβόαν
πορϑμὸν πεφευγότες 'Αχέροντος. . . .

But they, set free from sickness and eld and toils, having fled from the deeply
sounding ferry of Acheron. . . .

The adjective employed for the Acheron, *baryboan*, is striking; although gram-
matically modifying *porthmos*, its meaning applies to the waters of the river. The
thundering roar adds to the horror of the passage across Acheron, a voyage that
embodies the final and greatest of man's woes, death itself.

Following the archaic period in Greek literature, dating from Homer to around
500 B.C. and largely devoted to both the epic and lyric or elegiac poetry, a new
genre, tragedy, comes to the forefront in the classical period of the fifth century.
Except for a few historical works, tragedy, like epic, draws on myth for its subject
matter. By using myth to act out certain basic themes (such as revenge, the quest
for justice, punishment for sin, destiny, fatality, etc.), to study the forces at work
in the universe, and analyze the passions of human beings (ranging from pride
and violence to humility and suffering), fifth-century writers transform the elements of myth by emphasizing not the heroic so much as the tragic or comic features. The voyage to the underworld, for example, which in epic was treated in
part as adventure by phenomenological, anecdotal, and descriptive methods,
becomes fraught with mourning, lamentation, and scenes of blood and terror.
Death itself is no longer heroic but agonizingly horrific, and Hades' realm is
thought of less as a habitation for the dead and more as a place from whence
comes retribution. Concerning the underworld, then, tragedy is nondescriptive
but emotive; it employs the realm for the forces it embodies rather than for itself.
The dead, for example, are thought of as resting uneasily. They require retribution, pursuing the living as phantoms or in dreams, but most vividly through the
awful Erinyes, until some form of justice has been accomplished. The underworld, as a place of punishment for sin, of vindictiveness, and suffering, becomes
not merely gloomy but loathsome and terrifying.

While Greek tragedians occasionally refer to Charon or his boat, there is no
clear outline of the descent to Hades' nor of that realm's geography. Yet Aeschylus is not averse to representing on stage the terrors of the underworld, and Euripides, while sometimes attacking myth as a source of moral authority, refers still
more clearly to Charon. It is not until we reach Aristophanes and the comic theater, however, specifically in a play dealing with both Aeschylus and Euripides—the *Frogs*—that we find a major descent with Charon as a speaking per-
sonage.

The first ghost to appear on a Western stage is found in the oldest tragedy to
have come down to us, Aeschylus's *The Persians* (472 B.C.), one of the few plays
of the fifth century based on a recent historical event. Though the play belongs to
a comparatively early stage in the development of tragedy, Aeschylus himself was

over fifty when it was produced. The presence of the underworld in this play, the power of the dead, is evident everywhere. After the Chorus of Persian Elders have set the scene and spoken of the royal armament, Xerxes' deeds, and their fears, the queen mother speaks of her dismay and decides to offer rites to the underworld divinities in propitiation, much as Odysseus does in the *Odyssey*. But her aim is different: Odysseus desires to learn the future and talks to those with whom he has close ties; Queen Atossa (the name, incidentally, is unknown to Aeschylus), in response to an ominous dream, merely hopes to allay any nocent or malevolent power.

While she pours a libation, the Chorus beseeches "the conductors of the dead beneath the earth" to be gracious to the Chorus's prayers (625–627).[8] Whether the *pompoi* include Charon is not stated; rather, the Chorus invokes Hermes and Hades (Aïdoneus):

> Ye holy divinities of the nether world, Earth and Hermes, and thou, Lord of the dead, send forth to the light the spirit from below. . . .O Aïdoneus, Aïdoneus, thou who conveyest shades to the upper air, suffer our divine lord Darian to come forth! Ohe! (628–630, 649–651)

They are hopeful that his spirit may know a remedy for their distress (631–632), but they also wish to share their sorrows, "for a gloom, like that of Styx" hangs over them (664–667). At this, the ghost of Darius arises from his tomb, noting those who have invoked him and accepting his wife's libations kindly. But, "not easy is the path from out the tomb; for this cause above all—that the gods beneath the earth are readier to seize than to release" (688–690).[9] His time, in fact, is limited; "but speed ye," he says, "that I may be void of blame as to the time of my sojourn" (692).

While Darius's ghost refers to the "κατὰ χθονὸς θεοὶ" (689), no mention is made in *The Persians* of a boatman nor infernal rivers to be crossed. We must turn to the *Seven Against Thebes* (467 B.C.) for references to the waters of Kokytos and Acheron. When Eteocles prepares to meet his brother Polynices in combat at the seventh gate, the Chorus warns him: "Let not mad lust for battle fill thy soul and carry thee away" (686–687). Eteocles, however, as a son of Oedipus, is aware of his father's curse and responds:

> Since Heaven so urgently presses on the event, let all the race of Laïus, that hath incurred Phoebus' hate, drift adown the wind, apportioned to Cocytus's wave! (689–691)

The race of Laius is fated to die, a thought expressed through the vivid images of being hastened on the way by the wind and having been assigned the wave of Kokytos by lot.

The fate imagined by Eteocles is soon brought to pass, and the Chorus sees the bodies of both dead brothers, each killed by the other's hand. Aeschylus, with a magnificent metaphor, parallels the Chorus's lamentation and the crossing of the Acheron:

ἀλλὰ γόων, ὦ φίλαι, κατ' οὖρον
ἐρέσσετ' ἀμφὶ κρατὶ πόμπιμον χερῖν
πίτυλον, ὃς αἰὲν δι' Ἀχέροντ' ἀμείβεται
τὰν ἄστολον μελάγκροκον [ναύστολον] θεωρίδα,
τὰν ἀστιβῆ 'πόλλωνι, τὰν ἀνάλιον
πάνδοκον εἰς ἀφανῆ τε χέρσον.

(854–860)

But come, my friends, adown the wind of your sighs, ply with your hands about your heads the speeding stroke, which alway over Acheron wins passage for the dark and sable-sailed mission-ship unto the shore whereon Apollo sets not foot nor sunlight falls, unto the shore invisible, the bourne of all.[10]

That is, just as sailing with the wind speeds one's voyage, so sighs and lamentations hasten the crossing. The conducting or guiding oar strokes are visualized by the term πίτυλος—a word representing both the noise of repeated blows and the measured plashing of oars. Even the verb ἐρέσσω (Attic: ἐρέττω) means both to row and more generally to ply or urge. Unable to depict the descent on stage, the poet suggests the action through metaphor.[11] While doing so, he tells us more about the ship used to cross Acheron. There is no mention of Charon, but the boat itself is equipped with oars and black sails. The metaphorical language is further intensified through the use of the noun θεωρίς for ship. The θεωρίς was a sacred ship used to carry the θεωροί, state ambassadors sent to consult an oracle, to their destination. Thus as Herbert Smyth notes, the ship's mission stands in stark contrast to what we might expect from the noun employed. The poet has also described the underworld realm through the poetic device of litotes, a technique that renders the underworld's desolation more poignant by recalling what it is not. Of the six adjectives employed for the realm, a total of four are privative nouns.[12]

Vague and metaphorical references to Charon and his boat and to crossing underworld rivers become more substantial in Euripides. Rather than examine the underworld as seen in all his extant plays, I will concentrate briefly on two works that contain specific references to the boatman. Many have noted that with Euripides tragedy is in a process of change. The movement is from heroic tragedy to pathetic or romantic melodrama, perhaps most evident in the earliest play we possess by Euripides, the *Alcestis* (438 B.C.). In this play, after an initial confrontation between Apollo and Thanatos in which the death spirit affirms his right to bear off the wife of Admetus, Apollo claims that a man is on his way who will win her back. Soon after, a slave maiden announces Alcestis's last deeds, recalling with pathos her prayers for her children, her regret that another will take her place in the marriage bed, and her farewells to both children and servants (158–195). In the first stasimon, the Chorus asks Apollo to "oppose bloodthirsty

Hades" (225), but at their words, they see Alcestis carried from the house, dying, "doomed / to the Death God of the world below" (234–237). She herself apostrophizes the sun, sky and clouds, her land, home and bridal couch, in a last farewell, for her next words are:

> ὁρῶ δίκωπον ὁρῶ σκάφος [ἐν λίμνᾳ],
> νεκύων δὲ πορθμεὺς
> ἔχων χέρ' ἐπὶ κοντῷ Χάρων
> μ' ἤδη καλεῖ· τί μέλλεις;
> ἐπείγου· σὺ κατείργεις.
> τάδε τοί με σπερχόμενος ταχύνει.

$$(252–257)^{13}$$

> I see him there at the oars of his little boat in the lake,
> the ferryman of the dead,
> Charon, with his hand upon the oar,
> and he calls me now: "What keeps you?
> Hurry, you hold us back." He is urging me on
> in angry impatience.

While not present on the stage,[14] we hear the first words spoken by Charon and preserved in a complete work in Western literature.[15] His personality is captured through his speech and summed up by Alcestis. He is both impatient and surly; his tripartite discourse is irascibly succinct, composed of five words forming a question, a middle imperative, and an accusation. As Admetus laments, this is a bitter crossing. Charon's boat is also further characterized: the oars are two in number, and the boat is a *skaphos*, a hollowed-out vessel. While the diminutive *skaphis* is not used, the vessel is most likely a small boat or skiff, especially if only two-oared (δίκωπον). Charon, of course, is depicted as the ferryman of the dead, holding his hand, not on an oar, as in Lattimore's translation (252, 254), but on a *kontos*, a punting pole, which is most likely used for pushing off from the bottom in shallow water. The poet's use of κοντός and δίς κῶπαι seems strange; it would be difficult for Charon to handle two oars and a pole.[16] Perhaps as described in later poets, he forces those crossing to aid in rowing. Finally, the last adjective used to describe Charon, the present passive participle σπερχόμενος, may be interpreted in several ways. Simply, it means rapid or hasty; when referring to the mind, it can mean eager or vehement; or in respect to temper, it implies angry, hotheaded, and thus by inference impatient, impetuous, or brusque.[17] If Charon has only a small boat to transport the many dead, his haste and irascibility are understandable.

Alcestis cries that somebody is bearing her away to the dead, winged Thanatos himself, but she still has the strength for a lengthy pathetic speech to her husband. In his response, Admetus refers to both Orpheus and Charon:

> εἰ δ' Ὀρφέως μοι γλῶσσα καὶ μέλος παρῆν,
> ὥστ' ἢ κόρην Δήμητρος ἢ κείνης πόσιν

Alcestis says farewell to Admetus while Charun and Tuchulcha wait. Etruscan amphora
from Vulci. Cabinet des Médailles 918, Bibliothèque National, Paris. By permission of
Photographie Giraudon (8147).

ὕμνοισι κηλήσαντά σ' ἐξ Ἅιδου λαβεῖν,
κατῆλθον ἄν, καί μ' οὔθ' ὁ Πλούτωνος κύων
οὔθ' ούπὶ κώπῃ ψυχοπομπὸς ἂν Χάρων
ἔσχον, πρὶν εἰς φῶς σὸν καταστῆσαι βίον.

(357–362)

Had I the lips of Orpheus and his melody
to charm the maiden daughter of Demeter and
her lord, and by my singing win you back from death,
I would have gone beneath the earth, and not the hound
of Pluto could have stayed me, not the ferryman
of ghosts, Charon at his oar. I would have brought you back to life.

As Amy Dale notes (p. 80), after Alcestis's visionary encounter, the irony of Admetus's
hypothetical one is not to be missed. The passage is of great importance, for this is the
earliest reference in Greek literature to Orpheus's descent into Hades;[18] significantly,
Charon is identified with the Thracian poet's attempt to rescue his wife. Both he
and the unnamed *Ploutōnos kuōn* are seen as barriers. Here, incidentally, only
one oar is mentioned, and the boatman is called psychopompos, a common attribute of Hermes.[19]

   In the second stasimon, the Chorus offers us yet another vision of the crossing
to the beyond. Alcestis has died, and the Chorus says:

ὦ Πελίου θύγατερ,
χαίρουσά μοι εἰν Ἀίδα δόμοισιν
τὸν ἀνάλιον οἶκον οἰκετεύοις.
ἴστω δ' Ἀίδας ὁ μελαγχαίτας θεὸς ὅς τ' ἐπὶ κώπᾳ
πηδαλίῳ τε γέρων
νεκροπομπὸς ἵζει,
πολὺ δὴ πολὺ δὴ γυναῖκ' ἀρίσταν
λίμναν Ἀχεροντίαν πορεύ-
σας ἐλάτᾳ δικώπῳ.

(436–444)

O daughter of Pelias
my wish for you is a happy life
in the sunless chambers of Hades.
Now let the dark-haired lord of Death himself, and the old man,
who sits at the steering oar
and ferries the corpses,
know that you are the bravest of wives, by far,
ever conveyed across the tarn
of Acheron in the rowboat.

Charon is now "ἐπὶ κώπᾳ / πεδαλίῳ" (439–440)—which Lattimore translates as steering oar—rather than "ἐπὶ κοντῷ" (254). The use of the term *pedalion* is possibly proof that in Euripides' view, Charon does not row his boat. He uses either a punting pole to guide it through the shallows, or he sits at the tiller; in the latter instance, perhaps the boat is propelled by the wind in its sails. The earlier reference to two oars can possibly be interpreted now as referring to the two *pedalia* common on Greek ships. They were often joined by a type of yoke made of crossbars (ζεῦγλαι), which thus allowed one person to control both.[20] Concerning his personal appearance, Charon is now called an old man, as in the *Minyas*, and is the nekropompos over the Acheron, here called a λίμην, or marshy lake (cf. 902). In Aeschylus, where Charon is not specifically mentioned, the death passage is over Acheron, but only in Euripides are the boatman and the river clearly identified together. As a last note, Alcestis is ferried across by an "ἐλάτᾳ δικώπῳ" (444), again a twin-oared bark.[21]

Like Admetus, the Chorus also wishes it could rescue Alcestis:

εἴθ' ἐπ' ἐμοὶ μὲν εἴν,
δυναίμαν δέ σε πέμψαι
φάος ἐξ Ἀίδα τεράμνων
Κωκυτοῦ τε ῥεέθρων
ποταμίᾳ νερτέρᾳ τε κώπᾳ.

(455–459)

Oh that it were in my power
and that I had strength to bring you
back to light from the dark of death
with oars on the sunken river.

The realm of death is epitomized in its enclosed chambers and the streams of Kokytos (457–458), escape from which is aided by an oar from the nether river (459). The use of Kokytos and an implied boatman (whether Charon or not is unclear) suggests the intermingling of infernal rivers characteristic of later poets who employ Charon by turns on all four infernal rivers.

Herakles, who rescues Alcestis after a wrestling match with Thanatos (1140 ff.), finds that his own offspring confront Charon in the *Herakles* (ca. 417 B.C.), and now there is no thought of rescue. The action in this play begins with Amphitryon telling how Herakles, as a last labor for Eurystheus, ''descended down / to Hades through the jaws of Taenarus / to hale back up to the light of day / the triple-bodied dog'' and has not returned (23–25). Apparently his last deed has resulted in death (425–429). Now, adds the Chorus,

> στέγαι δ' ἔρημοι φίλων,
> τὰν δ' ἀνόστιμον τέκνων
> Χάρωνος ἐπιμένει πλάτα
> βίου κέλευθον ἄθεον ἄδικον·

(430–433)

> His friends have left his house,
> and Charon's ferry waits
> to take his children's lives
> the godless, lawless trip of no return.

The voyage is godless and unjust (433) because it is instigated by a tyrant. More importantly, unlike Herakles' return with Alcestis, this *keleuthos* is *anostimos*, without return. Charon's oar (*plata* by synecdoche may be translated as boat), which awaits the children, emphasizes the water barrier beyond which there is no return. The Chorus seems to asume that once the children have been ferried by Charon they are lost forever.[22]

When Megara brings the children on stage dressed in their funeral garments, she invokes Herakles in Hades (490 ff.): ''Come, even as a ghost even as a dream'' (494–495). Instead, the hero appears in his physical reality, his bow in hand. When Amphitryon finally asks if he has truly come from Hades, Herakles replies that he has, indeed, brought back the triple-headed dog (611), but his return was delayed by his desire to free Theseus (619). Whether or not he escaped by way of Charon's boat is not mentioned. The Chorus merely says he has returned from the Acherontian harbor (''λιμένα . . .'Αχερόντιον'' [770]), a reference to Hades by way of synecdoche.

When the figure of Madness suddenly appears on the roof of the palace, the tone again changes to horror and despair. Iris, the messenger of the gods, addresses Madness:

> ἔλαυνε, κίνει, φόνιον ἐξίει κάλων,
> ὡς ἂν πορεύσας δι' 'Αχερούσιον πόρον
> τὸν καλλίπαιδα στέφανον αὐθέντῃ φόνῳ.

(837–839)

drive him [Herakles], goad him, shake out the sails of death
and speed his passage over Acheron,
where he must take his crown of lovely sons.

Euripides here refers, it seems, to a ferry (*poros*) over Acheron; if so, it is surely to
that of Charon. The noun may, of course, be translated, as Lattimore does, by the
more general term *passage*. At any rate, the poet's variety of nouns for Charon's
boat is noteworthy.

Herakles' children, then, cross to the beyond to return no more. While the
crossing in Euripides is the result of a murderous and insane act, the situation
here also lends itself to pathos. In fact, as we will see when discussing the lyric,
one of the high points of the descent theme concerns the pathetic and poignant
crossing of a little child in Charon's boat.

In Greek tragedy, where references to Charon are especially brief, the structural
units most often emphasized are those of encounter. The actual descent is of little
importance, and any descriptive detail is included not to situate the nether realm
more clearly but to evoke a sense of horror at the awful power of the dead and the
gods of the underworld. Charon, by association, is one of the many malevolent
forces, and though not roaming in search of victims like the Erinyes or Thanatos,
he does seem to be waiting and hastening the dying.[23] The existence of rivers to
be crossed and references to Charon's ferry, now equipped with oars, sails, and a
punting pole, are standard features of tragic descents. Crossing the river is a vivid
image of the finality of death, beyond which there is no return, and often the
whole of Hades is succinctly epitomized by referring to either Acheron or Kokytos. Though full of horrors, the underworld itself is now seen as a continuation
of life on earth, with punishment for misdeeds and conscious existence for the
defunct.

Notes

1. Sapho is justly famous for her analysis of the passions of love, jealousy, and despair, emotions
that result at times in a desire for death. See, for example, fragments 31, 94, and 95, and cf. Archilo-
chos, fragment 112*D*, in which the poet hints at death through the Homeric expression of mist falling
on the eyes.

2. See, for example, Moschus of Syracuse (fl. ca. 150 B.C.) 1. 13–14, in *The Greek Bucolic Poets*,
ed. J. M. Edmonds.

3. While Homer employs the motif to stress the inevitability of fate (*Iliad* 6. 146–149), the elegist
Mimnermus of Colophon (fl. ca. 630 B.C.) uses the motif to emphasize the brevity of life and the fra-
gility of man. See fragment 2 in *A Short History of Greek Literature from Homer to Julian*, trans.
Wilmer C. Wright, p. 77. Bacchylides (fl. fifth century B.C.) employs the image of leaves in relation to
dead souls, which, through Virgil, is passed on to Dante. See Ode 5. 63–67 in *Lyra graeca*, ed. Edmonds, 3:144–149.

4. See, for example, Anacreon (fl. ca. 572 B.C.) as translated by J. M. Kirkwood, *Early Greek
Monody*, p. 173.

5. Let me mention the poems of the following poets: Asius of Samos (seventh or sixth century
B.C.) in *Early Greek Elegy*, ed. T. Hudson-Williams, p. 44; Alcaeus (fl. early sixth century B.C.) in
Greek Lyric Poetry from Alcman to Simonides, by C. M. Bowra, pp. 161–162; Theognis (fl. ca. 540

B.C.) in *Elegy and Iambus*, ed. Edmonds, 3:315; Theocritus (third century B.C.); 15. 102–103, 136–137, ed. by A. S. F. Gow; Bion (fl. end of second century B.C.), "Lament for Adonis" 1. 45–55, in *Greek Bucolic Poets*, ed. Edmonds; and the anonymous "Lament for Bion" under Moschus 3, in *Greek Bucolic Poets*.

6. Pindar, *The Odes of Pindar*, ed. and trans. Sir John Sandys.

7. The equality of all before inevitable death, a theme picked up by Latin poets, had been expressed much earlier by Solon (early sixth century B.C.) in an elegiac poem preserved by Plutarch. See Solon in *Elegy and Iambus*, ed. Edmonds, 1:139.

8. All translations of Aeschylus's works are those of Herbert Weir Smyth unless otherwise indicated.

9. Descent, however, is easy—at least according to another play of Aeschylus with which Plato, perhaps tongue in cheek, disagrees. Referring in the *Phaedo* most likely to the tragedian's lost *Telephus*, Plato through his mouthpiece Socrates says: "And the journey is not as Telephus says in the play of Aeschylus; for he says a simple path leads to the lower world, but I think the path is neither simple nor single, for if it were, there would be no need of guides, since no one could miss the way to any place if there were only one road. But really there seem to be many forks of the road and many windings; this I infer from the rites and ceremonies practised here on earth." Plato, *Phaedo* 107E–108A. I quote from the translation of Harold North Fowler, 1:371.

10. Smyth explains the image in these terms: "As the souls of the brothers are now being conveyed across Acheron in Charon's boat, the Chorus in imagination aid their passage by the ritual of mourning. Their song of lamentation stands for the wind, the beating of their heads by their hands are the strokes of the oars. Contrasted with the grim vessel that transports all spirits to the sunless land of Hades is the ship that goes to the festival at Delos, the 'clearly-seen' island, the land of Apollo, god of light and health" (1:395, note 1).

11. Aeschylus's use of metaphor and vivid language has aroused various critical judgments; Quintilian's expresses later divergencies: "sublimis et gravis et grande loquus saepe usque ad vitium, sed rudis in plerisque et incompositus" (cited in D. W. Lucas, *The Greek Tragic Poets*, p. 118).

12. Before leaving Aeschylus, I might add that one of his fragments preserved by Pollux (5. 47) refers to Χάρων as one of Actaeon's dogs; see Pollux in *Tragicorum graecorum fragmenta*, ed. Augustus Nauck, no. 245. For Charon as a dog's name, see the major classical dictionaries. Pollux, incidentally, refers to the stairway beneath the proscenium as χαρώνειοι κλίμακες, but both the stairway and the name have been considered much later Roman innovations. If so, we wonder how the ghosts of Darius and Klytaemestra in Aeschylus and Death in Euripides's *Alcestis* rose on stage. Ferguson claims that Klytaemestra rises "through a concealed entrance in the stage floor" (*A Companion to Greek Tragedy*, p. 102); he describes the action as shocking. Since most comments on staging and production and explanations of technical terms are found in scholia and lexica of the Alexandrian scholars, these are not always reliable for the fifth century B.C. (Lucas, p. 40). Carl Robert supposes that Charonian stairs were used in Sophocles' *Ichneutae*, where a cave that appears to be underground is indicated ("Zu Sophokles' *Ixneytai*," p. 536). In his translation of Euripides' *Hecuba*, where the ghost of Polydorus delivers the *prologos*, William Arrowsmith claims that the ghost enters above, *ex machina*. This would seem strange, since Polydorus's first words are, "Back from the pit of the dead, from the somber door / that opens into hell, where no god goes, / I have come" (1–3, quoted from Grene and Lattimore, *The Complete Greek Tragedies*, vol. 6). T. B. L. Webster claims that Darius enters through the stage building (*Greek Theater Production*, p. 8).

13. All Greek quotations of Euripides have been taken from the Loeb Library edition by Arthur S. Way, vols. 3 (*Herakles*) and 4 (*Alcestis*). Unless otherwise noted, all translations of Euripides are by Richmond Lattimore.

14. The vividness of the description has caused Thomas G. Rosenmeyer to write: "I like to think that Charon actually appears on the stage. Both the folk tale associations of the play, and its position in lieu of a satyr play, would encourage the utilization of the grotesque" (*The Masks of Tragedy: Essays on Six Greek Dramas*, p. 226). For comments on the imagery of Alcestis's three visions of death (Charon, Thanatos, and Night), see Shirley A. Barlow, *The Imagery of Euripides: A Study in the Dramatic Use of Pictorial Language*, pp. 56–57.

15. A younger contemporary of Euripides, Timotheus of Miletus (ca. 450–360 B.C.), who would have been about twelve when *Alcestis* was produced, apparently represented Charon on stage in an actual speaking role in his dithyramb, or *nomos*, entitled *Niobē*. If so, this might be the earliest known dramatic appearance of the boatman on stage. The appropriate extant speeches are the following: (1) Charon's "Make room in [or get in] the ferry" ("χωρεῖν δὲ πορθμίδ' ἀναβοᾷ," as cited by Machon and preserved in Athenaeus, *Deipnosophistai* 8. 341); (2) the response "I'm coming; why are you

shouting at me" ("ἔρχομαι· τί μ' αὖεις," quoted from *Niobē* by Zeno of Citium and preserved in Diogenes Laertius 7. 28) and possibly (3) "Get aboard the ferry, Hermes" ("ἔμβα πορθμίδος, Ἑρμᾶ," quoted by Teles and cited in Stobaeus, *Anthology* 5. 67). I quote with a revised translation of my own from J. M. Edmonds, *Lyra graeca* 3:326–327. See chapter 3 for Aristophanes' parody of this scene in *Lysistrata*.

16. Amy Dale would disagree. In a note on the phrase ἐν λίμνᾳ, she claims that "the water is the 'λίμνα Ἀχεροντία' of 443, with deep middle stream over which Charon rows with two oars, and stagnant marshy edges through which he poles the boat into the bank and holds it there" (see her edition of *Alcestis*, p. 72, notes).

17. Dale feels that the connotation is impetuous (p. 256). Herman W. Hayley, writing over a half century earlier, claims that "it is more probably that 'σπερχόμενος' is used absolutely, 'in haste,' as it so often is in Homer" (*The Alcestis of Euripides*, p. 99).

18. See Ivan M. Linforth, *The Arts of Orpheus*, pp. 16–17. Linforth claims that "it is significant, furthermore, that in the story to which Euripides alludes Orpheus must have been successful in his undertaking. If he had failed, any reference to the matter would be inappropriate" (p. 17). But this is not necessarily so. Admetus is boasting that if *he* had the voice of Orpheus, *he* would have succeeded (understood: where Orpheus himself failed; my emphasis). That is, Orpheus, despite his voice, failed to obey the prescription of the infernal deities, but I, Admetus, would have been more successful. Or we might understand: If I lost my wife a second time, neither Kerberos nor Charon could have restrained me from returning for her as they did Orpheus. The boast of course is empty, because first, Admetus does not have Orpheus's voice and second, in his attachment to life, Admetus has shown himself to be unheroic. It will be instead Herakles who by brute strength alone will conquer the forces of death.

19. Panayota Kyriazopoulou claims that psychopompos is attributed to Charon in confusion (p. 44).

20. Later poets, specifically Aristophanes and Lucian, describe the ferryman as requiring others to row his ship. Sometimes Charon is seen holding the steering paddles; at other times, he tends the sail.

21. I translate the noun ἐλάτη as *bark*, since the dual meaning of wood and boat is also inherent in Greek, where ἐλάτη is properly *fir* and may by metonymy be thought of either as an oar or an entire ship. Richmond Lattimore translates it as rowboat, while A. S. Way renders the noun as oar, specifically "twy-plashing oar."

22. Perhaps Alcestis, who the Chorus had envisioned as crossing the Acheron, had not yet arrived at Charon's boat. In the *Alcestis*, her body is being carried to its "burning place and grave" (608) when Herakles learns of her death. He himself asks where the funeral is being held (834) in order to find Death there and regain Alcestis (840–849). Only if Herakles is unable to find Death at the tomb will he have to go down to "the sunless homes of those below" (850–853). In fact, as he tells Admetus later (1142), Herakles found and fought Death by the tomb. Perhaps then in this instance Herakles did not overcome Charon! His descent for Kerberos, incidentally, as most older accounts present the story, was not by way of Charon's boat. Seneca is one of the first to describe an actual encounter between the two.

23. As one of the characters says in a play by the middle comedy poet Antiphanes (ca. 388–311 B.C.); "No one ever dies, master, who is ready to die. Charon draws the legs struggling to live and leads unwillingly on to his ferry those who are fed and lived in abundance. Hunger is the cure for immortality." Preserved by Stobaeus, *Anthology* 4. 53.3 ff. See Theodorus Kock, *Comicorum atticorum fragmenta*, 2:86; or J. M. Edmonds, *Fragments of Attic Comedy*, 2:200–201. I quote from the translation by Katherine Lever, *The Art of Greek Comedy*.

3

Greek Comedy: Aristophanes

The most extensive dramatic presentation of Charon in Greek or Latin literature belongs not to tragedy but to its counterpart, comedy. In the *Frogs* of Aristophanes, for example, the boatman appears as a speaking character. Details of the underworld crossing with Charon, however, are also found in two other Aristophanic works, the earlier old comedy *Lysistrata* (411 B.C.) and the later middle comedy *Plutus* (388 B.C). In *Lysistrata*, written during the darkest period of the Peloponnesian War, women from all the Greek states ally to deny sexual favors to the men in order to gain peace.[1] At one point, in full rebellion, they encounter a magistrate, drive off his archers, and mock him, first by dressing him as a woman and then as a corpse. Lysistrata says:

> σὺ δὲ δὴ τί μαθὼν οὐκ ἀποθνήσκεις;
> χοιρίον ἔσται· σορὸν ὠνήσει·
> μελιτοῦτταν ἐγὼ καὶ δὴ μάξω·
> λαβὲ ταυτί· καὶ στεφάνωσαι.

> (599–602)

> Truly, old fellow, 'tis time you were dead.
> So a pig shall be sought, and an urn shall be bought,
> And I'll bake you and make you a funeral cake.
>   Take it and go.

As Benjamin Rogers notes, the *melitoutta*, or honey cake, is for Kerberos, while the *tauti* (Attic for the neuter plural demonstrative ταῦτα) in the next line is the small change with which to pay Charon's fare. If this were true, this passage is the first to mention the necessity of paying for transportation to the beyond. Lysistrata's only words, however, are ''Take these things and be crowned''! She seems to be referring to a funeral wreath, since the aorist middle imperative στεφάνωσαι follows immediately. Also, it is unlikely that in mocking the magistrate she would actually give him money. (We note that she merely promises him the other items.) Rogers seems to be translating and commenting rather imaginatively, possibly influenced by later references to money in the *Frogs*.

When the magistrate stands dumbfounded, Lysistrata cries:

τοῦ δεῖ; τί ποθεῖς, χώρει 'ς τὴν ναῦν·
ὁ Χάρων σε καλεῖ,
σὺ δὲ κωλύεις ἀνάγεσθαι.

(605–607)

Take it and go.
What are you prating for? What are you waiting for?
Charon is staying, delaying his crew,
Charon is calling and bawling for you.

Outraged and frustrated, the magistrate runs off to complain to his fellow magistrates.

Charon himself is not characterized in this speech, nor as in the translation, does he have a crew; he merely calls the (imagined as) dying man, who is hindering the embarcation. The order to get into the ship is actually made by Lysistrata. I might note that line 606, "ὁ Χάρων σε καλεῖ," recalls Euripides' "Χάρων / μ' ἤδη καλεῖ" (*Alcestis* 254–255). Just as Alcestis hindered the boatman from cross-

Charon, by the Reed Painter. National Museum 1759, Athens. Photo of the Museum.

ing, so, too, does the magistrate. In the present context, of course, the pathos of the Euripidean scene is converted into farce, and the horror of the underworld is nullified by mocking buffoonery of the women.

In the *Plutus*, a mythological burlesque dealing with the god of wealth, Charon is referred to in a verbal conflict between Kario and the old koryphaios, where the young slave mocks the old age of the men in the Chorus. Since the play deals with wealth and specifically with why the evil prosper and the good are poor, it is appropriate that the reference to Charon concern the fare for the crossing:

ἐν τῇ σορῷ νυνὶ λαχὸν τὸ γράμμα σου δικάζειν,
οὐ δ' οὐ βαδίχεις; ὁ δὲ Χάρων τὸ ξύμβολον δίδωσιν.

(277–278)

Kario: You've drawn your lot; the grave you've got to
                                    to judge in; why delay now?
Old Charon gives the ticket there; why don't you pass away now?

The joke lies in parallels between the judicial system in Athens and the underworld reference. Rogers explains it as follows:

A dicast, wishing to exercise his judicial duties, would go in the early morning to the κληρωτήρια, and draw a letter, one of the second ten letters (from Λ onwards) of the Greek alphabet. Armed with this letter, he would present himself at the Court-house to which the same letter was affixed, and take his seat for the day. At the rising of the court he would receive from the presiding Archon a ξύμβολον, a ticket or certificate of attendance, on presenting which to the κωλακρέτης he would obtain his pay. (p. 386)

Kario thus tells the old Chorus leader that the latter has drawn by lot a letter that will allow him to enter his coffin (or burial urn) and he will receive his ticket from Charon (instead of from the Archon). As a scholiast points out, Charon is an anagram for the Archon. The ticket then is not for one's salary but passage across the river of death. The metaphorical language, equating the judicial procedure with the underworld crossing and thereby lampooning the Chorus leader's old age, is both highly irreverent and witty[2] and stands in contrast to the serious and grim metaphorical language of Aechylus in the *Septem*, where the acts of mourning are visualized in terms of passage across Acheron.

In discussing these two references in Aristophanes, I have recalled passages from both Aeschylus and Euripides. It is in the *Frogs* (405 B.C.), however, that the comic poet treats most fully the two Attic tragedians. But rather than examine in detail the extended contest of the two poets in the nether world, I would like instead to look first at the description of Hades by Herakles, then at the descent of Dionysos and Xanthias, and finally at the structural functions of the descent as a whole.

The action of the *Frogs* opens with Dionysos, who is disguised as Herakles and accompanied by his facetious servant Xanthias. Apparently preparing for a long journey, the god visits Herakles himself for instructions. When the hero suggests various manners of death, Dionysos says he wants to go as Herakles did. Herakles responds:

> Herakles: It's tough.
> It's a long trek. First
> You come to a huge lake . . .
> Bottomless. . . .
> Dionysus: How do I
>   Get across?
> Herakles: In a pram-
> Dinghy. An old man.
> The fare's two obols.

(PD, 136–140)[3]

Or as Rogers translates, "An ancient mariner will row you over / In a wee boat, *so* big. The fare's two obols."[4] The diminutive πλοιάριον (-αριον is usually contemptuous)[5] is employed by Herakles to frighten Dionysos. This little boat will transport the god "ἐπὶ λίμνην μεγάλην . . . πάνυ / ἄβυσσον" (137–138). The immensity of the bottomless lake stands in sharp contrast to the boat. The ναύτης himself is an old man (ἀνὴρ γέρων [139–140]), and for the first time, we learn that a fare of two obols is charged. Herakles continues with a parodistic description of the geography of Hades and its inhabitants.

Humorous exchanges between master and servant follow, during which the poet introduces a brief magnificent episode to further situate the descent; I refer to the corpse carried across the stage and to Dionysos's attempt to bargain with him to serve as porter. The vitality of the dead is hilarious,[6] and the scene, which ends with the dead man's striking imprecation, "Strike me alive again if,"[7] must have lingered in the spectator's mind. Coming as it does before the actual descent, this scene recalls in structure Odysseus's encounter at the thresholds of the beyond with the unburied ghost of Elpenor.

When the dead man has been carried off, Dionysos says: "Let's proceed to the boat" (χωρῶμεν ἐπὶ τὸ πλοῖον" [180]), and the next words are Charon's. Presumably, we have arrived at the Acherusian Lake (although many translators and commentators perversely call it the Styx), but exactly how Charon's boat appears is a matter of speculation. Some claim that his boat is conveyed around the orchestra, possibly by ropes, rollers, wheels, or stage hands, although it could have been drawn along in front of the stage backdrop.[8]

Charon's first words characterize him instantly as a boatman: "ὠόπ, παραβαλοῦ," the first word being a cry of the *keleustēs*, or boatswain, to stop rowing, the second an aorist imperative meaning put to land. Whether he is speaking to an imaginary (or real) crew or to himself is unclear; Charon must be just off scene because Xanthias asks, "Whatever's that?" (Rogers, 181). Dionysos, as if seeing a scene change, announces: "Why, that's the lake, by Zeus, / Whereof he spake, and yon's the ferry-boat" (Rogers, 181–182). As a final *didascalia*, Xanthias exclaims, "Poseidon! And that's Charon!" (PD, 183). Humorously, rather than repeat Dionysos's more general expletive νὴ Δία (181), the servant specifies the appropriate acquatic divinity "νὴ τὸν Ποσειδῶ" (183). With a triple greeting, Dionysos puns on the similiarity in sound between Charon's name and the imperative χαῖρε, welcome or hail (184).[9]

Oblivious to the greeting, Charon, the typical Greek ferryman it seems, sets about announcing his destinations:

> τίς εἰς ἀναπαύλας ἐκ κακῶν καὶ πραγμάτων;
> τίς εἰς τὸ Λήθης πεδίον, ἢ 'ς 'Όνου πόκας,
>
> (185–187)
>
> Who's for rest from toil and pain?
> Who's for Lethe's plain? Who wants
> Oblivion, land of Cerberus?
> This way to eternal Nowhere!
>
> (PD)[10]

Lethe, mentioned here for the first time in extant Greek literature, is clearly referred to as a plain (*pedion*) rather than a river.[11] The land of Nowhere is more comically described as the land where asses have wool.

Dionysos, without hesitation, answers I (188), and Charon tells him to get in quickly. As if having second thoughts, Dionysos in the same line asks him where he is really going. To the Crows? Charon responds, apparently politely but in reality jesting at Dionysos's expense, "Yes, by Zeus, because of you" (191). They are going to the Crows for Dionysos—perhaps implying, as Rogers notes, that Dionysos's manifest destiny is to be fed to the *korakes*.[12]

But no sooner does Dionysos say, "Come here, lad," than Charon responds, "I do not conduct a slave" (190). The assertion is astounding, though perhaps less so to a Greek of the time. Even in Hades, there is a class structure! Up to this point in the tradition, only those lacking funeral rites have been denied passage. But the reason behind this undoubtedly Aristophanic innovation becomes immediately clear when the boatman adds a political note: "Unless he has fought for his bodyrights at sea" (Rogers). As most commentators note, the reference seems to be to the Athenian naval battle and victory at Arginusae, where slaves helped man the ships and were afterwards freed (Stanford, p. 89). Having taken place just six months before the performance of the play, the battle undoubtedly was still a cause for high emotions. Here, Charon's disdain for a slave who neglected to fight must have reflected the sentiments of the Athenian citizens. Xanthias, in fact, offers a feeble excuse having to do with his eyes as the reason for evading military service. For the conservative poet, the draft evader is punished through Charon. A lesser poet might have been tempted at this point to put a tirade or bitter invective in the boatman's mouth, but Charon is somewhat perfunctory in his response: "Then fetch a circuit round about the lake" (Rogers, 193). Again, this is the first known indication of an alternative route around the water barrier; if not an Aristophanic invention, perhaps Theseus and Peirithoos in the *Minyas* were able to circumvent passage across the lake in the same fashion.

Ever practical, Xanthias wants to know where he should wait, and Charon's response again reminds us vaguely of Homeric underworld topography: "παρὰ τὸν Αὐαίνου λίθον" (194), he says in part, "beside the Withering stone" (Rogers). Hermes, of course, conducted the dead suitors by a rock on their downward journey; Aristophanes may be inventing a parallel landmark. Xanthias laments his ill-omened journey and starts out alone.

Charon and Dionysos are left on stage, and the following scene has great comic possibilities, especially regarding *commedia dell'arte lazzi*. For example, when Charon tells Dionysos to *sit to* his oar (my emphasis), he takes the boatman to mean *sit on* your oar (197), and the ferryman must give the god a detailed set of instructions to prepare him for rowing. Having called out to anyone else who wishes to cross to hurry, Charon directs his attention to the god, who is addressed with the comic name *gastron* (200). When the boatman tells Dionysos to stop playing the fool (202), he can hardly refer, as Stanford notes, to words, since the god has been unusually laconic (p. 91). With a series of compound privatives, Dionysos complains that he is "ἄπειρος, ἀθαλάττωτος, ἀσαλαμίνιος," "unskilled, unseamanlike, unsalaminian" (204). The sonorous sweep of the line recalls and parodies the grand Aeschylean manner. Charon counters his protestation of naval inexperience by announcing that once he dips his oar in the water, he will hear music of frog-swans (207), an oxymoronic admixture sure to cause some laughter. On the journey then, Charon will function as *keleustēs* and the frog chrous as the *triēraulēs*, or piper. While Aristophanes introduces Dionysos as a rower for comic purposes, the action also characterizes Charon: he is imperious enough to force even a god to aid in the crossing. Though a comic figure, or rather the straight-man of a comic team, Charon retains a hint of perhaps a more foreboding character in popular lore.

In the comic exchanges between Dionysos and the chorus of frogs, Charon has no part; I note in passing that these are dead frogs who once croaked on the marshy land in Athens! Like the animals hunted by Orion in Homer, they continue their earthly existence below the ground. Though lasting only sixty lines and perhaps never appearing on stage, this famous chorus gave the play its title. Charon himself speaks again but only briefly when the ferry reaches the far shore; his last words are:

> ὦ παῦε, παῦε, παραβαλοῦ τῷ κωπίῳ.
> ἔκβαιν', ἀπόδος τὸν ναῦλον.

(269–270)

Easy there! Easy! Push her in
With your oar! Now hop out,
And pay your fare.

(PD)

And in the same line, Dionysos takes his farewell with an abrupt, "Here's two obols," for his next words are addressed to Xanthias. Thus despite having to row himself across, Dionysos must still pay his fare to the boatman. Charon, though represented by later writers as parsimonious and avaricious, refers only once to the fare in Aristophanes, and it is Herakles and Dionysos who mention the exact sum.

Structurally, it is my contention that Aristophanes employed the descent motif much as did the poet of the *Odyssey*; that is, it functions as an extended frame for a lengthy episode or series of episodes incidental to the descent itself. In the *Frogs*, however, it should be noted that the frame is as lengthy as the enclosed episodes.

In the *Odyssey*, Odysseus descends for a prophecy much as Dionysos descends for a poet. Fulfillment of the initial happy thought in the *Frogs*, however, is of minor importance. Odysseus sees and carries on extended conversations with dead heroes and heroines while Dionysos witnesses as judge a lengthy contest between Aeschylus and Euripides. The closing of the frame in both cases is equally rapid: having detailed the descent at length, Homer for adventure and awe, Aristophanes for burlesque and laughter, each poet is little concerned with representing the actual return of their characters, a return that can only be anticlimactic, unlike that of an Orpheus, who truly descends to bring someone back to life. Dionysos's avowed purpose is incidental to the main action of the play, which is not to say that it is insignificant; in fact, his purpose, which begins somewhat lightheartedly, ends up being politically serious.

A few more parallels to the Homeric episode can be pointed out. Just as Odysseus receives advice from Kirke, so Dionysos questions Herakles and receives a description from him of what he will encounter. One important distinction is that while Odysseus goes alone, or rather with an amorphous crew who play no real part in the action, Dionysos is accompanied by a shrewd servant, whose inclusion has major implications. One of the most notable features of drama, of course, is action, represented, in part, through dialogue; the servant Xanthias allows that dialogue, and consequently the descent, to become comic. There is a further parallel, though tenuous, between Elpenor and the corpse. Neither has yet entered the depths of the underworld and both are encountered just before the major underworld episodes. Furthermore, just as some souls were denied passage in Homer, notably Patroklos, so Xanthias is refused by Charon. In both instances, a type of moral judgment is involved, one invoking the social and religious necessity of funeral rites, the other based on political considerations and social condition.

As a type of frame, however, the descent episode in the *Frogs* is quite different from that in the *Odyssey*; in simplest terms, Homer employs the descent as an epic motif in the return of a wandering hero, while Aristophanes uses the topos as pure comedy. A rapid descent might have permitted a more traditional structure for the entire play, but Aristophanes preferred to develop the underworld voyage at length because of its suitability for humorous confrontations, one of which is with Charon. The boatman himself has his comic moments but as a foil for Dionysos seems to retain some of his tragic seriousness; Charon, for example, is not really mocked. In denying Xanthias passage, he connects himself to the political current running throughout the play, and by forcing Dionysos to row, he evidences some pugnacious characteristics, though he seems neither sullen nor churlish. Without including Charon and his boat, the chorus of frogs would lose its comic undertones if not its very justification for being in the play.

As a figure mentioned in tragedy and appearing in comedy, Charon's role in the descent assumes increasing importance. He is rapidly becoming a canonical figure in any voyage to the beyond.[13] In Aristophanes, the descent becomes, in simplest terms, a necessary feature for getting Dionysos into the underworld to witness the *agōn*. But rather than treat the journey precipitously, the poet slows down the voyage by expanding comic episodes. The actual lake crossing is the predominate structural unit, but the initial encounter is also emphasized, for Charon arrives shouting an order, though not in the sterner imperatives of the tragedians, and details his destinations in humorous terms. Rather than directed at Dionysos as a living intruder, a fact that is ignored, Charon's initial speech is a general proclamation. Instead of a terrible underworld divinity, he seems to be an Athenian ferryman ready to transport whoever wishes to cross, provided she/he is not a slave. Even the details of Charon's ferry provide humor, with Dionysos first sitting on an oar and then rowing wildly in rhythm with the frogs' croaking. The price of the voyage itself may have also had humorous connotations. We do not know with what antics the boatman moved on stage, but in comedy the figure retains some of the seriousness of its tragic counterpart. Charon is present to remind us that in descending, even a god, Dionysos in this instance, is subject to the ferryman's imperious control.

Notes

1. All citations are from the Loeb Library edition in three volumes with translations by Benjamin B. Rogers; the *Lysistrata* and *Plutus* are in vol. 3.

2. The old koryphaios's response to Kario is, in fact, to call him an impudent rogue (μόϑων and κόβαλος, 279).

3. All Greek quotations and the numeration of all lines, including translations, have been taken from the edition by W. B. Stanford. I have also employed commentaries by Rogers (*The Comedies of Aristophanes*, vol. 5) and T. Mitchel (*The Frogs of Aristophanes*). The following are the translations employed: PD = Aristophanes, *Plays* II, trans. Patric Dickinson. Rogers = *Five Comedies of Aristophanes*, trans. Rogers. Any unacknowledged translations are my own.

4. The last two lines read: "ἐν πλοαρίῳ τυννουτῳί σ' ἀνὴρ γέρων / ναύτης διάξει δύ' ὀβολὼ μισϑὸν λαβών" (139–140).

5. Aristophanes, *The Frogs*, ed. Stanford, p. xl.

6. As Stanford says, "To the delight of the audience the Corpse sits up and takes an interest in Dionysus' offer " (p. 87). Katherine Lever picks this episode as one that never fails to strike her sense of humor (*The Art of Greek Comedy*, p. 130).

7. Stanford notes that the imprecation is a sardonic reversal of Achilles' affirmation in *Odyssey* 11. 489 ff. that any form of living is better than death. The corpse, then, implies that life in Athens is so bad that it would be terrible to have to return.

8. For the various critical stances mentioned, see the works listed in the Bibliography under Stanford (p. 88), G. Norwood (p. 130), A. L. M. Cary (pp. 52–53), T. B. L. Webster (p. 57), and K. J. Dover (pp. 179–180).

9. "χαῖρ', ὦ Χάρων, χαῖρ', ὦ Χάρων, χαῖρ', ὦ Χάρων." As Stanford notes, the Scholia list this line as a quotation from *Aithon*, a satyr play by the tragedian Achaeus. According to Rogers's notes, the poet put these words into the mouths of the riotous Satyrs as they, much to Charon's indignation, came tumbling into his ferry boat. It is easy to imagine Charon as a figure mocked in a mythological burlesque. Ludwig Radermacher, however, considers the greeting as solemn, perhaps a triple invocation, but to me this seems unlikely. As Stanford explains, the phrase with its heavy assonance is more likely intended to be comic; the derivation from a satyr play would support this.

10. In the Greek, a few more destinations are mentioned, specifically Taenarus and the Crows (or Ravens). Note the pun on Homeric names, for example, Kerberians for Kimmerians, also indicated by the Scholiast.

11. Plato (*Republic* 10. 621A) refers to Lethe as both a plain (πεδίον) and a river ('Αμέλητα ποταμόν [621A] and Λήϑης ποταμόν [621C]), while Virgil calls it a river (*Aeneid* 6. 714, 749).

12. Stanford merely claims that the polite response, "Just for *your* sake" is a "sardonic parody of an obliging ferryman" (p. 89).

13. It would be interesting to know if Charon appears in a burlesque of Odysseus's adventure, the *Nekyia* by the Alexandrian parodist Sopater of Paphos (early third century B.C.). For Sopater, see Norwood, p. 75. In his mythological burlesque *Heroes*, Timocles, a late middle comedy poet, apparently represented Charon on stage if an extant passage preserved by Didymus (ca. 80–10 B.C.) can be attributed to the boatman: Charon (?) says: "Hermes, if willing, helps me row at need [literally: "joins (me) in conducting these (scholia: ghosts)]; he's / Gladly come down to oblige fair Aristeomêdes." J. M. Edmonds, *The Fragments of Attic Comedy*, 2:613.

4

Hellenistic Poetry and the Later Greek Epigram

While early Greek lyricists develop motifs related to the underworld descent, most of the short poems in which Charon is referred to by name belong to pastoral or elegiac poets of the Hellenistic and later periods. As is true of the Alexandrians in general, poems where the boatman appears are brief, highly refined, and often clever. The epigram is especially apt to refer to the boatman, especially the sepulchral inscriptions in Book 7 of the *Anthologia palatina*.[1] The fictional epitaph, in fact, becomes a richly developed and artistic form, offering the poet an opportunity to develop a wide variety of sepulchral motifs.[2]

Along with the development of underworld themes, poets, much as mythographers, also offered explanations of infernal names; the origin of the name Acheron, for example, was sought in the name for pain (ἄχος). In his *Persephone*, the dithyrambic poet Melanippides (fl. ca. 480–450 B.C.) writes: "And because it goeth pouring forth pains within the bosom of Earth, it is called Acheron" (H. E. Smyth, *Greek Melic Poets*, pp. 453–454). And Licymnius of Chios, who taught that a name derives its beauty or its deformity partly from the sound and partly from the meaning, says that "'Αχέρων ἄχεα / βροτοῖσι πορϑμεύει" (ibid. p. 459)—"Acheron conveys the pains of men." From the fragment, it almost seems that Acheron is the name of the ferryman who conveys the dead across the stream. Stobaeus, who has preserved this fragment, adds another, again from Licymnius, which describes the Acheron: "Μυρίαις παγαῖς δακρύων ἀχέων τε βρύει" (ibid., p. 135); that is, "the river swells by means of ten thousand springs of tears and pains." The line recalls the general use of the expression *infinite sorrow* (ἄχος μυρίον) and brings to mind the phrase πηγαὶ δακρύων —the source of tears (one's eyes). The idea of the river being fed by the tears of man reappears in Dante, who makes the Gran Veglio of Crete responsible for the infernal rivers, formed from his many tears.[3] Here, Licymnius distills the horror of the underworld into one forceful image.

One of the motifs common to early Greek lyric and Hellenistic poetry is the imprisoning bank of Acheron, which reappears in Theocritus,[4] who not only refers, as did Pindar, to the ferry over Acheron, but who also alludes to Charon, though not by name. In Idyll 17 (ca. 273 B.C.), the "Panegyric of Ptolemy," Theocritus praises first Ptolemy's father and then his mother Berenice, who is deified by the poet;

> O Lady Aphrodite, chiefest beauty of the Goddesses, as 'twas thou hadst made her to be such, so 'twas of thee that the fair Berenicè passed not sad lamentable Acheron, but or e'er she reached the murky ship and that ever-sullen shipman, the ferrier of the departed, was rapt away to be a Goddess in a temple. . . . (45–50, trans. Edmonds, *The Greek Bucolic Poets*)

In the first reference to Charon in a pastoral poet (although this encomium lacks the pastoral motif),[5] the boatman is characterized by the phrase στυγνὸν ἀει (always gloomy) and his ship is dusky (κυανέαν, the hue of death,[6] even Acheron is πολύστονον, mournful or much lamenting. The tenebrous adjectives and somber underworld elements—river, ship, and ferryman—stand in sharp contrast both to fair Berenice and her fate.

One of the early elegiac poets to refer to the figure of Charon is Hermesianax of Colophon (third century B.C.), a poet influenced by both Mimnermus and Antimachus. Like Antimachus, he searched mythology for lovers, compiling the tales

Charon, by the Reed Painter. National Museum 1999 (from Eretria), Athens. Photo of the Museum.

in three books of elegiacs addressed to his mistress, Leontion. His use of the catalog, canonical in epic, for love stories has a long and felicitous tradition, beginning with the Hesiodic poets and continuing through the Italian Renaissance in such authors as Pulci and Poliziano. Central in these love affairs is the tale of Orpheus and his descent for his wife.[7] In a passage preserved by Athenaeus, Hermesianax describes Orpheus's encounter with Charon:

Such was she whom the dear son of Oeagrus [Orpheus], armed only with the lyre, brought back from Hades, even the Thracian Agriopê [Eurydice]. Ay, he sailed to that evil and inexorable bourne where Charon drags into the common barque the souls of the departed; and over the lake he shouts afar, as it pours its flood from out the tall reeds. Yet Orpheus, though girded for the journey all alone, dared to sound his lyre beside the wave, and he won over gods of every shape; even the lawless Cocytus he saw, raging beneath his banks [literally *brows*]; and he flinched not before the gaze of the Hound most dread, his voice baying forth angry fire, with fire his cruel eye gleaming, an eye that on triple heads bore terror. Whence, by his song, Orpheus persuaded the mighty lords that Agriopê should recover the gentle breath of life.[8]

Charon, by the Reed Painter. Greek lekythos. 5th cent. B.C. By permission of the Museum of Art (25.082), Rhode Island School of Design. Museum Appropriation and Special Gift.

With Alexandrian inventiveness and an all-inclusive manner, Hermesianax has enlivened the traditional story. Charon is not merely impatient; he actually drags souls into his boat; Cocytus, personified, and Kerberos, with his fire-breath, are magnificent. The "cruel eye gleaming" brings to mind later depictions of Charon himself; if we need more evidence of the poet's inventiveness—and apparent humor—the rest of the fragment will provide it. Hermesianax goes on to present Homer languishing over Penelope! And Hesiod is in love with Eoia, while Alcaeus and Anacreon are rivals for the love of Sappho, and so forth.

Aside from these extravagancies, the poet's representation of Orpheus's descent is quite lively and intriguing. Charon's shouting is familar from Euripides, while dragging souls into the boat very likely reflects his representation in middle comedy. The reeds in the river are a new element that others will imitate. Throughout the passage, emphasis is on not only underworld denizens, magnificently drawn, but Orpheus as musician. He descends armed with only his lyre; he dares to sing beside the lake; he wins over the gods and quiets even raging Cocytus; and he succeeds in winning to life Agriopê by his song.

Another poet, Leonidas of Tarentum, active in the middle of the third century B.C., refers in his epitaphs and poems of lament to not only Acheron and the ship across its waters (see *Ant. Pal.* 7. 648, 726) but the ferryman himself. The poet's fictitious epitaph for Diogenes is the first in a long line of similar renditions. The epigram presents the cynic addressing Charon himself:

> Ἀΐδεω λυπηρὲ διήκονε, τοῦτ' Ἀχέροντος
> ὕδωρ ὃς πλώεις πορθμίδι κυανέῃ,
> δέξαι μ', εἰ καί σοι μέγα βρίθεται ὀκρυόεσσα
> βᾶρις ἀποφθιμένων, τὸν κύνα Διογένην.
> ὄλπη μοι καὶ πήρη ἐφόλκια καὶ τὸ παλαιόν
> ἔσθος χὼ φθιμένους ναυστολέων ὀβολός.
> πάνθ' ὅσα κἠν ζωοῖς ἐπεπάμεθα ταῦτα παρ' Ἀιδαν
> ἔρχομ' ἔχων, λείπω δ' οὐδὲν ὑπ' ἠελίῳ.

(Gow and Page, *Hellenistic Epigrams*, 1:126)

Mournful minister of Hades, who dost traverse in thy dark boat this water of Acheron, receive me, Diogenes the Dog, even though thy gruesome bark is overloaded with spirits of the dead. My luggage is but a flask and a wallet and my old cloak and the obol that pays the passage of the departed. All that was mine in life I bring with me to Hades and have left nothing beneath the sun. (Paton, 7. 67)

Apostrophized as a troublesome (literally, *painful*) servant of Hades, Charon is described as sailing over the water of Acheron in a murky ferry. The adjective *kuaneos*, employed by Theocritus for Charon's ship (17. 49) and by Anyte for death (*Ant. Pal.* 7. 646.4) emphasizes the gloom of the crossing, while reference to the ship being overladen with spirits of the dead is an innovation. Like Diogenes, who carries the few items he possessed in life along with his one-obol fare,[9] these spirits have a weighty consistency. As well as being crowded, the *baris* is *okruoessa*, chill or dreadful; the adjective *icy* is elsewhere applied to Acheron itself,[10] and the term *baris* refers to the Egyptian barges used on the Nile. As we will see, Zonas of Sardis employs the same term, and it is used by Diodorus Siculus (1. 96) to support his claim that the mythological figure Charon originated in Egypt.

On the same theme, an anonymous epitaph reads: "O Ferryman of the dead, receive the Dog Diogenes, who laid bare the whole pretentiousness of life" (Paton, 1. 63). Here Charon is apostrophized as "νεκυστόλε . . . πορθμεῦ." Epitaphs by Honestus and Archias follow that of Leonidas more closely; while neither poet changes the basic concept, each adds a personal touch. Honestus, after describing Diogenes in one elegiac couplet, concludes with: "I bring all to the ferryman, for I left nothing on earth. But you, Cerberus dog, fawn on me, the Dog" (Paton, 7. 66). Addressed to Kerberos rather than Charon, the poem evinces its true purpose as a literary exercise through the final witty parallel between Diogenes' appellation and the infernal monster's essence. Given the dog's traditional fierceness, however, the request that he wag his tail in friendliness is quite appropriate.

Archias, whose epigram like Leonidas's, is composed of four couplets, mirrors more closely the model, both in structure and concept; consider the two couplets that refer to the crossing:

> O boatman of Hades, conveyor of the dead, delighting in the tears of all, who dost ply the ferry o'er this deep water of Acheron, though thy boat be heavy beneath its load of shades, leave me not behind, Diogenes the Dog. (Paton, 7. 68)

Again we note the literary elaboration, here dealing with Charon's name; Archias plays on the etymology that sees the verb χαίρω (to rejoice)[11] in Χάρων. Thus Charon is apostrophized not only as νεκυηγέ but also as "κεχαρμένε δάκρυσι πάντων" (1), rejoicing in the tears of all. The boatman's ship (ὁλκάς) is again weighed down with the souls of the dead ("ὑπ' εἰδώλοισι καμόντων" [3]), and to Acheron, Archias has added the adjective *deep*—"βαθὺ . . .'Αχέροντος ὕδωρ" (2).

Among the more interesting imitators of Leonidas is the first-century poet Zonas of Sardis (fl. ca. 90–80 B.C.), also known as Diodorus. A. S. F. Gow and D. L. Page, in fact, claim that he surpasses his model, being an exceptionally skillfull word-coiner and phrase-maker (*Garland* 2:413). In one epigram, far from being an imitator, Zonas describes a scene that is among the most poignant connected with the crossing theme:

> Ἄϊδη ὃς ταύτης καλαμώδεος ὕδατι λίμνης
> κωπεύεις νεκύων βᾶριν, *ἑλῶν ὀδύνην*,
> τῷ Κινύρου τὴν χεῖρα βατηρίδος ἐμβαίνοντι
> κλίμακος ἐκτείνας, δέξο, κελαινὲ Χάρον·
> πλάζει γὰρ τὸν παῖδα τὰ σάνδαλα, γυμνὰ δὲ θεῖναι
> ἴχνια δειμαίνει ψάμμον ἐπ' ἠονίην.

(7. 365)

Dark Charon, who through the water of this reedy lake rowest the boat of the dead to Hades . . . reach out thy hand from the mounting-ladder to the son of Cinyras as he embarks, and receive him; for the boy cannot walk steadily in his sandals, and he fears to set his bare feet on the sand of the beach.

What was earlier applied to the boat is here applied to Charon; he is now apostrophized as *kelaine*, black or gloomy. The adjective emphasizes the chthonic features of the ferryman and prefigures his demonic transformations. However, the fierceness of the boatman, who incidentally rows his own boat, is muted, we imagine, in the presence of the child. We expect that at least the speaker's request for aid and pity will soften the brusqueness of the traditional figure.[12] The poet begins with the death ship and the gloom of the underworld in order to conclude with the contrasting vision of the child, depicted with all the humanity of a living creature. The theme of the unjustness of an early death is completely lacking in the poem, which seems to reflect the Homeric acceptance of fate. What the poet expresses, however, is the desire that even in death the child find the care afforded on earth. Among the new elements in the poem are the ladder for embarcation and the sandy beach; the reeds are reminiscent of Leonidas. These details,

Child leading its mother to Charon's boat, probably by the Painter of Munich 2335. Greek lekythos. 2d half 5th cent. B.C. By permission of The Metropolitan Museum of Art, New York. Rogers Fund, 1909 (09.221.44).

which add to the reality of the scene, extend to the son of Cinyras: the boy's extreme youth is aptly characterized through his unsureness in his sandals, and his fear of the cold sand touches the heart. For its deep emotion and visual intensity, the poem is one of the the the crowning achievements of the epigrammatic works dealing with Charon. Andre Michalopoulos[13] has justly cited it as an example of "the deep humanity and the love of children which prevailed among the ancient Greeks.[14]

Another inscription, possibly intended for a relief or a painting, concerns the crossing of Niobe and her children. The author is Antipater of Thessalonica;[15] Niobe appeals to Charon as follows:

> Thou ferry-man of the dead, receive me, who could not hold my tongue, alone with my children; a boat-load from the house of Tantalus is sufficient for thee. One womb shall fill thy boat; look on my boys and girls, the spoils of Phoebus and Artemis. (Paton, 7. 530)

In two couplets, the poet captures the essential details of Niobe's pride and punishment. The immensity of her chastisement is reflected in her request that she and her children ride alone with none accompanying them in Charon's boat. The craft, elsewhere capable of carrying hosts of people, will be filled by her and the offspring of a single womb, her twelve children. Even in death, we detect the boast for which Leto punished her, although here the tone is one of lamentation. Charon himself, unmentioned by name, is merely a means of depicting the size and plight of Niobe's family.

The convivial and satirical epigrams of the *Anthology* also provide a glimpse of Charon.[16] Lucillius, a grammarian who lived under Nero, writes of the death of an especially bad poet who, we are told, left directions when he died that twelve lyres and twenty-five cases of music be cremated with him! As Hewitt translates the final rather pointed couplet:

> With five and twenty chests of tunes
> Charon's now entering your lagoons.
> O where in Hell is refuge please,
> When Hell contains Eutychides?

> (11. 133)

In the original, Charon is seen approaching Eutychides ("νῦν ὑμῖν ὁ Χάρων ἐπελήλυθε"), and the boatman's arrival signals upcoming suffering for the inhabitants of Hades, who must soon listen to the poet's wretched songs.

Two final epigrams of interest take us to the sixth century A.D. Written by Julian, the prefect of Egypt under Justinian, the first poem concerns the death of a sixteen-year-old wife, Anastasia. Having been married less than a year, the girl is much lamented; as the poet says, "Both thy father and husband shed bitter tears for thee, and perchance even the ferry-man of the dead weeps for thee" (Paton,

7. 600). Including fierce Charon in earthly mourning is unusual and effective; the pathos of Anastasia's death passes beyond men to the underworld divinities themselves! Though unstressed in the poem, the sense of marvel is implicit.

The second poem, composed of two couplets, expresses the contradictions inherent in death:

> A. "Charon is savage." B. "Kind rather." A. "He carried off the young man so soon." B. "But in mind he was the equal of greybeards." A. "He cut him off from pleasure." B. "But he thrust him out of the way of trouble." A. "He knew not wedlock," B. "Nor the pains of wedlock." (Paton, 7. 603)

As with Zonas, we find the motif of the death of a young person, even though the youth is no longer a child. But more importantly, rather than emphasizing the pathos of the child's death, the poet, in a stoic vein, attempts to find consolation in the fact that the youth thus avoids the troubles of life. In the dramatic opposition of the two speakers, Charon himself represents the good and bad faces

Youth preparing to step into Charon's boat, by the Painter of Athens 1934. Greek lekythos. 2d half 5th cent. B.C. By permission of The Metropolitan Museum of Art, New York. Gift of Samuel G. Ward, 1875 (75.2.6).

of death, the two sides of which are analyzed with some rhetorical detachment. Charon, who begins in classical and Hellenistic lyric as a figure of poetic vitality with evocative and descriptive traits, thus becomes in time, at least in one poet, a metonym of abstract death.[18]

To conclude, let me note that Charon's depiction in Hellenistic poetry, though brief, is often quite suggestive. Elegiac poetry, infused as it is with emotion, seems to permit descriptive adjectives and phrases expressive of the poet's inner feelings and attitudes. As a consequence, not only is the ferryman occasionally characterized in some detail but so are his boat, the Acheron, its banks, and the crossing itself. All are given emotive and empathetic qualities. Structurally, the unit of greatest development is the address to the ferryman, followed in importance by the description of his boat and the crossing. For the last aspect, of course, narrative detail is lacking; instead, the crossing is often included as an element in the description of Charon. The initial units then, those of preparation and descent and Charon accosting the descender, are relatively unimportant. Furthermore, those descending are rarely heroes and are not given to comedy, although both these motifs are found. Of greater interest to the Hellenistic poets are the dead souls who must pass by way of Charon's ferry. The felicitious decision of these poets is to have chosen the appeal to Charon as the moment of greatest elegiac intensity in the descent to the underworld.

Notes

1. For textual citations, I have employed both W. R. Paton's *The Greek Anthology* (Loeb Library, 1953) in five volumes and the editions of A. S. F. Gow and D. L. Page, *The Greek Anthology: Hellenistic Epigrams* (Cambridge: Cambridge University Press, 1965), vols. 1 and 2, and *The Greek Anthology: The Garland of Philip and Some Contemporary Epigrams* (Cambridge: Cambridge University Press, 1968), vols. 1 and 2. Book 7, devoted to sepulchral inscriptions, contains only a few that are genuine; as most scholars note, the rest are poetical exercises.

2. For an analysis of the variety of themes in Greek sepulchral inscriptions, see Richmond Lattimore, *Themes in Greek and Latin Epitaphs*.

3. *Inferno* 14. 112–120. Undoubtedly, Dante takes the idea from later poets if it is not a felicitous invention of his own.

4. See 12. 19. The adjective for Acheron is ἀνέξοδον, *without return*.

5. For a discussion of Theocritus's encomia and why they avoid the pastoral mode, see Thomas G. Rosenmeyer, *The Green Cabinet: Theocritus and the European Pastoral Lyric*, pp. 122–124.

6. Although the adjective need not be sinister, since it is applied elsewhere to normal ships (see, for example, Euripides, *Troades* 1094), in this context it seems forboding. Gow notes several parallel uses of κυάνεαν with death: Anyte's κυάνεος θάνατος (*Anthologia palatina* 7. 646); the κυανέου Ἄιδος cited in Kaibel (*Epigrammata graeca* 1046. 84); and references in Theognis (709) and Hesiod (*Scutum* 249). Charon is called dusky by Leonidas (*Ant. Pal.* 7. 67), and for Virgil, his ship is a "ferruginea . . . cymba" (*Aen.* 6. 303). See Gow, p. 334, note to line 49.

7. In Euripides' *Alcestis*, we have seen how Charon is integrated into the earliest known version of Orpheus's descent. Later writers, specifically Plato, make much of the dissimilarities in the parallel tales about both Alcestis and Orpheus. In Plato's *Symposium*, Phaedrus speaks of the courage instilled by love. Alcestis, he says, was willing to lay down her life for her husband, and the gods in admiration of her noble action granted her the privilege of returning to earth (179*B*). But he claims the gods sent Orpheus away empty, with only an apparition, because he contrived to enter Hades alive (179*D*). Other poets, however, notably Plato's contemporary Isocrates, felt that Orpheus had succeeded in bringing the dead back to life (*Busiris* 11. 7 ff.).

8. Hermesianax, in Athenaeus, *The Deipnosophists*, trans. Charles Burton Gulick. The passage from Hermesianax is found in Book 13. 597 ff. Athenaeus, a native of Naucratis, Egypt, lived in Rome at the end of the second and beginning of the third century A.D.

9. The ὀβολός is modified by the verb ναυστολέω in the sense of "that which carries the dead over Acheron" (Gow and Page). The form would be expected with Charon; here, it is used singularly for an inanimate object. According to Callimachus, fragment 278, one city is exempted from paying the fare: "That is why in this city alone even the dead receive no coin as fare, which is the custom for others to carry in dry mouths" (trans. C. A. Trypanis, *Callimachus: Aetia-Iambi-Lyric Poems*, p. 203). Trypanis notes that according to common belief, the poet is referring to the city of Hermione in the Argolid. Suidas, however (s.v. πορθμήιον), claims that the people of Aegialos, near Sicyon, were also excused by Demeter from the fare paid to Charon, because inhabitants of the region had informed the goddess of Persephone's fate when she was taken by Hades.

Callimachus, incidentally, also refers to Charon in fragment 628 in the phrase "ἄνωγε δὲ πορθμέα νεκρῶν" ("do you order the ferryman of the dead" [trans. Trypanis]). Among other poets in the *Anthologia* who refer to the obol are Antiphanes (11. 168), Lucillius (11. 171), and Ammianus (11. 209).

10. See, for example, Theocritus: "ἐπὶ ψυχροῦ Ἀχέροντος" (16. 31). The variety of adjectives and descriptive phrases employed by the Hellenistic and later poets for Acheron is truly outstanding. In Book 7 alone of the *Anthologia*, the Acheron is referred to as "the dark house of Acheron" (Andronicus, 181; Simias, 203), unknown (Anonymous, 482), "the pale stream of Acheron" (Anyte, 486), and all-subduing (Theodoridas, 732).

11. As Cornutus (first century A.D.) says: "ὁ δὲ Χάρων ἴσως μὲν κατ' ἀντίφρασιν ἐκ τῆς χαρᾶς ὠνομάσθη." See *De natura deorum* (Ἐπιδρομὴ τῶν κατὰ τὴν Ἑλληνικὴν θεολογίαν παραδεδομένων), ed. by Fridericus Osannus, chap. 35, p. 213; or the edition by Carolus Lang, *Theologia graecae compendium*, p. 74. Servius also gives us a definition by antiphrasis.

12. In an anonymous couplet, attributed by some to Bianor, Charon is also addressed in relation to a dead child, but the tone is no longer propitiatory: "Ever insatiable Charon (Πάντα Χάρων ἄπληστε), why didst thou wantonly take young Attalus? Was he not thine even had he died old?" (Paton, 7. 671). The thought reminds us of Euripides' *Alcestis*, where Apollo tells Death that he will get but one soul, whether now or later. I might add that another tragedian, namely, Aeschylus, is imitated by Callimachus in his depiction of the Acheron. In fragment 191, Hipponax of Colophon, who has returned from the dead, says: "I will not tell a long story . . . for not even I have much time to spare, as I must whirl back to the heart of Acheron" (32–35, cited in Callimachus, *Aetia, Iambi, Lyric Poems*, trans. C. A. Trypanis). The reminiscence of Darius in the *Persians* is evident.

13. Andre Michalopoulos, "The Classical Tradition," p. 3.

14. Another poem, under the name of Diodorus Grammaticus, and thus possibly by Zonas, refers to the water of Kokytos "where wailing is loud" (*Ant. Pal.* 7. 700). I refer to the poem because contemporary and later poets occasionally add interesting details about this underworld river. Erycius (? late first century B.C.), for example, speaks of a critic of Homer as suffering punishment in Kokytos (7. 377), and the Emperor Julian (A.D. 331–363) couples both Acheron and Kokytos in speaking about punishment (Oration 7 "To the Cynic Heracleios," cited in *The Works of the Emperor Julian*, 2:129). Antipater of Sidon (fl. ca. 120 B.C.) refers to a boat on the Kokytos (Paton, 7. 464), as does another poet, Aemilianus (Gow and Page, 9. 218). As a last source for the boat motif, let me mention two poems by Antiphilus (fl. ca. A.D. 53). The first is on Hieroclides, whose boat grew old with him "and when he died she buried him and shared his sailing even to Hades" (Gow and Page, 7. 635). Whether or not both went down together at sea is unclear. While this seems possible, Gow and Page, referring to other epigrams on the same theme (see, for example, Adaeus, 7. 305, and Etruscus, 7. 381, where Hieroclides is burnt with his ship), claim that the ship formed his funeral pyre. The second epigram of Antiphilus also seems to bear out the editors, for it refers to the death of the ferryman Glaucus, adding: "They burnt the shell over him, that the old man might sail to Hades in his own boat" (Gow and Page, 9. 242).

15. This Antipater is to be distinguished from the Sidonian, who also writes about the crossing to the beyond (7. 464). Unknown outside the *Anthology*, the Thessalonican flourished from around 11 B.C. to A.D. 15 (Gow and Page, *Garland*, 2:18–21; OCD, s.v.).

16. That Charon appeared earlier in satirical epigrams is attested by an epigram of Alcaeus of Messene (ca. 200 B.C.), who refers to a one-eyed monster as "the Charon of the wine-cup" (*Ant. Pal.*, 11. 12). The reference is to King Philip, son of Demetrius, who killed Epicrates the comic poet and Callias the tragic poet. Here, Charon seems to be a death-demon rather than a ferryman.

17. Joseph William Hewitt, "The Humor of the Greek Anthology," p. 72.

18. I might note that the influence of the poets extends to actual sepulchral inscriptions and epitaphs where Charon is occasionally mentioned. See, for example, the inscriptions cited by Richmond Lattimore (*Themes in Greek and Latin Epitaphs*, pp. 75, 87, 316). On page 287, reference is made to an epitaph for an historical doctor named Charon. Compare Paul Friedländer, *Epigrammata: Greek Inscriptions in Verse From the Beginnings to the Persion Wars*, p. 89: "χαῖρε Χάρων, οὐδ(ε)ίς τὺ κακῶς λέγει οὐδὲ θανόντα, / πολλοὺς ἀνθρώπων λυσάμενος καμάτου" ("Hail, Charon, no one speaks ill of you even in death [i.e., even when *you* are dead]; you have freed many mortals from sickness"). Were θανόντα not in the accusative case, this would seem to be an address to Charon the death-demon, who can be seen as freeing the sick by hastening their death. For other inscriptions, see the *Corpus inscriptionum graecarum*, ed. Ioannes Franzius, vol. 3, no. 6203.16, no. 6239.8, and vol. 4, no. 8139. The last reference is to the hunt of Calydonia. Among the dogs named, one is called Charon. See also *Epigrammata graeca ex lapidus conlecta*, ed. Georgius Kaibel, no. 302.2, no. 566.8, no. 646.3, and no. 647.16. For all these sources, full publication data can be found in the bibliography, primary sources, s.v. *Epigrams and Inscriptions*.

5

Latin Epic: Virgil and Lucan

Virgil is the first major Latin poet to present an extended portrait of Charon in a descent episode.[1] Just as Homer establishes the pattern of the underworld visit for the Greeks, Virgil, following in his footsteps, determines for Latin poets both the standard features of the descent episode and the description of Charon. But though guided by tradition, the Augustan poet enriches the theme with his own creative touches. Like later Greek depictions by Lucian, Virgil's representation of Charon is, in part, a result of *contaminatio*. The poet's awareness of previous epic (notably Homer, Hesiod, Apollonius, and the epyllia), Greek drama (see *Aeneid* 4. 469–473), Alexandrian poetry, Greek philosophical thought (including the mystery religions), and the Etruscan underworld has been attested by scholars.[2] The *Aeneid*, and Book 6 is an excellent example, illustrates the poet's eclectic use of his sources.[3] Before examining in detail Virgil's depiction of Charon in the *Aeneid*, however, I will first discuss the reference to the boatman in his shorter didactic epics, the *Georgics*, in many ways preliminary preparations for the *Aeneid*; and second, present briefly the poet's treatment of those underworld rivers connected with the crossing.

Early reference to Charon is found in Virgil's treatment of the Orpheus myth (*Georgics* 4. 454–506). While most accounts of Orpheus's descent for Eurydice in Greek and Latin mythographers do not contain references to Charon, both Virgil and Ovid mention the ferryman in their versions of the myth;[4] in this they reflect Euripides, who alludes to Charon as an obstacle in relation to Orpheus (*Alcestis* 357–362). As developed by Virgil, the story of Orpheus's descent begins in pathos. After Eurydice has been bitten by the serpent, not only her Dryad companions but even nature herself weeps in sorrow (*Georgics* 4. 460–463).[5] Orpheus, too, at first attempts to solace his grief in song—te dulcis coniunx, te solo in litore secum, / te veniente die, te decedente canebat'' ("[he] sang of thee, sweet wife—of thee, to himself on the lonely shore; of thee as day drew nigh, of thee as day declined [465–466]). But following these words, with no further explanation, we find the bereaved poet descending into Hades through the jaws of Taenarus (467–470). Arriving immediately before the underworld king, Orpheus attracts the bodiless shadows (*umbrae . . . tenues*), who are moved by his song to rise from lowest Erebus.[6]

Virgil sets the scene with a descriptive note before turning to the other inhabitants of the realm.

But round them are the black ooze and unsightly reeds of Cocytus, the unlovely mere enchaining them with its sluggish water, and Styx holding them
fast within his ninefold circles. (478–480)

The halls of death, Tartarus, and the Eumenides, all stand in amazement. Even
Cerberus's triple mouths are held open, and Ixion's wheel ceases to rotate (481–
484). The force of Orpheus's song is so great that the poet does not even bother to
detail a confrontation scene with Pluto; instead, we see him returning with Eurydice, who follows behind as ordered by Proserpine (485–487). Orpheus, of course,
unmindful of the restrictions, turns around in his frenzy and breaks the established pact.

Virgil extends this dramatic moment by portraying at length the grief of Eurydice and her words of farewell. She vanishes like "smoke mingled with thin air"
(499–500), an image that heightens the emotional tone of pathos[7] as does the
reference to Orpheus yearning to say more (501–502). The inexorable finality of
the separation is immediately felt when Charon enters the scene with the same
suddenness with which Orpheus first descended:

Charon holding a shade by a rope. Terracotta urn. Museo Etrusco, Chiusi. By permission of
Fratelli Alinari.

nec portitor Orci
amplius obiectam passus transire paludem.
Quid faceret? quo se rapta bis coniuge ferret?
quo fletu Manis, qua numina voce moveret?
illa quidem Stygia nabat iam frigida cumba.

(502–506)

Nor did the warden of Orcus suffer him again to pass that barrier of the marsh.
What could he do? Whither turn himself, twice robbed of his wife? With what
tears move Hell, with what prayers its powers? She, alas! even now death-cold,
was afloat in the Stygian barque. (HRF)

Following Charon's refusal of passage, the series of plaintive questions expresses
Orpheus's futility in pitting himself against the rigid ferryman in whose Stygian
craft cold Eurrdice is already sailing across the river.

Turning to Virgil's descriptions of the underworld rivers, let me point out that
contrary to Homer, Virgil situates the realm of the dead below the earth in Italy
rather than across the ocean in a vague, mysterious land. As in Homer, the underworld is characterized by its rivers; for Virgil, however, it is Styx with its nine
circles (*A* 6. 439; *G*. 4. 480) rather than Ocean, which surrounds all. Once, however, the Sibyl refers to the realm of Dis as girded by Cocytus (6. 132) and mentions a stygian lake to be traversed; most likely, she is not referring to the Styx
itself but employing the adjective *stygian* in the general sense of underworld. On
the actual trip, she points out the deep pools of Cocytus (''Cocyti stagna alta'')
and the stygian marsh (''Stygiam . . . paludem'' [6. 369]). The stygian mere, as
we will see, could easily be the Acheron, which is described as marshy by the
Greek tragedians.[9]

While almost all editors refer to Charon as being on the Styx, it is more likely
that he ferries souls over the Acheron, which is both a river and a lake. Or since
the underworld rivers often seem to be branches of each other, perhaps he ferries
the shades across more than one. The Acheron, for example, flows into Cocytus
(6. 295–297). While Charon is seen on the stygian wave (6. 385) with a stygian
boat (6. 391), he himself refers to a previous crossing as being over a lake (6. 393).
The use of the adjective *stygian*, again, does not necessarily imply the Styx itself
but merely the underworld. Likewise, when the Sibyl rebukes Palinurus for desiring to cross the ''stygian waters'' and the cruel river of the Furies (Cocytus, according to most editors, 6. 374–375), it is possible that she is referring in the first instance to the Acheron.

That the Acheron is considered a barrier is evident from its general use in
Aeneid 5. 99, where ghosts return to the earth, released from Acheron; also,
stygian marsh could be the Acheron or Cocytus, since Aeneas at one point refers
to ''the gloomy marsh from Acheron's overflow'' (6. 107). Elsewhere, to clarify
the point, we read that ''hence a road leads to the waters of Tartarean Acheron.
Here, thick with mire and of fathomless flood, a whirlpool seethes and belches
into Cocytus all its sand'' (6. 295–297). Whatever the body of water is called over
which Charon transports the dead, it does not seem to be the river Styx, as later

commentators (e.g., Servius) and most modern mythographers and critics state. When the poet refers to a barrier, he speaks of the Styx's ninefold circles as well as an "unlovely mere with its dreary water" that enchains the shades (6. 438–439). As we have seen in discussing the Greeks, they never place Charon on the Styx itself; later Roman poets who do so were possibly confused by Virgil's use of stygian waters for all underworld rivers. When Virgil writes that Charon bears shades over hoarse-voiced waters (*rauca fluenta* [6. 327]), he most likely has the Greek etymology of Acheron as much-lamenting in mind. Earlier in *Georgics* 2. 492, the poet had clearly referred to "the howls of hungry Acheron" ("sterpitum . . . Acherontis avari"). The use of *avaricious* with Acheron implies that the river is chary of releasing its souls to the upper world. It is perhaps from expressions such as this that among the Latins Charon is considered greedy and avaricious.

Virgil's use of the name *Acheron* is as confusing as his use of other underworld rivers; we are unsure whether the poet thinks of the Acheron as a body of water, a river god, or both. We read of the priestess who sees phantoms, hears voices, talks to the gods, "and speaks with Acheron in lowest Avernus" (7. 91). Here it is possible that rather than a personification Acheron is merely used metonymically for the shades of the underworld in general. Juno, for example, appears to use the Acheron as synonymous with the underworld when she claims that she will appeal to the lower gods (*Acheronta movebo* [7. 312]) if the upper ones will not help her. Elsewhere we read that the only honor that the dead have in the lower world— called Acheron—is to be buried: "interea socios inhumataque corpora terrae / mandemus, qui solus honos Acheronte sub imo est" (11. 23–24). The use of Acheron for the underworld is quite appropriate here, of course, since that river is traditionally a barrier for those lacking funeral rites. The river that Aeneas crosses is, in fact, that of no return (6. 425).

In turning to *Aeneid* 6, let me note that much has been written on the centrality of the descent in Aeneas's development. The importance of the book was pointed out even before Servius, who says:

> All Virgil is full of learning, but for learning this book takes the chief place. The greater part of it is from Homer. Some of it is simple narrative, much turns on history, much implies deep knowledge of philosophers, theologians, and Egyptians, to so great an extent indeed that many have written complete treaties on points of detail in this book.[10]

That Virgil in Book 6 tries to sum up the tradition, philosophies, and fancies of the past has been evident to many.[11] Most discussions of the structure of *Aeneid* 6 are based on a distinction between sources and aims, ranging from the dual division into mythological and philosophical to the triple division into mythological, moral, and philosophical.[12] But rather than examine in detail the structural principles of the book as a whole, let us turn directly to the encounter at the Acheron. After the description of personified horrors and supernatural monsters at the vestibule of Hades (264–294),[13] the representation of Charon follows that of an underworld deity in human form. Unlike other infernal inhabitants, such as Minos and

Rhadamanthus, who are not gods but great heroes, Charon is definitely described as a god.[14] Yet he is give a *terribilità* that adds to the gloomy atmosphere of the realm.

The depiction of the boatman is structured in three distinct moments, the first two of which are descriptive, while the third, delayed and prepared by the encounter with Palinurus, is dramatic. The first moment, following the hectic passage in which phantom terrors are mentioned in rapid profusion and Aeneas, in fear, draws his sword against them, represents a momentary withdrawal from active involvement on the part of the descender. Whereas Aeneas springs immediately to action when faced with the classical monsters, he is not at first directly threatened by Charon; in fact, the picture that Virgil now leisurely unfolds remains detached from the descent movement as such for over twenty lines. The description of Acheron begins in line 295, and Aeneas's first response to the sight is delayed until line 317. In the meantime, we are offered first an extended portrayal of the boatman, one of the hightlights of Virgil's descriptions, and then an example of the boatman's effect, not on Aeneas but on the souls of the dead. After these two descriptions, the poet pauses to allow the Sibyl to explain further the significance of the event, and her discourse prepares the way for the Palinurus episode. In all, forty-two hexameters are devoted to these first two moments, while the entire Palinurus episode has only forty-seven.

Aside from its own significance, the encounter with Palinurus serves to vary the narrative pace. By changing the emotional tone from awe and horror to pity, that is, by moving from the violent activity of underworld monsters to the sad tale of a former comrade of Aeneas, Virgil prepares for the sudden drama of the actual encounter with Charon on the banks of the Acheron. In this third and final moment, which extends over another thirty-three lines, Charon is seen in action, both physically and verbally, in direct relation to the descender and his guide. The three moments as a whole comprise one of the major panoramic tableaux of the underworld, rivaled by only descriptions of Tartarus (also introduced with a glimpse of an infernal river—Phlegethon, the rushing flood of flames) and Elysium, with its Valley of Lethe.

With the narrative pattern in mind, I can now analyze in greater detail the separate scenes at the river. Virgil begins with three lines devoted to the Acheron:

> Hinc via, Tartarei quae fert Acherontis ad undas.
> turbidus hic caeno vastaque voragine gurges
> aestuat, atque omnem Cocyto eructat harenam.

> (6. 295–297)

> Hence a road leads to the waters of Tartarean Acheron. Here, thick with mire and of fathomless flood, a whirlpool seethes and belches into Cocytus all its sand. (HRF)

The separation of noun and adjective, *turbidus . . . gurges*, emphasizes the vastness of the watery gulf, while the two forceful verbs heighten the description of the water's incessant movement. The hectic swirling of the boiling mud and sand prefigures the confusion of the souls at the place of embarcation.

From the Acheron's seething waves, we turn to the *portitor*, a noun more properly interpreted as harbor master (from *portus*) but extended after Virgil to include the meaning of ferryman (from its resemblance to *portare*):[15]

> portitor has horrendus aquas et flumina servat
> terribili squalore Charon, cui plurima mento
> canities inculta iacet, stant lumina flamma,
> sordidus ex umeris nodo dependet amictus.
> ipse ratem conto subigit velisque ministrat
> et ferruginea subvectat corpora cumba,
> iam senior, sed cruda deo viridisque senectus.
>
> (6. 298–304)

A grim warden guards these waters and streams, terrible in his squalor—Charon, on whose chin lies a mass of unkempt, hoary hair; his eyes are staring orbs of flame; his squalid garb hangs by a knot from his shoulders. Unaided, he poles the boat, tends the sails, and in his murky craft convoys the dead—now aged, but a god's old age is hardy and green. (HRF)

Interweaving the adjective *horrendus*, which separates the rhyme of *has . . . aquas*, extends the adjective's force beyond the strict reference to Charon to include as well the river that he guards. Later poets, influenced perhaps by Virgil's displacement of attributes, often apply Charon's features to other aspects of the crossing. In this instance, the adjective itself is intensified by the ablative of quality: Charon is not simply dreadful or horrid, but horrid "with terrible squalor." His awesome roughness is particularized in verse 300 by reference to both his mass of gray hair, which lies neglected on his chin, and his eyes, which stand with flame.[16] The two verbs, placed side by side, seem to freeze the action; the technique is ekphrastic. It is as if Virgil is describing in vivid terms a work of art, where the sartorial reference completes the picture, reinforcing the boatman's maniacal look by emphasizing the shabbiness of his garment, which hangs from a knot tied at his shoulders.

Though a guardian and an aged deity, Charon guides his ship with a pole, tends the sails, and ferries the dead in the dusky craft:

> ipse ratem conto subigit velisque ministrat
> et ferruginea subvectat corpora cumba,
> iam senior, sed cruda deo viridisque senectus.
>
> (6. 302–304)

From the motionless verbs describing Charon's features, the poet passes to a series of verbs—*subigit, ministrat,* and *subvectat*—indicating action. Though old, Charon's age is that of a god, fresh and hardy; thus he tends not only the sails of his boat but propels his ferry with a punting pole, a feature mentioned as early as Euripides' *Alcestis*.

Throughout these verses, the poet's mastery of poetic technique is especially evident; the syntax is pleasingly varied, as illustrated, for example, by the two noun-verb clauses in verse 302, which are followed by the reversed structure, verbnoun, in verse 303. At times, nouns and adjectives are interwoven; at times, they enclose an entire hexameter, as in verse 301. Phonic patterns are equally varied, with continuity provided by the recurrence of sounds and concepts located at either some distance—for example, *squalore* (299), *sordidus* (301)—or close together—the *m*'s in *plurima mento* and *lumina flamma* or the reverberating *d*'s in "sordidus ex umeris nodo dependet amictus" and so forth (301).

Having depicted Charon in some detail, Virgil passes to the throng of souls arriving for passage. The scene illustrates not only the sad plight of the dead but also the unchecked authority of Charon:

> Huc omnis turba ad ripas effusa ruebat,
> matres atque viri, defunctaque corpora vita
> magnanimum heroum, pueri innuptaeque puellae
> impositique rogis iuvenes ante ora parentum:
> quam multa in silvis autumni frigore primo
> lapsa cadunt folia, aut ad terram gurgite ab alto
> quam multae glomerantur aves, ubi frigidus annus
> trans pontum fugat et terris immittit apricis.
> stabant orantes primi transmittere cursum
> tendebantque manus ripae ulterioris amore.
> navita sed tristis nunc hos nunc accipit illos,
> ast alios longe submotos arcet harena.
>
> (6. 305–316)

Hither rushed all the throng, streaming to the banks; mothers and men and bodies of high-souled heroes, their life now done, boys and unwedded girls, and sons placed on the pyre before their fathers' eyes; thick as the leaves of the forest that at autumn's first frost dropping fall, and thick as the birds that from the seething deep flock shoreward, when the chill of the year drives them overseas and sends them into sunny lands. They stood, pleading to be the first ferried across, and stretched out hands in yearning for the farther shore. But the surly boatman takes now these, now those, while others he thrusts apart, back from the brink. (HRF)

To the multitude of souls described by Homer (see above, chap. 1), Virgil adds two autumnal images, those of leaves, found in Apollonius of Rhodes (*Argonautica* 4. 216 ff.; cf. *Iliad* 6. 146–149 as well as Bacchylides, *Ode* 5. 63–67), and migrating birds; both images describe not only the number of souls but also their movement. Their desire to cross to the farther bank is hindered by Charon, who is now seen fulfilling his duties as guardian of the realm and ferryman.

In the description, Virgil employs his first adjective for Charon's internal state; the *navita* is *tristis*, an adjective suggesting not sadness but a surly harshness, which is both gloomy and forbidding.[17] Denying passage to the unburied until a hundred years have passed, as the Sibyl soon explains in response to Aeneas's questions (317-30), Charon ferries only those who have been *sepulti*.[18] That the boatman does not row his boat alone during the crossing seems to be suggested by Aeneas, who asks: "By what rule do these leave the banks, and those sweep the lurid stream with oars?" ("quo discrime ripas / hae linquunt, *illae remis vada livida verrunt?*" [319-320, my emphasis]). Furthermore, other descriptive notes increase the gloomy atmosphere of the infernal landscape. To the *vada livida* (320), the poet soon adds the *stagna alta* of Cocytus and the stygian *paludem* (323) as well as the *ripas . . . horrendas* and *rauca fluenta* (327) of Acheron.

Following the change of pace offered by the Palinurus episode, Virgil once again returns to the actual descent of Aeneas, who with the Sibyl now draws near the river:

> Ergo iter inceptum peragunt fluvioque propinquant.
> navita quos iam inde ut Stygia prospexit ab unda
> per tacitum nemus ire pedemque advertere ripae,
> sic prior adgreditur dictis atque increpat ultro:
> "quisquis es, armatus qui nostra ad flumina tendis,
> fare age, quid venias, iam instinc, et comprime gressum.
> umbrarum hic locus est, Sommi Noctisque soporae;
> corpora viva nefas Stygia vectare carina."
>
> (6. 384-391)

So they pursue the journey begun, and draw near to the river. But when, even from the Stygian wave, the boatman saw them passing through the silent wood and turning their feet towards the bank, he first, unhailed, accosts and rebukes them: "Whoso thou art that comest to our river in arms, O tell me, even from there, why thou comest, and check thy step. This is the land of Shadows, of Sleep and drowsy Night; living bodies I may not carry in the Stygian boat. (HRF)

From his boat in the river, Charon accosts the living descenders as they approach the place of embarcation. The verb *adgredior* indicates the force of his verbal attack; he approaches—almost assaults the descenders—with words, reproving their intentions.[19] His first words are both a question and a command, with the abrupt and jerky syntax reflecting the boatman's initial agitation. Having referred to Aeneas as armed, Charon contrasts the presence of the living to the state of the dead: this is the land of shadows, sleep, and night. In refusing to transport the *corpora viva* (we might contrast and compare Dante's use of *anima viva*), Charon refers to his boat with the noun *carina*, a variation of the earlier use of *ratis* (302) and *cumba* (303, cf. 413); later, the boat is mentioned through the metonymic use of *puppis* (410) as well as the noun *alveus* (412). This technique is employed by later poets, most notably Dante.

As if to explain his denial of passage to the living, Charon tells of previous descents, those of Hercules and Theseus and Pirithoüs, and the disastrous results for the realm. Charon does not mention any personal harm, although Servius claims that the boatman was shackled for a year as punishment "ob quam rem anno integro in compedibus fuit" [*ad Aen.* 6. 392]). In response, the Sibyl denies any intent to harm the realm, referring to Aeneas's filial piety and desire to see his father in lowest Erebus. Apparently her words are of no avail, for she continues: "If the picture of such piety moves thee in no wise, yet know this bough!" (HRF, 405–407).

The effect of the bough on Charon is immediate: "tumida ex ira tum corda residunt. / nec plura his" ("thereon, after his anger, his swelling breast subsides.

Aeneas, the Sibyl, and Charon, by G. M. Crespi. Kunsthistorisches Museum, Vienna. By permission of Photo Marburg, courtesy of the Art Reference Bureau.

No more is said" [407–408]). Deflated, the ferryman speaks no more, nor does the Sibyl. Admiring the fateful bough, not seen for a long time (we are not told when it was seen), Charon returns to action:

> Caeruleam advertit puppim ripaeque propinquat.
> inde alias animas, quae per iuga longa sedebant,
> deturbat laxatque foros; simul accipit alveo
> ingentem Aeneam. gemuit sub pondere cumba
> sutilis et multam accepit rimosa paludem.
> tandem trans fluvium incolumis vatemque virumque
> informi limo glaucaque exponit in ulva.
>
> (410–416)

[He] turns his blue barge and nears the shore. Then other souls that sat on the long thwarts he routs out, and clears the gangways; the while he takes aboard giant Aeneas. The seamy craft groaned under the weight, and through its chinks took in a marshy flood. At last, across the water, he lands seer and soldier unharmed on the ugly mire and grey sedge. (HRF)

While Servius does not comment on the adjective *caeruleus*, later commentators have been perplexed by the apparent contrast between it and *ferrugineus*. Perhaps the best explanation, aside from attempts to equate the hues of both colors, is W. McLeod's, who discusses it in the light of literary devices of "elegant variation" and "vivid particularization," that is, as an imitation of Homer's apparent contradictions.[20]

But the boat is not the only element described in terms of color: Graphic details of the far edge of the swamp, with its green sedge and amorphous slime, add a note of gloom to earlier references to the lurid stream (32) and hoarse-voiced waters (327). The groaning of the flimsy boat that has cracks where the seams are sewn together is a particularly effective detail that catches the danger of the crossing. The heaviness, both conceptually and phonetically, of words like *ingentem* and *sub pondere* contrasts to the lightness inherent in the sibilant sounds of the adjective *sutilis*.

When we think of the episode as a whole, and especially of the portrayal of Charon, it is difficult to accept critics like R. D. Williams and R. C. Austin, who emphasize the comic effects in the encounter with Charon, claiming that the boatman is a mock-heroic figure.[21] It seems unlikely that the first true barrier to Aeneas's progress would be treated with ironic detachment. Rather than mocking the boatman, Virgil steeps him in gloom, adding details typical of the Etruscan divinities, fierce creatures of horrific appearance.[22] The pathos of unburied souls desiring to cross or of Palinurus is only effective if set off by a glimpse of what these souls must face.

In examining the depiction of Charon as a whole, we note that Virgil portrays first the boatman's features, then his functions, and finally his speech; each stage serves to develop the solidity of the figure. Initially, Charon is seen in isolation,

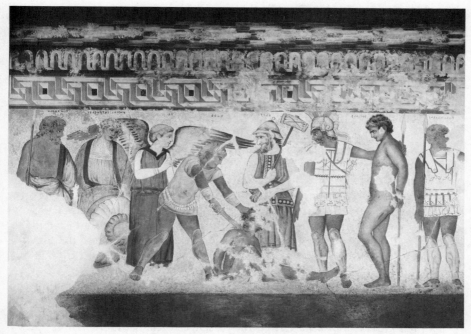

Sacrifice of Trojan prisoners with Charun. Reconstruction of an Etruscan wall painting in the François tomb, Vulci. Museo Archeologico, Florence. By permission of Fratelli Alinari.

immobile as it were, his features captured with a few brief strokes. Following this introduction to the external traits of the guardian, Virgil integrates the figure into the underworld tableau: Charon is silent, but depicted in action. Finally, after the tale of Palinurus's earthly fate, the poet presents the ferryman dramatically: Charon breaks into a speech directed against the living descender despite the fact that the boatman is in midstream with a load of souls. Aeneas himself does not respond to the underworld god, perhaps still awed by the entire experience at the river. His feelings during the crossing, while not stated, are implicit in Virgil's concise description of the voyage's hazards.

Structurally, the descent episode is developed with epic fullness. Perhaps the most interesting feature is the break between the third unit in which the guardian is first seen and the following units of confrontation. In addition to varying narrative flow, this device permits the reintroduction of a more forceful boatman. Interestingly, the ferryman's discourse involves not only interrogation and commands but a lengthy explanation for his actions. It is as if he recognizes the authority of the two descenders but is aware that even "sons of gods and invincible in valour"—"dis . . . geniti atque invicti viribus" (HRF, 394)—earlier caused havoc in the realm. The Sibyl, aware of the power of the fateful branch, responds with directness, mentioning Aeneas's reasons, but does not wait to see if they have any effect, perhaps equally aware of Charon's obduracy. Unmoved by pleading souls, Charon, we imagine, would be indifferent to filial piety, his anger soothed only by a magical object.

The sixth and seventh units, embarcation and passage, are also of interest. Charon not only accepts the two descenders but clears out the ship before doing so. While not described in detail, we can imagine the force needed to expel the souls desirous of crossing. The ship itself, apparently stitched together with skins,[23] is vividly fragile; perhaps Charon's relief at landing the two on the far side is as great as theirs.

Within the units, Virgil's descriptive technique is *pauca e multis*; that is, from the logical fullness of a scene, he selects only a few detailed and vividly impressive items, allowing the reader to imagine the rest. Kenneth Quinn discusses Virgil's elliptical narrative technique, with the episode of the crossing as an example.[24] While Virgil, for example, mentions Aeneas's embarcation, that of the Sibyl is left aside. Quinn continues:

> There is no description of the boat getting under way; nothing is said of the journey itself; the disembarkation is cut to a terse statement that both passengers arrived safely; if *tandem* suggests the trip was slow and painful business, coupled with *incolumnis* it reflects the passengers' feelings more than it states a fact. We do not see them take their leave of Charon—all the details of arrival are eliminated so as not to detract from the impact of the last line and the impression the slime and sedge convey of the horror of Aeneas' reaction as he sets foot upon the farther shore. (P. 79)

The movement is thus from descriptive point to descriptive point with "a minimum of connecting reportage" (p. 78). And within the descriptions themselves, only those features are detailed that strike a sense of marvel or horror, that is, evoke an emotional reaction in the poet or his audience.

Later epic poets employ the boatman in a variety of ways but with less epic fullness where the eight structural units in the Virgilian descent are concerned.[25] Rather than analyze all the references in depth, I will examine Charon's appearance in Lucan's *De bello civili*, sometimes called *Pharsalia*, as an example of alternative depiction. Charon is described in this historical epic in Books 3 and 6 in tones that, as we will see in discussing drama, seem to reflect Seneca's view of a weary ferryman. In the first instance, based on a tragic topos, in fact, the boatman is mentioned by the ghost of Julia when she appears to Pompeius in a dream:

> diri tum plena horroris imago
> uisa caput maestrum per hiantis Iulia terras
> tollere et acenso furialis stare sepulchro.
> sedebus Elysiis campoque expulsa piorum

ad Stygias, inquit, tenebras manesque nocentis
post bellum ciuile trahor. uidi ipsa tenentis
Eumenidas quaterent quas uestris lampadas armis:
praeparat innumeras puppes Acherontis adusti
portitor: in multas laxantur Tartara poenas.

(3. 9–17)[26]

Julia, a spectre full of dread and menace, raised her sorrowful head above the yawning earth and stood in the guise of a Fury amid the flames of her funeral pyre. And thus she spoke: "Now that civil war has begun, driven forth from the Elysian Fields and abode of the blest, I am dragged to Stygian darkness and the place of guilty spirits. There I saw with these eyes the Furies, and in their hands were torches, to brandish for kindling the strife between you; the ferryman of scorched Acheron is geting ready countless boats; Tartarus is making wide its borders for the punishment of many sinners. (JDD)

We are reminded of tragic prologues in which spirits of the dead initiate the action. That Charon should have fleets at his control is astounding. The image intensifies the horrors of war by emphasizing the number of dead who descend for passage.

But more important as an epic pattern worthy of imitation is the conjuration scene in Book 6. In this instance, the Haemonian witch Erichtho is consulted by Sextius Pompeius and decides to raise a corpse from the dead to answer some questions. She addresses the underworld beings:

"Eumenides, Stygiumque nefas, poenaeque nocentum
et Chaos innumeros auidum confundere mundos:
et rector terrae quem longa in saecula torquet
mors dilata deum: Styx et quos nulla meretur
Thessalis Elysios: caelum matremque perosa
Persephone, nostraeque Hecates pars ultima, per quam
manibus et mihi sunt tacitae commercia linguae:
ianitor et sedis laxae, qui uiscera saeuo
spargis nostra cani: repetitaque fila sorores
tracturae: tuque o flagrantis portitor undae
iam lassate senex ad me redeuntibus umbris:
exaudite preces, si uos satis ore nefando
pollutoque uoco. . . ."

(6. 693–707)

"I invoke the Furies, the horror of Hell, the punishments of the guilty, and Chaos, eager to blend countless worlds in ruins; I cry to the Ruler of the world below, who suffers age-long pain because gods are so slow to die; to Styx, and Elysium where no Thessalian witch may enter; to Persephone who shuns her mother in heaven, and to her, the third incarnation of our patron, Hecate, who permits the dead and me to converse together without speech; I call on the custodian of the spacious dwelling, who casts the flesh of men to the ravening hound; on the Sisters, who must spin a second thread of life; and on the ancient ferryman of the fiery river, whose arms are weary of rowing the dead back to me—hear ye my prayer. If these lips that address you have enough of horror and pollution. . . ." (JDD)

It has been noted that the conjuration motif is a conscious poetic substitution for the Virgilian descent topos. That is, where Virgil textually situates a significant other-world episode affirming Roman destiny (Book 6), Lucan situates an episode that undermines the imperial ideology.[27] A monstrous witches' rite results in an evocation of a soldier who details a vision of the carnage caused by civil war. Whatever the political message of the diverse topoi of descent and conjuration, it is significant that Charon appears in both. Later epic poets are, in effect, offered a choice of important episodes into which underworld figures can be integrated. In Lucan's model, Charon is listed in a catalog of infernal powers, with little external description; rather than being a fully developed figure of interest in his own right, he illustrates the effects of civil wars on mankind and the underworld. Located on a fiery stream, a descriptive Senecan note apparently employed to increase the horror of the underworld realm, Charon is tired of transporting souls back to Erichtho. While Lucan does not place an antiwar invective in Charon's mouth, later poets are happy to do so. As the ferryman of the dead, Charon is, in effect, a victim of evil events on earth.

Thus to conclude the presentation of Charon in classical Latin epic, let me note not only the existence of modes providing full elaboration of all units of the descent episode but also the dual pattern available to poets using the ferryman. While extant Greek epic has left little concerning the representation of the boatman himself, it does provide important models of both evocation and descent. And when developed by the Latin poets, both topoi often contain allusions to the figure of Charon, some authors referring to the boatman with extensive description, others with brief but evocative touches.

Notes

1. Earlier Latin writers, such as Cicero (*De natura deorum* 3. 43), had spoken of both Charon and the underworld, but no extant fully developed literary use of the figure predates Virgil. The extant early dramatists contain no representation of the boatman, although one of Plautus's characters does speak of paintings he has seen, depicting the torments of Acheron (Tindaride says: "Vidi ego multa saepe picta quae Acherunti fierent / Cruciamenta, verum enim vero nulla adaeque est Acheruns / Atque ubi ego fui in lapicidinis" [*Captivi* 5. 4, 1]).

2. For comments on Virgil's use of sources, see the works listed in the bibliography under Cyril Bailey, Franz Cumont, Franz De Ruyt, T. R. Glover, Eduard Norden, Friedrich Solmsen, and R. D. Williams. More specific studies are cited where appropriate.

3. All quotations from Virgil's *Georgics* or the *Aeneid* are drawn from the edition of H. Rushton Fairclough. Volume 1 contains the *Eclogues*, *Georgics*, and *Aeneid* 1-6, while vol. 2 contains *Aeneid* 7-12 and the minor poems. Fairclough's translation is hereafter referred to in the text as HRF.

4. See, for example, Conon, *Narrationes* 45; Apollodorus, *Bibliotheca* 1. 3. 2; and Hyginus, *Fabula* 164. For a thorough study of the Orpheus myth with an attempt to reconstruct a lost Greek

original, see C. M. Bowra, "Orpheus and Eurydice," pp. 113–126. A recent work of interest, appearing after this study was in press, is *Orpheus: The Metamorphoses of a Myth*, ed. John Warden.

5. All Latin quotations are from *The Works of Virgil with a commentary* by John Conington and Henry Nettleship. Translations by Fairclough (HRF).

6. Virgil employs the images of birds hiding in leaves to express the number of souls and also refers to the dead in lines reminiscent of Homer (*Od.* 11. 36–43) and repeated in the *Aeneid* (6. 305–316).

7. The image is discussed by Segal, " 'Like Winds and Winged Dream,' " pp. 97–101, in relation to Virgil's other scenes of attempts to grasp shades.

8. *Stygian* is a popular adjective for underworld features; see the stygian groves, *lucos Stygis* (6. 154), stygian gloom (*Georgics* 3. 551), stygian waters (7. 773), stygian lakes (8. 296), stygian wave (12. 91) in which Turnus's sword is dipped, stygian waves in the plural (3. 215), stygian boat (*Aeneid* 6. 391, *Georgics* 4. 506), and stygian applied to Jove (i.e., Pluto [4. 638]), Orcus (4. 699), and king (6. 252). At one point, Jove swears by the waters, in this case obviously Styx, of his stygian brother (9. 104). In *Georgics* 1. 243, *Styx atra* however merely refers to the underworld in general. Compare *Aeneid* 5. 854–856 where Somnus puts Palinurus to sleep by shaking over his head a bough dipped in Lethe, thus lending it stygian power; By the way, Allecto also flies on stygian wing (7. 476).

9. The Styx itself is referred to several times by its traditional feature as a river of oath. Of Jupiter or Jove, we read that "by the waters of his Stygian brother, by the banks that seethe with pitch and black swirling waters, he nodded assent . . ." (10. 113–115; cf. 9. 104–106). Juno also swears "by the inexorable fountain-head of Styx, sole name of dread ordained for gods above" (12. 816–817).

10. Trans. T. R. Glover, *Virgil* p. 233.

11. Servius says: "Miscet philosophiae figmenta poetica, et ostendit tam quod est vulgare, quam quod continet veritas et ratio naturalis" (*ad Aen.* 6. 719).

12. For the relevant discussions, see the works listed in the bibliography under Eduard Norden, Albrecht Dieterich, Robert S. Conway, Cartault, Frances Norwood, L. A. MacKay, and Brooks Otis.

13. We are reminded of the terrors of popular folklore that Lucretius had tried to expel. See *De rerum natura* 1. 115 ff. and 3. 37, 978–1023.

14. Cyril Bailey, *Religion in Virgil*, p. 254. MacKay, however, emphasizes that in the descent, "the central episode in a poem instinct [*sic*] with divinity, the gods are notably lacking. Charon, though *deus*, is a subordinate figure at best, and is left behind at the entrance; he is a link with that upper world of poetic legend in which gods do intervene" ("Three Levels of Meaning in *Aeneid* VI," p. 182). Or to look at the boatman from a different perspective, Frances Norwood, in discussing Virgil's humanistic approach, writes: "Charon, a divine being, looks like an ordinary seaman rather the worse for wear (301); his rough bullying ways (316) are reflected in his address to Aeneas and the Sibyl (389); his bad temper (407) is hardly worthy to be called *ira caelestis*" ("The Tripartite Eschatology of *Aeneid* 6," p. 18). H. E. Butler, incidentally, notes that Cicero discusses the question of whether or not Charon is a god in his *De Natura Deorum* 3. 43. See *The Sixth Book of the Aeneid with Introduction and Notes*, p. 154.

15. See Fairclough's edition, 1. 526–527, note 2, and the classical commentaries cited by Norden, *Aeneis Buch VI*, p. 221.

16. W. F. Jackson Knight describes Charon's eyes: "Charon's eyes 'glare starkly', *stant lumina flamma*. This is strange; eyes do not usually stand, though *stare* is a very favourite Vergilian word, with many meanings, especially 'be still', for example of the sea, a Greek idea originally. If eyes 'stand', it is surprising that they should do it 'with flame'. There is an alternative reading, *stant lumina flammae*, 'eyes of flame stand', which is inferior in authority, but sometimes chosen. . . . Charon's eyes are . . . suddenly impressive to the sight, intensely real in their steady, stark, still, 'standing' glare. They glare, of course, with flame; for Vergil's Charon is not only the Greek ferryman of Aristophanes, but more than half his Etruscan self, Charun, the Etruscan torturing death-devil, no ferryman at all. But Vergil has meanwhile got something else quite right. For the name Charon or Charun in Greek means something like 'bright eyed'." *Roman Vergil*, p. 257. We might ask if Charon's eyes are fiery merely in an etymological sense or are they indicative of an internal state? If Virgil is recalling *Iliad* 1. 104, where an enraged Agamemnon is seen with eyes "like blazing fire" (ATM), then Charon is characterized above all by his ire. Franz De Ruyt claims that Virgil assuredly had no idea of the foregoing etymology (*Charun: Démon étrusque de la mort*, p. 247).

17. Servius glosses *tristis* as "asper, inmiserabilis, severus" (*ad Aen.* 6. 315).

18. The *turba* denied passage is not only *inhumata* but *inops* (325), the latter adjective perhaps suggesting the lack of an obol, which is otherwise unmentioned in the scene. Servius, however, interprets the adjective as follows: "inopem enim dicit sine pulveris iactu—nam 'ops' terra est—id est sine terra, sine humatione" (*ad Aen.* 6. 325).

19. As Servius notes, "*Adgreditur dictis* hoc sermone ostendit iratum" (*ad Aen*. 6. 387).

20. W. McLeod, "The Wooden Horse and Charon's Barque: Inconsistency in Virgil's 'Vivid Particularization'," p. 145. Other studies on this problem are cited by McLeod.

21. R. D. Williams holds that Charon, part of the "traditional machinery" of Hades, is "stylized and unreal" compared to the personal reality of a ghost like Palinurus (*The Aeneid of Virgil, Books 1-6*, p. 484). An effective contrast to this statement is found in Glover's *Virgil*, where we read about Charon: "The poet draws him in a few lines with extraordinary life and power; no one would take him for a ghost or spirit, too lifelike he is . . ." (p. 260). For Williams, however, rather than being a figure of gloomy horror, Charon presents no real terror. "Virgil's presentation of him is to some degree mock-heroic. . . . We cannot quite call the scene comic, but it is handled with a certain irony and detachment" ("The Sixth Book of the *Aeneid*," p. 53). Detachment? Hardly. Williams burlesques the confrontation scene in his article "Virgil's underwold—the opening scenes (*Aen*. 6. 268–416)," pp. 1–7. Compare both the earlier article by R. C. Austin, which I have not seen ("*Aeneid* VI, 384–476," pp. 51–60) and Conway, "The Structure of the Sixth Book of the *Aeneid*," in E. C. Quiggin, pp. 1–26.

22. De Ruyt writes about Virgil's Charon as follows: "Il est un exemple frappant de cette compénétration des cultures grecque, étrusque et italique, dont sortira l'originalité romaine" (*Charun*, pp. 247–248). After comparing Virgil's boatman to that of the Greek comedians, De Ruyt adds: "Mais le batelier de la comédie grecque n'est que grossier et d'une avarice sordide. Le Charon de Virgile a un caractèr de puissance effroyable et odieuse, où l'on ne peut pas ne pas reconnaître un souvenir du terrible et redouté Charun" (p. 248).

23. For an extended discussion of the meaning of *sutilis*, see James Henry, *Aeneidea, or Critical, Exegetical, and Aesthetical Remarks on the Aeneis*, 3:307–309.

24. Emmanuel Hatzantonis notes the use of the same device in Dante; see "Variations of a Virgilian Theme in Dante and Lope de Vega," p. 36 and note 9. For Kenneth Quinn's comments, see *Virgil's Aeneid: A Critical Description*, pp. 78–80.

25. Along with the reference to Charon in the *Culex*, the ferryman is mentioned more than once in the *Punica* by Silius Italicus, the *Argonautica* by Valerius Flaccus, and the *Thebaid* by Statius. In the *Culex*, the gnat saves the sheperd from a serpent, whose "blazing eye gleams with a savage look" ["aspectuque micant flammarum lumina torvo," (173; HRF)] and then having returned from Hades as an *effigies*, relates the manner of its descent. Though just a gnat, it was compelled by the *manes* to cross over Lethe, driven like a *praeda Charonis* (216). One expects, as Anthony A. Barrett notes ("The Topography of the Gnat's Descent," p. 255), to find Lethe only at the end of the underworld, but here it is strangely connected with Charon. Statius, incidentally, also refers at one point to Charon as the "Lethaei portitor amnis" (*Thebaid* 12. 559).

Among the outstanding references to the boatman, let me quote the following with little comment:

> tunc regemunt pigrique lacus ustaeque paludes,
> umbriferaeque fremit sulcator pallidus undae
> dissiluisse novo penitus telluris hiatu
> Tartara et admissos non per sua flumina manes.

(Statius, *Thebaid* 8. 17–20)

Marino in his *Idilli favolosi* also refers to Charon as a *pallido Nocchiero* (*Orfeo* 159). In *Thebaid* 11. 587–593, the boatman is compared to Oedipus, who displays his ghastly body after his horrid deed:

> qualis si puppe relicta
> exosus manes pigri sulcator Averni
> exeat ad superos solemque et pallida turbet
> astra, nec ipse diu fortis patiensque superni
> aeris; interea longum cessante magistro
> crescat opus, totisque exspectent saecula ripis:
> talis init campum. . . .

Lucian, of course, dramatizes just such an event in one of his dialogues. Silius Italicus has this to say:

" 'nullo non tempore abundans / umbrarum huc agitur torrens, vectaque capaci / agmina mole Charon, nec sufficit improba puppis' " (*Punica* 13. 759–761).

Charon's roomy boat, as we will see, is derived from Seneca.

> tergeminam tum placat eram Stygiasque supremo
> obsecrat igne domos iam iam ex orabile retro
> carmen agens; neque enim ante leves niger avehit umbras
> portitor et vinctae primis stant faucibus Orci.
>
> (Valerius Flaccus, *Argonautica* 1. 812–815)

> gaudet Averna palus, gaudet iam nocte quieta
> portitor et tuto veniens Latonia caelo.   (*Argonautica* 6. 158–159)

Quotations are from the Loeb Library editions, Statius and Valerius Flaccus, trans. J. H. Mozley; Silius Italicus, trans. J. D. Duff.

26. Lucan, *Pharsalia* ed. C. E. Haskins, pp. 76–77. Haskins compares Petronius 121 where we read: "uix nauita Porthmeus sufficiet simulacra uirum transducere cumba; classes opus est." All English translations of Lucan are by J. D. Duff, referred to hereafter as JDD.

27. See David Quint, "Epic Tradition and *Inferno* IX," pp. 204–205.

6

Latin Lyric and Related Poetic Forms

In turning to Latin poetry, let me note that despite Lucretius's insistent denial of underworld terrors (see *De rerum natura* 3. 978–1023, for example),[1] poets continue to employ the boatman as a characteristic feature of the underworld. One of the more common themes with which Charon is likely to be connected is that of a common doom. That all must cross Acheron is attested by Horace in his *Odes*; in Carmen 2. 3, Horace counsels Dellius to enjoy life while he is able, for death is close at hand. It is of no avail whether one is wealthy or of illustrious descent:

> Omnes eodem cogimur, omnium
> versatur urna serius ocius
> sors exitura et nos in aeternum
> exsilium impositura cumbae.
>
> (25–28)[2]

We are all being gathered to one and the same fold. The lot of everyone of us is tossing about in the urn, destined sooner, later, to come forth and place us in Charon's skiff for everlasting exile.

The crossing by way of Charon's boat is effectively seen as an eternal exile.[3]

While one is constrained to accept the fact that everyone must die, the elegist Tibullus laments the fact that war brings death before one's time; he asks:

> quis furor est atram bellis accersere Mortem?
> imminet et tacito clam venit illa pede.
> non seges est infra, non vinea cultu, sed audax
> Cerberus et Stygiae navita turpis aquae;
> illic pertussisque genis ustoque capillo
> errat ad obscuros pallida turba lacus.
>
> (1. 10. 33–38)[4]

What madness is it to call black Death to us by warefare! It is ever close upon us: it comes unseen on silent feet. Below there are neither cornlands nor well-kept vineyards; only wild Cerberus and the ill-favoured mariner of the stream of Styx. There wanders a sallow throng beside the dusky pools with eyeless sockets and fire-ravaged hair.

The underworld is characterized by both what it is not and what it is. Fierce Cerberus and the ugly sailor on the stygian wave are representative terrors; rather than concentrating on the infernal inhabitants, however, Tibullus turns to the fate of humanity. The pale crowd, its essence captured by reference to empty eye-sockets and fire-singed hair, wanders toward the dark pools.

Propertius is more interesting, since he integrates Charon into his love poetry as well as employing the ferryman more conventionally.[5] In Book 2 of his *Elegies*, the poet notes that while most men are uncertain of the time of their death, the lover is different:

> solus amans novit, quando periturus et a qua
> morte, neque hic Boreae flabra neque arma timet.
> iam licet et Stygia sedeat sub harundine remex,
> cernat et infernae tristia vela ratis:
> si modo clamantis revocaverit aura puellae,
> concessum nulla lege redibit iter.
>
> (27. 11–16)

The lover only knows when and by what death he shall perish, and fears nor weapons nor blasts of the north wind. Yea, even though he sit at the oar among the reeds of Styx and gaze on the dismal sails of the boat of hell, if the faint whisper of his mistress's voice cry out and call him back from the dead, he will return over that road that the eternal ordinance hath sealed.

The power of love, capable of revivifying a dead shade, is masterfully illustrated. In another elegy, Propertius asks for mercy for his ailing beloved, imagining that her beauty has offended some goddess, such as Venus. If his mistress dies, he says, he, too, will cease to live and "one murky boat of destiny shall bear our loves together, setting sail to the pools of Hell" (28. 39–40). Employing, incidentally, the same adjective for Charon's boat as Virgil (*caerula*), Propertius attests the strength of his love through his willingness to cross to Hades.

In a later poem, following the death of Cynthia, the poet feels constrained to affirm the reality of an afterlife: "The Shades are no fable: Death is not the end of all, and the pale ghost escapes the vanquished pyre" (4. 7. 1–2). His proof is that his beloved returned to him as he slept, castigating him for his failure to perform proper funeral rites for her. In the description of her fate, Cynthia refers to the nature of the underworld, noting that "two mansions are there allotted beside the foul stream of Hell, and all the dead must ply the oar this way or that" (55–56). While some are ferried to a realm of punishment, others are transported to Elysium. But contrary to most accounts, Cynthia claims that at night the spirits are freed to wander on earth (89). Even Cerberus wanders at will, a situation that Seneca later uses to represent, as we will see in examining tragedy, an unnatural state. The practice results in more labor for Charon, since, as Cynthia tells us, the boatman is not only obliged to ferry the souls once again across the river but to count them as well: "At dawn Hell's ordinance bids us return to the pools of Lethe: We are ferried over and the mariner tells o'er his freight" (91–92).

Propertius's early hyperbolic claim that love has the power to bring the dead back to life gives way to an awareness of the finality of death in Book 4. In an elegy addressed to her spouse Paullus, Cornelia, now dead, asks that her grave no longer be burdened with tears, for "no prayers may open the gate of darkness; when once the dead have passed beneath the rule of Hell, the ways are barred with inexorable adamant" (4. 11. 2–4). As she says soon after, "When the ferryman has received his toll, the pale portal closes on the world of shadows" (7–8). In this instance, of course, the poet, in his attempt to console Paullus, counsels him through Cornelia's speech to reconcile himself to her death. When faced with the reality of death, Propertius can only claim that the soul continues to exist in the beyond.

Ovid, however, returns to the theme of the power of love in his depiction of the Orpheus myth (*Metamorphoses* 10. 1–74). Although the main details of the myth in both Virgil (*Georgics* 4. 454–506) and Ovid are similar—for example, neither refers to Charon as a hindrance on Orpheus's downward journey[6]—the tale in Ovid's hands is treated with less pathos and greater rhetorical flourish. Following Eurydice's sudden death (*Met.* 10. 10), Orpheus, we are told, mourned on earth and then descended to Styx by way of Taenarus in order to try the lower shades. Instead of presenting the poet's lamentation, Ovid details at length his song to Pluto and Persephone (note the Greek form of the goddess, verse 15).[7] In his appeal, Orpheus, after asserting that he is not lying, says that he has come down, not to see dark Tartarus (20–21), not to bind the three throats of the Medusean monster (22), but to gain his wife. We are reminded of the Sibyl's response to Charon in the *Aeneid*.

Orpheus claims that he has tried to bear his grief, but love has conquered him just as, he imagines, it conquered the infernal king, who abducted his beloved (25–29). Having introduced the reference to love's power, a force that extends even into the underworld, Orpheus launches into a prayer, preceded by an abbreviated invocation typical of epic (29–30). To further convince the underworld powers to release his beloved, he touches on the theme that sooner or later all descend to Hades' realm. The motif, familiar to both Greek and Latin poets (see Horace, *Ode* 2. 3. 25–28), is popular among Italian poets who deal with this myth.

Having detailed Orpheus's speech, Ovid now describes its effect on the underworld denizens. Here, too, with epic fullness and perhaps a touch of humor, he expands on Virgil's brief note: The bloodless spirits weep; Tantalus does not strive for water; Ixion's wheel is still; the vultures no longer pluck at the liver (of Tityos); the Belides with their urns are idled, and Sisyphus sits on his rock (40–44). Even the Eumenides' cheeks are wet with tears (45–46). Giving in to Orpheus's plea, the underworld rulers release Eurydice, first, however, establishing the condition that Orpheus not look back until he has left the Avernian valley.

Orpheus, of course, turns around, both in love and fear that Eurydice is not behind him. In Ovid, Eurydice does not bother to lament, for "What was there to complain of?," says the poet, "One thing, only: / He loved her" (61). Instead, she breathes a final *vale* (62) and returns to Hades; stunned by this double

Charon with mallet and the voyage to the underworld. Funeral urn. Museo Guarnacci, Volterra. By permission of Fratelli Alinari.

death (64), Orpheus is compared to another man who was petrified at the sight of Cerberus. Following the simile, Charon is briefly introduced: "Orantem frustraque iterum transire volentum / Portitor arcuerat" ("In vain the prayers of Orpheus and his longing / To cross the river once more; the boatman Charon / Drove him away" [72–73]). As in Virgil, where he is also unmentioned by name, Charon is seen simply as an immovable force, untouched by the poet's prayers. The finality of Charon's denial is evident in the absence of an extended epic confrontation.

Another poet who, like Propertius, employs Charon and the crossing in poems of consolation is Statius. In an epicedion describing the arrival in the underworld of Glaucias, the favorite of Atedius Melior, Statius writes that the youth will be well received. Cerberus will not bark at him, nor will the Furies terrify him; in fact, even Charon, a fierce sailor with a greedy boat, will draw his ship near the banks to ease the embarcation:

> quin ipse avidae trux navita cumbae
> interius steriles ripas et adusta subibit
> litora, ne puero dura ascendisse facultas.
>
> (*Silvae* 2. 1. 186–187)[8]

Nay, even the grim sailor of the greedy boat will draw nearer to the barren shores and fire-scorched bank, that the boy's embarking may be easy.

Charon, though often described as a severe ferryman,[9] defers to the worthy. Thus, in another *consolatio*, again in hexameters, Statius describes what will happen to Priscilla, the wife of Abascantus, secretary of state to Domitian. Cerberus, in her case, wil not howl, because "he is silent for the blessed" (5. 1. 250). And what of Abascantus's other fear?

> ne tardior adsit
> navita proturbetque vadis? vehit ille merentes
> protinus et manes placidus locat hospite cumba.
>
> (250–252)

Lest the sailor be slow to draaw nigh her, or disturb her on the waters? He conveys deserving souls forthwith, and quietly sets them in his welcoming craft.

The hospitable boat is a novel conception.

Elsewhere, the poet takes nothing for granted and implores underworld horrors, among them Cerberus, Hydra, Scylla, and the Centaurs, to disappear and not to molest the descending soul. The wish is expressed that Charon receive the shade, scattering the throng in order to accept him without delay, and that the boatman set him softly in the middle of sea grasses:

> umbramque senilem
> invitet ripis, discussa plebe, supremus
> vector et in media componat molliter alga.
>
> (5. 3. 281–283)

Let the ferryman of the dead invite to the bank the aged shade, and lay him gently to rest amid the grasses.

The poet's concern is perhaps greater because he is dealing with the death and descent of his own father. Charon, referred to as a *supremus vector*, is imagined as being respectful and kind to the old man. The image of the boatman in the *Silvae* is intriguing when compared to the more traditional representation in Statius's *Thebaid*, where Charon, as noted earlier, is a ghastly sight (see, for example, 11. 587–593).

While other funeral poems and inscriptions also refer to the boatman,[10] let me mention as a brief example of Charon's presence in Latin satirical poetry the poems of Juvenal, who both satirizes the notion of an infernal boatman and employs the concept when it suits his purposes. In the hexameters of *Satyra* 2, for example, Juvenal mocks the common beliefs much as Lucretius had:

> Esse aliquos manes et subterranea regna
> et contum et Stygio ranas in gurgite nigras,
> atque una transire vada tot milia cumba
> nec pueri credunt. . . .
>
> (149–152)[11]

That there are such things as Manes, and kingdoms below ground, and punt-poles, and Stygian pools black with frogs, and all those thousands crossing over in a single bark—these things not even boys believe. . . .

But when criticizing life in Rome, Juvenal avails himself of Charon in order to render more vivid his reproof of the rich. In Rome, he says, it is impossible for honest men to make a living, and for the poor, life entails endles troubles. As an example, the poet refers to a poor man crushed to death by an overloaded wagon belonging to a rich man. While the dead man's family waits for him, unaware of his fate, the fellow is already in Hades: "at ille / iam sedet in ripa taetrumque novicius horret / porthmea" ["their master is already sitting, a new arrival, upon the bank, and shuddering at the grim ferryman" (3. 264–266)]. Unlike the other shades, however, this man has no hope of passage: "He has no copper in his mouth to tender for his fare and no hope of a passage over the murky flood, poor wretch" (266–267). As a satirist, Juvenal criticizes belief in underworld terrors; as a poet, however, he employs these same terrors with descriptive detail in order to create a picture of an immoral situation. In the Italian Renaissance, the poetic use of the underworld and its more famous inhabitants, as evidenced in Juvenal, is not lost on lyric poets.

Claudian, the last notable representative of the classical tradition in Latin poetry (OCD), follows the pattern of descent developed in the Orpheus myth by Virgil and Ovid despite the fact that Claudian deals with a different story. In his *De raptu Proserpinae*, he describes the descent of Pluto with his bride-to-be and subsequent changes in the realm. As the returning couple enter Tartarus, the shades assemble, "thick as the leaves the stormy south wind shakes down from the trees, dense as the rain-clouds it masses, countless as the billows it curls or the sand it scatters'' (2. 308–310).[12] Although imitating the images of such poets as Virgil and Seneca, Claudian employs the similes in a new and unifying way—a storm.

With the arrival of Proserpine, Hades is filled with unusual joy. In describing the inhabitants of the realm, Claudian lingers over each with epic fullness. Among the inverted aspects of the underworld, we find the infernal rivers:

> Then, too, the birds flew unhurt over the now appeased stream of poisonous Avernus, and Lake Amsanctus checked his deadly exhalations; the stream was stayed and the whirlpool grew still. They say that then the springs of Acheron were changed and welled up with new milk, while Cocytus, enwreathed with ivy, flowed along in streams of sweet wine. (2. 348–353)

The most startling and original detail is that the Acheron now flows with milk, while Cocytus has become wine; this description will attract Marino when he retells the myth.

Since the underworld is rejoicing, death itself no longer stalks the living and mankind flourishes. The absence of dead souls brings to the poet's mind the infernal boatman, who is the last of the chthonic figures to be pictured. Claudian portrays him with brevity and originality:

Pluto in his quadriga accompanied by Charun and Vanth. Etruscan amphora. Museo Faina, Orvieto. By permission of Fratelli Alinari.

impexamque senex velavit harundine frontem
portitor et vacuos egit cum carmine remos.

(2. 359–360)

Charon crowned his uncombed locks with sedge and singing plied his weight-less oars.

With no shades to ferry, the old boatman, his unkempt forehead wreathed with reeds, celebrates with song while rowing his boat.[13]

To conclude briefly, Charon is rarely pictured at length by the Latin poets, although descriptive adjectives do accompany nouns referring to the boatman. As a well-known figure, Charon is rarely mentioned by name, appearing instead as a *navita* (or *nauta*), *portitor, vector, porthmeus,* and so forth. The brevity of the references precludes, in effect, a meaningful discussion of structural units in a descent topos. Rather, what is significant is that the motif of crossing the infernal river in Charon's boat is employed with a variety of lyric themes, including elegiac, amorous, and satirical.[14]

Notes

1. For a discussion of Lucretius's view of the afterlife, see Cumont, "Lucrèce et le symbolisme pythagoricien des enfers," pp. 229–240.
2. Horace, *The Odes, Epodes and Carmen Saeculare*, ed. Clifford H. Moore. All translations are by C. E. Bennet.
3. Horace repeats the motif in Carmen 2. 14 where he laments the fleeting nature of life. Part of his message is that all are equal in death: "No, not if with three hecatombs of bulls a day, my friend, thou strivest to appease relentless Pluto, who imprisons Geryon of triple fame and Tityos, by the gloomy stream that surely must be crossed by all of us who feed upon Earth's bounty, be we princes or needy husbandmen" (5–12).
4. *Catullus, Tibullus and Pervigilium Veneris*, trans. J. P. Postgate (New York: MacMillan, 1912).
5. Among the conventional uses of the crossing motif, let me cite the following two examples:

Yet no wealth shalt thou carry to the waves of Acheron: naked, thou fool, thou shalt be borne to the ship of Hell. There victor and vanquished shades are mingled in equality of death: captive Jugurtha, thou sittest beside the consul Marius. . . . (*Elegiarum liber* 3. 5. 13–16)

And yet hither at last come all, come noble and come base; bitter is the way, but all must tread it; all must assuage the triple throat of the baying hound, and climb the boat of that grim greybeard that waits for all. (3. 18. 21–24)

The reference to the *publica cumba* of the fierce old man (*torvi . . . senis*) recalls the κοινὴν . . . ἄκατον of Hermesianax. References are to Propertius, trans. H. E. Butler.
6. Contrast Seneca, who describes Orpheus on his first descent as drawing Charon's boat to him *nullo remigio*, by the power of his song (*Hercules oetaeus* 1072–74).
7. *Ovid's Metamorphoses: Books 6–10*, ed. William S. Anderson. Translations are those of Rolfe Humphries.
8. Statius, trans. J. H. Mozley. Elsewhere in this poem, the ferryman is referred to as a *portitor* (299).
9. See, for example, *Silvae* 2. 6. 80–81: "iam litora duri / saeva, Philete, senis, durumque Acheronta videbas." In this case, the dead person, Philetus, is a favorite slave.
10. Among the more famous examples are the *Elegiae in Mecenatem* and the *Consolatio ad Liviam*. In the first poem, we read that

irreligata ratis, numquam defessa carina,
it, redit in vastos semper onusta lacus:
illa rapit iuvenes prima florente iuventa,
non oblita tamen sed repetitque senes.

(5–8)

The barque that knows no fastening, the never-wearied keel,
goes and returns for ever with its load across the vasty pools:
it carries off the young in the first bloom of their youth,
yet unforgetful claims the old as well.

(J. W. Duff, *Minor Latin Poets* [Loeb Library, 1934]), pp. 120–21)

For a textual emendation of interest, see J. A. Richmond, "Charon's Boat," p. 388. The *Consolatio* refers to the boatman as follows: "omnes expectat auarus / portitor et turbae uix satis una ratis" (357–358). Charon also appears in Franz Buecheler's *Carmina latina epigraphica* (Leipzig: Teubner, 1895). See especially no. 1109, with the lines: "Non Acherontis transvehar umbra vadis, / Non ego caeruleam remo pulsabo carinam, / Nec te terribilem fronte timebo Charon" (20–22). Cited in Franz Cumont, *After Life in Roman Paganism*, p. 85. The popular motif that all must cross by way of Charon's boat is expressed in no. 1223. J. A. Tollman compares the latter reference to Horace. See *A Study of the Sepulchral Inscriptions in Buecheler's "Carmina Epigraphica Latina*," pp. 76 ff. Richmond Lattimore also discusses some Latin epitaphs with Charon in his *Themes in Greek and Latin Epitaphs* (e.g., pp. 39–40).

11. G. G. Ramsay, *Juvenal and Persius* (Loeb Library, 1960), pp. 28–31.

12. Maurice Platnauer, *Claudian* (Loeb Library, 1922), vol. 2.

13. Elsewhere, specifically in his invective against Rufinus, Claudian refers to Charon and his crowded boat. Among the crimes committed by Rufinus and the wicked is that of war: The slaughtered victims crowd through the entrance to Avernus "and weigh down Charon's crowded barque" (*In Rufinum liber secundus*, 503, in *Claudian*, ed. Platnauer, 1:94–95).

14. While medieval Latin poets are chary regarding specific details about the classical underworld and of little influence on vernacular poets regarding the use of Charon with lyric motifs, several do mention Charon by name. As examples, let me refer to the secular poet Festus Rufius Avienus, *Aratea*, 208–211 (ed. Alfredus Breysig, p. 10) and the Christian poets Prudentius, *Hamartigenia*, 501–503; *Contra orationem Symmachi libri duo*, 1. 386–387 (*Corpus scriptorum ecclesiasticorum latinorum*, vol. 61), Paulinus of Nola, Carmina 31. 477 (*CSEL*, vol. 30, p. 324), and Gunzo of Novara, *Oratio* (*Patrologia latina*, vol. 136, col. 1302A). A thorough study of medieval poets would reveal other similar references.

7

Latin Tragedy: Seneca

Seneca, imitating in part the Greek tragedians and influenced as well by Virgil's infernal tableau, develops his underworld scenes with great detail. The *contaminatio* of sources and the elaborate attention lavished on the underworld are especially evident in *Hercules furens*. While the first reference to the ferryman is brief, the second occurs in Theseus's lengthy description of Hercules' descent.[1] After graphically recounting Hercules's downward voyage through the cavern of Taenarus to the infernal rivers (662–696), depicting Tartarus (709–727),[2] and speaking of infernal justice for crimes committed, Theseus tells of his famous rescuer's descent for Cerberus:

> Ferale tardis imminet saxum vadis,
> stupent ubi undae, segne torpescit fretum.
> hunc servat amnem cultu et aspectu horridus
> pavidosque manes squalidus vectat senex.
> inpexa pendet barba, deformem sinum
> nodus coercet, concavae squalent genae;
> regit ipse longo portitor conto ratem.
> hic onere vacuam litori puppem applicans
> repetebat umbras; poscit Alcides viam
> cedente turba; dirus exclamat Charon:
> "quo pergis, audax? siste properantem gradum."
> non passus ullas natus Alcmena moras
> ipso coactum navitam conto domat
> scanditque puppem.   cumba populorum capax
> succubuit uni; sidit et gravior ratis
> utrimque Lethen latere titubanti bibit.

(762–777)

A rock funereal o'erhangs the slothful shoals, where the waves are sluggish and the dull mere is numbed. This stream an old man tends, clad in foul garb and to the sight abhorrent, and ferries over the quaking shades. His beard hangs down unkempt; a knot ties his robe's misshapen folds; haggard his sunken cheeks; himself his own boatman, with a long pole he directs his craft. Now, having discharged his load, he is turning his boat towards the bank, seeking the ghosts again; Alcides demands passage, while the crowd draws back. Fierce

97

Charon cries: "Whither in such haste, bold man? Halt there thy hastening steps." Brooking no delay, Alcmena's son o'erpowers the ferryman with his own pole and climbs aboard. The craft, ample for whole nations, sinks low beneath one man; as he takes his seat the o'erweighted boat with rocking sides drinks in Lethe on either hand. (FJM)

As in Virgil, Charon, as old man in squalid garb with an unkempt beard, guards the sluggish swamp; rather than describing his eyes, however, Seneca appears to mention the boatman's sunken cheeks, which are rough and dirty. Virgil himself, incidentally, had previously employed the verb *squaleo* with a beard. But while the translator renders the phrase "concavae squalent genae" as "haggard his sunken cheeks," it is possible to translate *genae* as eye sockets. If this is the actual meaning, Seneca follows the Virgilian pattern in almost every detail, though varying his choice of vocabulary: Where Virgil begins his depiction of the underworld encounter with the verbs *aestaut* and *eructat*, Seneca employs *stupent* and *torpescit*. Both poets use *servat*, but then Seneca substitutes *pendet* for Virgil's *iacet* and *coercet* for *dependet*. For Virgil's "stant lumina flamma," the tragedian writes "concavae squalent genae." Instead of Virgil's two-line description of the means of transportation ("ipse ratem conto subigit velisque ministrat / et ferruginea subvectat corpora cumba"), Seneca uses one line ("regit ipse longo portitor conto ratem"), although he had earlier used the verb *vectat*, substituting *pavidos . . . manes* for Virgil's *corpora*.

The ensuing confrontation also owes much to Virgil's similar scene, except that Hercules, of course, overpowers the ferryman with his own strength. The image of Hercules subduing Charon with the boatman's own pole is a felicitous note, which Dante perhaps had in mind when describing Charon in the act of beating the arriving souls. Seneca also portrays the boat as sinking low under the weight of the descender's body and like Virgil, varies his nouns for the craft itself, employing *ratis, puppis,* and *cumba*. To the last noun, Seneca adds the descriptive phrase *populorum capax*, an influence on later epic poets.

In looking at the description as a whole, we note the nondramatic nature of the descent episode. In the economy of the play, apparently meant to be read rather than acted, the long narration by Theseus serves, at best, to increase the suspense of the main action. Prior to Theseus's lengthy speech, Hercules has just returned from the underworld and leaves the scene to attempt to rescue his wife and children from the evil tryant Lycus. The protracted exposition of Hercules' underworld task is only interrupted nearly two hundred lines later by the arrival of a throng of people, rejoicing at Hercules' victory over Lycus.

In Seneca's *Oedipus* a play in which the poet describes a horrific conjuration scene, Charon is portrayed in a manner that influenced Lucan. It has been noted that less than one half of the play is devoted to dramatic dialogue and Seneca seems to focus on the long scenes of sacrifice and necromancy.[3] The poet's intention appears to be to increase the atmosphere of horror. The reference to Charon is found in a description of an unnatural state, that is, the plague ravaging

Thebes. Not only has the earth been suffering but so, too, has the underworld. As the Chorus of Theban elders says in the parode:

> Rupere Erebi claustra profundi
> turba sororum face Tartarea
> Phlegethonque suam mutat ripam;
> miscuit undis Styga Sidoniis.
> Mors atra avidos oris hiatus
> pandit et omnes explicat alas;
> quique capaci turbida cumba
> flumina servat durus senio
> navita crudo, vix assiduo
> bracchia conto lassata refert,
> fessus turbam vectare novam.

(160–170)

They have burst the bars of abysmal Erebus, the throng of sisters with Tartarean torch, and Phlegethon, changing his own course, has mingled Styx with our Sidonian streams. Dark Death opens wide his greedy, gaping jaws and unfolds all his wings, and the boatman who plies the troubled stream with roomy skiff, though hardy in his vigorous old age, can scarce draw back his arms wearied with constant poling, worn out with ferrying the fresh throng o'er. (FJM)

It is almost as if the two realms have become one; the horrors of Hades have, in fact, been transposed to earth. Even Cerberus, the Chorus says later, is rumored to have burst his chains and be wandering in Theban fields.[4] The ferryman himself (note again the verb *servat*), though identified with Virgilian traits, is pictured in a new situation. Virgil's old man with his hardy, green age is still a *"durus . . . navita"* with *"senio . . . crudo,"* but despite the boatman's vigor, the number of dead is so great that he can hardly move his arms, tired by the constant poling. By introducing these underworld horrors at the outset of his play, Seneca prefigures the disastrous and unnatural deeds yet to come.

The ferryman of the dead reappears in Seneca's *Agamemnon* in a passage reminiscent of Aeschylus. In Aeschylus's homonymous work, Cassandra, late in the play, breaks into a lament, contrasting what was with what is to be. She was raised, she says, by the banks of the Skamandros, her native stream, but now she will chant her prophecies by the banks of Kokytos and Acheron (1157–1161). This technique of opposition (earth versus Hades) is varied by Seneca, who elaborates on the underworld aspects and also depicts Cassandra not as lamenting but foreseeing in a frenzy the doom of Agamemnon and herself. In her vision, Cassandra feels kindred shades summoning her to the beyond:

> iuvat per ipsos ingredi Stygios lacus,
> iuvat videre Tartari saevum canem
> avidique regna Ditis! haec hodie ratis

Charon, Hermes, and Cerberus. Etruscan amphora. Museo Faina, Orvieto. By permission of Fratelli Alinari.

> Phlegethontis atri regias animas vehet,
> victamque victricemque.
>
> (750–754)

'Tis sweet to fare along the very Stygian pools; sweet to behold Tartarus' savage dog and the realms of greedy Dis! To-day this skiff of murky Phlegethon shall bear royal souls, vanquished and vanquisher. (FJM)

That the poet places the underworld ship on murky Phlegethon is unusual; most likely, as in the case of his imitator Lucan, Seneca employs the fiery stream because of its grimmer and more sinister aspects. The extent of Cassandra's raving is such that she now desires this horrible scene rather than the kindly streams of her childhood.[5]

As a final example of Charon's appearance in Senecan tragedy, I refer to *Hercules Oetaeus*, a long play of dubious authenticity, in which the underworld crossing is treated in both traditional and novel ways. Influenced by both Ovid and Sophocles, Seneca, with a profusion of Stoic philosophy, recounts the death and deification of Hercules. When Deïanira learns of the disastrous effects of her love potion, she departs, resolving to kill herself. In response, the Chorus refers to Orpheus's statement that "naught for endless life is made" (FJM, 1035) and having recalled the Thracian poet, sings of his descent for Eurydice:

> Quin per Taenarias fores
> manes cum tacitos adit
> maerentem feriens chelyn,
> cantu Tartara flebili
> et tristes Erebi deos
> vicit nec timuit Stygis
> iuratos superis lacus.
>
> . . . .
>
> audis tu quoque, navita;
> inferni ratis aequoris
> nullo remigio venit.

(1061–1067, 1072–1074)

Nay, when through the gates Taenarian to the silent ghosts he came, smiting his mournful lyre, with his sad song he conquered Tartarus and the sullen gods of Erebus; nor was he daunted by the pools of Styx, by which the high gods swear. . . . Thou also, ferryman, didst hear, and thy boat that plies the infernal sea came oarless on. (FJM)

While Orpheus's descent ended in failure, thus verifying the statement that "all which has been and shall be born shall die" (FJM, 1099) and following the Virgilian and Ovidian patterns, the detail of the boat responding to Orpheus's song is a felicitous innovation that influences later poets.[6] Like Virgil and Ovid, Seneca does not detract from the tale by describing the boatman himself at length; Charon merely stands as an obstacle easily overcome by Orpheus's song.

In a later episode, when Hercules goes off to die on the pyre prepared for him, the Chorus pictures his shade as it descends to the underworld:

> Vadis ad Lethen Stygiumque litus,
> unde te nullae referent carinae;
> vadis ad mane miserandus, unde
> Morte devicta tuleras triumphum,
> umbra nudatis veniens lacertis
> languido vultu tenuique collo;
> teque non solum feret illa puppis. . . .

(1550–1556)

Thou farest to Lethe and the Stygian shore whence no keel will ever bring thee back; thou farest, lamented one, unto the ghosts whence, overcoming Death, thou didst once return in triumph, now but a shade, with fleshless arms, wan face and drooping neck; nor will that skiff . . . bear thee alone. (FJM)

Hercules descending a second time to Hades, now, however, as a dead spirit, is an intriguing and poetically novel situation. Whereas living, he required the entire boat because of his weight, now, a pale soul, he will pass with many others.

Soon after, Alcmena herself, bearing Hercules' funeral urn, launches into a formal song of mourning in which she wonders what is happening during Hercules' final descent: Is he in Elysium or did dark Styx bar his way because of the theft of Cerberus?

> quis nunc umbras, nate, tumultus
> manesque tenet?
> fugit abducta navita cumba?

(1922–1924)

What confusion now, my son, seizes the shadowy spirits? Does the boatman draw away his skiff in flight? (FJM)

But she soon realizes that no ghosts or shadows are afraid of him (1931). As a shade, he no longer has his earthly strength. The momentary and original vision of a fleeing Charon emphasizes the contrast between what Hercules was and now is.

Hearing the voice of Hercules from above, Alcmena is at first stunned, thinking her son has escaped yet another time from the realm of Styx:

> vicisti rursus mortis loca
> puppis et infernae vada tristia?
> pervius est Acheron iam languidus
> et remeare licet soli tibi
> nec te fata tenent post funera?

(1949–1953)

Hast escaped once more death's stronghold and the infernal skiff's dark pool? Is Acheron's wan stream retraceable and mayst thou alone recross it? And after thy death do the fates hold thee no more? (FJM)

But Charon has not been lax; instead Hercules has ascended to the stars and the gods above. As he says, "the pools of groaning Cocytus hold me not, nor has the dark skiff borne o'er my shade" ["Non me gementis stagna Cocyti tenent / nec puppis umbras furva transvexit meas" (FJM, 1963–1964)]. In fact, according to the poet's final message, glorious valor is never borne to the stygian realms.

In conclusion, Seneca's most noteworthy innovation is to have combined elements of the Greek tragedians with narrative techniques of Latin epic. In his greater attention to descriptive detail, much of it concentrating on the horrors of the underworld, Seneca represents Charon in several innovative ways. He is the first to my knowledge to relate in such clear detail the conflict between Hercules and Charon. Seneca presents a vivid picture of the power of Orpheus's song on Charon's boat and sets forth an intriguing scene, the imagined descent of Hercules after his death, now in the form of a shade. To the boatman's Virgilian portrayal, Seneca adds such novel features as an exhausted ferryman whose boat is ample enough for nations. Furthermore, influenced by Homer's evocation of the dead, by similar scenes in Greek tragedy, and possibly the contemporary interest in exotica, such as witches and their rites, Seneca employs Charon in a conjuration scene, a scene that influences later epic poets such as Lucan. Seneca is also inventive enough with mythological materials to place Charon not on the Acheron but on Phlegethon. Therefore, though following on the whole the traditonal features of the descent motif, Seneca is, at the same time, capable of innovation.

Notes

1. In the first reference, the Chorus, lamenting Hercules' fortune, refers to his many tasks, among them the voyage to Hades. The underworld scene is succinctly but vividly described: "stat nigro pelagus gurgite languidum, / et cum Mors avidis pallida dentibus / gentes innumeras manibus intulit, / uno tot populi remige transeunt" ("sluggish stands the mere with black abyss, and, when Death, pale-visaged with greedy teeth, has brought countless tribes to the world of shades, one ferryman transports those many peoples" [554-557]). All quotations and translations of Seneca are by Frank Justus Miller, hereafter referred to as FJM.

2. The poet, in part, writes: "There is a place in a dark recess of Tartarus, which with a heavy pall dense mists enshroud. Hence flow from a single source two streams, unlike: one a placid river (by this do the gods swear), with silent current bears on the sacred Styx; the other with mighty roar rushes fiercely on, rolling down rocks in its flood, Acheron, that cannot be recrossed" (FJM, 709-716).

3. George E. Duckworth, *The Complete Roman Drama*, pp. 671-672.

4. Later still, when the Theban priests conjure up the shades in a gruesome rite, the gloomy setting is typical of underworld potamography. The scene takes place appropriately beneath a tree, where a chill spring flows untouched by light. Furthermore, an "oozy swamp surrounds the sluggish pool" (FJM, 547). Seneca seems intent on infusing the play with the horror of the lower realms.

Let me mention in passing that Seneca not only employs the traditonal similes for the dead but enriches them with his own additions. His description includes the images of clouds, leaves, flowers, with swarming bees, waves, and birds (598-607).

5. Otto Regenbogen interprets Cassandra's attitude as one of extreme courage and ecstatic jubilation in the face of death. In effect, death is seen as an escape from the horrors of life. "Schmerz und Tod in den Tragödien Senecas," pp. 409-462.

6. Compare, for example, the *Orfeo* by the Spanish poet Juan de Jáuregui, where Orfeo's singing both stops the boat (2. 16) and guides it across the river (2. 19). For an analysis of similar episodes, see my article on "The Representation of Charon in the *Siglo de Oro*: Innovation in the Myth of Orpheus," pp. 345-364.

8

Prose Dialogues and Narrative

In discussing Lucian, whose works contain the most extensive references to Charon in antiquity, let me first mention briefly the poet's concept of the underworld crossing and then analyze at greater length five sources where Charon is a major character.[1] With this and a brief discussion of the myth of Psyche in Apuleius, the survey of the infernal boatman in classical literature will have been completed.

Despite the fact that mythology was the repository for many of the philosophical and religious traditions that Lucian mocked, his use of the mythical mode was dual. At times, he speaks of certain customs, practices, or beliefs merely to mock them;[2] on the other hand, although criticizing the foolish exaggerations of the poets, Lucian often employs myth as if accepting its reality, at least on a poetic level. In this instance, fantasy, adopted as both a literary and philosophical tool and thus functioning for a moral purpose, becomes superreal. The technique is especially evident in the depiction of Charon. Lucian's genius is, in fact, to have created an original representation of the ferryman and the underworld crossing by fusing classical material and his own keen sense of reality.

Turning specifically to Lucian's portrayal of the underworld crossing, we note his satirical creativity, expressed through an innovative *contaminatio*. In his dialogue, *The Liar* (*Philopseudes*), Lucian speaks of Odysseus, who is seen as a liar with the noble purpose of getting his comrades home safely.[3] His example, however, brings to mind the "vice of romancing" and those poets, among them Homer, who prefer mendacity to truth. Tychiades, one of the interlocutors, speaks of the weird tales he heard when visiting an ill friend. Cleodemus, one of those gathered around the sick bed, tells of a magician who performed an enchantment by digging a trench at night in order to summon dead souls. The ill man, Eucrates expounds, in turn, on his personal knowledge of the supernatural, referring among other things to the horrible goddess Hecate, who appeared to him and then disappeared into a vast chasm. Looking over the edge, he says, "I saw the whole of Hades: There was Pyriphlegethon, the Lake of Acheron, Cerberus, the Shades; (FF, 3:243). The influence not only of Homer but also Plato is evident, for when Eucrates describes the activities of the spirits, Ion exclaims, "There now! after that I should like to hear the Epicureans say another word against the divine Plato and his account of the spiritual world" (ibid, 243).[4]

104

Not to be outdone, Cleodemus relates a similar experience: Once when ill, a young man "conducted me through a chasm into Hades; I knew where I was at once, because I saw Tantalus and Tityus and Sisyphos. Not to go into details, I came to the Judgement-hall, and there were Aeacus and Charon and the Fates and the Furies" (ibid, 244). Interestingly enough, Lucian here places Charon at the scene of judgment itself. Also of interest is the fact that we find first someone who merely looks into a chasm, thus seeing deeper into Hades (as apparently Odysseus does), and then another who actually descends to see the great sinners (as the later episodes of the *Odyssey* imply). Tychiades, of course, not having seen these marvels, does not believe in the supernatural.

Another influence on Lucian's representation of the underworld is Menippus of Gadara (third century B.C.), to whom some would attribute the origin of the seriocomic style. As a major dramatic character, Menippus appears in seventeen out of thirty *Dialogues of the Dead* and is the title figure in *Menippus, or The Descent into Hades (Nekyomanteia)* and *Icaromenippus, or The Sky-Man*.

In the *Nekyomanteia*, the initial ceremony, where a pit is dug and sheep slaughtered, recalls *Odyssey* 11. As an added feature, the incantation of the magician rends the ground asunder and the barking of Kerberos is heard (AMH, 4:89). The following depiction of Charon's boat recalls the epigrams of Leonidas of Tarentum and Archias. In Lucian, however, the emphasis is not only on the overloaded boat but the lamentation of the spirits as well:

> When we reached the lake, however, we came near not getting across, for the ferry was already crowded and full of groaning. Only wounded men were aboard . . . through some war or other.
> However, when good old Charon ["ὁ βέλτιστος Χάρων] saw the lion-skin he thought that I was Heracles, so he took me in, and not only ferried me across gladly but pointed out the path for us when we went ashore. (Ibid., 4:89–91)

Lucian's original note is depicting Charon as happy to see one whom he thinks is Herakles. In Aristophanes, Charon is less easily fooled, for he makes no comment on Dionysos's appearance or identity. Traditionally according to the mythographers, Charon paid dearly for aiding Herakles. Servius (*ad Aen.* 6. 392), for example, relates that Charon, frightened into ferrying Herakles, was put in chains for a year by Hades as a punishment. We might expect the boatman to be more truculent; in fact, this is the first example in extant Greek literature of Charon making room in his boat for a living descender. The motif has a long and felicitous fortune, more likely due, however, to Virgil than to Lucian. Furthermore, the boatman is seen as aiding the descenders by pointing out the path to be taken. Charon is apparently, to the living at least, no sullen ferryman.

Another work dealing with the underworld in general is *Of Mourning (De lucto)*, a summary, inspired by the absurdities observed in mourners, of popular beliefs found in the poets. In summarizing their views, Lucian refers to Hades, which Pluto has organized so that none may return above except for very important reasons. Pluto is aided in his aim by the geography of the realm:

His country is surrounded by great rivers, fearful even in name; for they are called "Wailing," "Burning Fire," and the like. But the principal feature is Lake Acheron, which lies in front and first receives visitors; it cannot be crossed or passed without the ferryman, for it is too deep to ford afoot and too broad to swim across—indeed, even dead birds cannot fly across it! (AHM, 4:115)

As in previous writers, we find dead animals in Hades; here, birds that are unable to fly across the lake, presumably because of its deadly vapors or distance. While this is the first time this feature is attributed to the Acheron by a Greek writer, the Latins had often referred to this aspect of the Aornum.[5] Charon's importance is emphasized, since there are apparently no alternative routes around Acheron.

Having detailed the poetic representation of the underworld rivers, Lucian criticizes some of the beliefs of the people, such as the notion that an obol must be placed in the mouth of the dead in order to pay the ferryman (ibid., 119). Lucian's satirical comment is that people neither consider which coinage is used in Hades nor the fact that without it the dead would be refused by Charon and thus escorted back to life.

Two final works refer briefly in a more descriptive vein to the popular conception of Charon. In his *Life of Demonax*, Lucian reports the philosopher's witty response to a question about the condition of his legs:

A man saw on the legs of Demonax a discoloration of the sort that is natural to old people, and enquired: "What's that, Demonax?" With a smile he said: "The ferryman's toothmark!" (AMH, 1:165)

Literally, he responds, "Charon bit me" ["Χάρων με ἔδακεν" (45)]. In this context, we sense the idea of a death-demon rather than a "ferryman," the word employed by the translator Harmon.[6] Finally, in his *Prolalia*, or introductory lecture, entitled *Herakles*, Lucian compares the Gaul's portrayal of Herakles to Charon:

To their notion, he is extremely old, bald-headed, except for a few lingering hairs which are quite gray, his skin is wrinkled, and he is burned as black as can be, like an old sea-dog. You would think him a Charon or a sub-Tartarean Iapetus—anything but Heracles! (Ibid., 63)[7]

The parallel to Charon illustrates Lucian's conception of the boatman, who in the major works is most often represented through speech and action rather than description.

Works dealing more directly with Charon are the *Dialogues of the Dead* (parts 4, 10, and 22), *Voyage to the Lower World (Cataplus)*, and *Charon, or the Inspectors*. The three vignettes from the Νεκρικοὶ διάλογοι are the briefest works but do not lack descriptive detail. Other fragments in the series of thirty also offer a glimpse of the crossing; in Dialogue 20, for example, Menippus asks Aiakos for a guided tour of Hades, and the gate-keeper (πυλωρός) replies: "This is Cerberus, as you know, and on your way in you've already seen the ferryman here who brought you over, and the lake and Pyriphlegethon'' (MDM, 7:25). In Dialogue 13, Diogenes tells Alexander the Great that "none may reascend who has once sailed the lake and penetrated our entrance; Aeacus is watchful and Cerberus an awkward customer'' (FF, 1:130). The theme of the impossibility of return is familiar from the lyricists.

As in previous writers, the necessities of realistic plot and action also require the shades to be depicted as substantial. In Dialogue 27, for example, Crates describes how one soul was conveyed to the ferry:

> As for Oroetes, he was so tender-footed that he could not stand, far less walk. . . . He threw himself down and there he lay; nothing would induce him to get up; so the excellent Hermes had to pick him up and carry him to the ferry; how I laughed! (Ibid., 150)

Antisthenes replies that he, too, enjoyed himself:

> When I came down, I did not keep with the crowd; I left them to their blub-berings, ran to the ferry, and secured a comfortable seat for the passage. Then as we crossed, they were divided between tears and sea-sickness, and gave me a merry time of it. (Ibid.)

The seasickness of the passengers adds a novel element to the crossing![8]

Even more intriguing for its originality is the glimpse of the crossing referred to by Alexander the Great in Dialogue 12. Claiming that he is superior to Hannibal, Alexander boasts of the number of dead whom he sent to Hades in one day:

> The ferryman certainly says that his boat could not cope with them on that occasion, but that the majority of them made their own rafts [σκεδίας] and crossed over in that way. (MDM, 7:151)

It is interesting that the noun for Charon's ferry is σκάφος, used to emphasize the volume of dead souls sent below, rather than the diminutive σκαφίς, which appears, as we will see, in the *Dialogues of the Dead*, part 4. Since we also know that none may cross except by way of Charon's boat (see *De Lucto* 3), Alexander's exaggeration is obvious when he claims that the dead constructed their own means of transportation. But even if an exaggeration, the image of souls crossing on rafts is masterful.

Let us turn to those works where Charon has a speaking role. Part 4 of the *Dialogues*, entitled "Hermes and Charon," has as its main theme the praise of times past, with special reference to the present passion for money. The dialogue between porthmeus and psychopompos, developed with great brevity, begins with the realistic encounter between a ferryman and a supplier of equipment: "If you don't mind, ferryman, let's work out how much you owe me at the moment, so that we won't quarrel about it later'' (ibid., 73). Hermes wisely requests an accounting in order to avoid a quarrel later. The situation is typical of Lucian, who renders visible daily activities in the underworld and establishes action there on the level of strict reality: While dealing with what is traditionally a realm of poetic fantasy, Lucian depicts it as prosaically as possible, thereby divorcing the realm and its inhabitants from their usual sense of religious mystery and awe. Hermes, like Charon, is preoccupied with earthly concerns.

Initially, then, Hermes sets the commonplace tone by evincing characteristics of a good businessman. He is politely concerned about his payment, for what we do not yet know, and is aware of a potentially irascible Charon; Hermes' caution is expressed in the phrase "εἰ δοκεῖ" ("Let us calculate, *if it seems best* [to you], what you owe me").

The boatman's response, however, establishes him as an amicable sort, a forthright person with a commonsense approach to business matters: "Let's do that, Hermes. It's better to have this settled, and it'll save trouble." Hermes begins his accounting by listing an anchor that he brought as ordered, costing five drachmae. Charon is surprised by the expense—"Πολλοῦ λέγεις"—but when Hermes protests that he bought it for five drachmae himself, exclaiming "by Hades" to reinforce his sincerity, and spent two obols for an oar thong, Charon resignedly concedes: "Put down five drachmae and two obols." The rise in tone produced by Hermes' exclamation is immediately quieted. While later poets see the boatman as avaricious and miserly, Lucian merely allows him the normal human reaction to high prices. Later, in fact, he reacts to other supplies as being worth the price. If Charon and Hermes are later to castigate the living for their concern with money, they themselves must be untainted by greed. The motif of money, however, is established early for a purpose.

Charon's ferry will not only have a new anchor, the first mention of this accoutrement, but other supplies as well; in fact, from the list of items provided by Hermes, it appears that the boat has become quite dilapidated. The next item listed is a darning needle for the sail, for which Hermes says he paid five obols. Charon's reply is again laconic—"καὶ τούτους προστίθει" ("add those also"). Two more drachmae are due as well for wax to plug leaks in the boat, nails, and a small piece of rope that Charon has already made into a brace. Again the mention of these practical provisions, common to the life of a sailor, intensifies the reality of the scene. Lucian seems more concerned with establishing a realistic tone, a scene of visual clarity and great actuality, than with developing a moral or philosophical message.

When the accounts have been settled, Hermes asks when he will be paid. The response is again that of a shrewd businessman rather than a miser:

> For the moment, Hermes, it's impossible, but if an epidemic or a war sends me down a large batch, I can then make a profit, by overcharging on the fares in the rush. (Ibid., 77)

The ill fortune of mankind is Charon's livelihood. As Hermes says, "So, for the present, I'll have to sit down and pray for the worst to happen so that I may be

Charon and his boat, probably by the Sabouroff Painter. Greek lekythos. 2d half 5th cent. B.C. By permission of The Metropolitan Museum of Art, New York. Rogers Fund, 1921 (21.88.17). All rights reserved.

paid?'' (ibid., 77). The humor in Charon's comment, if there is any, lies in his ig-
noring the burial customs: The dead are given what the living deem to be the
normal fare; how the dead are to pay a higher rate is unclear.

Hermes, surprisingly, is quite humane in his response to Charon's next statement that since it is peace time, few arrive for embarcation. "Better so," he says,
"even if you do keep me waiting . . ." (77). The enforced leisure of the moment,
however, brings to his mind the past, when brave men used to arrive, many
wounded and covered with blood. In contrast, those arriving now are more likely
to have been poisoned by a wife or son, or they are fat from rich living, quite
unlike the old ones. He blames their deaths most often on money—"They
scheme against each other for it, apparently" (ibid., 77).

Having struck this ethical note almost in passing, Lucian ends the dialogue
with a sudden humorous twist. When Charon responds, "Πάνυ γὰρ περιπόθητά
ἐστι ταῦτα" ("certainly, it is much desired by everyone"), Hermes proves the
boatman's point by adding, "Then you won't think it wrong of me if I dun you
for my debt" (ibid., 79)!

Part 10 of the *Dialogues of the Dead*, "Charon and Hermes," begins in more
auspicious times, for Charon has a host of men waiting for passage. Unfortunately, the *skaphis* is just as small and apparently as beaten-up as ever. Given this
situation, the ferryman's concern is no longer merely with money but the safety
of his ship. Despite the length of the dialogue, which is about four times as long
as part 4, Charon's role is much reduced, and this reduction of the picturesque
and material aspects of Hades parallels an expansion of moralistic and satirical
features. Lucian's aim is to satirize the ephemeral values of the living as seen by
comparing life after death. His method is to employ a repeated situation—individual embarcation on Charon's ferry—in order to expand the targets of his
criticism.

The framework for Hermes' interrogation of souls is established with Lucian's
characteristic attention to detail. Though brief, the depiction of Charon and his
ferry is especially vivid; we begin in mediis rebus, with no indication of who is
speaking or where we are:

> Let me tell you how you stand; your boat is small, as you can see, and unsound,
> and leaks almost all over; if it lists one way or the other, it will capsize and sink.
> Yet you come in such numbers all at once, each of you laden with luggage. If,
> then, you take all this on board, I'm afraid you'll be sorry for it later on, parti-
> cularly those of you that can't swim. (Ibid., 101, 103)

It is only when someone asks, "Well, what shall we do to have a good passage,"
that the boatman in his response refers to Hermes. Charon's solution is to have
the shades strip themselves of all possessions, "for, even then, the ferry will
hardly hold you" (ibid., 103). It is up to Hermes to allow no one on board who
has not complied with the boatman's request; as Charon tells him, "Go and
stand by the gangway, and sort them out for admission. Make them strip, before
you let them on board" (MDM).

Menippus, the "best of men," gladly throws his wallet and staff into the water and takes the seat of honor "up beside the steersman" where he can keep his eye on the others. Among those to follow and be interrogated are a male prostitute, a Sicilian tyrant, a hefty athlete, a wealthy man, an armed soldier, and a false philosopher. All are divested of their possessions. As an example of Lucian's technique, the philosopher, who is full of talk about marvels and hides under his cloak such vices as hypocrisy, ignorance, contentiousness, vanity, unanswerable puzzles, thorny argumentations, complicated conceptions, wasted effort, nonsense, idle talk, hair splitting, gold, soft living, shamelessness, temper, luxury, effeminacy, falsehood, pride, and notions of superiority, is stripped of not only these vices but his beard as well, which Menippus cuts off with a shipwright's axe (ibid., 109, 111). The reiteration of each man's possessions, culminating in this display, becomes overwhelming. In the case of the philosopher alone, the possessions are heavy enough, says Hermes, that not even a battleship (literally a *pentēkontoros*, or ship with fifty oars) would be sufficiently big. Lucian renders visible the vanity and ephemerality of most human values, which because of their apparent "weightiness" are left behind when one travels to the realm of truth and equality.

Finally ready for departure, Hermes shouts, "Loose the cable, and pull in the gangway; haul up the anchor; spread the sail" (FF). The boatman himself is even told to take the *pēdalion*, or steering oar. Though undescribed, we apparently witness an actual crossing, for the passengers begin grieving, and during the voyage, Menippus and Hermes talk of what is happening on earth in relation to the recently dead. Hermes soon announces that they have reached port and directs the group to follow the straight path to the court. As he says, he and the ferryman are off for another lot of shades.

The peculiar character of Menippus is rendered more clearly in a delightful dialogue entitled "Charon and Menippus" (22) in which both the boatman and the philosopher are depicted with unusual vitality. In fact, the dialogue opens with an angry Charon shouting, "Pay the fare, curse you" (MDM, 7:9). The recipient of his wrath is unnamed until near the end of the dialogue, although clues are given as we proceed as to who this rascal (κατάρατος) actually is. Charon himself is apostrophized in line 2, and the boatman's name situates the dialogue in the underworld.

Menippus is unaffected by the boatman's angry words, replying, "Shout away, Charon, if that's what you prefer." When the ferryman protests again, asking for his due fee, the Cynic responds by saying that he has absolutely nothing. The statement astounds the boatman, who is forced to switch from imperatives to an incredulous question: "Is there anyone who doesn't have an obol?" Menippus, of course, cannot respond for the rest of mankind, but he is without his fare. Outraged, the god threatens to use physical force: "But by Pluto, I'll throttle you, you blackguard, if you don't pay" (ibid., 11). But, instead of the cowering shade we might expect, Charon's opponent is as virulent as Charon himself. The passenger's response—"And I'll smash your head with a blow from my stick''—seems less a threat than a matter-of-fact statement. The boatman can only resign himself to the situation and refuse to let the shade disembark. As in Aristophanes' *Frogs*, the passengers pay on leaving the ship.

Menippus suggest that Hermes pay for him, since the god delivered him. The idea is humorous in its novelty, but the god, of course, exclaims, ''Heaven help me, if I'm going to pay for the dead too'' (11). Charon's repeated threat to keep Menippus from disembarking has no effect, for the Cynic remains indifferent to the situation. When Charon asks if he did not realize that he had to bring an obol with him, Menippus professes his awareness of the custom but also his inability to fulfill it. ''Did that make it wrong for me to die?'' he asks.

Apparently none of Charon's previous passengers have ever traveled free of charge, for the boatman's next comment is again a question: ''So you'll be the only one to boast of a free passage?'' (13). Whether Charon is thinking only of shades or whether the famous living descenders also paid, is incidental but interesting. Menippus claims he did not travel free, apostrophizing Charon as ὦ βέλτιστε (cf. *Nekyomanteia* 10–11; AMH 4:90), and adding, ''I baled, I helped at the oar, I was the only passenger who wasn't weeping'' (13). Even this does not satisfy the ferryman, who remains adamant; no other alternatives to the obol are allowed.

Menippus's carefree response is to request to be taken back to life then. Charon betrays his ranking in the infernal hierarchy by noting that he would get a good beating from Aiakos if he did so. Instead, he searches through the Cynic's bag but finds no money. The boatman asks Hermes where he found this dog (punning on the origin of the word *cynic*) and describes how the shade acted during the passage: ''How he chattered on the crossing too, mocking and jeering at all the passengers and singing on his own while they were lamenting!'' (MDM, 7:13, 15). In Hermes' rejoinder, we find the first reference to Menippus by name, with an added comment that ''he is absolutely independent and cares for nobody'' (15). The dialogue closes with an impotent threat by the ferryman and a characteristic witticism from Menippus:

> Charon: But if I ever get my hands on you—
> Menippus: If you get your hands on me, my good fellow! But
>   you won't get them on me a second time.
>
> (Ibid. 15)

Unlike a ferry passage on earth, this one takes place only once.

Throughout this work, which embodies a confrontation, the dramatic nature of the dialogue is evident structurally, since neither interlocutor has more than one or two lines per discourse. The technique reminds us of dramatic stichomythia and possibly reflects the influence of middle comedy or the satry play. The humor of the piece lies not only in the outrageous responses by Menippus but the incongruity of having no fare. Lucian had satirized the custom of placing an obol in the mouth of corpses in his discursive treatis *On Mourning (De lucto)*, and now he offers the same criticism in dramatic form. It is the satirist's genius to incarnate the ridiculousness of popular belief in a vivid and convincing manner. By forcing his audience to think through their beliefs, to see how they would function if put into practice, that is, dramatized in realistic terms, Lucian attacks the custom in a manner comprehensible to all.

The last two works to be considered are Lucian's masterpieces; both are too long however to be examined in great detail. Rather than looking at the extended satire in each, I will concentrate solely on the artistic representation of Charon in each work. Since he is a major interlocutor in both, Charon has much to say but not always of a personal, or self-descriptive, nature. In *The Downward Journey, or The Tyrant (Cataplus)*, Charon relinquishes the scene to Clotho for the main episode, which satirizes the tyrant Megapenthes. The dialogue also extends beyond the actual crossing, since the shades, after disembarcation, continue on to the judgment seat of Rhadamanthus, where the tyrant is prosecuted for his misdeeds on earth.

What, we might ask, is Charon's role in this dramatic and satirical dialogue? As usual, he is the point around which infernal activity is ordered; that is, all souls must arrive at his landing and await passage across the lake. Their marshaling together for embarcation provides an opportunity for contrasts and lengthy discussions. In addition, the actual crossing permits a continued depiction of the true nature of the dead. As the focus of life in Hades, Charon is portrayed with the usual attention to realistic detail; he is neither an abstract ferryman nor a stock figure to be mentioned and dispensed with. The dialogue opens with the boatman addressing Clotho, an interesting departure from tradition. Clotho, of course, as one of the three Fates and the spinner of the thread of life, is normally an abstraction or when personified, is not described as dwelling in Hades; Lucian is the first to my knowledge to depict her so actively involved in the death and descent of the shades.

Charon's first words are a complaint: The ship has been fixed up and ready to sail for some time, but Hermes has failed to arrive. The actual preparations that Charon has undertaken are somewhat humorous. The water has been bailed out, bringing to mind the leaky boat in part 10 of the *Dialogues of the Dead*; the mast is in place with the sail hoisted, and all the oars are tied down with lanyards. There is nothing, he says, to hinder them from weighing anchor and sailing. It is almost dusk—as if Hades had days and nights—and Charon has yet to earn an obol. As a servant of Pluto, mirroring the role of the slave in human society, the boatman fears his master will blame him for taking it easy, when all is the fault of the nekropompos. The ferryman's witty comment is that Hermes must have had a drink of the water of Lethe.

The description of the boat presents some variation from the little skiff seen elsewhere in Lucian. The mention of both a sail and oars implies a much larger craft; in fact, as we learn when Hermes and the dead finally arrive, the boat holds thousands. Before Hermes' appearance, however, Charon has time to lament the guide's preference for his celestial duties:

Here with us there is nothing but asphodel and libations and funeral-cakes and offerings to the dead, and all else is misty, murky darkness; in heaven, however, it is all bright, and there is ambrosia in plenty and nectar without stint, so it is likely that he finds it more pleasant to tarry there. And when he leaves us he flies up as if he were escaping from jail, but when it is time to come down he comes with reluctance, at the last moment, slowly and afoot. (AMH, 2:5)

With his usual subtlety, Lucian burlesques the simplistic notions of the poets.

When Hermes finally arrives, he is waving along the souls with his wand, dripping with sweat, dusty-footed, and panting. His delay, he explains, was caused by a tyrant who kept trying to escape. In his discourse, Hermes discloses a few more details of underworld life: It is Atropos who turns the souls over to the guide, and the descent to Charon is preceded by counting the souls at the entrance to Hades. Aiakos is found there with a tally sheet sent by one of the Fates, and he verifies the number of dead souls before they continue on to the ferry. On this particular trip, Hermes was found one short of the tally of a thousand and four and was accused of thievery by Aiakos. Hermes realized that the tyrant must have escaped and pursued him aided by a Cynic.

This little scene of underworld job hazards is interrupted by Charon, who urges them about their business. Clotho's task is to hold the account book near the gangway and record the name, city, and manner of death of each soul as she/he embarks. The first consignment to the ferryman are three hundred babies, many of whom were abandoned. The boatman's comment is quite imagistic: "I say, what a rich haul! It's green-grape dead (ὀμφακίας ... νεκρούς) you have brought us" (11). Following these clusters of unripe grapes, the unmourned, or old people, are brought on board, they, too, without interrogation. Deaf with age, they have to be carried on by Hermes, who announces to Charon: "Here you are again, three hundred and ninety-eight, all tender and ripe and harvested in season." The boatman's humorous response continues and sharpens the metaphor: "Good Lord, yes! They're all raisins (ἀσταφίδες) now!" (11). The reference is possibly a take-off on the traditional image of the souls as dead leaves, dry and shriveled.

Among those to board, of course, is the tyrant. Due to his attempts to escape, Charon decides to lash him to the mast. The tyrant naturally claims to no avail that he should have the *proedria*, or privileged seat. Finally, when Charon is ready to cast off, the poor neglected cobbler Micyllus calls out to be allowed on board. In contrast to the tyrant, he is eager to cross in order to leave behind his miserable life on earth and enjoy the equality found in Hades. Clotho is all set to allow him in when Charon cries out that the boat is full. Micyllus, told to wait until the next morning, threatens Charon—"I'll have you up before Rhadamanthus for breaking the law"—but the ship is already sailing.

The situation results in one of Lucian's most hilarious artistic innovations. Micyllus decides to swim across in the boat's wake, for, as he says, "I'm not afraid of giving out and drowning, seeing that I'm already dead! Besides, I haven't an

obol to pay my passage'' (ibid. 37). The cobbler does as he says to the horror of
Clotho. A short dramatic scene develops, with the result that the poor man is
pulled on board despite Charon's protest that the boat is full. Hermes solves the
dilemma by suggesting a seat on the tyrant's shoulders.

During the crossing, the philosopher Cyniscus tells Charon that he has no obol
but offers to bale or help row. The ferryman, with no recriminations, accepts the
offer of aid and sets him rowing. Cyniscus asks if he should sing a few sailors'
songs to set the rhythm, but his intentions are foiled by the lamentations of the
other shades. Hermes notes that Micyllus is not grieving and informs him that no
one may cross without a tear. Micyllus laments ''for custom's sake,'' bemoaning
that he will no longer be able to suffer (41)! Our last glimpse of Charon soon
follows, for the ship has arrived at the far side. The boatman collects his fares
from all but Micyllus, who is allowed to descend with only a slight protest from
Charon. In leaving the scene, Charon disappears with yet another droll twist; his
final words are: ''I am going after horses and cattle and dogs and the rest of the
animals, for they have to cross now'' (ibid., 43).

The final dialogue of interest to us, *Charon, or the Inspectors*, illustrates by its
very design Lucian's innovative abilities, for the situation is a reversal of the descent motif. Instead of souls descending to Charon, we find the ferryman ascend-
ing to examine life on earth. Traditionally, of course, playwrights had represented
the evocation of souls from Hades. I refer, for example, to both Cratinus's *Chi-
rons*, where the ghost of Solon rises from Hades, and the *Demoi* of Eupolis,
where great Athenians of the past rise to give advice for the present. While Lucian
may have been influenced by these or similar works, this is evident not so much
in *Charon* as in *The Fisher (Piscator)*. In this latter dialogue, the famous philosophers of the past receive ''a short leave of absence from Hades'' (FF, 1:208) in
order to persecute Lucian for abuse, which leads to a defense of the satirist's actions. The situation in *Charon*, however, requires a creative leap of the imagination: Dead spirits had always been evoked, in both popular belief and literature,
but never the ferryman himself.

The work begins with Hermes, who asks Charon not only what he is laughing
at but why he has left his ferry and come up to earth. The action strikes even the
psychopompos as unusual: ''You are not at all in the habit,'' he says, ''of concerning yourself with affairs up above'' (AMH, 2:397). Claiming that he wishes to
see what life is like and why people grieve when they die, Charon says that like
Protesilaos, he has obtained permission from Hades to come up to the sunlight
for a single day. Furthermore, he hopes Hermes will consent to guide him, since
Hermes knows all about these matters.

After some initial hesitation, with fear expressed that Zeus may confine him to
Hades for his delay or cast him from heaven as he did Hephaestos, Hermes yields
to the boatman's persuasive request. As Charon tells him, ''I have never ordered
you to bale or take an oar. On the contrary, you stretch yourself out on deck and
snore, in spite of those broad shoulders of yours, or if you find a talkative dead
man, you chat with him throughout the trip, while I, old as I am, row both oars

of my boat alone'' (ibid., 399). Interestingly, the term for *old* used by Charon is πρεσβύτης, which is only the sixth stage of seven in a person's life. Also, he himself rows his boat, which is propelled by two oars, a feature reminiscent of the tragedians.

Hermes notes that it is impossible to see everything in detail:

> In that event Zeus would be obliged to have me advertised by the crier, like a runaway slave, and you yourself would be prevented from doing the work of Death and compelled to embarass the revenues of Pluto's government by not bringing in any dead for a long time; besides, Aeacus the toll-taker would be angry if he did not make even an obol. (Ibid., 309, 401)

His solution is to see the principal things from some high mountain. He would take Charon to heaven, he says, were it not for the fact that someone conversant with shades is prohibited from setting foot in Zeus's realm.

Charon gives himself into Hermes's care with a lengthy epic simile taken from the life of a sailor. The boatman's literary talents, evidenced in his use of imagery in *The Downward Voyage*, continue to be illustrated:

> You know, Hermes, what I am in the habit of telling you and the others when we are on the water. When we are close-hauled and the wind in a sudden squall strikes the sail and the waves rise high, then you all in your ignorance tell me to take the sail in or slack the sheet off a bit or run before the wind; but I urge you to keep quiet, saying that I myself know what is best. Just so in this case; you must do whatever you think is right, for you are skipper now, and I will sit in silence, as a passenger should, and obey your orders in everything. (Ibid., 401)

Not only is the boatman poetic, he is also wise. Hermes, in turn, resorts to a poetic solution. He and Charon will pile mountains on top of each other as the sons of Aloeus (the giants Otus and Ephialtes) did according to Homer. When Charon doubts their own ability to do so, Hermes says that they are gods and ought to be able to surpass the deeds of mere children. His technique is to read a few verses of Homer, who ''puts the mountains together as easily as that'' (405), and the poetic description becomes reality. Lucian is not content to satirize myth by presenting it in the light of reality; he also parodies poetry itself, lending the verses of Homer a material efficacy.

Charon's only fear is that this ''experiment in Homeric building'' (407) may tumble down. With a humorous reference to the techniques of the playwrights he says, ''This is an uncommonly big piece of stage-machinery (*mēchanē*) that you are mounting me on'' (407). Hermes is undaunted, however, and sets the two of them on the twin peaks of Parnassus. Having gotten this far, Charon can only make out the outlines of Greece, which incidentally has ''rivers bigger than Cocytus and Pyriphlegethon.'' Unhappy with this, he tells Hermes that he wants to observe people themselves; another pair of Homeric verses remedies this obstacle as well.

Charon's progressive talents as a student of literature are next revealed when he asks if Hermes would like questions formed in Homeric language. To the doubting response of Hermes—"How can you know any of it when you are always on shipboard and at the oar?"—he replies:

When I set him [Homer] over the ferry after his death, I heard him recite a quantity of verses and still remember some of them, although a good bit of a storm caught us then. You see, he began to sing a song that was not too auspicious for the passengers, telling how Poseidon brought the clouds together, stirred up the deep by plunging in his trident as if it were a ladle, excited all the gales and a lot more of it. Thus he put the sea in a commotion with his verses, and a black squall suddenly struck us and just missed capsizing the boat. Then he became seasick and jettisoned most of his lays, including Scylla and Charybdis and the Cyclops; so that it wasn't hard for me to get a little salvage out of all that he let go. (Ibid., 411, 413)

This underworld student of Homer goes on to analyze the foibles of mankind; among their faults is their failure to pay heed to Death. The ferryman, for example, sees an athlete basking in the applause of the crowd and informs Hermes that in a little while he will be thrown by Thanatos, "the most invincible of all antagonists," and seized and heaved aboard the boat by Charon himself.

The philosophical discussions between the two gods are enlivened by the overheard conversation of two sixth-century-B.C. figures, Solon and Croesus. A reference by them to gold produces a brief Charonian disquisition on the stupidity of those who seek it (419, 421): None will board his skiff carrying any (427). In the air above the earthly activity, Hermes points out the Fates spinning the threads of life from which like puppets hang the citizens of earth. As Charon says, "all this is very funny, Hermes" (431).

The humor of the situation takes on tragic tones in the discussions that follow. Their details are beyond the scope of this study, but one aspect must be pointed out in relation to Charon's use of imagery. He sums up his opinion of humanity and life as follows:

You have noticed bubbles in water, caused by a streamlet plashing down—I mean those that mass to make foam? Some of them, being small, burst and are gone in an instant, while some last longer and as others join them, become swollen and grow to exceeding great compass; but afterwards they also burst without fail in time, for it cannot be otherwise. Such is the life of men; they are all swollen with wind, some to greater size others to less; and with some the swelling is short-lived and swift-fated, while with others it is over as soon as it comes into being; but in any case they all must burst. (Ibid., 435)

Hermes' witty comment is "Charon, your simile is every bit as good as Homer's, who compares the race of men to leaves" (437).[9]

Charon would like to shout to the citizens of earth to desist from their vain labors and live always with death before their eyes. Despite all their striving for possessions, he says, they must all come down to us with but a single obol (437). "Nothing that is in honour here is eternal, nor can a man take anything with him when he dies . . ." (437). The boatman's comment is appropriately a reminiscence of Solon, whose words he has praised earlier in the dialogue.

As a last appraisal of mankind, Charon asks to see the tombs, which is a stimulus for yet another discourse criticizing funeral practices (cf. *De lucto*). The ferryman marvels when told that prominent cities like Troy exist no more; he remembers, "I set a great many from that place across the ferry, so that for ten whole years I couldn't dock my boat or dry her out" (443). But in Hermes' words, "Cities die as well as men." Finally, thanking Hermes for his aid, Charon prepares to return to his ferry. He closes the dialogue with one last remark on the silly concerns of unhappy mankind, adding "but never a thought of Charon."[10]

With this work, Charon has reached his culmination as a dramatic character in Lucian's satirical dialogues. As Hermes tells the boatman at one point, "εὖ γε παρῳδεῖς, ὦ Χάρων"—"You are good at parody, Charon." In addition, Charon has shown himself to be a master of poetic knowledge and moral philosophy. Lucian's brilliance is to have realized the satirical possibilities of the very myths he originally set out to criticize. Rather than doing away with Charon and his more notable colleagues, Lucian establishes them as philosophers and critics. At the same time, of course, through his unremitting sense of reality, he mocks popular beliefs in the mysterious and terrifying underworld.

In conclusion, I refer to the polemic regarding Lucian's originality. I think it is evident that regarding the portrayal of Charon and the underworld crossing, Lucian is not only much more detailed than his predecessors but also quite innovative. As Barry Baldwin notes, "Lucian was the first to admit that he based his key work on classical models, and was sensible enough to admit that the label of originality was not the holy grail. But his work is not a pallid pastiche of the classics of Greek literature" (*Studies in Lucian*, p. 118). In fact, Lucian went far beyond his sources. What is most unconventional and striking, in my opinion, is his point of view. Hades has become not only a secular realm, a model of what earthly life should be like, but has acquired a reality so sharp that its details are more actual and graphic than those of earth. In turn, the descenders, now dead, reveal more clearly their true nature, since they are stripped of the concealing trappings of their earthly existence.

The inhabitants of Hades, especially Pluto's servants, are, in effect, "depoeticized"; that is, as figures represented with absolute reality—Charon, for example, is a vivid Greek ferryman—they are divorced from fantasy while being entirely mythical. Charon gains a new solidity, a personality: Not only a ferryman with the nautical concerns of his craft, Charon demonstrates an awareness of more important values; in his most developed state, he is both a philosopher and moralist. The shrewd insights and criticisms expressed by the boatman and the descent motif, however, are never arid. Due in large part to the novel portrayal of the underworld in which Charon plays a major role, Lucian's satire is above all entertaining—and thus more memorable and effective.

It is apparent that all structural elements of the descent are employed by Lucian. The later features of crossing and disembarcation, ignored in most treatments of the myth, find a purpose in Lucian. Above all, they enable discussions begun in the confrontations at Charon's ferry to be continued and developed in the light of the passengers' increasing fear. The realization that all must face judgment becomes most intense at this stage of the descent. The embarcation, when the souls leave behind their possessions, and the disembarcation, when the ferryman collects his fee, give rise as well to satire of not only funeral customs connected with the obol but the acquisition of money itself. All of the units, however used for satire, are filled out with descriptive detail. And finally, even the descent itself is turned upside down when Charon ascends to visit this world. The popularity of the descent motif, and the figure of the boatman is confirmed by later Byzantine writers[11] as well as by the Italians. The latter poets' fondness for the ferryman is studied in part 2.

Before turning to the Italians, however, let me discuss briefly the representation of Charon in the only Latin novel that has survived in its entirety, Apuleius's *Metamorphoses*. This work contains a reference to Charon in a myth of great importance for later Italian poets of all literary genres[12]—the myth of Cupid and Psyche, which Lucius, in the shape of an ass, overhears related by an old woman, a cook of the young bride Charite. Narrated in Books 4-6 in a central position in the novel, the myth of Psyche unifies the thematic motifs of the work as a whole. But rather than discuss at length the nature of the *Metamorphoses* or the poet's intent, I will analyze the narrative elements in Psyche's descent to the underworld, the last and greatest of the tasks imposed on her by an angry Venus.

In Book 6, Psyche, realizing she is being sent to her destruction, resolves to kill herself by leaping from a tower, death being the easiest method of descent. But the tower turns out to be Psyche's "donor," to use Vladimir Propp's terminology, providing information essential for successfully completing her task.[13] Provided with what we might call "magical agents," honey sops for Cerberus and coins for Charon, Psyche overcomes the obstacles in her path and gains the object of her quest. Yet though having successfully returned from the underworld, she again succumbs to her curiosity, violating Venus's interdiction much as she had earlier violated Cupid's and in the end must be rescued by Cupid himself.

Within the framework of this folktale, there appears a mythological figure traditionallly associated with the classical underworld—the boatman Charon. In Apuleius, the greatest development of the descent theme and Charon's roles in it is found in the tower's instruction to Psyche, since the narration of the event itself is summarized with great rapidity. The tower's first directive concerns the location of an entrance to the underworld, which, in this case, happens to be Taenarus. In describing the downward voyage and the necessary accoutrements—"offas polentae mulso concretas ambabus . . . manibus, at in ipso ore duas . . . stipes" ("two sops sodden in the flour of barley and honey in thy hands and two half-

pence in thy mouth")[14]—the tower warns Psyche of certain *villains* whom she is
to avoid. If she passes by the first of these, she will come to a river (Book 6, sec.
18):

> Nec mora, cum ad flumen mortuum venies, cui praefectus Charon protenus ex-
> petens portorium, sic ad ripam ulteriorem sutili cymba deducit commeantes.

> By and by thou shalt come unto the dead river, whereas Charon is ferryman,
> who will first have his fare paid him before he will carry the souls over the river
> in his patched boat.

By employing the motif of the boatman and his fare, Apuleius emphasizes the
ferryman's avarice, a vice hinted at by others but expressed most clearly by the
Latin storyteller:

> Ergo et inter mortuos avaritia vivit, nec Charon ille vel Ditis pater, tantus deus,
> quicquam gratuito facit, sed moriens pauper viaticum debet quaerere, et aes si
> forte prae manu non fuerit, nemo eum expirare patietur.

> Hereby you may see that avarice reigneth even amongst the dead; neither Cha-
> ron nor Pluto will do anything for nought: for if it be a poor man that is near to
> die, and lacketh money in his hand, none will allow him to give up the ghost.

Given this situation, the tower advises Psyche what to do:

> Huic squalido seni dabis nauli nomine de stipibus quas feres alteram, sic tamen
> ut ipse sua manu de tuo sumat ore.

> Wherefore deliver to the foul old man one of the halfpence which thou bearest
> for thy passage but make him receive it with his own hand out of thy mouth.

There is no hint of a confrontation between the squalid, old ferryman and the living descender. Since Psyche will offer the coin in her mouth, presumably as the
other shades do, she will be received by Charon without oppositon. Perhaps the
boatman's avarice overrides any fear of intruders.

During the ferry passsage in Charon's *sutilis cymba*, Psyche will face another
obstacle:

> Nec setius tibi pigrum fluentum transmeanti quidam supernatans senex mor-
> tuus putres attollens manus orabit ut eum intra navigium trahas: nec tu tamen
> illicita affectare pietate.

> And it shall come to pass as thou sittest in the boat, thou shalt see an old man
> swimming on the top of the river holding up his deadly hands, and desiring
> thee to receive him into the bark; but have no regard to his piteous cry, for it is
> not lawful to do so.

The significiance of this figure, beyond his role as an impeding villain, is unclear. If we interpret Apuleius's tale allegorically as the voyage of the rational soul toward intellectual love,[15] perhaps the *senex mortuus* with his *putres manus* represents the sins of the flesh, which are capable of submerging the boat. At any rate, prefiguring Filippo Argenti, who in Dante's *Commedia*, also tries to enter a boat but is repelled with disdain, he is a character to be avoided. After describing other underworld hazards, the tower informs Psyche that she is to return as she went, giving the other coin to the *avaro navitae*.

In looking at the episode as a whole, we find that Apuleius deals mainly with the more narrative elements of the descent theme—the actual downward voyage, paying the fare, and the crossing—avoiding the dramatic units of confrontation. Charon, as one of the several figures encountered in the beyond, receives little description, unlike Cerberus, who is depicted with more frightening features.[16] Rather than serving as an object of horror, the boatman embodies a moral principle; that is, he represents one of the vices characteristic of the lower realm in popular lore—avarice. Apuleius's brief portrayal of the *avaro nocchiero* initiates the allegorical exegesis of Charon by later poets and commentators and Charon's avarice becomes a standard feature not merely in narrative works but in all genres.

Notes

1. For the varied works that I have used in this chapter, see the following in the bibliography: F. G. Allinson, Barry Baldwin, Alfred R. Bellinger, Jacques Bompaire, Marcel Caster, Maurice Croiset, Joseph W. Hewitt, Barbara McCarthy, Emily J. Putnam, Jacques Schwartz, William H. Tackaberry, and Paul Turner (the latter under Lucian in the primary bibliography).

2. See, for example, *Amber or the Swans (De Electro)*. Regarding just one aspect of contemporary life—the interest in dreams—I would like to refer to the work by Artemidorus, because he himself refers to Charon. In Artemidorus's *Oneirocritica*, he relates the following: "Someone dreamt, for example, that Charon was playing with pebbles with a man and the dreamer took the side of the man. Consequently, Charon lost the game and he was angry and pursued the dreamer. The dreamer turned and fled. . . . The deity, therefore [unable to catch him], turned and departed. . . . Charon playing at pebbles foretold a relationship with death. The fact that Charon did not catch him indicated he would not die, but rather that his feet would be in danger because of the pursuit" (1.4, trans. Robert J. White). The vitality of Charon in popular belief is attested by his appearance in dreams.

3. All titles are cited according to both the English of the Loeb edition (or the Fowlers) and the standard Latin form. The following translations have been employed throughout this chapter: LC = Lionel Casson, *Selected Satires of Lucian*. FF = H. W. Fowler and F. G. Fowler, *The Works of Lucian of Samosata* in 4 vols. AMH = A. M. Harmon, vols. 1–6 and MDM = M. D. MacLeod, vols. 7–8, *Lucian*. PT = Paul Turner, Lucian, *Satirical Sketches*.

4. Mocking a poet or philosopher, of course, requires acquaintance with her/his works. Plato does not mention Charon, incidentally, when speaking of the underworld but he does refer to the topography and practices (especially the infernal judgment and resultant punishment) of the realm. See, for example, *Republic* 10. 614A–621C (the vision of Er the Pamphylian), *Phaedo* 107D–108C and 111D–114D (where vessels on the Acheron are mentioned in 113D), and *Gorgias* 523A–526D.

The Epicureans, who are mentioned as being critical of Plato, sought to free man from fear of death and after-life punishment of the soul. An expression of their ideas about the underworld can be found in the first century B.C. Latin poet Lucretius (see especially 1. 115 ff. and 3. 37, 978–1023). A sepulchral inscription cited by Lattimore offers perhaps the most succinct example of their attitude:

οὐκ ἔστι ἐν "Αιδου πλοῖον, οὐ πορῦμεὺς Χάρων,
οὐκ Αἴακος κλειδοῦχος, οὐχὶ Κέρβερος κύων.
                                    (*Themes in Greek and Latin Epitaphs*, p. 75)

There is no boat in Hades, no ferryman Charon,
no Aeacus keepter of the keys, nor any dog called Cerberus.

The later Stoic philosopher Epictetus (ca. A.D. 55–135) sounds the same note in his *Discourses*: "οὐδεὶς "Αιδης οὺς οὐ 'Αχέρων οὐδὲ / Κωκυτὸς οὐδὲ Πυριφλεγέθων, ἀλλὰ πάντα / θεῶν μεστὰ καὶ δαιμόνων" ("There is no Hades, nor Acheron, nor Cocytus, nor Pyriphlegethon, but everything is filled with gods and divine powers" [*The Discourses as Reported by Arrian*, 3. 13–15, trans. W. A. Oldfather]).

I note in passing that other writers of dialogues also influenced Lucian, specifically Plutarch (ca. A.D. 50–120). For his description of the afterlife, see *On the Delays of Divine Justice (De sera numinis vindicta)* 563E ff. Here much like Plato's Er, Thespesius tells what he saw on his visit to the underworld. In doing so, Thespesius refers to the previous descents of Dionysos and Orpheus but spends most of his time on infernal punishments. Elsewhere the similar tale of Timarchus is told, in which islands, lakes, and a great abyss appear. See *On the Sign of Socrates (De genio Socratis)* 590A ff.

5. "Αορνος, meaning birdless, was a fanciful Greek translation of the Italic Avernus, the lake near Cumae. Virgil speaks of this gulf in *Aeneid* 6. 237–242. For the same legend, cf. Lucretius 6. 740 and Livy 24. 12. Among the Greeks, Strabo refers to this legend in describing Aornum (5. 4. 5) and also speaks of other Charonia (Χαρώνια) where poisonous vapors rise. See, for example, 12. 8. 17 and 14. 1. 11 and 44. Gulf Aornum, of course, is a separate entity from the Acheron; Lucian has transferred its features to the Acheron.

Regarding the Charonean caverns, see Pliny, *Historia naturalis* 2. 95, 208 ("spiracula vocant, alii Charonea, scrobes mortiferum spiritum exhalantes, item in Hirpinis Ampsancti ad Mephitis aedem locum, quem qui intravere moriuntur"). Compare Cicero, *De divinatione* 1. 79. Iamblichus also refers to these in his Greek work *On The Mysteries of the Egyptians, Chaldeans, and Assyrians*; see the translation by Thomas Taylor, chap. 1, p. 205 (= 182. 9 in the edition of Édouard des Places, p. 147).

6. Later authors note this tradition in which Charon has many features of Thanatos. The *Suidae lexicon*, for example, refers to "Χάρων ὁ Θάνατος" (ed. Bekkeri, p. 1120). Compare the *Glossaria duo*, ed. Henricus Stephanus (= Henri Estienne), col. 150 (p. g. ii^v), where we find *Orcus* defined as Charon. Isidore is more inclusive yet; he writes: "Pluton Graece, latine Diespiter, vel Ditis pater, quem alii Orcum vocant, quasi receptorem mortuorum. Ipse est Graece Charon" (*Origines* 8. 11. 42).

7. Elsewhere Charon is employed in a metaphor to describe old age. Lucian refers to himself late in life, saying, "He is nearly in the clutches of Aeacus, one foot is in the ferryman's boat" (*Apology for the Dependent Scholar*, FF, 2:27).

8. In the same dialogue, Diogenes tells an old pauper that he should not have feared death, because he is "as old as our ferryman" (MDM, 7. 133).

9. More to the point, perhaps, would have been a reference to Plutarch, who in talking of metempsychosis depicts those to be reborn as rising into the air in a "flamelike bubble." When these πομφόλυγα gently burst, a human form comes forth. See *De sera numinis vindicata* 563F–564A.

10. As Rocco and others note, the phrase has become a proverb in France—"et de Charon, pas un mot," as Mme. de Sévigné says (p. 42).

11. See, for example, the great tenth- or eleventh-century *Epic of Digenis Akritas*, considered the most ancient monument of neo-Hellenic literature in a popular language, where Charon comes to earth as an insatiable death-demon; the thirteenth-century epic *Achilleis*, where he is again a death-demon and Ployxena asks Achilles (her spouse) to fight Charon; the early fifteenth-century work, Mazaris's *Journey to the Underworld*, a Byzantine imitation of Lucian's *Nekyomanteia*; the *Plague of Rhodes* by Emmanuel Georgillos, written around 1498, where Charon rides on a horse called Kerberos! (*Carmina graeca mediiaevi*, ed. Wilhelm Wagner [Lipsiae: Teubner, 1874], pp. 32–82); the sixteenth-century *Rhymed Complaint of Jean Pikatores* (ed. Wagner, *ibid.*, pp. 224 ff.), where Charon, carrying a bow and arrows for his victims, appears on horseback; he claims that he obeys the will of God, and offers a religious exposition on cosmogony, including material from the Bible; the *Apokopos* of Bergadis (*Bibliothèque grecque vulgaire* ed. Emile Legrand, vol. 2 [Paris: Maisonneuve, 1881], pp. 94 ff.); the tragedy *Erophile*, an imitation of Giraldi's *Orbecche* by Georges Chortatzis, in which Charon (in the form of a skeleton) rather than Nemesis delivers the prologue and speaks of his own appearance and functions; and many other works of popular poetry too numerous to detail. See Panayota Kyriazopoulou, *Le personnage de Charon de la Grèce ancienne à la Grèce moderne*, pp. 59–111.

12. Let me mention in passing that Charon is found in other fragmentary Latin prose works. As an example, see Petronius's *Satyricon* 121 (where the allusion occurs in verse, however). Other references can be found in the rhetoricians, but I should note that where prose fiction is concerned the classical world is rather lacking. The causes lie in part with the prestige of verse for works of imaginative literature.

13. Vladimir Propp, *Morphology of the Folktale*, chap. 3.

14. Apuleius, *The Golden Ass*, trans. W. Adlington (1566), rev. S. Gaselee, Book 6, secion 18, (p. 274).

15. See Robert Graves, *The Golden Ass of Apuleius*, p. xvi. Michael Grant, while stating that "the indications of allegory in this fairy-tale are not very extensive," notes the significance of the names of Psyche (the soul) and Eros (love) as well as the other characters in the story (*Myths of the Greeks and Romans*, p. 421). Grant adds that the myth was treated allegorically by Martianus Capella and Fulgentius, among others (pp. 422–423).

16. Apuleius describes Cerberus as follows: "Canis namque praegrandis, teriugo et satis amplo capite praeditus, immanis et formidabilis, tonantibus oblatrans faucibus mortuos, quibus iam nil mali potest facere, frustra territando ante ipsum limen et atra atria Proserpinae semper excubans servat vacuam Ditis domun" ("For there is a great and marvellous dog with three heads, huge and horrid, barking continually at the souls of such as enter in, to frighten them with vain fear, by reason he can now do them no harm; he lieth day and night before the gate of Proserpina, and keepeth the desolate house of Pluto with great diligence").

PART II

Charon in Italy from Dante to Marino

9

Epic Forms

But if our Italy can rightly boast of being epically superior to ancient Rome, modern England, and all the rest of the world, thanks to Dante, Ariosto, and Tasso, with much more reason yet can our Italy glory in having produced other poems that cannot be registered in any other class but that of epics, and which are hers alone, with no other nation, either ancient or modern, able in this respect to compete with her for the record.

Giuseppe Baretti, *La frusta letteraria*

In discussing poems as varied as Boiardo's *Orlando Innamorato*, Pulci's *Morgante*, Frezzi's *Quadriregio*, Tassoni's *Secchia Rapita*, and Lippi's *Malmantile*, Giuseppe Bareti, too, found it necessary to group dissimilar works in one epic category. The range of generic material that I will treat in this chapter is quite extensive. Although the differences are often subtle, let me point out several major distinctions before presenting the material itself.

Due in large part to his unparalleled originality, Dante's poem has evaded any direct classification. Although commonly referred to as an epic, the *Commedia* is actually a sacred poem of allegorical intent. The works that follow Dante's are at times equally difficult to classify, if not for their originality, then for their bizarreness. Therefore, in order to discuss these works of varied epic design more cogently, I have grouped them into four main categories. The first contains sacred poems, allegorical-didactic works, and Christian epic, three subtypes related through their use of religious themes. Poems in the second group range from epic of classical imitation, most notably of Virgil, to chivalric romance, often based on medieval *chansons de geste*;[1] within this category, of course, are many heroic poems that fuse the classical with the medieval. The third group consists of mock-heroic poems, varying from those satirizing chivalric romance to those mocking epic. And finally, as a fourth type, I discuss the mythological epic of the Seicento.

Despite the range of generic subtypes, all the poems discussed in this section are based to some extent on the classical form of epic as found in the *Iliad*, the *Odyssey*, and the *Aeneid*, models themselves of varied form. All the poems are in verse, usually quite lengthy, and narrative in intent; most deal, whether seriously or mockingly, with some aspect of heroism—that is, majestic deeds, grand figures, and important events often of universal scope. Among the romance elements introduced into epic are the themes of heroic love, adventure, and the quest. Concerning the approach most often taken by epic poets, both personal and general experiences are unified through the writer's individual vision as conveyed through traditional material and well-known structural formulas. Among the most popular of these structural features is, of course, the canonical episode of the descent to the underworld, an episode transformed in Italy with surprising vitality and for various artistic purposes. It is the range of these transformations that I will study, dating from the thirteenth century to the arbitrary, but I believe justifiable, limit of early to mid-seventeenth century.

i. Sacred Poems, Allegorical-Didactic Poems, and Christian Epic

Dante. Given the scarcity of mythological figures in Christian medieval poetry, Charon's appearance in Dante's *Commedia* signals a new awareness of classical material and its adaptability to a Christian scheme. The remarkable fusion of the sacred and the secular in Dante's vision of the underworld is prefigured when the pilgrim notes that both Aeneas and St. Paul have preceded him on his voyage (*Inf.* 2. 13–30). In fact, while Charon and other classical divinities were rarely mentioned in medieval theological excursions into the beyond,[2] in the *Commedia*, the boatman is merely the first of several mythological figures to appear. Dante's genius is to have blended so thoroughly the material of classical epic and pagan mythology with the topics and concerns of sacred literature.

Soon after the poet and his guide Virgil pass through the gates of hell,[3] Dante notices a group of souls on the banks of a great river (3. 71). But when he asks Virgil about them, his guide silences his curiosity by saying that these things will be made known when they actually arrive "su la trista riviera d'Acheronte" (3. 78).[4] Virgil's response rebukes Dante for his haste to know and is followed by a tercet of silence and shame, a technique of great ingenuity, for from this silence, the majestic figure of Charon rises before us.

> Ed ecco verso noi venir per nave
>   un vecchio, bianco per antico pelo;
>   gridando: "Guai a voi, anime prave!
> Non isperate mai veder lo cielo:
>   i' vegno per menarvi a l'altra riva
>   ne le tenebre etterne, in caldo e 'n gelo.
>
>   82–87

And behold, an old man, his hair white with age, coming towards us in a boat and shouting, "Woe to you, wicked souls! Do not hope to see Heaven ever! I come to carry you to the other shore, into eternal darkness, into fire and cold.

Caronte, by Luca Signorelli. (1499) Capella di San Brizio, Duomo, Orvieto. By permission of Fratelli Alinari.

Unlike Virgil's picturesque boatman, Dante's Charon does not merely float into view. Signaled by the staccato of harsh consonants (*ecco, vecchio, bianco, antico, pelo*) and the interrruption implied by the initial *ed*, Charon literally bursts into the scene, his swiftness captured phonetically by the interespersed soft sounds of *v*'s, *n*'s and *r*'s in "verso noi venir per nave." Rather than an external portrait of his features, Dante's presentation is dramatic and emotive. The boatman seems to advance not just across the scene but toward us as a direct threat.

From sight, we pass instantly to sound: Charon appears *gridando* with devilish vehemence. It has been said that his first words reveal the lack of pity that characterizes hell.[5] Addressing the wicked souls with an imprecation, Charon, in effect, repeats the terrible message over the entrance to hell; "Hope never to see the sky." The negative import of *non isperate*, reinforced by the adverb *mai* that hangs in the middle of verse 85, is rendered even darker by contrasting hell to what it is not—*lo cielo*. Not only will these souls not go to heaven, they will never again see the sky. The dark horror of hell, which lies in good part in its eternity, is further summed up by Charon in the contrast of hot and cold. The realm is above all a place of punishment for sin. In describing what awaits the souls, Charon also defines his own role—he is an instrument to aid their passing. While his own task is merely to carry souls to the other bank, his significance, it has been pointed out, lies in the fact that he is part of the greater chain that will carry the wicked to the depths and extent of hell, which he synthesizes into the sensations provoked by fire and ice. The infernal landscape converges in the boatman, then, and as a minister of God, he is no longer a minor classical divinity (as in Virgil) but a cruel and intimidating demon.

> "E tu che se' costí, anima viva,
>   pàrtiti da cotesti che son morti."
>   Ma poi che vide ch'io non mi partiva,
> disse: "Per altra via, per altri porti
>   verrai a piaggia, non qui, per passare:
>   più lieve legno convien che ti porti."

(3. 88–93)

"And you there, living soul, stand aside from these that are dead." But when he saw that I did not do so, he said, "By another way, by other ports, not here, you shall cross to shore. A lighter bark must carry you."

Immediately aware of Dante the pilgrim, the diabolical ferryman turns from the lost souls to him, sputtering a series of similar phrases. As a living soul, Dante is ordered to leave; Charon, in effect, seems to prophesy Dante's end, for he tells him that he will pass elsewhere by a lighter boat.[6] If he is referring to the ship of purgatory, he possesses an aspect of divine knowledge unusual for a demon. While Dante emphasizes the boatman's demonic characteristics, in part to serve as a greater contrast to the celestial ferryman, Charon still retains perhaps a hint of the classical divinity. He acquires a greater significance, since it is apparently through him that Dante chooses to express his own salvation. Thus I would agree with many modern critics that the boatman is not referring to crossing the Acheron in another boat, an idea espoused by early commentators. Charon does refuse to transport Dante initially, but the pilgrim is hindered at many stages of his descent only to triumph in the end. If Dante is able to cross other barriers aided by infernal beings (Phlegyas, Nessus, and Geryon, for example), there is no good reason why he cannot be transported in Charon's boat. Dante, of course, is unaware of the passage, having fainted, perhaps in symbolic death.

Dante, faltering at the boatman's verbal onslaught, trades no words with Charon;[7] Virgil, however, unintimidated, silences him with a response that resounds with the might of God's will:

> E 'l duca lui: "Caron, non ti crucciare:
> vuolsi così colà dove si puote
> ciò che si vuole, e più non dimandare."
>
> (3. 94–96)[8]

And my leader to him, "Charon, do not rage. Thus is it willed there where that can be done which is willed; and asked no more."

The absolute inclusiveness of God's authority is expressed through the chiastic structure of the three-verse speech itself. Virgil's response both opens and closes with a command. The phrase expressive of God's power begins and ends with the same verb and inverted syntax (*vuolsi . . . si vuole*) followed and preceded by two words of similar sound (*così colà . . . ciò che*). In the midst, lies the verb *potere*, signifying the dominance of God's power, at one with his all-encompassing will.

Silenced, Charon seems to burn in impotent anger:

> Quinci fuor quete le lanose gote
> al nocchier de la livida palude,
> che 'ntorno a li occhi avea di fiamme rote.
>
> (97–99)

Thereon the grizzled cheeks of the ferryman of the livid marsh, who had wheels of flame about his eyes, were quiet.

Dante's mastery of poetic technique is again evident: Rather than merely telling us that Charon remains silent, he describes the result of his silence—the woolly cheeks that move no more—and at the same time situates and further describes the boatman. From an initial note telling us that an old man is coming by ship and the subtle introduction of his name in Virgil's speech, we pass to his occupation (*nocchiero*), his location (the deathly hued marsh), and other details of his personal appearance. The use of the term *livida* for the *palude* recalls the long tradition of similar adjectives describing Charon, his boat, and surroundings. Amidst this ghastly darkness and lack of color, Charon's eyes stand out, rimmed with wheels of flame. Again, the idea has a long history, from Homer's heroes whose eyes blaze to Virgil's boatman with his eyes of flame, and Dante's use of the motif must be understood in the light of the medieval tradition as well. In Dante, the wheels of flame hint at Charon's diabolical traits.[9] The brevity of Dante's description, which concentrates on just two aspects of Charon's face, is nevertheless amply indicative of his nature.

The effect of Charon's words and appearance on those less fortunate than the poet is now dramatized:

> Ma quell'anime, ch'eran lasse e nude
>   cangiar colore e dibattero i denti,
>   ratto che 'nteser le parole crude.
> Bestemmiavano Dio e lor parenti,
>   l'umana spezie e 'l loco e 'l tempo e 'l seme
>   di lor semenza e di lor nascimenti.
>
> (3. 100–105)

But those forlorn and naked souls changed color, their teeth chattering, as soon as they heard the cruel words. They cursed God, their parents, the human race, the place, the time, the seed of their begetting and of their birth.

It is as if Charon has turned his anger on these souls, devoid, we understand, of not only clothing but divine protection.[10] Weary and vulnerable, the souls turn pale and shiver in fear; verse 101 with its clicking *d*'s and *t*'s phonetically mirrors the chattering teeth.[11] The corporeality of the souls is striking: These are not Virgil's "tenuis sine corpore vitas" who flit about "cava sub imagine formae" (*Aen.* 6. 292–293). The horror of the situation overwhelms the wicked, and they vent their inner feelings in blasphemy. Once when first beginning my study of Charon, I wrote that any feeling of pity we have for the souls disappears as Dante's sense of justice comes into view; that is, pity gives way to the realization that these souls are true rebels. But I am not so sure that this is Dante's intent. It seems, instead, that he emphasizes not the wickedness of these souls so much as their tremendous feelings of grief and regret, feelings that are also part of their punishment. Now that it is too late to repent, it is as if they wish never to have been born. The extent of their remorse is indicated by the tremendous weight of the last two verses with the anaphoric build-up of cursed subjects. Unable to do otherwise, the souls, crying loudly, gather at the *riva malvagia* (107).

Outside the picture at the moment, Dante describes the infernal boatman and the scene at the crossing of the Acheron. Three powerful lines beginning solidly with *Caron dimonio* add to the force of this classical ferryman turned devil:

> Caron dimonio, con occhi di bragia
>   loro accennando, tutte le raccoglie;
>   batte col remo qualunque s'adagia.
>
> (109–111)

The demon Charon, his eyes like glowing coals, beckons to them and collects them all, beating with his oar whoever lingers.

Again as an indication of his internal nature, his diabolical ferocity, the eyes are mentioned. As if frustrated in his attempt to drive off the living intruder, Charon continues to seethe inside; his anger is not only evident in his eyes of burning coals, but it vents itself in blows on the backs of those who linger or sit in the boat.[12]

Changing the tone from violence to elegy, Dante develops a beautifully evocative double image in the next two tercets. The desolation of the scene is impressed on the reader:

> Come d'autunno si levan le foglie
>   l'una appresso de l'altra, fin che 'l ramo
>   vede a la terra tutte le sue spoglie,
> similemente il mal seme d'Adamo
>   gittansi di quel lito ad una ad una,
>   per cenni come augel per suo richiamo.
> Così sen vanno su per l'onda bruna.
>
> (112–118)

As the leaves fall away in autumn, one after another, till the bough sees all its spoils upon the ground, so there the evil seed of Adam: One by one they cast themselves from that shore at signals, like a bird at its call. Thus they go over the dark water.

Seen as autumn leaves falling—literally "lifting themselves—one by one until the branch is bare, the souls are isolated not only from God but from each other. The effectiveness of the initial image lies partly in the fact that the tree itself is personified; that is, the bare branch *sees* all its leaves on the ground.[13] The reference to the souls as the evil seed of Adam intensifies the biological parallels. Charon's control of the embarcation is again emphasized when the souls are compared to birds obeying their master's signal. Jumping into the boat like birds being recalled to the lure, the souls are carried across the river, disappearing into the gloom. Many have noted that unlike Virgil's quantitative use of the Homeric image, where the souls are as *numerous* as leaves, Dante's simile stresses with elegiac intent not the leaves' number but the fact that they fall one by one from the branch in autumn.

Dante's crossing of the Acheron, by whatever means, is not related; when Canto 4 opens, he is on the far side of the barrier. As noted earlier, Dante's early commentators (mirrored by modern ones) were perplexed by this and postulated a variety of reasons for the poet's failure to specify the manner of transportation.[14] Whatever the mode of passage (and I suggest, as have others, Charon's boat), Dante clearly intended the matter to remain a mystery or thought it too obvious to merit comment. An actual crossing of an infernal swamp, is, however, detailed in Canto 8. The crossing is important as a source for later poets who do depict the passage with Charon.

Descending to the fifth circle, the two poets find themselves at the Styx, a *tristo ruscel* in the form of a swamp. At the sight of some puzzling signal fires that pass from tower to tower, Dante again turns to Virgil with questions, and the guide's answer not only sharpens the descriptive detail of the setting but adds to the suspense by telling Dante that he will see for himself what is occuring:

> Ed elli a me: "Su per le sucide onde
> già scorgere puoi quello che s'aspetta,
> se 'l fummo del pantan nol ti nasconde."
>
> (8. 10–12)

And he to me, "Over the foul waves you can already make out what is expected, if the fumes of the marsh do not hide it from you."

Almost instantly Dante sees "una nave piccioletta / venir per l'acqua verso noi" ("a little bark . . . come towards us then through the water" [15–16]). With an effect similar to that of the Charon episode, a single boatman comes into view shouting "or se' giunta, anima fella!" ("Now you are caught, fell spirit!" [18]). The sailor's joy at what he thinks is the arrival of a new sinner is succinctly and masterfully captured in his brief speech, but as with Charon, Virgil recognizes him instantly and just as quickly deflates him:

> "Flegïàs, Flegïàs, tu gridi a vòto"
> disse lo mio segnore, "a questa volta:
> più non ci avrai che sol passando il loto."
>
> (19–21)

"Phlegyas, Phlegyas, this time you shout in vain," said my lord. "You shall not have us longer than while crossing the mire."

The demon's anger ("fecesi Flegïàs ne l'ira accolta" [v. 24]) is all the greater for being contained.

Virgil enters the *barca* and Dante follows. As in Virgil's *Aeneid*, only with a living descender on board does the boat sink low—"e sol quand'io fui dentro parve carca" (27).[15] Once in the *legno*, they proceed to cross, the boat cutting deep into the water:

> segando se ne va l'antica prora
> de l'acqua piú che non suol con altrui.
>
> (8. 29–30)

The ancient prow moves off, cuting more of the water than it is wont with others.

Dante and Virgil ferried by Phlegyas, by Eugène Delacroix. (1822) Musée du Louvre, Paris. By permission of Photographie Giraudon.

Aside from the descriptive note, reinforced by the verb *segando*, I call attention to Dante's variation in nouns for the *boat*—from *nave* and *barca* to *legno* and the metonymic *prora*.

One episode that occurs while the two are crossing the *morta gora* (31) is significant for it parallels the Psyche myth related by Apuleius. I refer to Filippo Argenti's attempt to pull himself into the boat: "Allor distese al legno ambo le mani" (40). Whether Dante knew of Apuleius's account, where an old man swimming in the river holds up his hands in his desire to enter the boat, is questionable, however. At any rate, having crossed the swamp, the pilgrim and his guide descend from the boat:

> Non sanza prima far grande aggirata,
>   venimmo in parte dove il nocchier forte
>   "Usciteci," gridò: "qui è l'intrata."

(8. 79–81)

And not until we had made a great circuit did we come to a place where the boatman loudly cried, "Out with you here! This is the entrance."

The departure of Phlegyas is as rapid as his arrival.

Before leaving Dante, it is instructive to compare the contrasting figures of Cato and the Celestial Ferryman in *Purgatorio* 1 and 2; Dante, as we saw, referred to this crossing in Charon's prophecy. Just as Charon, who prefigures the initial crossings in both purgatory and paradise, embodies in his appearance, actions, and effect on others the essence of hell, Cato and the Celestial Ferryman embody the tone, atmosphere, and binding principles of purgatory.

Like Charon, Cato first appears to Dante as an old, solitary man. This *veglio solo*, however, is "degno di tanta reverenza in vista, / che più non dee a padre alcun figliuolo" ("worthy in his looks of so great reverence that no son owes more to his father" [1. 32–33]). Cato's description focuses on his physiognomy—his beard, hair, and eyes—much as was Charon's. In contrast to the infernal wheels of fire around Charon's eyes, we see adorning Cato's face "li raggi de le quattro luci sante" ("the rays of the four holy lights" [1. 37–39]), as if the sun, God's splendor, were before him.

As a guardian of purgatory, Cato fires a series of questions at the two poets, and again as with Charon, Virgil takes command. Dante the poet, however, emphasizes a significant change in status regarding Virgil the guide. Having subdued the infernal ferryman with the phrase "vuolsi così colà dove si puote / ciò che si vuole," Virgil now recognizes Cato's authority, saying, "esser non puote il mio che a te si nieghi" ("mine it cannot be that to you this be denied" [1. 57]). In answering Cato's questions, Virgil speaks for thirty-three lines (52–84), whereas he devotes only three lines to Charon.

Later after Cato has left us, toward the end of Canto 2, he returns paralleling Charon's first arrival. "Ed ecco il veglio onesto / gridando: 'Che è ciò, spiriti lenti?' " we read, followed by the repetitive " 'Qual negligenza, quale stare è questo?' " ("When lo, the venerable old man, crying, 'What is this, you laggard spirits? What negligence, what stay is this?' " [2. 119–121]). But the intention of this scolding is quite different from Charon's: Cato is moved by love, not wrath. Even the image that comes to Dante's mind, in comparison to autumnal falling leaves and returning birds in *Inferno* 3, is warm, pastoral, and delicate. The spirits, like startled doves who have been feeding at peace and are surprised, rush off, and Dante, now a part of what he sees, is not less quick to do likewise.

Just as Cato fulfills in a heavenly manner Charon's duty as guardian, the angel pilot in *Purgatorio* 2 represents the aspect of ferryman, and it is in this figure that we encounter a more deliberate contrast to the demon *nocchiero*. Our introduction to this boatman is less abrupt. Beginning with line 13 of the second canto, we have the first indication of an impending arrival, but not until five lines later do we learn that *un lume* (a light) has appeared, moving so rapidly toward us that no flight equals it. Though this voyage takes place with supernatural speed, six lines from the appearance of the *lume*, during which time the poet looks away to question Virgil, we still see "un, non sapea che, bianco . . ." ("a something white"). We sense hesitancy in the repeated caesura, also noting the emphasis, caesura on both sides, of *bianco* (2. 23). Charon burst before us menacingly; this ferryman rises majestically, coming from a light on the horizon to envelop our view. Another two tercets (31–36) point out the immense power of this figure: He needs neither oar nor sail. In direct contrast to *Caron dimonio*, we see *l'uccel divino* on whose brightness Dante cannot look (37–40). And unlike Phlegyas's boat in *Inferno* 8, which sinks under the poet's weight to plow a deeper path, this "vasello snelletto e leggiero" ("a vessel so swift and light")—the double diminutives support the statement—"l'acqua nulla ne 'nghiottiva" ("the water took in naught of it" [2. 41–42]). In opposition to Charon's evil burning eyes, this *celestial nocchiero* appears "beato per iscripto" ("at the stern stood the celestial steersman, such, that blessedness seemed to be inscribed upon him" [43–44]).

The next two tercets epitomize the pervading spirit of purgatory. The sense of brotherly love, *caritas*, and unity overflows. Of the spirits who have just arrived, we read:

> "*In exitu Israel de Aegypto*"
> cantavan tutti insieme ad una voce
> con quanto di quel salmo è poscia scripto.
>
> (46–48)

"*In exitu Israel de Aegypto*" all of them were singing together with one voice, with the rest of that psalm as it is written.

No oar beats these souls. Making the sign of the cross, they jump, not one by one like falling leaves but all together at once on the beach (49–50). From the *selva oscura* crossing water barriers with Charon's and Phlegyas's ferries and viewing a third, that of the celestial ferryman, we have finally come to *migliori acque*.

Looking at both infernal crossings as a unit, certain structural features stand out. Dante as a descender to the lower world follows in the steps of more famous heroes. He descends, however, not to rescue a friend, liberate a spouse, gain an infernal object, nor learn of the future of his race but to acquire knowledge of a different sort. His descent is a journey of redemption, the archetypal journey of the soul from sin to salvation, from a state of guilt to one of grace. A first and necessary stage in this journey is recognition of sin in itself and in oneself, followed by purification, and finally an ascent to all that is heavenly. Dante's poetic technique, his vision, does not remain abstract, however. Following models both classical (underworld descents) and medieval (underworld visions), Dante adheres to a strictly realistic depiction of the beyond. The poet's actual descent, then, passes rapidly from a vague and allegorical *oscura costa* (2. 40) to the reality of the doors of an infernal city (3. 1–11). Passing easily through the vestibule of the negligent, the two descenders arrive at the first infernal barrier, *un gran fiume* (71). As a poet faced with what I have called the second structural unit in the descent theme, Dante chose to follow the classico-mythological scheme with a boatman rather than the theological models of the Middle Ages with their supernatural bridges. The barrier is thus named immediately by Virgil as the

Acheronte (3. 78). This, the first of the infernal rivers, is characterized as large
(71), having sad banks (78), being a river (71, 81, 124), a livid swamp (98), and
having dark waves (118). The banks of the river await all those who fear not God,
and the crossing itself signifies the loss of all hope. Though the river is described
in some detail, it is done so throughout the episode rather than on introduction
of the barrier itself. Later when the two poets arrive at a second water barrier—the
Styx—Dante describes it at greater length initially and also throughout the
episode. It is a *palude* called Stige (7. 106), a *tristo ruscel* (107) with *maligne
piagge grige* (108).[16] In its mire (*in quel pantano* [110; cf. 8. 12]) swim muddy
people; soon after, we learn that the water bubbles (119) from those stuck in its
limo (121) or *belletta negra* (124). Elsewhere, the swamp is called a *lorda pozza*
(127) and has *sucide onde* (8. 10), with smoke rising above (8. 12). As a further
characteristic of the swamp, the poet mentions its stagnant water (*morta gora*
[31]).

Perhaps the most dramatic unit is that of the boatman's appearance; Dante's
technique here is to fuse the descriptive with the dramatic. Charon both verbally
assaults the souls and physically beats them with his oar. Descriptive detail is
added throughout the central units of confrontation where Charon addresses
Dante and is quieted by Virgil. Charon's refusal to transport Dante is not coun-
tered with physical force, music, a golden bough nor money but by divine pre-
rogative. God's will requires no physical instrument. Paralleling the conflict in
classical epic where superior force, often divine, aids the hero's mission, in
Dante's poem, Charon's attempt to retard the pilgrim's progress is abruptly
quashed. The response of the evil souls to Charon's threats is typical of dead souls
in classical literature: They do not reply to the boatman himself but chatter in
fear, lamenting the irrevocability and eternity of their situation.

The unit of embarcation is well developed in Dante. Concentrating on Charon
again, Dante depicts an intimidating demon who allows no delays. As in Seneca
and Lucan, among others, Charon is a busy ferryman—not because of war but
because so many men die evil. As the poet says, before the boatman can reach the
far side (presumably he rows with his oar), a new group gathers on this bank
(3. 119–120). The souls themselves receive equal attention in the lengthy similes
employed to describe their fate. But concerning the means of transportation,
despite the many nouns employed for the ferry itself, we learn almost nothing of
its nature; in Dante's scheme, it is incidental.

The unit in which the boundry is crossed is best developed in the Phlegyas
episode. As with Aeneas in Virgil's poem, Dante's weight is immediately noticed. But whereas Aeneas crosses uneventfully, Dante the pilgrim experiences a
confrontation characteristic of Lucian's crossings, during which much is likely to
happen. And as in Lucian, with whom Dante was unfamiliar, such a confrontation is in part comic, part philosophical. The burlesque verbal battle between
Dante and Filippo Argenti ends with symbolic import, illustrating the nature of
just wrath.

Finally, the disembarcation, mentioned only in the Phlegyas episode, is brief and nonconsequential. Let me note in passing that neither boatman—Charon nor Phlegyas—is used to emphasize infernal avarice or greed. No coin is needed to cross Charon's river; the only prerequisite is to have died wicked. Unlike the Virgilian boatman, Charon does not choose whom to ferry but instead accepts all those arriving for the passage.

Taken together, the two infernal crossings contain almost all the structural units of the mythological model; in this, Dante's poem is characteristic of classical epic, with its all-embracing inclusiveness. Later imitators of Dante and classical epic, especially poets who develop varied forms of epic in the Renaissance, are often not so inclusive, just as Virgil's followers were not. Perhaps the change in Italy, most notable in the lack of detailed underworld scenes in the chivalric romance, reflects a new outlook on life in which the beyond is no longer so important as the present. Despite the popularity in classical and medieval times of eschatological episodes, writers of the Renaissance quite often treat the descent as merely another convention. But before going on to references to Charon in Renaissance secular epic, I will examine a few other portraits in predominantly religious works.

Frezzi. One of the earliest full-length treatments of Charon following Dante's is Federico Frezzi's *Quadriregio* or *Libro dei quattro regni*, a poem of allegorical-didactic intent.[17] While most critics who have dealt with the poem classify it as a pedestrian imitation of the *Commedia*, [18] the episode with Charon offers some details of interest.[19] Written between 1400 and 1403 and composed of seventy-four *canti* in *terzine*, this didactic poem treats the journey of man aided by first the false guide Cupid and later Minerva, goddess of wisdom, through four realms from vice to virtue. Along the way, various monsters of moral import are described, as are the benefits of virtue. Charon himself appears in Book 2, chapter 7 in the kingdom of Acheronte. Arriving at the river Acheron, the author sees thousands of monsters waiting to cross; after a description of these allegorical beasts representing humanity in the various stages of life, the poet says:

> Vidi Caròn non molto da lontano
> con una nave in mezzo la tempesta,
> che conducea con un gran remo in mano.
>   E ciascun occhio, ch'egli avea in testa,
> parea come di notte una lumiera
> o un falò, quando si fa per festa.

> (7. 28–33)

I saw Charon not far off in the middle of the storm with a ship which he was guiding with a large oar in his hand. And each eye in his head seemed like a chandelier at night or a bonfire, when one is made for a festival.

While Frezzi has obviously been influenced by Dante, he chooses the less dramatic descriptive presentation of Virgil; the tone, however, has fallen to the casual.
It is almost as if we stumble accidently on Charon rather than see the boatman
burst into the scene with the alertness of a careful watchman or the fierceness of a
demon. Furthermore, we are not shown the boatman in action but are told about
him, with comparisons to objects drawn from everyday life. In this, we sense
perhaps the influence of Boccaccio and the novelistic tradition in Trecento Italy.
Though the descriptive detail remains somewhat external to the ferryman's character, aesthetic pleasure can be derived from the images themselves. Comparisons
of Charon's eyes to a light at night and a festive bonfire add a popular touch that
has its own effectiveness when compared to the more aulic poetry of the time.

But Frezzi, unable to compete with the stylistic brilliance of Dante, takes an
entire verse to tell us how far away the boatman is, having earlier referred to him
as "non molto da lontano" (28):

> Quand'egli fu appresso alla riviera
> un mezzo miglio quasi o poco manco,
> scòrsi sua faccia grande, guizza e nera.

(7. 34–36)

When he was close to the shore, a half mile almost or a little less, I spied his
large face, wrinkled and black.

While the adjective *guizza* (*vizza*), referring to Charon's wrinkled face, stands
out, *grande* seems to be mere padding,[20] and *nera*, while recalling medieval
demons (and bringing to mind Michelangelo's later Dantesque Charon in "The
Last Judgment"), remains extrinsic and unmotivated by action. It seems that the
rhyme scheme and the necessities of the meter control the selection of adjectives,
rather than the figure of the boatman himself.

The *contaminatio* of Virgil and Dante becomes more evident as the description
of the boatman continues:

> Egli avea il capo di canuti bianco,
> il manto addosso rappezzato ed unto;
> e volto sí crudel non vidi unquanco.

(7. 37–39)

He had a head, white with gray hair, his cloak on, patched up and greasy; and I
never saw a face so cruel.

Canuti (from the Virgilian *canities* [*Aen.* 6. 300]) referring to hair and *capo bianco* are repetitive in a way that Dante's "un *vecchio* bianco per *antico* pelo" is
not (my emphasis). Interestingly, though Frezzi has modified the Dantesque
verse, he has maintained the staccato effect of the consonants *c, p, t,* and *b*; but
whereas in Dante the sound mirrored the action, in Frezzi action is lacking entirely. Charon's mantle is effectively described as tattered and greasy, an

The boat of Charon (detail of the Last Judgement), by Michelangelo. (1535–41) Sistine Chapel, Vatican. By permission of Fratelli Alinari.

amplificatio of the Virgilian *sordidus* (6. 301), but the final verse returns to the face merely to tell us that the poet had never seen one more cruel. Lacking the force of Dante's verses, Frezzi's replace poetic expression with pale exposition. As yet, there has been no action nor forceful words to underline Charon's fierceness. When the boatman finally addresses the souls gathered on the bank, his words are those of a rhetorician, a theologian, rather than an angry demon:

> Non era ancor a quell'anime giunto,
> quando gridò: —O dal materno vaso
> mandati a me nel doloroso punto,
>   per ogni avversità, per ogni caso
> vi menerò tra la palude negra
> incerti della vita e dell'occaso.
>   Pochi verran di voi all'età intègra;
> spesso la vita alli mortali io tollo,
> quand'ella è piú secura e piú allegra.—
>
> (7. 40–48)

He had not yet reached those souls, when he cried: "O you sent to me from the maternal vessel in the moment of pain, through every adversity, through every eventuality, I will take you, uncertain of life and death, amidst the black swamp. Few of you will come to a full age for often I snatch life from mortals, when it is most secure and happiest.''

The length of this speech as well as its syntax epitomizes Frezzi's expansive methods and diffusive style. The paratactic repetition, employing both asyndeton (''per ogni avversità, per ogni caso'') and polysyndeton (''della vita e dell'occaso, piú secura e piú allegra'') is typical of the technique of Trecento *cantari* who composed orally and needed verse fillers. The circumlocutions almost overshadow one of the noteworthy aspects of Charon's speech—he receives the souls at birth for their life's journey and ends their life at his discretion, a feature reminiscent of the boatman's identification with a death-demon among the Byzantines but more likely to be traced to the medieval allegorization of Charon as time. The swamp, by the way, Virgil's ''*vada livida*'' (6. 320) and Dante's ''*livida palude*'' (3. 98), is simply black in Frezzi. Also, in expanding Charon's speech from Dante by moralizing, Frezzi has lost sight of what the boatman threatens. While Dante's Charon emcompasses with his speech of doom all the horror of hell: ''i' vegno per menarvi all'altra riva / nelle tenebre etterne, in caldo e 'n gelo,'' Frezzi's boatman merely says ''vi menerò tra la palude negra'' (44); Charon's task in Dante is rendered somewhat insignificant in Frezzi.

When Charon is finally seen in action, he exhibits a Dantesque cruelty:

> Dava col remo suo tra testa e 'l collo
> a' mostri, che mettea dentro all cocca;
> e forte percotea chi facea crollo.
>
> (7. 49–51)

With his oar he was hitting between head and neck the monsters that he was putting inside his boat, and was beating hard those that fell.

The ferryman beats even those who stumble and fall. When the boatman turns to the intruder, his words are reminiscent of both the Charon and Phlegyas episodes in Dante:

> Poscia rivolto a me, colla gran bocca
> gridò:—Or giunto se', o tu, che vivi,
> venuto qui come persona sciocca.—
>
> (7. 52–54)

Then turning to me, with his large mouth he cried: ''Now you have arrived, O you who are living, having come here like a stupid person.''

The trivial third line is Frezzi's originial touch.

Minerva's response, ''Costui convien ch' arrivi / all'altra ripa sotto i remi tui, / 'nanzi che morte della vita il privi'' (''it is necessary that he arrive at the other bank under your oars, before death deprives him of life'' [55–57]), evokes a reply from Charon imitative of Virgil's guardian:

>—Su la mia nave non verrete vui
>—rispose a noi con ira e con disdegno,—
>ché altre volte giá ingannato fui.
> Un trasse Cerber fuor del nostro regno,
>l'altro la moglie; or simil forza temo:
>però voi non verrete sul mio legno.—

$$(7.\ 58–63)$$

"On my ship you won't come" he responded to us with anger and disdain, "because I've already been deceived other times. One dragged Cerberus outside our realm, another the wife; now I fear a similar force: So you won't come on my ship."

Unlike Virgil, however, Frezzi has been constrained by his meter to enclose the boatman's recollection in a childlike and repetitive denial of embarkation.

Minerva, possessing neither the power of a golden bough nor a Christian god, asks the *vecchio lordo* ("filthy old man") for the oar in order to row the boat herself (64–66). "Lassame andar," she says, "consumator ingordo, / ché a te non è subietta quella vita, / per la qual vive uom sempre per ricordo" ("let me go, greedy consumer, because that life is not subjected to you for which one lives always for remembrance" [67–69]). Apparently Charon is easily conquered, for

> Ratto ch' egli ebbe esta parola udita,
>si vergognò ed abbassò le ciglia,
>e senza più parlar ne die' la ita.

$$(70–72)$$

The second he had heard this word, he felt ashamed and lowered his eyes, and with no more words gave us passage.

The poet's reliance on Dante, who describes Charon's abrupt surrender with vivid brevity ("quinci fuor quete le lanose gote" [*Inf.* 3. 98]), extends to this description of shame, which is taken from Dante's description of himself before Virgil's subtle reproach for curiosity: "Allor con li occhi vergognosi e bassi / . . . infino al fiume del parlar mi trasse" ("Then, with eyes downcast and ashamed . . . , I refrained from speaking till we reached the river" [*Inf.* 3. 79, 81]).

The following tercets, again of Dantesque imprint, illustrate Frezzi's use of the *quotidiano*:

> Navigato avevam ben giá due miglia,
>ed io mi volsi addietro, e vidi ancora
>venuta alla riviera altra famiglia,
> Solcando noi per quella morta gora,
>con gran tempesta tra le morte schiume,
>col vento non da poppa, ma da prora.

$$(73–78)$$

> We had already navigated a good two miles when I turned around and saw still
> another family gather on the coast, we plowing through that dead pool, with a
> great storm amidst the dead froth, with the wind not from the stern, but from
> the bow.

Frezzi details the exact distance traveled and the direction of the wind, typical in
a sailor's narration of events, but neither is important for the crossing; rather than
being evocative, Frezzi is precise and grounded in the factual. Also, though the
content (the image of new souls) and language is Dantesque, with *morta gora*
rhyming with *prora* (from the Phlegyas episode), for example, the structure is
assuredly Frezzian. Unlike Dante's hypotactic syntax with incidents motivated
by previous action, Frezzi's paratactic flow results in a lack of continuity and
causation.

During the crossing, we are treated to an allegorical episode. The monster of
seven faces, representing the various ages of mankind, is gradually transformed
(in fact, step by laborious step: *prima*, [82], *seconda* [83], *terza* [85], *quarta* and
quinta [86], *sesto* [88]) to *un sol vecchiaccio* ("one ugly old man"), *sol* meaning,
as the poet explains, that "non sette piú, ma un tutti pariéno" ("no longer
seven, but one they all seemed" [90]). As a poet, Frezzi is bound to the particular, diffusive, and given to lengthy moralization. The explanation of mankind's
transformation, for example, occupies the poet from verses 91–129, after which
Minerva delivers a small sermon (133–150). Among the original aspects of the
allegorical discourse is the fact that Charon, called a cruel pirate (104), is ferrying
the negligent, who once ferried are formed anew on the near bank to await an
endless cycle of passage.

When Minerva finishes her sermon, Charon, "ad ira . . . commoto" ("moved
to anger" [151]), shouts out his own message and in doing so continues the long
line of medieval allegorizers. He compares the passage of time to a *nocchiero*
(154) much as Fulgentius and Boccaccio, to mention two outstanding mythographers, compared Charon himself to time. From the boatman's perspective, the
traditional parallel is ironically inverted. With the ferryman's speech at an end,
one final verse closes the canto: "Poi si partí Caròn fiero e rubesto" ("Then Charon left, wild and fiery" [160]).

While Frezzi like Dante returns to a classical pattern to represent a Christian
message, the *Quadriregio* illustrates what happens to poetry when it is suffocated
by didacticism. Charon's portrayal is indicative of the change: Rather than a full-
bodied demon of dramatic incisiveness, we find a two-dimensional figure employed above all as a didactic tool. The boatman, whose task is openly allegorized, becomes a spouter of allegorical truth. Though belonging to a work of the
Quattrocento, he thus becomes more medieval than Dante's ferryman. While the
Virgilian features of Charon employed by Dante, who borrows only what is significant for his own scheme, serve a purpose, Frezzi, on the contrary, contaminates
the two sources without successfully integrating them. Frezzi calls Charon black, a
typically medieval demonic quality, and then adds that he has white hair; Frezzi

mentions the Virgilian mantle only to return to Charon's cruel face. While following on the whole the Virgilian pattern, Frezzi is most original when employing realistic images and striving for allegorical significance; transforming Charon into a ferryman for the negligent, who then reform and pass again in an endless cycle, is a felicitous innovation. From a Dantesque demon who embodies the characteristics of the entire realm of hell, Charon has become both a descriptively detailed ferryman and a Christian rhetorician.

With the development of the sacred poem in the Cinquecento, Charon recedes to the background. When he is referred to, it is usually in passing and as a fixed and nondescript feature of the underworld. Poets who choose to depict hell in pagan terms feel constrained, like Curzio Gonzaga (A 19), to excuse themselves by imputing blame to ancient writers who were lost in darkness, whereas now "palesato il vero / Per Cristo, siamo a l'ignoranza tolti" ("the truth having been revealed by Christ, we are freed from ignorance" [*Fidamante* 22. 97]). Others, like Luigi Tansillo, integrate the classical with the biblical but avoid pagan names in doing so (see A 21). In religious works where a traditional descent is lacking, we often find at least an infernal council, an old motif renderd canonical for Italian poets by Tasso (see, for example, Grandi's *Tancredi*, A 20).[21]

The form of epic most popular near the end of the sixteenth century when Counter-Reformation fervor was strong seems to be Christian epic wirtten along classical lines. Although religious in purpose, these epics lack overt allegory and didacticism, features that give way to Christian history, as in Tasso's *Gerusalemme liberata* (A 18), or biblical narrative, as in Valvasone's *Angeleida* (A 22). While such poets as Tasso and Valvasone did not feel compelled as Trissino did in *L'Italia liberata dai Goti* to ignore the figure of the boatman, they treat him as only a minor character in the ranks of demons. The external traits, even his occupation, are most often forgotten.

Erasmo da Valvasone. As an example of Christian epic, I will discuss briefly Erasmo da Valvasone's *Angeleida* (1590), an epic narrating the war of the good angels against Lucifer and his rebels (A 22). The poem describes the new realm of Satan in Canto 3. Cast into the depths of the earth, the infernal lord prepares to establish his kingdom. As the protagonist, Satan assumes aspects of the boatman described by Dante; at one point, for example, Satan swells his *lanose gote* in anger. Charon, relegated to a minor position, is referred to only once and shares half an octave with Cerberus. Satan assigns each of them their duties as follows:

> Cerbero, Tu che di questo mondo basso
> La prima cura, il primo honor ti prendi:
> Vegghia a la porta, et custodisci il passo
> Con occhi sei, con tre latrati horrendi:
> Charon, et Tu d'ogni pigritia casso
> A traggittar sul tristo fiume attendi:
> Verracci d'alto ogni hor tributo grave
> Tu lo raccogli, et ce la reca in nave.

(11)

Cerberus, you who of this low world take the first care, the first honor: Watch at the door and guard the passage with six eyes, with three horrendous barks; and Charon, you free of all laziness, attend to ferrying over the sad river. Every hour a solemn tribute will come to us from above. You collect it and bring it to us by ship.

The poet's innovation is to regard the tribute paid not as the money but the souls themselves. Like Virgil's watchful guardian or Lucan's busy ferryman, Charon also stands out for his lack of laziness. The boatman's most original and startling feature, of course, is that he appears to be one of the fallen angels, although the poet does not explicitly state this.

Ghelfucci. In the early Seicento, religious poems along epic lines also continued to be written. The sacred was fused with both the *romanzesco* and the *eroico* to such an extent that, as Belloni says, "Vediamo dare il nome di eroici a poemi che sono essenzialmente sacri e il nome di sacri a poemi che in realtà sono epici" ("we see the name of heroic given to poems which are in essence sacred and the name of sacred to poems which are in reality epics").[22] Napoleone Ghelfucci's *Il Rosario della Madonna* (1616) is an example of a sacred poem that is called heroic. One of the elements found in this largely religious poem that pertains to the epic tradition is the familiar descent into the underworld; only now, the descent is a Christian harrowing of hell, set in the framework of a Virgilian Hades. In the long description, Charon assumes some originality; the boatman's first appearance is descriptive:

> Da la spelonca à la Città di Pluto,
> Fende il terren, da sconosciuto fonte
> Quel fiume sì nocente, e sì temuto,
> De la trista riviera d'Acheronte:
> Qui varca l'alme, come augel pennuto
> Con leve cimba il passeggier Caronte;
> E pur son d'Acheronte al paragone,
> Poveri d'acqua il Nilo, e 'l Maragone.

(A 25, 24. 33)

From the cavern to the city of Pluto, that river so harmful and so feared, of the sad shore of Acheron, splits the earth from an unknown source. Here with a light craft the traveler Charon, like a feathered bird, transports the souls. And yet, in comparison with the Acheron, the Nile and Maragone are poor in water.

Despite the immensity of the river, Charon, like a winged (literally, feathered) bird, transports the souls of the dead with his light boat. The image has some novelty, although it reflects the influence of Dante's celestial ferryman as well as Erasmo da Valvasone's evil angel. I am reminded of an illustration attributed to the Dutch artist Marten Van Heemskerch (1498–1574) entitled "Divitium misera sors" in which Charon is so depicted as well as Luca Signorelli's fresco in the Duomo of Orvieto, where in a Dantesque scene, Charon, seen rowing his boat, has wings and a red halo around him.

The final reference to the ferryman occurs during the harrowing:

> De le genti d'Averno, altre ne l'onde
> Del lago, altre attuffarsi 'n Acheronte;
> Lasciò la barca, e dileguossi altronde
> Con leve corso, il suo nocchier Caronte.

(52)

As for the people of Avernus, some dived in the waves of the lake, others into Acheron; its ferryman Charon left the boat and disappeared elsewhere with a light step.

The unintentional veiled humor of souls diving into Acheron—Charon's departure is more dignified—brings to mind an earlier religious poem, Francesco Bracciolini's *Croce racquistata* (see A 24), where the underworld episode results in some apparent buffoonery.

On the whole in the poems in this first category, Charon stands out as a demon ferryman. The influence of Dante is pervasive, even in works based on a Virgilian descent. Although Charon begins as a vibrant figure, described at length and of some significance, he eventually becomes, possibly under the influence of Counter-Reformation reforms, a minor and often unnamed accoutrement of the infernal regions. When rehabilitated, so to speak, Charon has a new significance: Rather than a diabolical ferryman smacking of an ancient underworld divinity, he acquires a Christian and biblical provenance, being seen now as one of the fallen angels, a servant of Satan, not God. As a result, since Satan is the figure of greatest interest to late Cinquecento and early Seicento poets, Charon is denied an extended portrait, characterized sufficiently, according to the new scheme, by his wings and his boat.

ii. Classical Epic and Chivalric Romance

Petrarch. While the portrayal of Charon in Dante is related to the sacred as well as the epic traditions and in Mussato to Senecan tragedy as well as epic (see A 2), in Petrarch's *Africa*, we find a representation of the boatman belonging to the lyric (A 3).[23] Petrarch, joining historical elements to fantastic, inspired by Christian as well as classical sentiments, and unifying moralism with the marvelous, introduces the elegiac motifs of lyric into the grandeur of epic and specifically into the descent scene. In Book 5, the poet, drawing from Livy but inspired by Virgil as well, narrates the story of Sophonisba. Masinissa, under the restless spur of his love for her, is described with Petrarch's typical psychological penetration. Having married Sophonisba with the promise to provide her with poison should the situation require it, Massinissa finds himself faced with Scipione's ultimatum to leave her.

In a long lament during which he decides he must send Sophonisba the poison, Massinissa in his woe foresees his beloved crossing the Acheron. The episode has deservedly been indicated as one of the high points of Petrarch's lyricism. Touching on human passions, lofty affections, and restless conflicts of the soul, the situation is reminiscent of the poet's vernacular love poetry.

At one point, Massinissa imagines Sophonisba dead:

> Risus qui ferrea figit
> pectora, qui celum, qui circumfusa serenat
> nubila, tartareum ruit irrediturus ad antrum.
>
> (5. 643–645)

> That smile, so quick to pierce
> a breast of iron or shatter clouds that blot
> the skies, is doomed alas to sink for aye
> beneath the Stygean depths.

The contrast, intensified by the adynata, recalls traditional elegiac comparisons between the sky above and life in the underworld. Sophonisba's smile, indirectly compared to the sun in its power to render serene, will have a force in Hades similar, as it were, to that of Orpheus's song: "Heu michi! Felices anime, quibus illa repente / lux oriens veteres veniet purgare tenebras!" ("Ye happy souls / to whom that quickening light will come to break / the gloom of centuries!" [5. 646–647]). The smile has become pure light. The contrast of sky to underworld and of light to darkness continues when Massinissa laments that Sophonisba's *pes lacteus* must enter the *atram . . . cimbam* (649–650). But though ferried by Charon, she will cross not the Acheron but the "lethei gurgitis estum" (651), described in Acherontian fashion as agitated ("That milk-white foot / with god-like step will board the dreary bark / and soon be carried over Lethe's wave" [649–651]). Lethe, of course, as the river of oblivion is more appropriate in elegy.

The thought of Sophonisba being ferried across the river results in a lover's feelings of envy: Massinissa is even jealous of Charon!

> Fortunate Charon! utinam michi flectere clavum
> contingat, neutramque diu contingere ripam;
> tuque mei interea serves moderamina regni!
>
> (652–654)

> Ah, happy Charon, would it were my task
> to steer your skiff; I'd linger between shores
> and leave to you the ruling of my realm.

The king not only wishes to change places with the infernal boatman but would not touch either bank with Sophonisba in the boat for a long time. The latter emotional comment saves from rhetorical coldness the obviously artificial twist that Charon can take Massinissa's place on earth. Had Petrarch read Lucian, where Charon does visit the earth, the latter comment would have seemed less startling, less an unexpected *trouvaille*.

From an exclamation, the poet passes to a rhetorical question: "Invidiose senex, quando hec tibi monstra videre / contigit, aut ullo posthac continget in evo?" ("O enviable ancient, have you seen / a paragon like this, and can you hope / hereafter ever to look on its peer?" [655–656]). The question introduces a small catalog of women whom Charon has transported by means of his ferry. While Ovidian in detail, the catalog recalls, in form and location, the lists of women in earlier epic descents (e.g., *Aen.* 6. 445–451). Included are Proserpina, Dido, the horrid Gorgon (whom Hesiod by antiphrasis had called fair-cheeked and who was described, as we saw, in Lucian as beautiful),[24] Laodamia, Procris, Helen, and Phaedra. But who, Massinissa asks his imagined Charon, "Who had so much honor and so much glory for beauty?"

Massinissa's love for Sophonisba and his jealousy of Charon lead Massinissa's imagination to new heights of fancy. Charon himself will fall in love with her!

> Crude senex, michi crede, parem non ulla videbunt
> secula, nec rerum laudatrix magna suarum
> etas prima tulit. Visa tangere iuventa;
> ardebis, michi crede, senex.
>
> (665–668)[25]

> Doubt not my word, old man:
> no age to come will look upon her like,
> nor did the first age, though it vaunt its worth,
> behold such rare perfection. Aye, that sight
> will stir your passion, old man; have a care.

The speech, enclosed by the chiastic apostrophe to the old boatman, is a hymn to Sophonisba's unparalleled beauty. From her fate, however, Massinissa turns to his own: He, too, will soon cross in Charon's boat, following the "coniugis infauste vestigia cara" ("footsteps I adore / of my unhappy wife" [669]); thus recalling Orpheus rather than more traditonal epic descenders. The disconsolate youth continues, adding that he will not remain long imprisoned in life; a greater grief would be rebirth before seeing his beloved. The thought inspires him once again, and for the last time, he addresses the boatman: "Tu parce, senex, atque arbiter equus / igne pari flagrans iuvenilibus annue flammis" ("Old man, take pity; as an honest judge, / and burning with a flame akin to mine" [673–674]). Rather than a severe guardian, Charon will be indulgent, he, too, in love with Sophonisba.

The absense of epic tones in this imagined crossing is evident when we ask which of the descent units are employed by the poet. As in classical lyric, we have no clear sequence of descent, confrontation, and crossing; instead, Charon is invoked in elegiac tones as the ferryman for the crossing from life to death. But rather than lament the boatman's cruelty or the gloom of the crossing, the poet uses the motif for marvel; that is, the cruel old man himself will fall in love with this *monstra* (655) of beauty. Thus, Charon is not invoked as a figure in his own right but as an element of Hades upon whom Sophonisba can work her charms. Petrarch's skill, beyond the rhetorical virtuosity of the praise-lament, lies in restricting the field of infernal beings largely to Charon.[26] Instead of detailing in Ovidian fashion all the infernal denizens affected by Sophonisba, the poet uses an epic figure, familiar above all from the Virgilian underworld, who requires no lengthy description that would detract from Sophonisba. While Massinissa's lament is artificial in its rhetorical development, his imaginings avoid the detachment of an extended infernal vision.

Sophonisba's actual descent takes place in Book 6 and follows in abbreviated form the Virgilian pattern; we should note, however, that the tone is not one of heroism but lament. It is characteristic of Petrarch's psychology that the only descent he chooses to narrate is not a male hero's but rather a woman's, a victim of greater powers.[27] As in the *Canzoniere*, more attention is paid to the mournful presentment of death than to the actual moment of dying itself, since Massinissa torments himself more vividly before the catastrophe than afterward. In the imagined descent, attention is on Massinissa's own passions rather than what Sophonisba will feel. In this self-portrait of a lamenting lover, Charon serves as a foil for Massinissa's own emotions. Had we read of Sophonisba's fears, Charon would probably have appeared as an element of death, horrific and ghastly; instead, he is a lover's rival, an old man easily overcome by the queen's great beauty. Though lacking physical description, the boatman acquires a new and human passion: He is not characterized by his furious wrath but by love.

La Discesca di Ugo d'Alvernia. Although the themes of love and arms are commonly fused in the *poemi cavallereschi* as well, most Italian chivalric romances restrict heroic deeds to actions on earth, to duels and battles performed in the service of love. The problem of an afterlife, eschatological anxiety, is most often ignored. Despite the lack of developed descents, however, Charon continues to appear in brief scenes and occasionally in major episodes. The latter situation is perhaps best illustrated in a *chanson de geste* written in a Franco-Venetian dialect in the late fourteenth or early fifteenth century. I refer to an unpublished poem on Carlo Martello and Ugo, Count of Alverna (A 5), a work that A. Graf has shown rather conclusively to be a direct translation of a French romance.[28] It would appear from the description in D. D. R. Owen's recent book that the poem in question is based on a lost romance on Huon d'Auvergne.[29]

Instead of the more common themes of chivalric epic, such as war between Saracens and Christians, duels of knights, and love episodes, all of which appear but are of secondary importance, the predominant motif, the principle action, is outside the confines of earthly endeavors. The plot in briefest terms runs as follows: Carlo Martello, in love with Ugo's wife, sends the count on a journey to hell to ask the demon Lucifer to recognize Carlo's sovereignty and pay tribute to him. After innumerable difficulties, Ugo, sustained by his religious fidelity to

Carlo, fulfills this task and returns safely to France, at which time Carlo, overtaken finally by God's justice, is fittingly carried by devils to eternal damnation.

Ugo's journey to find the entrance to the lower world is an Odyssean account
full of strange encounters in foreign lands. Somewhere in Asia, the count arrives
in the region of hell and after various adventures meets Aeneas, who like Dante's
Virgil offers to be Ugo's guide. They are soon joined by St. William of Orange,
sent from heaven as a fellow guide, recalling Dante's references to Aeneas and
St. Paul. The author of this poem, influenced greatly by Dante, as we will see, has
decided to provide both a secular and spiritual guide. St. William, of course,
a medieval knight who defeated the Saracens at Orbien (793) and later founded
and retired to the monastery of Gellona, where he died (812), is more contemporary in spirit to the author of the poem. A principal figure in a cycle of French
epics, the most important of which is the eleventh-century *Chanson de Guil-
laume d'Orange*, William is a more appropriate patron saint of Ugo than one of
the apostles would be.[30]

Ugo and his guides are transported in an unpiloted boat to hell proper. The influence of Dante's *Commedia* soon becomes evident when the poet describes the
different categories of sinners. The first group are "la zente chi non feno ny ben
ni male" ("the people who did neither good nor evil"), followed by the lustful,
the proud, and the panderers, who

> biastemano lor padre e quily che lor batezono,
> biastemano la morte che a lor sorpresse:
> "ziossy seresemo se zamay non fosemo nate."
>
> > (A 5; Graf, p. 107)

Blaspheme their father and those who baptized them; they blaspheme death
who surprized them: "We would have been happy if we had never been
born."

Proceeding onward, Ugo sees the first infernal river, Acharonte, "donde l'aqua
reuerdisse / piena de vermy e de serpente assaie" ("where the water turned green
full of worms and numerous snakes" [Renier, p. 31]) and then encounters the
boatman:

> me ynversso lor vene vno corando et destesso
> vna gran naue ed è vechiardo fiorito:
> Charonte auea nome al dolorosso paiesse,
> dolente coloro che vano a suo servisio
> e lla lor schera.
>
> > (A 5; Renier, p. 32)

But towards them one came running and readied a large ship, a vigorous old
man; Charon was his name in the land of sorrow, sorrowful are they and their
group who go to his service.

Charon arrives, as in Dante, shouting at the spirits: "Za venite tristy male-
dety, / condurò vuy a la ynfernal masone" ("you're coming already, you wicked
damned; I'll conduct you to the infernal abode" [ibid]), and Ugo like Dante asks
his guide Aeneas, "per che ano ily cosy per tropo gran volere / del trapassare
l'aqua?" ("why do they have such a great and excessive desire to cross the
water?" [ibid]). The response, however, is original—an armed centaur drives
them on.[31] Of those who plunge into the river, "ly vermy li engiotisse" ("the
worms swallow them" [Renier, p. 33]). Other spirits enter the boat, where *Charon
demonio* beats them with his oar.[32] When the boatman sees Ugo arrive, he
shouts: "me quelo stranio chi è senza morte arivato / portà nol vollio, tropo seria
agreuato" ("but I don't want to take that strange one who has arrived without
dying. I would be too offended" [ibid]), but Aeneas silences him with words
similar to Virgil's in the *Commedia*. Before the voyagers can enter the ship, the
sagitario shoots a flaming arrow into the boat, burning the souls contained therein. On Charon's return, they pass the Acheron with him ("cosy sen uano per lo
lago tenembroso" [Renier, p. 36]), the only incident being Ugo's request for a
drink; San Guielmo, orders a spirit to bring wine, and Ugo's thrist is quenched.[33]
No sacred or allegorical significance seems to be lent to this enigmatic feature. On
disembarking, Ugo and his guides continue their voyage, undergoing adventures
too numerous to relate.

   Although the portrayal of Charon lacks descriptive detail, the ferryman's words
and actions are clearly derived from Dante's poem. Like Dante, the anonymous
poet stresses the fierceness of Charon. But rather than emphasizing the moral
features of the episode; injecting the emotions of fear, regret, sadness, and pity in
his poem; and stressing the significance of the embarcation and crossing, the poet
treats the scene as an element of wonder. In fact, he feels compelled to introduce
yet another strange being, the hybrid beast shooting arrows at the souls. The effect on the whole is less one of religious terror than secular marvel; that is, the
poet develops a world of fantasy, which is only externally moral. Ugo is not descending for his own salvation but merely to fulfill a duty to his sovereign.
Dante's vision, on the contrary, is entirely based on a moral and religious scheme.
Perhaps above all, the significance of Charon in this chivalric romance is that the
poet is the first to integrate Dante's portrait into the secular world of chivalric
deeds.

   Ugo's descent seems to have had little influence. In the chivalric romance that
dominates the first half of the Cinquecento, Charon is a figure of less consequence, mentioned most often in passing with little external description. When
he is described at greater length, however, it is often, but not always, with
Dantesque features. As examples of the peculiar ways in which Charon is employed, let us look at the brief references in Boiardo, Bello, Ariosto, and the Seicento poet Pancetti.

Boiardo. In Matteo Maria Boiardo's *Orlando Innamorato*, where classical myth
merges into the chivalric, Charon is not mentioned by name, but the crossing via

his boat is employed in an unusual situation. In Book 3, Canto 1, Mandricardo, the pagan son of Agricane, journeys from Tartaria to seek vengeance for his father on Orlando. The necessity of doing so had been announced to him in the following terms by an old man:

> L'anima del tuo patre maledetta
> Non può il mal fiume allo inferno passare,
> Perché scordata se è la sua vendetta.
> Sopra alla ripa stassi a lamentare:
> Stassi piangendo e tien la testa bassa,
> Ché ogni altro morto sopra li trapassa.
>
> (A 10; 3. 1. 8)

The soul of your cursed father cannot cross the evil river to hell, because his revenge has been forgotten. He sits on the bank lamenting; he sits crying and holds his head low, because every other dead one crosses over him.

As in earlier references to classical myth, where basic details are made a part of the world of chivalry and classical names discarded,[34] the myth of an infernal crossing is employed in modified form. As in the *Aeneid*, Charon refuses passage to certain souls, but the motivating force of denial is now one peculiar to the world of knighthood—vegeance unsought rather than funeral rites forgotten. The poet, who is more concerned with human passions than infernal machinery, effectively captures the situation of the unavenged king, who weeps in sadness. The rhythmic flow of the verses, with the soft *s*'s and repeated *p*'s and *t*'s ("Sopra alla ripa stassi . . . / stassi piangendo e tien la testa bassa") recalls an elegiac litany. Boiardo shows himself a master at underlining sense with sound in poetry of great sensitivity. From this glimpse of a lamenting father, related to touch Mandricardo's passions, the old man passes to a vision designed to arouse the pagan's pride: All other dead pass above his father. Though unmentioned by name or occupation, Charon is behind this situation as the party responsible for denying passage, a denial that serves to arouse Mandricardo and initiate the action in the poem's last book.

Boiardo's technique of absorption and transformation serves at times to veil the possible classical sources of his narration. One example of this, possibly related to a descent myth, is his allegorization of a quest tale. The obvious sources are the myths of Perseus and Medusa along with the Garden of the Hesperides. In Book 1, Canto 12, Fiordelisa narrates the story of Tisbina, Iroldo, and Prasildo. Iroldo and Tisbina share a mutual love, but she is bothered by a rich baron, Prasildo, who lives nearby. As in Boccaccio's tale of Federigo degli Alberighi (*Dec.* 5. 9), Prasildo ennobles himself in his love for Tisbina. Failing in his attempts to win her love, however, he becomes thin and pale and contemplates suicide. Hearing this, Tisbina decides to set a task for him to win her love. He is to journey to the garden of Medusa, which is surrounded by walls and has only four doors—those of Life, Death, Poverty, and Riches. In the middle of the garden is a tree guarded by Medusa, with branches of gold, one of which is desired by Tisbina.

This seemingly impossible task is facilitated by a pilgrim who tells Prasildo to enter nude through Poverty's door, employ a mirror to get the branch, give Avarice nearby some of the gold, and exit at Riches's door. When Prasildo successfully returns, Tisbina cries in distress, "Deh quanta è paccia quella alma che crede / Che Amor non possa ogni cosa compire!" ("oh how foolish is that soul who believes that Love cannot accomplish everything" [oct. 45]).

Apparently there is no hint of Charon, but when we compare the story to the descents of such classical heroes as Orpheus or Psyche, a possible parallel to Charon emerges. First, Medusa's garden could easily be a symbol of the underworld itself and the golden branch, reminiscent of Aeneas's, represents a desired object to be found there—whether one's wife, as Eurydice, or an object belonging to Proserpina. Guarding the exit is Avarizia, a figure who must be paid before passage can be permitted. Charon himself, of course, in the Psyche myth, among others, is a symbol of avarice. Whether or not any of these mythical figures were in Boiado's mind is difficult to ascertain; if so, he has managed to merge disparate elements and various sources with his own imagination to create a new myth of poetic originality.

Francesco Bello. Francesco Bello, Il Cieco da Ferrara, mentions Charon in his *Libro d'arme e d'amore nomato Mambriano*. Imitative of Boiardo, Bello relates how Mambriano, king of Bitinia, wages war against Rinaldo in order to avenge his uncle's murder. On his way to France, a storm carries Mambriano to an island, the home of Carandina, a *fata* who surpasses in magic arts Zoroastro, Circe, and Medea (1. 32). Her castle, at the top of a mountain, is described:

> Quindi costei sopra un picciolo monte
> S'ha edificato per arte un castello,
> Al qual sudan Vulcan, Sterope e Bronte,
> E quanti fabri stanno in Mongibello.
>
> (A 11; 1. 33)

Here she has built a castle by artifice on top of a small hill, for which sweat Vulcan, Steropes, and Brontes and however many smiths are in Mongibel.

But these traditional builders are not the only figures who aided the fairy; Charon himself took part!

> Più volte gl'intervenne anco Caronte,
> Conducendogli sopra il suo burchiello
> Materia da componer soda e dura,
> Della qual poi fur fatte l'alte mura.
>
> (33)

More than once Charon, too, intervened there, transporting material for it in his little barge, material solid and strong, from which next were built the tall walls.

Bello demonstrates his free use of classical mythology by employing the boatman as a shipper of supplies.

The poet's familiarity with Dante is also evident in a variety of episodes; in one of which, Charon is briefly described. Besides the Dantesque demons depicted in Canto 1, Bello describes a monster in part in the following terms: "Nel fronte ha un occhio assai più rosseggiante / Che non son quei del nocchier di Plutone" ("in his forehead he has an eye much more ruddy than those of the ferryman of Pluto" [4. 41]). Unwilling to compete with Dante's portrait of the boatman, Bello employs the ferryman either outside of tradition, with slightly humorous results, or as a figure of comparison.

Ariosto. Ludovico Ariosto also demonstrates his familiarity with Dante's depiction of the boatman as well as with classical portrayals.[35] In the *Cinque canti* written to enrich the *Furioso* but never included in it, Ariosto describes a flying vessel of the good fairy Gloricia. Imprisoning the traitor Gano and his men, Gloricia flies with them into the sky (1. 86–87). The inhabitants of different regions, seeing them pass, formulate various explanations for the marvel:

> Alcuni imaginar che di Carone,
> lo nocchiero infernal, fosse la barca,
> che d'anime dannate a perdizione
> alla via di Cocito andasse carca.
> Altri diceano, d'altra opinïone:
> —Questa è la santa nave ch'al ciel varca,
> che Pietro tol da Roma, acciò ne l'onde
> di stupri e simonie non si profonde.—
>
> (A 12; 1. 91)

Some imagined that the ship belonged to Charon, the infernal ferryman, and that it was heading towards Cocytus, loaded with souls damned to perdition. Others, with a different opinion, were saying: "This is the holy ship which crosses to heaven, which took Peter from Rome, so that he not become immersed in the waves of rape and simony.

While the second reason is more logical and biting, the first illustrates the poet's interest in Charon, here seen as crossing Cocytus rather than Acheron. The tendency to see Charon in any sailor, any old man, is evident in Canto 4 of the *Cinque canti*, where Ruggiero jumps off a burning ship and is swallowed by a whale of Alcina (4. 31–32). Unaware of what has happened, the hero assumes that he is dead and is now a spirit in purgatory or hell (33).[36] Ruggiero, having been converted earlier, is praying that he is not in hell when he sees a light appear:

> Esser Caron lo giudicò da lunge,
> che venisse a portarlo all'altra riva:
> s'avvide, poi che più vicin gli giunge,
> che senza barca a sciutto piè veniva.

(4. 36. 1–4)

He judged him from far off to be Charon, coming to take him to the other bank; he realized, as the fellow came closer to him, that he was coming without a boat and with dry feet.

Just as biblical commentators saw Jonah's descent into the whale as prefiguring Christ's descent into hell, so Ariosto allows us to combine the imagery of both (a whale and a descent) in this episode.

While Ariosto relates no extended descent to the underworld—in the *Furioso*, Astolfo merely descends to the first level of hell—he does refer to Charon as ferryman of the dead.[37] The two references are brief but interesting. When Atlante stops the duel between Ruggiero and Marfisa, telling them that they are brother and sister, he relates how at his death he asked for a special dispensation, knowing the two would fight in this particular place:

> Ma inanzi a morte, qui dove previdi
> che con Marfisa aver pugna dovevi,
> feci raccor con infernal sussidi
> a formar questa tomba i sassi grevi;
> et a Caron dissi con alti gridi:
> "Dopo morte non vo' lo spirto levi
> di questo bosco, fin che non ci giunga
> Ruggier con la sorella per far pugna."

(36. 65)

> Before I died, here, where I had forseen
> That pre-ordained you were one day to come
> And would engage in combat with your twin,
> I gathered heavy stones to form this tomb
> (With Hell's assistance) and to Charon in
> Loud tones I thus decreed: "When I succumb,
> My soul must tarry in this cypress-glade
> Until my wards to battle here are led.

(BR)

What is most astounding about this unusual request is the implication that Charon is a death-demon who comes to earth for the dead. This concept of Charon, familiar in Byzantine literature, may very likely have been known to the poet.[38] Reinforcing such a hypothesis is the last Ariostean passage to be discussed.

In Canto 42, the poet describes the havoc created by Orlando, enraged at the death of Brandimarte. First to die is Agramante:

Orlando giunse, e messe il colpo giusto
ove il capo si termina col busto.
　Sciolto era l'elmo e disarmato il collo,
sí che lo tagliò netto come un giunco.
Cadde, e diè nel sabbion l'ultimo crollo
del regnator di Libia il grave trunco.
Corse lo spirto all'acque, onde tirollo
Caron nel legno suo col graffio adunco.

(42. 8–9)

On him Orlando came and smote him just
Where with the helmet head confined the bust.
Loosed was the helm, the neck without its band:
So, like a rush, was severed by the sword.
Down-fell, and shook its last upon the sand
The heavy trunk of Libya's mighty lord.
His spirit, which flitted to the Stygian strand,
Charon with crooked boat-hook dragged aboard.

(WSR)

When the spirit rushes to Acheron, we find not a Dantesque Charon beating souls with his oar but a figure bearing a hooked grappling iron, reminiscent perhaps of the Malebranche in *Inferno* 21. The late arriving soul is pulled into the boat by the grapnel as Charon prepares to shove off from shore; the image, though brief, has pleasing vitality. The grasping nature of the boatman is amply and physically illustrated by his use of the *graffio adunco*.

Ariosto's characteristic use of Charon is defined by attempts to merge the classical and Dantesque figure with the world of fantasy found in romance. In the *Cinque canti*, where the boatman is mentioned in relation to a flying vessel, the traditional myth is transformed into a fairy tale. Charon is a fantastic being who conducts his ship into the sky. In the second reference, he is also a creation of someone's fancy, namely Ruggiero in the whale; both images are connected as well with Danteque thoughts on perdition. In the *Furioso*, the poet depicts the boatman in equally original situations. The concept of a classical ferryman is present as well as the Byzantine idea of Charon as a death-demon. In neither instance, however, does the poet describe the figure's physical features; at most, his nature is represented through his actions and the reaction of the other characters to him.

Pancetti. In the Seicento, the most unusual representation of Charon in a work combining classical epic and *romanzo* elements is found in Camillo Pancetti's *Venetia libera*. Mirroring in inverted form Trissino, who gave pagan names to angels, Pancetti gives demons names of pagan divinities. Thus we find devils called Mars, Bacchus, Cerberus, Erebus, Demogorgone, and Alcides under the power of a *maga* Venus, all intent on destroying Venice. Charon is mentioned in

Canto 22 where the virtuous Venetians succeed in defeating the demon-aided French. In the midst of the tremendous battle, the Venetian hero Hector kills one of the seven sons of Erebus called Morte:

> Non si sgomenta il pio Campion dal viso
> Vestito a doppio di color di morte,
> Si incontra col fratel, di chi have ucciso,
> (Custode è ognun de le infernali Porte)
> Questo è Caron, che lui fece un sorriso,
> Come al reo par, che 'l manigoldo apporte,
> E disse: Il mio fratel da me n'aspetta,
> Morte imbianca il tuo volto, ecco vendetta.
>
> (A 30; 22. 59)

The pious captain is not dismayed by the face dressed in a double color of death; he clashes with the brother of the one he killed (each is a guardian of the infernal gates). This one is Charon, who gave him a smile which seemed like that of an executioner to the culprit and said: My brother expects it from me; death whitens your face, here is vengeance.

That is, after killing the one son Death, Hector, undismayed, passes to fight Death's brother, Charon, who is depicted with an executioner's grin. All seven sons are parenthetically referred to as guardians of hell's gates. Charon—a demon warrior—threatens vengeance and succeeds in the following octave in wounding Hector:

> Lo spadon, come un'hasta in aria gira,
> E smaglia l'elmo, e rode il gran cimiero,
> Crollò il capo d'Hettor, che'n se delira,
> Stà per cader, per deviar sentiero.
>
> (22. 60)

His broadsword, like a spear, turns in the air and smashes the helmet and knaws at the crest; the head of Hector slumps down, delirious; he is about to fall, to swerve from the path.

Hector's wife Artemisia, however, rushes in and kills the demon (60).

After killing the next four sons of Erebus (Spavento, Tenebra, Dolore, and Pertinace), Hector and Artemisia face the seventh son, Acheronte (22. 64), who arrives too late to save his brothers. Breathing *horribil fumo*, he cries, "O fratelli d'ira mi consumo" and falls dead under the blows of the two Venetians. Thus in the most unusual extension of Charon in an historical epic infused with *romanzo* elements, the demon becomes a warrior fighting on earth to aid the French against the Venetians. As a warrior, of course, he has lost all his traditional attributes and functions, retaining only his name and infernal origin.

In conclusion, the representation of Charon in poems blending epic and romance elements can perhaps best be defined as strikingly original. In fusing the variety of traditions available to them, these poets exhibit a greater degree of freedom concerning established motifs and figures. No longer an intimidating guardian, Charon is imagined in an elegiac context in Petrarch as being in love. In the Dantesque framework of *La discesa di Ugo d'Alvernia*, Charon is a figure of marvel coupled with a centaur who shoots flaming arrows; in Boiardo, Bello, and Ariosto, Charon forbids passage to the unavenged; ships supplies for a fairy to build her magic castle; and is thought to guide a flying ship, seek the dead on earth, and pull souls into his boat with a hook. Finally, in Pancetti, Charon becomes a demon knight fighting on earth for the French. What is perhaps most noteworthy, besides the originality with which the figure is treated, is that Charon is rarely described physically. Instead, as a character belonging to a magic world of fantasy, he is defined above all by the situation in which he is employed. And since these situations are always highly characteristic of the world of chivalric romance, Charon assumes an identity that is both varied and modern.

iii. Mock-Heroic Poems

Although Alessandro Tassoni wrote his *Secchia rapita* with the intention of creating a new poetic form, the *poema eroicomica*, a subgenre that thrived in the Seicento, the origins of the form can be found as early as the late Quattrocento. We should perhaps more accurately speak of early mock-chivalric romance and later mock-epic. Supporting this early origin of the mock heroic are several representations of Charon, ranging, among others, from those of Pulci, Folengo, and Legname in the fifteenth and sixteen centuries to those of Bracciolini and Lalli in the seventeenth.

Pulci. In Luigi Pulci's *Morgante*, Charon first appears in Canto 2 in a speech of the recently converted giant. Excited by his and Orlando's victory over a demon, Morgante expresses his desire to invade hell itself "e far tutti i dïavoli sbucare"! ("and drive out all the devils" [A 9; 2. 37]). In the following two octaves, the gaint imagines what he would do on his voyage to the underworld:

> E si potessi entrar di qualche loco,
>   ché nel mondo è certe bocche, si dice,
>   donde e' si va, che di fuor gettan fuoco,
>   e non so chi v'andò per Euridice,
>   io stimerei tutti i dïavol poco.
>   Noi ne trarremo l'anime infelice;
>   e taglierei la coda a quel Minosse,
>   se come questo ogni dïavol fosse;

> e pelerò la barba a quel Caron,
> e leverò della sedia Plutone;
> un sorso mi vo' far di Flegeton,
> e inghiottir quel Fregiàs con un boccone;
> Tesifo, Aletto, Megera e Ericon
> e Cerbero ammazzar con un punzone;
> e Belzebù farò fuggir più via
> ch' un dromedario non andre' in Soria.

$$(2.\ 38–39)$$

And if I could get in at some spot, since there are certain openings in the world, they say, where one can go, which spout out fire and I don't know who went there for Eurydice, I would hold all the devils in low esteem. We will drag the unhappy souls out of there; and I would cut off the tale of that Minos, if every devil were like this one; and I will pluck out the beard of that Charon, and knock Pluto off his chair; I want to finish off Phlegethon with one sip, and swallow that Fregyas in one mouthful; and kill Tisiphone, Alecto, Megera and Erichtho and Cerberus with a punch; and Belzebub I'll make flee farther off than a dromedary would go in Syria.

With his humorous references to half-remembered mythological lore, Morgante illustrates the common person's conception of the beyond, most of which is derived from Dante's poem. Morgante begins with a reference to the various entrances reputed to lead to hell; mentions an illustrious predecessor, Orpheus, whose name, however, he cannot remember; and boasts of what he, Morgante, will do to the inhabitants in the lower realm. Devoting one verse to each, Morgante captures an important detail of each underworld being: He will free the unhappy souls; cut off Minos's tail; pull out Charon's beard; dethrone Pluto; drink up Phlegethon in one swallow—as well as Phlegyas, whom he calls Fregiàs —slaughter the Furies, Erichtho, and Cerberus, and chase off Belzebub.

This would-be harrower of hell is soon discouraged, however, when Orlando tells him there is nothing to eat in hell and offers the advice that one should always choose the easy, level road rather than ascent or descent (2. 40–41).

Much later in the poem, Charon reappears in Canto 26, which tells of the battle of Roncisvalle. At one point, the poet pauses to describe how busy the devils were with the dead souls of the pagans:

> e bisognoè che menassin le mane
> e che battessin tutto 'l giorno l'ali
> a presentarle a' giudici infernali.

$$(26.\ 89)$$

and it was necessary that they keep their hands busy and beat their wings all day in order to present them to the infernal judges.

Those in hell responsible for judgment and transportation had to work especially hard; the poet asks us to imagine their activity:

Pensa quel dì se menoron la coda
　　Eaco, il gran Minòs e Rodomanta;
　　e quel Satàn, se tu credi che e' goda;
e se Caron nella sua cimba canta,
　　rassetta i remi, e la vela rannoda
　　col mataffione, e le vele rammanta;
e se si fece più d'una moresca
　　giù nello inferno, e taferugia e tresca!

(26. 90)

Think if that day Aeacus, the great Minos, and Rhadamanthys moved their tails; and that Satan—if you believe he enjoys himself; and if Charon in his boat sings, arranges his oars, reties the reef, and corrects the sails; and if down in hell they didn't dance more than one moresca, and scuffle, and tresca.

Typical of the popular tradition, Christian devils and pagan semidivinities are treated as one. But whereas the classical judges and Satan are merely mentioned in passing, Charon's task catches the fancy of Pulci, who details in technical language the boatman's activities much as Lucian depicts the practical aspects of Charon's work. Pulci imagines the ferryman singing in his boat (*cimba* recalls the Latin *cumba*, commonly used for Charon's boat by Virgil, Horace, Statius, and other poets), a picturesque way of expressing a typical boatman's joy at receiving more fares. The alliterative *c*'s in verse 4 add to the musicality of the first concept, while the repeated *r*'s in verses 5 and 6 as well as the parallel structure of "e la vela rannoda" and "e le vele rammanta" add to the impression of ceaseless and hectic activity. Charon is seen arranging his oars, retying his sails with cords, and maneuvering them with the halyards. Meanwhile, the other inhabitants of hell are dancing and carousing.

Finally, near the end of the poem, Charon is referred to for the last time by Pulci. The emperor Carlo, speaking to the traitorous Marsilio, tells him that he will soon be in hell. Marsilio, trying to save his life, asks to be baptized, knowing that no Christian can kill another. His hypocrisy is recognized, however, and his request denied. Carlo addresses him as follows: "Io non credo che l'acqua di Giordano, / dove fu battezzato Gesù nostro, / ti potessi lavar come cristiano" ("I don't believe that the water of Jordan, where our Christ was baptized, could wash you as a Christian" [27. 277]). Instead, Marsilio will receive another type of baptism:

　　—Con Bianciardino e col tuo Falserone
　　　　giù nello inferno ti battezzerai—
　　　　disse Carlo—in quelle acque di Carone,
　　quando la sua barchetta passerai.

(27. 278)

With Bianciardino and your Falserone you will baptize yourself down in hell —said Carlo—in those waters of Charon, when you cross in his little boat.

The irony of the situation—crossing the Acheron as a baptism into hell—is superb, the concept pleasantly original. Charon, of course, as a means of transportation is mentioned in this instance only in passing.

Among the parodistic elements of the *Morgante* is the manner in which classical underworld divinities are treated. Influenced in part by the more popular singers of the time and the culture of bourgeois Florence, Pulci exagggerates the heroic traits of his characters. In doing so, Charon becomes a comic figure, characterized by his grotesque beard and his excited activity; his features inspire not awe or terror but ridicule.

Folengo. The boatman becomes yet more buffonish in an underworld episode in Teofilo Folengo's *Baldus* (A 13).[39] Mocking the heroic topoi of chivalric romance, Folengo describes Baldus's strange adventures, including confrontations with witches, devils, monsters, pirates, poets, and other marvelous creatures. Among the caricatures of classical themes in Book 24, we find the descent into the infernal regions with which the work ends. The parodistic treatment of this descent extends as well to the *Divina Commedia*.

In the middle of Book 24, Baldus and his companions find themselves entering a dark woods leading to a gate and the realm of Lucifer. After an episode in an infernal inn, Baldus and his friends arrive at the *nigras . . . undas* of Acheron (492):

> Illic circa suas testas hinc inde volazzant
> innumerae flentes animae, vocitantque Charontem,
> quas ille ad ripam debet passare sinistram,
> sed non, transactis iam giornis octo, videtur.

> (494–497)

Here around their heads innumerable weeping souls flutter on all sides and shout for Charon to carry them to the other bank, but eight days have passed and he has not been seen.

The humor lies not only in the length of Charon's delay but in the specification of eight days.

Near the river, Cingar comes on a nearly dead youth whom he revives with urine (!), since odiferous medicinal sprays are lacking and Acheron's water ''venenosis . . . fluctibus ardet'' (''burns with venomous waves'' [530]). The youth, a lost son of Baldus called Grillus, tells how he and his twin brother Fanettus came to hell searching for their father:

> Ast ubi nos fortuna locum deduxit ad istum,
> nos, inquam, medios longa stracchedine mortos,
> affuit ecce Charon, praesentis nauta riverae,
> qui tenet officium curvo transferre batello
> damnatas animas et ademptas morte secunda.

> (559–563)

But when fortune brought us here to this place, half dead, I say, with exhaustion, behold Charon comes gliding in, the ferryman of this shore, who performs the duty of transporting in his hollow boat the damned souls, taken away to a second death.

Dante's influence extends from the situation—the abrupt introduction of Charon —to the language—"la seconda morte" (*Inf.* 1.117).

Grillus asks the ferryman to transport them, alleging in Virgilian fashion the affection, love, and fidelity that they owe their father, but

> Ille ribaldonus, crestosus vecchius, et omni
> fraude sat impressus, velut omnis nauta catatur,
> promisit nos velle quidem passare delaium,
> sed non insemmam, dicens quod transiet unus
> post alium, fietque duplex vogatio nostra.
> Et causam tulit hanc: "ne scilicet ipsa periret
> gundola, corporibus sic sic onerata duobus."

$$(567–573)$$

That great knave, that crusty old man with every fraud imprinted on his face, as is true of all ferrymen, promised us he meant to carry us to the other side but not both together, saying that he would ferry one after the other and that our rowing across would be double. And the reason he alleged was this: that the gondola not sink, weighed down by two bodies.

As in Lucian, the humor lies in the introduction of realistic elements into a scene of fantasy. The denunciation of Charon characterizes him not only in physical terms but also morally. He is both old and deceptive, so much so that his crafty nature is embedded in his features. His crossing will not only suppposedly be double but also duplicitous. In fact, Charon, having ferried Fanettus over, has been gone, says Grillus, for six days.

Rejoicing at his good fortune, Cingar leads the youth toward the Acheron. Baldus, meanwhile, is at the river shouting fiercely for Charon and threatening to break his back if he does not appear immediately with the boat (589–591). The banks of the river, he says, are filling up with souls (592–593). But Baldus, we learn, shouts in vain, for Charon, marvel of marvels, has fallen in love (!), and it is not, as imagined by Massinissa in Petrarch's *Africa*, with a descending soul. Instead, he burns with love for the nymph Tisiphone to whom he has handed over the youth Fanettus.

While Tisiphone enjoys the youth's company, Charon has been standing outside, waiting to satisfy his carnal desires:

> Ille stat indarum, stat mattus, statque balordus,
> seria postponens carnali cuncta desio:
> cui propria utilitas, cui barchae puzzat aquistus,

> et quod aquistatur seu stento sive salaro
> dilectae tribuit, velut est usanza, bagassae.
>
> (600–604)

He stands there in vain, stands a madman, and stands stupid, postponing all his serious business because of carnal desire; he doesn't care about his own good; the gain of his boat stinks, and all that he has acquired whether by skimping or by salary he bestows on his beloved whore, as is his custom.

It is as if a moralist were describing the vices of an evil man.

From lustful Charon, the poet turns back to his heros, who are hard pressed by the arriving souls. Thousands pile up on their backs; their ears fill up, their noses; even their beards and hair are entwined with spirits. Folengo offers a buffonish picture of the descenders shaking their heads, clearing their throats, and sneezing souls! The Virgilian image of the souls is given a new and humorously realistic treatment; Fracassus, in fact, is compared to an old ox bothered by bees: "Hinc examen apum cunctis sua testa vedetur, / agmine quae denso se circa foramen adossant" ("his head seems to everyone a swarm of bees, when they gather in a thick bunch around the hole" [616–617]).

Finally, after Baldus has met his son Grillus, an incident that allows Folengo to satirize the idea of one's offspring as the flower generated by the plant, the fruit of one's tree,

> ecce venit sbraiando Charon, chiamatque bravazzus:
> "Papa Satan, o papa Satan, beth, gimel, aleppe.
> Cra cra, tif taf noc, sgne flut, canatauta, riogna."
>
> (638–640)

Behold Charon comes yelling and shouting like a bully: Father Satan, o Father Satan, beth, gimel, aleppe. Cra cra, tif taf noc, sgne flut, canatauta, riogna.

Scholar of Dante or not, any reader will break out laughing at this humorous display of infernal language.[40]

A description of Charon follows, developed along Virgilian lines, with each element grotesquely exaggerated. Charon's uncombed beard, for example, covers his belly and touches his knees; his head is completely bald. He wears a ragged *schiavina*—a pilgrim's gown or coarse blanket—called, says the poet, a *sattinbarca* by the Chioggian rabble.

Charon's arrival brings to the page a ten-line vignette of Venetian boatmen who stand precipitously on the edge of their gondolas, not caring if they fall and drown. Charon meanwhile approaches the shore and frightens the souls with his "mala fazza . . . / cumque bravariis . . . acerbis" ("evil face and with his harsh blustering" [661–662]). Baldus, however, angrily calls him a *poltrone* and tries to get in the boat, but no sooner is the anchor dropped than the souls rush in filling all the holes and taking the seats (663–666).

Charon, on seeing Baldus and his companions, asks them why they have come, who they are, and then tells them if they wish to enter his boat they will have to leave behind their baggage of flesh. We are reminded of the souls waiting to board in Lucian's *Dialogues of the Dead*, part 10. Baldus calls Charon a liar and tells him to keep quiet or he will throw him headfirst into the water. The descender recalls a past hero, namely, Meschino, who was allowed passage, but finds his threats useless, for Charon shoves the boat away, already full of souls, and refuses to listen.

Fracassus's solution is to make a tremendous leap across the river. Marveling at the deed, Baldus tells him to pull out Charon's beard, hair by hair, break his head and all the bones in his body, and then try to guide the boat back himself (691–694).

Charon is also thunderstruck by the leap but continues his voyage, unloading the souls finally at the far shore. Afraid to return for Baldus, Charon sets about repairing his boat and performing other tasks to delay his return. The situation leads to a scene of pure farce: Fracassus sneaks out of the bushes on tiptoe, creeps up behind the boatman, grabs him by the neck, twirls him around three or four times, and heaves him far off into the darkness (706–717).

The episode at the river has not yet finished. Finding the boat unable to bear his weight, Fracassus "cum pede dat calzum retro in culamina barchae" ("from behind gives the boat a kick in the ass with his foot" [734]), and it flies off to his companions. Guided by Cingar rather than Charon, the boat makes seven trips with the heroes. Baldus, laughing, praises Cingar as an excellent ferryman:

> "Certe hic nec forma nec discrepat arte Charontis.
> Cernite terribiles oculos magramque figuram.
> Quis nam illum guardans non dixerit esse diablum?"
>
> (748–750)

"For sure he's not different from Charon, neither in appearance nor in occupation. Look at his terrible eyes and his thin figure. Who in looking at him wouldn't say he was a devil?"

Thus, the river is crossed, and the canto comes to an end.

Following in basic outline Virigl's account of the infernal river and its crossing, Folengo has enlivened the episode not only through satirical treatments of both Dantesque and Virgilian elements but also creative innovations of his own. The humor of his presentation is of varied origin: At times it is found in language, at times in situation. Folengo's versatility as a comic artist extends from the bawdry to the witty, from the exaggerated to the grotesque, from satire to farce, and from mock fantasy to ridiculous realism, all expressed in a language combining the loftiness of Latin with the coarseness of the vernacular dialects. Folengo seems to have been influenced in depicting the boatman by the grotesque portrait of the *senex amans* so familiar in classical and early Cinquecento comedy. Without doubt, Charon's age and dreadful aspect invite irreverence. The burlesquing of the ferryman is completed by comparisons to modern Venetian gondoliers and Chioggian bravoes.

Legname. Though not sharing Folengo's comic intentions nor his poetic skills, the Paduan Antonio Legname treats the figure of Charon with humorous results in his *Astolfo innamorato, libro d'arme, e d'amore* (A 15). While Charon is mentioned as early as Canto 1. 15,[41] an extended portrayal of the boatman is reserved for Canto 8, where Astolfo and Malagigi ponder how to conquer Carlo and take Paris. When Malagigi fails to arouse any demons, he decides to travel to the stygian realm and haul up Pluto himself (8. 12). Traveling south past Rome, Malagigi meets the Sibyl and tells her his plan:

> Disse a lui la Sibilla, almo barone,
> quando ti piaccia ti darò le chiave,
> ch'andar potrai per l'oscuro valone
> dove si trova tante anime prave.
> A lei rispose il filiuol di Buone
> dammi ti prego anco un palo grave,
> ch'a Caronte vo far un gran servizio,
> romper la cimba, e cacciarlo d'officio.

(18)

The Sibyl said to him, immortal baron, when you wish I will give you the keys, so that you can go through the dark valley where one finds so many wicked souls. The son of Buone responded to her, give me I beg you a heavy pole also, since I want to do a great service to Charon, break his boat, and chase him off his job.

Calling Charon a "miscredente ladro, e insano" ("an insane, misbelieving thief"), Malagigi threatens to lead him so far away that he will never be able to return to hell and harm others in his *palischermo* (dinghy [19]). Using his key, Malagigi passes through a gate and descends to the center of the earth.

An octave of Virgilian inspiration describing the symbolic figures, such as old age and poverty, near the entrance to hell (23) soon gives way to an Ariostean picture of dense smoke (24). Having passed through this, Malagigi finds himself in a large plain "dove ogn'alma si sta senza paura / nè v'è demonj più che quelle offende" ("where every soul lives unafraid, nor are there any more devils to offend them" [26]). Proceeding to Charon's river, the magician reverses the traditional confrontation; in this, he is reminiscent of Folengo's crafty Fracassus:

> Malagigi gli aggionge d'improviso,
> adesso che 'l meschin pur non si puote
> levar non ch'alla cimba sua provista
> corresse, che l'avea già per le gotte

il negromante preso, ed ei s'attrista,
benchè lui si dimena con gran rote
di su, di giù, e cerca con inganno
farli restar di se vota la mano.

(27)

Malagigi comes upon him suddenly, before the wretch can even get up let alone run to his provided boat; already the necromancer has grabbed him by the cheeks, and he soon weakens, although he twists with great wheels up and down and tries with deceit to get himself out of Malagigi's grip.

The distance from Virgil's august and watchful figure and Dante's majestic and cruel demon to this pathetic, struggling wretch is immense. The satiric disparagement of Charon, begun by Pulci and carried to its height in the comic work of Folengo, continues in the basically serious poem of Legname. Here, in fact, Morgante and Baldus's threats to tear out Charon's beard are carried out in reality:

che Malagigi gl'avea a pelo, a pello
gli strappa la barba via dal mento,
nè di sì poco far resta contento.

(29)

Now that Malagigi has him, he pulls his beard out of his chin hair by hair, nor does he remain content to do so little.

Despite Charon's *urli, gridi*, and *spaventevol voce*, the necromancer continues to beat the boatman until he has him tied up in chains.
Malagigi considers smashing Charon's boat but changes his mind:

anzi salisce in poppa, el remo toglie
per gir all'altra ripa il sir benigno
traendo tuttavia seco in catena,
Caront' il vecchio per più darli pena.

(31)

Instead the benevolent sire climbs in the stern and takes the oar in order to go to the other bank, dragging with him in chains, however, the old Charon in order to punish him some more.

On the far side, the magician finds an inscription reminiscent of Dante's in *Inferno* 3, to which, incidentally, the poet refers (34), but passes on unafraid, taking with him "quello sì indegno ladro di Caronte" ("Charon, that so unworthy thief" [36]).
In the midst of this descent modeled along pagan lines, Malagigi comes across a soul (Mandricardo) who speaks of the Messiah and introduces the motif of his harrowing of hell (40–41). From the praise of those who worship the true God—

"e non li nostri Dèi vani, e bugiardi" ("and not our vain and lying gods" [43])—the poet falls again into the comic:

> In questo ragionar l'alma feroce
> del già morto superbo Rodomonte
> verso di lor venia con aspra voce
> gridando, per un piè prese Caronte,
> e correndo via passa veloce.

(44)

While they were talking, the fierce soul of the already dead, proud Rodomonte came toward them shouting with a harsh voice; he took Charon by one foot and running away passes by swiftly.

Malagigi, of course, follows him to regain his prisoner.

Charon's vicissitudes are not quite over; in fact on reaching Pluto's city, Rodomonte unties Charon, twirls him around a few times, lifts him into the air, and hurls him against the wall! Our final glimpse of the battered boatman comes when a subdued Pluto asks Malagigi to pardon his servant (51). Unlike Folengo, who has comic intentions throughout his poem, Legname returns to more serious events on earth following this farcical descent.

In analyzing the reasons for Legname's burlesque depiction of Charon, we must consider several points, among them the growing tendency to mock fantastic elements in romance. Perhaps the bizarre features of not only Malagigi but the Astolfo story itself lend themselves to a humorous approach in general. And of course, the descent topos, being one step removed from earthly reality, invites yet more exaggeration. Charon, finally, is vulnerable because of his traditionally grotesque features. His distortion can be traced from the ambiguous portrait of a squalid god in Virgil through the demonic transformation by Dante to the parodistic displacement brought about by writers like Pulci and Folengo. Legname, perhaps in disdain for the "Dèi vani e bugiardi," chooses to describe the infernal regions as populated by inept demons and classical monsters no longer awesome or horrific but simply pathetic. At best, then, the encounter with the ferryman is a moment of comic relief; Charon, as a result, becomes a stick-like figure, lacking the character development typical of epic.

In the Seicento, the epic and chivalric ideals of the past, ideals that had dominated European literature for four centuries, are generally said to have come to an end.[42] While epics of various types continue to be written, the new genre catching the imagination of seventeenth-century poets is the *poema eroicomico*. Despite the fact that most works of this type mention the boatman only in passing,[43] Charon's role in the new form occasionally reemerges with broadly comic tones.

Bracciolini. Francesco Bracciolini's *Lo scherno degli dei* (A 27) is an example of a mock-heroic poem that contains several references to Charon but does not develop him as a character. Though deriding extensively other figures of pagan mythology, Bracciolini chooses to mock the boatman with much less satirical intensity.

Charon is mentioned most conspicuously in the story related by Morfeo to Venus. The episode as a whole has great comic possibilities, for it deals with the descent to the underworld of Morfeo himself, disguised as Amore. While Charon offers no resistance to his passing ("E da Caronte fuì subito accolto" [11. 19]), other spirits rush to tell Pluto that Love (Morfeo disguised) has penetrated their realm. A host of demons gather in an attempt to expel him, but Pluto decides a council is needed to consider the matter at length (11. 22).

Integrating the themes of the infernal council and the descent, Bracciolini describes the controversy that rages over whether Love is good or bad. To Proserpina who wishes to keep Love, since he is the cause of hell on earth, Alecto counters by saying Love is too sweet: "E non vo' che quaggiù tra queste pene, / Si comincia l'un l'altro a voler bene" ("I don't want people to begin loving each other down here among this suffering" [11. 43]). She continues to explain why Love is incompatible with the other guardians of hell:

> Che non è già la barca di Caronte
> Sola, che ci difenda il nostro regno,
> Che Giove e Marte con le mani si pronte
> Sopra il fiume farian ponti di legno;
> Ma quei che guardian noi dalle lor onte
> Son l'Odio e l'Ira, e il Canchero e lo Sdegno,
> Tutti quanti nemici capitali
> D'Amor, come dell'acqua gli stivali.

(11. 44)

It's not only Charon's boat alone which defends our realm, since Jove or Mars with their ready hands could build wooden bridges over the river; but the ones who guard us from their insults are Hatred and Anger, Cancher and Disdain, all capital enemies of Love, like boots are of water.

Charon, in fact, has been an ineffectual guardian, since he allowed Love to pass with ease. His unimportance is emphasized when the Fury notes that the gods could always bridge the infernal rivers if they wished! With Love in hell, the gods will come in swarms.

Pluto recognizes that Alecto has spoken "prudentemente per ragion di stato" (11. 50), and Amore is expelled. Morfeo describes his expulsion in Dantesque terminology:

> Via, via, tutti in un tempo, fuora, fuora,
> E da quell'ombre a Cerbero cagnaccio,
> Mi fan gridar in bando allhora, allhora,
> Senza processo, e dannomi lo spaccio.

Mi ripassa Caron la morta gora
Ed io da lor me ne diparto e taccio,
E 'l piè rivolgo alla Tenarea buca,
Dove l'aria migliore me riluca.

                                                            (11. 57)

Away, away, all at once, out, out, and from those shades to the cur Cerberus
they shout for me to be exiled—right away, without a trial—and kick me out.
Charon transports me back across the dead pool, and I depart from them and
keep silent, and turn my foot back to the Tenarean hole, where better air
shines for me.

As a minor figure in this mini burlesque of the underworld, Charon is mocked for
the ease with which the disguised Morfeo passes. Rather than a true guardian,
Charon has become an accommodating ferryman.

Lalli. The boatman is perhaps parodied most extensively in Giambattista Lalli's
grotesque version of Virgil's poem, entitled *Eneide travestita* (A 32). With the
supposed intention of making the *Aeneid* more popular, Lalli burlesqued this
work by filling his translation with anachronistic events, caricatures, and trivial
episodes. The encounter with Charon is described as follows:

Giunser, tra questo mentre, a una fiumana
D'un'acqua puzzolente d'Acheronte:
Acqua, ch'è nera come inchiostro, e strana,
Che non saprìa nuotarvi un Rodomonte.
Sgorga in Cocito, e per la via piana
Ha una barchetta, ed è il nocchier Caronte;
Caronte un bestìale, un spiritato,
Barba di becco, e cera d'impiccato.
      E' vecchio rimbambito, accesi ha gli occhi,
Come carboni dentro un forno ardenti:
La bocca è grande, e larga, e senza denti:
Appeso al collo ha un ferraiuol da scrocchi:
Un'asta lungha tien sopra i ginocchi,
Di remo in cambio, per varcar le genti;
Le genti, dico, afflitte e sconsolate,
Ch' in posta di qua su sono spacciate.

                                                            (p. 75)

Meanwhile they arrived at Acheron's broad stream of stinking water, which is
black as ink and strange, which even a Rodomonte would not know how to
swim. It disgorges into Cocytus, and where it levels out there is a little boat and
the ferryman Charon—Charon, a beast, a possessed man, with beak beard and
hanged-man's face. He's a childish old man, has inflamed eyes, like burning
coal in an oven; his mouth is large and wide, and toothless; he has a sponger's
cloak hung around his neck; he holds a long pole on his knees, instead of an

oar, to transport the people; the people, I say, afflicted and disheartened, who are dispatched in the post from up here.

From the grim warden of Virgil, Charon has become a beast, a possessed being. The description of his bearded face as that of a hanged man is effectively grotesque. Rather than translate Charon's green age as an indication of robust strength, Lalli classifies him, in effect, as a senile or childish old man, hence, his large toothless mouth. Instead of simply being called tattered, his short cloak is compared to a sponger's.

The parody continues in the following scene of confrontation, falling at times into the bawdry. Charon, for example, apostrophized by the Sibyl as ''Caronte di vellutto,'' says, in referring to previous descenders, that ''ci fecero restar tanti castroni'' (''they made us seem castrated dolts''). When he is quieted by the golden bough, ''mandò tutta la collera in bordello: / Poichè in tanti anni appena ha nella mente / Di averne visti, e n'avea un gran martello'' (''he dispelled all his anger in a brothel, since for so many years he barely recalls having seen any, and he had a great hammer'' [pp. 80–81]). Finally, the episode comes to a close with a comic reference to Aeneas's weight in the boat:

The Entrance to Erebus, by Luca Giordano. (1684–86) Palazzo Medici-Riccardi, Florence. By permission of Fratelli Alinari.

> Ma perch'ella intessuta, e un po' sdrucita
> Era intorno la sua circonferenza;
> Dubitò Enea, con l'acqua sul ginocchio,
> Di diventare o gambero, o ranocchio.

(p. 81)

But since it was patched together and a bit torn around the edge, Aeneas, with the water to his knee, was afraid he might become either a crawfish or a frog.

To summarize Charon's representation in mock-heroic poems, I think it is evident that the range of comic portraits is quite extensive: The boatman is mocked in his own right—both as a wretched underworld servant and an old man in love. Particular descriptions of Charon in Dante and Virgil are also parodied; Bartolomeo Bocchini, for example, does to Dante's oar-swinging ferryman what Lalli does to Virgil's aged god (see A 34). In effect, Charon becomes not only a plaything of the poets but a bauble to be tossed around by various descenders. As a stick-like figure, he has lost all physical reality; what features are mentioned are grotesquely exaggerated. Rather than repeat specific examples, let me reemphasize the importance of comedy for this form of epic. Writers of the mock-heroic seize the boatman as a type of stock figure comparable to the *senex* in Roman and Cinquecento comedy. Charon's vain blusterings also bring to mind those of the *miles gloriosus*, a character who is also thrashed in spite of his frightening bombast. Fierce Charon, of course, has a long history of succumbing to descenders. As an impotent guardian and an aged and squalid servant of the infernal gods, he is a figure easily ridiculed.

iv. Mythological Epic

Marino. As a final epic type, let me mention Marino's lengthy mythological poem, the *Adone* (A 31). As in the mixed works of romance and epic, Charon's part is relatively small. In the description of the underworld home of the infernal fury Jealousy in Canto 12, Charon is absent, although Cerberus is mentioned as is "il gorgoglio di Stige e d'Acheronte" ("the gurgling of Styx and Acheron" [12. 13]). Jealousy, herself, like Mussato's Charon (see A 2), has "Un rospo . . . in bocca" ("a toad in her mouth" [12. 21]) and is surrounded by symbolical monsters of Virgilian origin (12. 22 ff.). And like the traditional underworld ferryman, from her eyes she, too, casts flames—"Luce fiammeggia torbida e sanguigna" (12. 27). When through fear of evil Jealousy, Venus urges Adonis to flee, he wanders guided by the nymph Silvania into the realm of Falsirena, which is far below the surface of the earth in an underworld cavern. Here Adonis hears the noise of a large river and other horrible sounds:

> Passa, dietro a colei, ch'è sua maestra,
> De la cieca caverna entro la bocca;

Quando sente scrosciar de la man destra
Gran fiume, che con impeto trabocca;
Ed ecco rimbombar l'atre spelonche
D'un orribil romor come di conche.

(12. 153)

He passes into the mouth of the blind cavern, behind her, his teacher; then he
hears on the right the roaring of a large river, which flows along with vehemence; and behold the gloomy caves thunder with a dreadful din like that of
conches.

By the light of gems shining in the cavern, Adonis sees the banks of the river,
"E vide a gola aperta un crocodilo, / Di cui forse maggior non nutre il Nilo"
("and he saw a crocodile with open mouth, of which perhaps the Nile nurtures
none larger" [154]). In this underworld descent, interestingly, the crocodile is a
Charon figure! There is evidence of this in the following stanza, where we read
that the crocodile "Vennegli incontro e cominciò parole / Minacciose a formar
d'uman linguaggio" ("came toward him and began to form threatening words in
human language" [155]). And as in traditional descents, the youth's guide counters the guardian's opposition:

—Taci, bestia malvagia, odiosa al sole,
Non impedir nostro fatal passaggio.
Così vuol chi quaggiù può quanto vole,—
Disse Silvania e seguitò 'l viaggio.
Fuggì la fera ubbidiente e tacque,
E ritornossi ad appiattar ne l'acque.

(155)

Keep quiet, evil beast, hateful to the sun, don't impede our destined passage.
Thus wills she who down here can do what she wills," said Silvania and continued the voyage. The obedient beast fled and was silent and returned to hide
in the water.

Rather than refer to God's will as Dante does, Marino refers to the will of the enchantress Falsirena. The baroque playfulness of the episode, which is clearly
modeled on a traditional descent, lies in the substitution of this natural monster
for the boatman Charon. Marino's contamination of disparate sources is also illustrated in Silvania's explanation of this creature's origin, an explanation based on
the myth of Actaeon. The crocodile was once a man who saw Falsirena naked and,
splashed in the face with a magic liquid, was turned into a beast by her (cf. Ovid,
Met. 3. 138 ff.; Nonnos, *Dionys.* 5. 287 ff.).

An actual refernce to Charon occurs in the following canto, when Adonis resists
Falsirena's love. In her despair—"Da me l'inferno stesso è vinto e domo, / Nè
son possente a soggiogare un uomo" ("by me hell itself is conquered and tamed,
yet I am not powerful enough to subjugate a man" [13. 25]—the enchantress

calls up from hell the spirit of a dead warrior. Her aim is to learn the identity of Adonis's true beloved. In describing the *maga*'s incantation, Marino brings to mind Erichtho's evocation of a corpse in Lucan's *Pharsalia*. Like Erichtho, Falsirena invokes Pluto (*Tartareo Giove*, [13. 57]), Persephone, Hecate, the Fates, and Charon as well as other underworld powers. The ferryman and Cerberus are grouped together in octave 61:

> E tu, vecchio nocchier, ch'altrui fai scorta
> A quelle region malvage e crude,
> solcando l'onda ognor livida e smorta
> De la bollente e fetida palude;
> E tu, vorace can, che 'n su la porte
> De la gran reggia, ov' ogni mal si chiude,
> Perchè chi v'entra più non n'esca mai,
> con tre bocche e sei luci in guardia stai;
> . . .
> Assistete propizii a l'opra mia.
>
> (61, 62. 8)

And you, old ferryman, who guide others to those wicked and cruel regions, furrowing the wave always livid and wan, the wave of the boiling and fetid swamp; and you, voracious dog, who at the gate of the great realm where every ill is enclosed stand watch with three mouths and six eyes, so that he who enters never leaves again; attend propitious to my work.

The invocation, typical of Marino's eclecticism, contains reminiscences of not only the Latin classics (Lucan, for example, places Charon on Phlegethon, the *bollente*; Virgil on the *livida . . . palude*) but his Italian predecessors, notably Dante and Erasmo da Valvasone.

To conclude the discussion of Charon's representation in Marino's mythological epic, let me point to not only the skillful contamination of his varied sources and his wit but to his tendency to transform reality into myth, or to speak more exactly, to render myth into fable. The effect desired, of course, is marvel or pleasing novelty. Instead of a traditonal ferryman over an infernal river, we find the more exotic crocodile as guardian of an underworld realm. Even more surprising, of course, is the fact that this crocodile speaks much as Charon usually does; thus a beast that we might expect to find in popular lore is substituted for a figure familiar in mythology.

v. Conclusion

In summing up Dante's depiction of Charon, I spoke of the fullness of his descent model, noting all the various structural features and the poet's method of employing them. Concerning the later epic kinds, various in form and content, few develop a descent episode with equal completeness. Of those poems that do, most follow the pattern established by Virgil, although integrating Dantesque features into their descriptions of Charon. Dantesque language even appears in translations of Virgil, for example, that by Annibal Caro, published posthumously in 1581 and called "la bella infedele." So masterful a translation that it is treated as a work of art in its own right, this work contains a description of Charon's eyes as "occhi accesi / come di bragia." Following the extended imitations in the Quattrocento, most writers seem to shy away from lengthy portrayals, perhaps aware of the difficulty of emulating the *Commedia*'s representation of Charon. The predominance of chivalric romance and mixed chivalric epic in the Cinquecento results in fewer underworld adventures also. The lack of extended descent episodes in this form reflects the influence of both the more imitated French romances, romances that rarely depict Charon at length, and the increased interest in life on this earth, typical of the high Renaissance. When in the late sixteenth century attempts were made to return to a stricter epic type, the model was more often Homer than Virgil.[44] What happens to Charon, however, is interesting, since the name of the infernal boatman if not always the function continues to endure. Most outstanding, and perhaps traceable to the widespread practice of *contaminatio*, is the great variety of episodes in which Charon figures. In Petrarch, Charon is integrated into amorous elegy; in Pulci, he sings, and Morgante threatens to debeard him; in Bello, Charon ferries building supplies; in Folengo, he is threatened and beaten and also burns with lust; in Legname, he is enchained, hauled off by his foot, and hurled against a wall. In these and later poets, Charon becomes a comic figure with hilarious results. In Boiardo, the crossing is connected to a chivalric motif of revenge; in Ariosto, some identify Charon with a flying boat. Atlante refers to Charon as a type of death-demon, and elsewhere he hooks a swimming soul. In Christian epic, Charon is regarded as a demon and occasionally even as one of the rebellious angels. Pancetti, who sends devils to earth to take part in the battle between Venice and the French, no longer depicts Charon as a boatman but a warrior. Others working within tradition deform not only the boatman's features but also his actions. Marino with veiled wit goes so fare as to substitute a crocodile for Charon's role as guardian. In short, through their varied portrayals, these writers, whether medieval, Renaissance, or baroque, demonstrate both the vitality and the adaptability of myth.

Notes

1. I do not plan to concern myself with the polemic regarding the differences (or their lack) between the *poema epico* and the *romanzo cavalleresco*, a controversy occupying much of the latter half of the sixteenth century. Admittedly, there are variations of significance in both form and content between epic and romance. None, however, are major enough to prohibit the unified examination of the references to Charon they contain.

2. Despite the appearance of infernal rivers (some flaming and most crossed by bridges), fiery demons, and beasts with flaming eyes, Charon is absent, for example, from the descents found in the apocryphal *Gospel of St. Peter* and the *Gospel of Nicodemus*, both of the second century A.D., as well as in *The Voyage of Bran* (ca. A.D. 545) and St. Patrick's Purgatory (A.D. 1153). Nor is Charon mentioned in the famous visions of the *Apocalypse of Peter* (first century A.D.), St. Paul (fourth century),

Gregory the Great (sixth century), St. Furseus (ca. A.D. 640), Drihthelm (A.D. 696, as narrated by Bede), the Monk of Wenlok (eighth century), Wettin (A.D. 824), Bernold (mid-ninth century), the Monk of Eyrisham (A.D. 1196), Alberic (A.D. 1206), and Thurcill (A.D. 1206).

The closest possible references to Charon are perhaps those of the apocryphal *Acts of Thomas* (trans. Walker in the *Anti-Nicene Christian Library*, vol. 26) and the *Vision of Tundal* (A.D. 1149). In the earlier work, we read of a woman who, when restored to life by St. Thomas, relates her vision of hell. She speaks in part as follows: " 'A certain man,' she said, 'received me, hateful in appearance, all black, and his clothing exceedingly filthy' " (138–139). In *Tundal*, the best known and most elaborate of all medieval visions, we read about a monstrous beast, called Acharon (or Akyron), who swallows the souls of covetous men. Apparently a reminiscence of the classical Charon or the Acheron itself, this beast, into whose mouth nine thousand men might ride, provides an example of how classical mythology was often grossly transformed in the Middle Ages. For references to these visions, see works listed in the bibliography under Alessandro D'Ancona, Ernest J. Becker, C. S. Boswell, and Marcus Dods. I might add that Charon's influence is evident in sculpture in a legend connected with the death of Dagobert (ca. A.D. 628–638). In a monument to the right of the high altar in the Church of St. Denys near Paris we find a group of demons in a boat, one of whom wears a mantle and holds an oar. See Adolphe N. Didron, *Christian Iconography: The History of Christian Art in the Middle Ages*, 2:131.

3. The writing over the doors of hell underscores a significant difference between Dante's *Inferno* and the underworld of his model, the *Aeneid*. Whereas in Virgil the return from Dis is difficult, in Dante's hell, it is impossible: "Lasciate ogne speranza, voi ch'intrate" (3. 9). All quotations are from the editon of G. Petrocchi, *La Commedia secondo l'antica vulgata* (Florence: Società Dantesca, 1966). All translations of Dante are by Charles S. Singleton, *The Divine Comedy* (Princeton: Princeton University Press, 1970, 1973).

4. While Dante's ancient commentators have much to say about both the Acheron and Charon, as well as about other features of Canto 3, I will not burden the notes at this point with their ideas. Since many comments are in actuality quite external to the poem, I treat the commentators as a separate group in chap. 12, dealing with prose works. Following in the tradition of Servius and the medieval allegorizers, the commentators can be studied in relation to the mythographers.

5. I am indebted throughout my discussion of the *Commedia* to the many works on Dante listed in the bibliography. For an excellent bibliographical orientation to Canto 3, see Francesco Mazzoni, "Il Canto III dell'*Inferno*," pp. 321–322. Two later works of interest dealing with Dante's Charon are Paolo Nicosia, "Il Caronte dantesco ovvero della frodolenza demoniaca (III, 82–99 e 127–129)," pp. 81–98 and Emmanuel Hatzantonis, "Variations of a Virgilian Theme in Dante and Lope de Vega," 35–42.

6. The verses in question have been subject to much discussion despite their apparent simplicity. Most modern scholars accept the reference as implying that Dante will pass from the mouth of the Tiber to purgatory on the "vasello snelletto e leggiero" referred to in *Purgatorio* 2. 41. No early commentators before Alessandro Vellutello (1544), however, ever came to that conclusion. Those who commented on the passage interpreted it in the light of Dante's miraculous crossing at the end of the canto. See Francesco Mazzoni, "Il Canto III dell'*Inferno*," pp. 425–426.

7. While there are psychological reasons for Dante's silence, it is interesting to note that he often does not speak with classical figures, the most notable case being that of Ulysses and Diomedes. In this, Dante possibly reflects his reverence for Virgil, his intermediary, through whom he has acquired a knowledge of the figures of Greek myth.

8. The same words are used before Minos (*Inf.* 5. 22–24) and in varied form before Pluto (*Inf.* 7. 10–12).

9. Giacomino da Verona's description of demons might be cited as an example of the type. In his *De Babilonia infernale*, we read:

Lì è li demonii	cum li grandi bastoni,
Ke ge speça li ossi,	le spalle e li galoni,
Li quali cento tanto	plu è nigri de carboni,
S'el no mento li diti	de li sancti sermoni.
Tant'à orribel volto	quella crudel compagna
K'el n'ave plu plaser	per valle e per montagna
Esro scovai de spine	da Roma enfin en Spagna
Enanco k'encontrarne	un sol en la campagna.
K[i] i çeta tutore,	la sera e la doman
Fora per me' la boca	e rubel fogo çanban;

La testa igi à cornua   e pelose è le man;
Et urla como luvi;   e baia como can.

(97–108)

Esther Isopel May (ed.), *The "De Jerusalem Celesti" and the "De Babilonia Infernali" of Fra Giacomino da Verona.*

10. The moral sense of the adjective *nude* was first pointed out by Boccaccio, who says that the souls are "nude di consiglio e d'aiuto" (*Il comento alla Divina Commedia* 1:252). Others take the term in the sense of deprived of a body.

11. Natalino Sapegno refers to the equally onomatopoeic *stridor dentium* in Matthew 13. 42. *La Divina Comedia. I. Inferno,* p. 37.

12. It is very possible that the widely accepted meaning of *s'indugia* for Dante's *s'adagia* is incorrect. This intriguing verb, which has resulted in a host of studies, is discussed at length by Francesco Mazzoni, who cites the various critical positions of the ancients and moderns (pp. 439–442). The most logical interpretation of *s'adagia* would seem to be *si siede.*

13. While the image of leaves in the *Aeneid* (6. 309–310) lacks the Dantesque personification, Virgil elsewhere personifies a grafted tree that sees new leaves sprout and fruit that is not its own: "miraturque novas frondas et non sua poma" (*Georgics* 2. 82).

14. Some of these reasons will be examined in chapter twelve when the ancient commentators are discussed. Let me merely note that the range of speculation includes Charon, an angel, Virgil, Beatrice, Lucia, the wind itself, a supernatural force, and divine grace. See Francesco Mazzoni, pp. 452–455.

15. Cf. *Aeneid* 6. 413–414 and Seneca, *Hercules Furens* 776–777.

16. While Dante avoids an etymological treatment of the Acheron—his commentators amply fulfill this task—here, Dante apparently seizes on Servius's etymology "a tristia Styx dicta est" (*ad Aen.* 6. 134). Etymological and allegorical interpretation, as we will see later, have a long and felicitous history, extending through Macrobius and Fulgentius to Bernard Silvestris of Tours and on to the Italian Trecento.

17. The edition employed is cited in the bibliography (Primary Sources: Part 2, A 6). Hereafter all references to primary sources for part 2 will be indicated by the letter A and the number of the entry.

18. See for example Carlo Cordié, *Dizionario letterario Bompiani: Opere,* vol. 6, p. 9.

19. As Giuseppe Baretti says, imitators of great poets like Dante, Petrarch, Ariosto, or Tasso "hanno talvolta avuta la fortuna di scrivere qualche verso, che que' poeti non si sarebbono recati a grand'onta d'adottare per roba loro. Il Frezzi, esempigrazia, nel suo *Quadriregio* ha una buona quantità di terzine, che sono sputate dantesche" (*La frusta letteraria,* no. 3, 1 nov. 1763).

20. Elsewhere in this episode, for example, the adjective *grande* is used for Charon's mouth (52), a storm (77) and an old man (92). The paleness of the adjective is evident throughout but especially in the last instance where the size of the man is not only incidental but already included in the form of the noun itself, *vecchione.*

21. For the history of the topos, see Olin H. Moore, "The Infernal Council," as well as M. Hammond, "*Concilia deorum* from Homer through Milton."

22. Antonio Belloni, *Storia dei generi letterari italiani: Il poema epico e mitologico,* p. 344.

23. All translations of the *Africa* are by Thomas G. Bergin and Alice S. Wilson. See the primary bibliography, A 3.

24. H. J. Rose refers to the ugliness of the Gorgons but also to artistic representations of Medusa as a beautiful woman, common in the third to the fourth century B.C. (*A Handbook of Greek Mythology,* p. 30).

25. The adjective *crude* is a traditional epithet of little contextual significance and seems employed for its phonetic similarities to the word *crede.*

26. Massinissa refers briefly near the end of his lament to Cerberus and the underworld king. The youth asks Cerberus what Sophonisba's beauty will do if Orpheus's song conquered Cerberus's fierceness. Her beauty will soften not only Cerberus but will cause Pluto to forsake Proserpina.

27. An interesting though most likely fortuitous parallel to a traditional confrontation with Charon can be found in Petrarch's letter on climbing Mt. Ventoux. While any force of hindrance has aspects typical of Charon, the old man who attempts to discourage the two climbers at the foot of the mountain reacts much as an infernal guardian. After attempting to hinder the climbers in vain, he accompanies them a little way, points out the correct path, utters admonitions and sees that they leave behind all garments of burden. *Familiarum rerum libri* 4. 1.

28. References to Charon, while not common, are found in medieval French romances. The most noteworthy examples are the extended portrait of the demonic figure Caro in the twelfth-century *Roman d'Eneas*, a representation more terrifying than Virgil's, and the two ferryman Acharon and Acheron on the river Cochiton in the *Roman de Thèbes*.

29. See Douglas Owen, *The Vision of Hell: Infernal Journeys in Medieval French Literature*, pp. 183–185.

30. For the details on William, see Giorgio Sibzehner-Vivanti, *Dizionario della Divina Commedia*, p. 290.

31. "[E] vite venire corando a gran furore / vna ombra ydiose dal tempo anticho, / dal mezo yn zossa era un chaualo coredore / et vmana forma era quel de sopra" (Rodolfo Renier, A5, pp. 32–33).

32. [Q]uel prende suo remo quando y sono dentro yntrate, / gran colpy li dona per fianche e per costate" (Renier, A5, p. 34).

33. The spirit moves so fast to comply with the Saint's request that "sageta d'archo sì tosto non se descrocha" (Renier, A5, p. 37). One is reminded, of course, of *Inferno* 8. 13–14 where Phlegyas arrives with equal speed.

34. See, for example, the story of Circe and Ulysses in Book 1, Canto 6; that of Hippomenes who races Atalante and wins through the strategym of dropping three golden apples in Book 1, Canto 21; and that of Cadmus and the teeth of the dragon in Book 1, Canto 24. Numerous other examples of the integration of classical myth into the world of chivalry might be cited.

35. The poet was especially attracted by Dante's description of Charon's eyes. In Canto 2 of *Orlando furioso*, he refers in a simile to dogs who approach in anger "con occhi bieci e piú che bracia rossi" (A 12; oct. 5). And when St. John becomes angry, "gli occhi infiammò, che pareveno duo fuochi" (35. 30). Elsewhere in referring to the strength of old Sobrino, the poet recalls Virgil's description of Charon (*Aen*. 6. 304):

> D'una vecchiezza valida e robusta
> era Sobrino, e di famosa prova;
> e dice ch'in vigor l'età vetusta
> si sente pari alla già verde e nuova.

(40. 54)

Ariosto also referred more than once to ferrymen in terms reminiscent of Dante's celestial *nocchiero*. In the *Furioso*, when Ruggero flees from Alcina's domain to Logistilla's realm of virtue (10. 43–44), he finds a *vecchio nocchiero* who is described as *tutto benigno* and later referred to with the Dantesque term *galeotto* (*Inf*. 8. 17 and *Purg*. 2. 27).

36. Reminiscent of Jonah's situation, this episode also has many close parallels with Lucian's *True History*.

37. I have employed the following translations of the *Furioso*, indicated in the text by the translator's initials: BR = Barbara Reynolds, *Orlando furioso* (*The Frenzy of Orlando*): *A Romantic Epic by Ludovico Ariosto* (See A12). WSR = William Steward Rose: Ludovico Ariosto, *Orlando furioso* (see A12).

38. For Byzantine references to Charon, see chapter 8, note 11, and Panayota Kyriazopoulou, pp. 59–111. The *Apokopos* of Bergadis, first published in 1519, often refers to Charon, although without a precise description. The poet, after falling asleep one night, sees a dragon, falls down its throat, and finds himself in Hades, in Charon's realm. The episode brings to mind the later prose works of Anton Francesco Doni, where the boatman is found inside Lucifer (see chap. 12). For other early Italian editions of Bergadis, see Lino Politis, "Venezia come centro della stampa," vol. 2, pp. 443–482, especially pp. 452–456.

39. For an excellent article on Folengo's methods as illustrated in the Charon episode, see Emilio Bigi, "L'episodio di Caronte nel 'Baldus' e il metodo del Folengo," pp. 32–49.

40. While the situation is that of *Inferno* 3. 83–84, Folengo mocks Dante's use of infernal jargon in *Inf*. 7. 1, where Pluto shouts "Papé Satàn, papé Satàn aleppe!" For a further discussion of Charon's language, see Giorgio Bàberi Squarotti, "L'inferno del 'Baldus'," pp. 175–176.

41. A giant appears at a feast of Carlo Magno and kills Arcibaldo of Cremona "che più non ritornò in Lombardia, / anzi più presto a ritrovar Caronte." Cerberus is mentioned in 2. 5–6.

42. Giuseppe Toffanin, *Storia letteraria d'Italia: Il Cinquecento*, p. 407.

43. In Tassoni, for example, Charon is referred to in lines reminiscent of Lucan's portrayal of a tired ferryman: "Caronte lasso in trasportar gli uccisi, / ch'a passar Stige scenderan sotterra, / bestemmierà

la maledetta sorte / che gli diè in guardia il passo de la morte'' (7. 39). Giove, who is talking of how many will be killed in an upcoming battle, has just compared the dead to fallen trees, perhaps a mock exaggeration of the traditional image of men as leaves. Interestingly, we find Charon, rather than the souls as in Dante, cursing his fate.

44. I refer, for example, to the varied attempts represented by Trissino's *L'Italia liberata dai Goti,* Alamanni's *Avarchide*, Giraldi's *Ercole*, Bernardo Tasso's *Amadigi* and *Floridante*, and Torquato Tasso's *Rinaldo*, none of which, to my knowledge, contains depictions of Charon.

10
Dramatic Forms

Turning to dramatic productions of the fifteenth to the seventeenth century in Italy, we are again struck by the variety of generic types. They range from medieval *sacre rappresentazioni*, early mythological fables, farces, and *intermedi* to comedy, serious comedy, tragedy, tragicomedy, pastoral plays, sacred drama, and melodrama, not to mention other more minor subtypes. What is most surprising is that Charon appears as a character or is mentioned in almost all of these generic variations, with the possible exception of the more regular sacred drama of the Cinquecento and Seicento, ranging from Cecchi's *Figliuol prodigo* (1560s) to Andreini's *Adamo* (1613).[1] While later dramatic works, influenced by Aristophanes and Lucian, develop the boatman at much greater length,[2] I restrict the chronological range of this chapter to works from the Renaissance, extending exclusively from Poliziano's *Orfeo* (1480) to Alessandro Mattei's *Morte di Orfeo* (1619).[3] Charon's possibilities in drama are amply represented during these years.

Not surprisingly, the representaion of Charon is most extensive in the so-called irregular forms—the *favola mitologica*, the *intermedio* (or *intermezzo*), and melodrama. It is well known that learned writers producing standard drama most often chose the plays of Plautus and Terence (and occasionally Aristophanes) as models for comedy and for tragedy, the works of Sophocles, Euripides, and Seneca. Whatever the model, however, sixteenth-century works of classical imitation tend to be based on the Ciceronian formula of "imitatio vitae, speculum consuetudinis, imago veritatis." With this orientation, writers of the time rarely delve into the underworld and as a result hardly ever refer to Charon; the fact that some occasionally do so attests the boatman's popularity in other genres. To facilitate my analysis, then, I group the works to be discussed into four categories: (1) early mythological drama; (2) farce and tragicomedy; (3) *intermedi*, dating to the second half of the Cinquecento; and (4) later mythological drama or melodrama. For other works of tragicomedy, tragedy, comedy, serious comedy, and the pastoral where Charon's role is more minor, let me merely refer the reader to the bibliography (Primary Sources: Part 2).

i. Mythological Fables

Poliziano. Angelo Poliziano's *Favola di Orfeo*, the first major effort in the vernacular to combine medieval form (the *sacra rappresentazione*) with classical content (pagan myth) in drama, contains an episode patterned on the denial of crossing related by Virgil and Ovid.[4] Although Charon is absent, the play provides a structural pattern that when imitated by others includes the boatman. The descent motif enters the play when Orfeo has been informed of Euridice's fate and resolves to liberate her from the underworld. In hell, he addresses first Cerberus and then the Furies, asking them to calm their anger, weep with him, and open the iron doors. Plutone marvels at the power of the descender's music, which has stopped the wheel of Ixion; calmed the ceaseless activity of Sisyphos, the Danaids, and Tantalos; and quieted Cerberus and the Furies (230–237).

Minos, fearful of deceit, takes the part of Charon in epic and opposes this descender, warning Plutone by recalling previous heroes who descended with evil intentions. Orfeo, like Aeneas, denies any intention of harming the realm.[5] Reminding Plutone of his own love for Proserpina, he asks for Euridice, referring to her as "la tenera vita e l'uva acerba" ("the tender vine and unripe grape" [272]), an image reminiscent of Charon's comparison in Lucian's *Cataplus*. Later, having once again lost his beloved, Orfeo resolves to return to the *plutonia corte* (317), but now his singing is of no aid. A Fury opposes his progress, saying, "Più non venire avanti: anzi el piè ferma" ("do no come any further; on the contrary, hold your foot firm" [318]), thus fulfilling the role of Charon in the story told by both Virgil and Ovid.[6]

Favola di Orfeo e di Aristeo. Near the end of the fifteenth century and beginning of the sixteenth, an anonymous *Favola di Orfeo e di Aristeo* was written in which Caronte appears in act 3 in a dialogue with Orfeo and Plutone. The situation is not Orpheus's second attempt to enter hell but parallels Minos's speech in Poliziano's *Orfeo*. The boatman tells the descender, "Pastore, il tuo volere è troppo ingordo: / tu credi ognor trovar quai giù pietade, / ma del tuo credar troverai discordo" ("shepherd, your desire is too greedy; you believe you will always find pity down here but you will find your belief to be mistaken" [A 37; 3. 109–111]). That Charon was chosen to counter Orfeo's plea instead of Minos is due not only to the author's adherence to his classical sources but perhaps also to the influence of Dante and the classical epic poets in whose works the boatman is a hindrance. The anonymous author, in fact, seems to be acquainted with both the *Commedia* and *Vita Nuova*.[7]

Niccolò da Correggio. Aside from the early Orfeo works, Charon is also mentioned in the *Fabula di Cefalo* of Niccolò da Correggio (A 38). Based on Cefalo's story related in Ovid's *Metamorphoses* (7. 690–862), with a modified happy ending, the play also reflects the influence of Poliziano's *Orfeo*. At one point, Cefalo for example, tells Aurora, "dunque, madonna, il tuo desio correggi" ("well then, my lady, correct your desire" [25]), recalling Pluto's words to Orfeo, and later when Cefalo's wife Procri flees, he cries, "Deh non fugire" ("Oh, don't flee"), much as Aristeo to Euridice. When Procri is struck by Cefalo's spear, her last words recall those of Euridice to Orfeo on their separation: "Cagione è stato el troppo ardente amore, / e sola intendo de passar quel rio" ("the reason has been your too ardent love and alone I intend to cross that river'' [99–100]). The allusion to the river, of course, introduces the motif of the underworld crossing. Cefalo, in fact, laments as follows:

> Questa fu la mia vita, viva e morta,
> questa al mondo mi fe' viver felice,
> questa mi fia seguendo optima scorta,
> questa mi fu più ch'al suo Orfeo Euridice,
> questa seguendo, al fiume mi trasporta,
> ché 'l legno di Caron tocar non lice,
> questa è colei per cui vivea contento,
> questa morî per gielusia del vento!

(174–181)

This one was my life, living and dead; this one made me live happy in the world; may this one for me, following, be an excellent guide; this one was more to me than Eurydice to her Orpheus; this one will bear me, following, to the river, since it is not permitted to touch the bark of Charon; this one is the one for whom I used to live content; this one died out of jealousy of the wind!

Every verse of the octave except that devoted to Charon's boat begins with the pronoun *questa* referring to Procri. In the elegiac refrain, the reference to Charon's boat stands out as an exclamation of grief. Despite Cefalo's protestations, he realizes that he cannot pass beyond the barrier of Charon's boat; as Procri says, she will cross the river alone.

The final allusion to crossing the underworld river recalls Virgil's depiction of Charon and his refusal to transport anyone who is unburied. As one of the Muses says to a nymph: "Tu, Galatea, con quella ardente face / la pirra accendi, e sia Procri sepolta, / e poi in quella urna el cener sia servato, / che 'l passo in Stigie non li sia negato" ("you, Galatea, light the pyre with that burning torch, and let Procri be buried, and then let her ashes be preserved in that urn, so that the passage across Styx not be denied to her" [218–221]). While the act concludes with a lyric lamentation by the chorus, "piangete, silve alpestre, fiumi e rive" (222), the play itself, much like the *Orfeo*, which ends with a bacchanalian celebration, continues on to a festive denouement. Diana, in fact, stops the proceedings, brings Procri back to life, and reconciles the couple in lasting peace.

ii. Farce and Tragicomedy

Caracciolo. Before passing to the *intermedi*, I will discuss two early, irregular works with mythological episodes; I refer to Caracciolo's literary farce *Lo imagico* (A 39), where Charon appears as one of the dramatis personae, and Epicuro's *La cecaria* (A 40), a strange work that is professedly a tragicomedy. Pier Antonio Caracciolo's farce begins with the entrance of an aged and bearded magician accompanied by four disciples, one bearing a golden bough ("insegno de quello hebe da Sybilla Enea"), one a book on magic arts, one *un vase grande* for fire and incense, and the last a knife to cut magic circles. Following this initial *didascalia*, we read: "Appresso venea Charonte in una barcha con Aristippo et Diogene philosophi et Catone Censorino" ("next, Charon came in a boat with the philosophers Aristippus and Diogenes and Cato the Censor" [A 39; p. 429]). In effect, within the dramatic framework, we find a dialogue of the dead.

Rather than descending to the underworld, the magician invokes souls through an incantation. Drawing several circles on the ground, the necromancer invokes Hecate, asking that his power equal that of others such as Iosue, who stopped the sun, Amphione, who called the rocks to form Thebes, and Orpheo, who descended to hell and put Cerberus to sleep. From Hecate, the magician turns directly to Charon:

> Festina il tuo uiagio el remo prendi
> Charonte et presto actendi ad quel che dico
> Et mena in lo tuo antico et leue grippo
> Diogene Aristippo; et in unione
> C'ze uenga ancor Catone censorino
> Per lo uoler diuino che te incita
> Menar ad questa uita in le toe riue
> Ogne animal che uiue alto et directo
> Ornato di ragione et de intellecto.

(A 39; pp. 434–435)

Hasten your voyage, take the oar Charon and attend quickly to what I say; and bring Diogenes and Aristippus in your ancient and light craft; and let Cato the Censor come also. In accord with divine will, which moves you, bring from your banks to this life every soul who lives lofty and straight, endowed with reason and intellect.

The spirits—cynic Diogenes, hedonistic Aristippus, and virtuous Cato—appear at this and talk in philosophical terms of their lives. Their discourse is finally put to an end by Charon, who interrupts Cato's comment that death comes on one suddenly like the wind, by saying:

> Conuien che ormai festina perchio sento
> chiamarme con lamento al triste lito
> Da un numero infinito dalme infrecta
> Che con la mia barchetta allaltra riua
> Dogne letitia priua le conduca
> che essendo io lloro Duca et scorta fida
> Bisognia che le guida et piu non resti
> Pero siati presti intrati in barcha
> Che troppo e stata scarcha and'amo via
> Ch'io uo lassarui oue ui tolsi pria.

(p. 443)

By now we must needs hasten because I hear myself called with lamentation to the sad shore by an infinite number of souls in haste, so that I may take them with my little boat to the other bank, destitute of all joy. Since I am their leader and faithful guide, I must escort them and remain no more. Therefore, be quick, get in the boat, which has been empty too long; let's go away because I want to leave you where I picked you up before.

Characterized by his haste and solicitude, Charon desires to fulfill his task as a faithful servant of the gods; any signs of anger or belligerence are absent from his speech. Instead, he reminds us of the scrupulous but congenial ferryman familiar from Lucian. Charon is not employed for comic nor heroic effects but as a simple narrative (or dramatic) tool to facilitate the entrance and departure of the invoked characters.

Epicuro. Just as Caracciolo's farce is, in effect, a work of narrative, Marc'Antonio Epicuro's *tragicommedia* is in large part a lyric work. Consisting of one act with three scenes, the play voices the love laments of three *ciechi* (blind men). Each man, relating his tale of woe, touches on a wide variety of lyric motifs. Charon enters the picture in a lengthy baroque mataphor when in narrating the beauty of his beloved, the *Vecchio cieco* compares his pains to those of hell:

> Disposto dunque a entrare
> per la dolente porta,
> presi il desir per scorta;
> Amor mi fu Caronte,
> ma non varcommi per l'usato fiume,
> ma per la riva sol di Flegetonte;
> per l'aria senza lume,
> la barca, che nel fondo ognor s'apria,
> fu tema e gelosia;
> li remi fûr pensier, vela il tormento,
> a cui li miei sospir fean sempre vento.
>
> (A 40; scene 2)

Disposed then to enter the gates of sorrow, I took desire as my guide; Love was my Charon, but he didn't carry me across the usual river, just along the bank of Phlegethon; through the air without light the boat, which was always coming open at the bottom, was fear and jealousy; the oars were thoughts, torment the sail, to which my sighs were always a breeze.

Inverting the typical medieval allegorization of the infernal crossing, Epicuro depicts falling in love as a descent to the underworld. Guided by his desire, the Vecchio is ferried into hell/love by Charon/Cupid. The boat, always leaky, is fear and jealousy; the oars his thoughts, the sail his torment, filled by the wind of his sighs. While the imagery is startling and developed with originality, we are reminded of Petrarch's sonnet 189 "Passa la nave mia colma d'oblio," where the poet sees himself as a ship guided by his enemy Love. In Epicuro, the incongruity of the extended metaphor lies above all in equating Caronte and Amore. Because of the nature of love, Charon, of course, is placed on the fiery river Phlegethon rather than the cold Acheron.

In these early dramatic forms, Charon's role is based most often on his functions in nondramatic classical forms. The Orpheus and Cefalo myths belong traditionally to lyric and mythological poetry, forms in which Charon's role is relatively minor. When a dramatist, such as the anonymous poet of the *Favola di Orfeo e di Aristeo* introduces a more fully developed boatman, the author adheres to not only the narrative tradition of mythological poetry but also to the structural pattern of epic. Thus in the descent episode, the ferryman becomes a form of hindrance, a guardian who verbally accosts the descender. Correggio and Epicuro, on the contrary, avoid the typical narrative and epic pattern, since they merely refer in passing to Charon in their dramatic works. The boatman, physically nondescript, is mentioned in conjunction with lyric motifs, first in an elegiac lament and then in a lover's plaint. Finally, Caracciolo employs the ferryman in a dramatized dialogue of the dead, but the evocation of Charon and his boat of souls perhaps owes more to Lucan and the epic tradition than to Lucian, with whom the author may have been unfamiliar.

iii. *Intermedi*

With the advent in the sixteenth century of regular drama based on classical form and verisimilar content, underworld mythology becomes merely a verbal accoutrement, and as a consequence, descents are rarely dramatized. Charon does appear as a character, however, in lighter mythological scenes serving as *intermedi* between the five acts of the erudite forms.[8] While at first of minor importance, though always of popular appeal, the *intermedi* in time acquired a prominence in their own right as a dramatic form of festive brilliance and grand spectacle.[9] Prominent among the spectacular effects is the underworld display, a scene familiar from the *sacre rappresentazioni* but carried to new heights of extravagance. With the inclusion of classical monsters, and especially Charon and his ferry, the poet and scenographer induce a sense of marvel in the audience. Most often, this effort seems to entail not only vivid costumes, both Virgilian and Dantesque, but the actual process of ferrying a boat on stage.

Cini. One of the more celebrated productions is the myth of Cupid and Psyche for the marriage of Francesco de' Medici and Giovanna d'Austria in 1565 (see A 43). Written by Giovan Battista Cini, the *intermedi* develop Apuleius's story in six stages and in doing so bring to the stage a variety of sumptuous scenic effects, including carts descending from heaven, Charon's boat in hell, and musical instruments disguised as swans, weapons, and serpents.

Charon himself appears in the fifth *intermedio*, where Psiche, accompanied by Gelosia, Invidia, Sollecitudine, and Disprezzagione, is sent to Proserpina. After Psiche has sung a madrigal, the spectators see an opening in the floor

> di cui fumo e fiamma continua e grande pareva che uscisse, e si sentí con spaventoso latrato, e si vide con le tre teste di essa uscire l'infernal Cerbero, a cui ubbidendo alla favola si vide Psiche gettare una delle due stiacciate che in mano aveva, e poco dopo con diversi mostri si vide similmente apparire il vecchio Caronte con la solita barca, in cui la disperata Psiche entrata, gli fu dalle quattro predette sue stimulatrici tenuta noiosa e dispiacevol compagnia
> (A 43; Vasari, pp. 140–141)

From which it appeared that smoke and a continuous large flame were coming out, and we heard and saw the infernal Cerberus come out of this opening with a frightening bark and with his three heads. In agreement with the fable, we saw Psyche throw him one of the two mashes which she had in her hand, and soon after we saw Charon, along with several monsters, appear in the same way with his accustomed boat, into which hopeless Psyche entered and was accompanied by the annoying and disagreeable presence of her four prementioned tormentors.

While Charon's appearance is not described in detail, it is clear that he was an old man, probably dressed in Virgilian fashion, and with his boat, easily identifiable. With the disappearance of the infernal ferryman and his passengers, the fifth *intermedio* comes to a close. When the sixth begins, all has been resolved happily, for Psiche and Amore appear on Mount Helicon rejoicing that she has returned safely from hell.

Leone De Sommi. The same myth was employed by Leone De Sommi Hebreo in his *intermedi* represented shortly before 1573 in Mantova; according to Bonilla, the work as a whole, found in the Biblioteca Nazionale di Torino (Codice IV, 58), is still unpublished.[10] De Maria, however, has edited a fragment of *intermedio* 3, where Charon appears as one of the characters (A 44) and is listed as well in the index of *personaggi*. In the passage cited by De Maria, Astrea is counseling Psiche about her voyage to the underworld:

> Chiedi prima a Caron di qua dal fiume
> che trapassar ti voglia a l'altra riva
> et lassa ch'ei dalla tua propria bocca
> tolga una delle due monete ch'io
> a questo fin ti porgo, et l'altra poi
> si pigliarà nel tuo tornare indietro.

First ask Charon if he wants to carry you from this side of the river to the other bank and let him take from your mouth one of the two coins which I am giving you for this purpose; the other one will be taken on your trip back.

Psiche's response is enclosed in two resounding hendecasyllables: "Invido avaro inessorabbil vecchio / che vuol mercede, al suo dovuto officio" ("envious, avaricious, inexorable old man who wants pay for his due function"). The buildup of adjectives describing the *vecchio* is especially effective; as in Apuleius, Charon is defined above all by his avarice.

The actual crossing appears to take place on stage; it is signaled by the loud sound of water and chains:

> Si udì un grande mormorar d'acque et con istrepito di catene e di foco si scoperse la bocca de l'inferno et si vide appresso comparir di là dal fiume Caronte sopra la sua barchetta. . . .(A 44; pp. 288–289)

> We heard a great murmuring of water and the mouth of hell came into view with an uproar of chains and fire, and then we saw Charon appear from the far side of the river in his little boat.

Just as in Cini's representation, the effect of a boat moving across the stage must have appealed to both the poet and his audience desirous of unusual stage effects.

Giovanni de' Bardi. The only actual description of Charon's physical features in these works that I have been able to find comes from one of six *intermedi* performed in Florence for the marriage of Ferdinando I de' Medici with Cristina di Lorena in 1589. Writtten by Giovanni de' Bardi, with stage machinery and *apparati* designed by the ducal architect Bernardo Buontalenti, the *intermedi* were among the century's most elaborate. Described, in fact, as "singolari e con rappresentazioni e macchine quasi soprannaturali" ("singular and with almost supernatural machinery and representations" [Settimani, *Diario*, ms. del R. Arch. di Stato di Firenze, vol. 5, c. 130]), they were given several repeat performances (see A 46).[11]

In order to allow for a greater degree of inventiveness, each *intermedio* was a unit complete within itself. While the first, for example, represented the harmony of the spheres and several others developed varied mythological tales, the fourth depicted the "demoni celesti e infernali." The action, initiated by a magician who first summoned the celestial spirits, was accompanied by the music of Giulio Caccini. Playing a lute and backed by the harmony "di lire grandi, e di bassi, di viole, di liuti, d'un violino, d'arpe doppia, bassi di tromboni, e organi di legno che sonavano dentro," the magician next evoked the demons:

> All'entrar dell'Inferno si vedeva il vecchio Caronte, con la sua barca, come par che 'l dipinga Dante, con barba lunga e canuta; intorno agli occhi, simili a fuoco, alcune ruote di fiamme; e empieva la barca d'anime che facevano a gara per imbarcarsi, perchè egli con lo infocato remo batteva chi s'adagiava. Per tutto l'Inferno, come è detto, [c'erano] infinite schiere di brutti *Diavoli* e d'anime tormentate, e spezialmente intorno a Lucifero. (A 46; pp. 30–31)

At the entrance of hell we saw the old man Charon, with his boat, similar it seems to how Dante paints him, with a long and hoary beard; around his eyes, similar to fire, some wheels of flame. He was filling the boat with souls who were competing to embark because he with his inflamed oar was beating anyone who delayed. Throughout all of hell, as I said [there were] infinite groups of ugly devils and of tormented souls, and especially around Lucifer. . . .

Along with other Dantesque and classical creatures who are described at length are Gerione, Plutone, Satan, Minos, the Arpie, Centauri, Minotauro, and Cerbero. With its vividness, baroque profusion of color and monstrous action, the scene brings to mind the work of such modern cinematographers as Fellini. Although Lucifer, who is described at great length, steals the scene in this particular instance, Charon stands out as one of the spectacular aspects of the underworld. Not only does he appear with his boat, but his eyes have wheels of flame, probably painted on the actor, and he swings a burning oar. (Whether the oar was lit like a torch or merely painted to seem on fire is unclear.) At any rate, the Dantesque episode appears to have been brought to life on the stage with startling verisimilitude.

Le nozze de Mercurio e Filologia. De Sommi, who helped initiate such spectacular effects with his *intermedi* on Psyche previously mentioned, is also the author of a pastoral play, *Le nozze di Mercurio e di Philologia* (1584), which very possibly was adapted or served as a source for the *intermedi* performed with Battista Guarini's *Il Pastor fido* in the fall 1598 in Mantova. As related by an eye witness, the Neapolitan Battista Grillo, the *intermedi* were "bellissimi, et pomposi, sì per la molta spesa de i vestiti, com'anco per l'apparato, et gran numero delle machine, che intervennero ne gl'intermedij" ("very beautiful, and grand, both for the high cost of the garments, and for the apparatus and great number of machines which took part in the intermedi" [A 47; p. 406]).

The fable itself was presented as an allegory of the marriage of Philip III of Spain (Mercurio) and Queen Margherita of Austria (Filologia). Juno, in the scene following act 1, tells Iride to spread the news of a divine marriage. The messenger goddess is to descend to earth, "anzi sin'all'inferno" ("on the contrary all the way to hell"), to invite the gods to attend the celebration (p. 408). After Iride has announced the wedding in the Elysian Fields,

s'aprì la terra, et essa penetrò a basso, et tutto ad un tempo s'aprì parimente una gran voragine, et se vidde l'inferno aperto co 'l Can Cerbero, et la città di Dite in mezz'a molte fiamme. . . . (p. 408)

The earth opened and she descended to its depths, and all of a sudden a great chasm opened in the same way, and hell was seen open with the dog Cerberus and the city of Dis in the middle of many flames.

From these flames appears "Plutone, con i tre Re suoi sudditi," and the god expresses his desire to attend the wedding—"voleua prima de tutti gl'altri andarsene a rallegrare.'' With these words, Charon appears in his boat and transports Pluto across Lethe: ''all'hora Caronte nella sua barchetta s'appresentò, et postolo dentro, lo fece trauersare il fiume Lethe . . .'' (pp. 408–409). Having arrived at the Elysian Fields, Pluto ascends in a cloud toward the sky, accompanied by music. Even the ascent, like the appearance of Charon's boat, pertains to the marvelous. A cloud from heaven meets the infernal lord halfway, absorbing him and his cloud and carrying them out of sight. The *intermedio* closes with a group of poets singing in praise of the couple, saying, among other things, ''quest'alme felici hoggidì han fatto all'inferno i cieli amici'' (''these happy souls today have made friends of heaven and hell'' [p. 409]).

Schiafenati. As a final example of an *intermedio* where Charon appears, let me refer to one performed in Milan in 1599 for the entrance of the infanta Isabella, wife of the archduke Alberto d'Austria. The *intermedio*, one of five written by Camillo Schiafenati, all with different plots, deals with the popular topic of Orpheus and Eurydice, a myth congenial to musical treatment. Foreshortening the fable, the *intermedio* begins with Euridice dead and Orfeo resolving to go to hell for his beloved.

At his singing, the doors of hell open, and Orfeo contemplates the underworld scene. Along with Plutone and Proserpina on a throne, the musician sees the infernal judges, the three Furies, infernal spirits, damned souls, classical sinners and their punishments (specifically Tantalo, Iscone, and Sisifo), and the Elysian Fields, where Euridice dwells.

Vedevasi altresì Caronte varcar con la sua barca Euridice, vedevasi anche alla porta dell'Inferno Cerbero, e in somma tutte quelle cose rappresentate, che si leggano nella descrittione dell'Inferno fatta da Virgilio, da Ovidio e da altri Poeti. (A 48; p. 226)

Charon was seen also, transporting Eurydice with his boat; also Cerberus at the door of hell, and in short all those things were represented which one reads in the description of hell made by Virgil, Ovid, and other poets.

Stage effects, again then, include a ferrying by boat. Having observed the surroundings, Orfeo begins to sing and brings *grandissimo refrigerio* to the damned. The ensuing dialogue between Orfeo and Plutone was also put to music despite the fact that as the narrator notes, ''non pare che il decoro, e verisimilitudine della favola admetta musica in Plutone,'' adding that ''fù ciò introdotto per maggior sodisfattione de gli aspettatori, e ascoltanti, e per gusto di chi poteva commandare'' (''it does not seem that decorum and the verisimilitude of the fable would allow music in Pluto. That was introduced for the greater satisfaction of the spectators and listeners and for the pleasure of he who could so command'' [p. 227]).

In the resolution of the fable, Charon appears again:

Tosto che la gratia fù da Plutone conceduta comparve Caronte à passare Euridice con la sua barchetta, e perchè contra 'l patto Orfeo riguardò indietro,
venne di traverso 'l Fato in habito di diavolo, che la riportò, donde s'era par-
tita, e chiusesi l'Inferno, e tornaronsi à sentire le pene, e gli stridi de
dannati. . . . (P. 227)

As soon as grace was conceded by Pluto, Charon appeared to carry Eurydice
across in his little boat, and because Orpheus looked back contrary to the pact,
Fate came from the opposite way dressed as a devil and took her back from
where she had departed. Hell closed itself and the sufferings and screams of the
damned were heard once more.

Whether or not Charon has a speaking (or singing) role in this work is not stated.
Given the author's lack of compunction concerning verisimilitude, perhaps the
boatman does break into song or speech. Whatever the situation, later musicians
and poets, such as Monteverdi, are uninhibited, adding to the heritage of
Charon's representations an aria-singing ferryman.

Before turning to *melodramma* proper, however, let me emphasize again in
conclusion that the appearance of Charon in these *intermedi* not only functions to
further the narrative but more importantly as an element of marvel. However
staged, the river crossing must have offered the poet a chance to indulge in unusual scenic effects. The actual representation of the boatman, moreover, varies
according to the subject. In some instances, notably when a classical fable is
dramatized, Charon embodies in his functions the essence of the classical underworld as opposed to a Christian hell with medieval demons. In other essentially
nondramatic extravaganzas, such as the "Comparsa di demoni," he reflects the
influence of Dante. In effect, the scene at the Acheron in *Inferno* 3 is reproduced
on stage. In either instance, Charon adds to the rich display of the *intermedi*.

iv. Melodrama

The classical tales that were developed in both the early mythological plays and
the *intermedi* continue to be employed by writers of melodrama. In fact, the
birth and development of melodrama in Seicento Italy owes much to the *intermedi* of the preceding half century. As Enrico Furno has noted,

né il melodramma, né gran parte del teatro secentesco hanno caratteri così
propri, che molti dei loro elementi non debbano rintracciarsi in quella speciale
forma di drammatica spettacolosa, allegorica . . . fiorita superbamente in
Firenze, durante tutto il Cinquecento. ("Il dramma allegorico," 12:103)

neither melodrama nor a large part of the theater of the seventeenth century
have characteristics of their own, because many of their elements must be
traced back to that special form of spectacular, allegorical drama . . . which
flourished superbly in Florence during the sixteenth century.

As we have seen from the *intermedi* discussed, Florence is not the only city where this type of drama flourished. It was in Florence, however, that melodrama found its first practitioners, although representations of their work soon spread to Mantova and other cities.[12] As examples of Charon's appearance in this new genre, I will examine *Euridice* and *Arianna* by Rinuccini, *Orfeo* by Striggio, and the *Morte di Orfeo* by Mattei.

Rinuccini. Ottavio Rinuccini's *Euridice* (A 49) is ostensibly a tragedy, although the poet has superimposed a happy ending on the familiar story. The descent of Orpheus into the underworld is depicted in scene 4.[13] Unsure of his surrroundings, the musician questions his guide Venus. Her response situates the scene at the Acheron and establishes Orpheus as the first mortal to descend into Hades:

> L'oscuro varco, onde siam giunti a queste
> rive pallide e meste,
> occhio non vide ancor d'alcun mortale:
> rimira intorno, e vedi
> gli oscuri campi e la città fatale
> del re che sovra l'ombre ha scettro e regno.
>
> (430–435)

The dark passage, through which we have reached these pale and sad shores, no mortal eye ever saw before; look around and see the dark fields and the fatal city of the king who rules and holds sway over the shades.

Orfeo's song, asking the shades of hell to cry at his lament, leads to a confrontation with Plutone. As in Poliziano, Orfeo reminds the infernal lord that he also desired and pursued his beloved. At Plutone's hesitance, Proserpina adds her urgings, followed by the encouragement and rationalizations of the other infernal beings. Radamante, for example, implies that as lord of the underworld, Plutone is free to break its rigid laws; even Caronte adds his consent in a five-verse speech:

> Quanto rimira il sol, volgendo intorno
> la luminosa face,
> al rapido sparir d'un breve giorno
> cade morendo e fa qua giù ritorno:
> fa' pur legge, o gran re, quanto a te piace.
>
> (559–563)

All that the sun sees, turning around his luminous torch, falls dying at the rapid disappearance of a brief day and returns down here. Make a law, O great king, such as pleases you.

What Orfeo himself claims in Ovid and Poliziano ("Ogni cosa nel fine a voi ritorna, / ogni vita mortale a voi ricade") is here espoused by the infernal boatman himself. To Poliziano's note of human fatality, Rinuccini adds the Petrarchan motif of the fleetingness of time. As the boatman responsible for the return of all souls, these words are appropriately expressed by Charon. In the context of the drama, Charon is never referred to by name, but his identity was undoubtedly easily established by his physical attributes. Following Charon's words, Plutone yields, and the *canoro amante* (593) is praised by the chorus for his daring deed. The final two scenes of the brief work are devoted to celebration and rejoicing. With a series of adynata, the chorus closes the drama, prasing the triumphs of Orfeo and his poetic power.

Besides making an appearance on stage in a singing role in the *Euridice*, Charon is also referred to in Rinuccini's *Arianna* (1608), another *tragedia di fin lieto* (A 52). Performed in Mantova with music by Claudio Monteverdi, the melodrama reflects the influence of Ariosto just as the *Euridice* reflected that of Poliziano. The eight scenes of the play relate the story of Arianna's abandonment by Teseo and her subsequent marriage to the immortal god Bacco. The action, initially tragic, permits the development of much lyric lamentation, the most famous being Arianna's ode "Lasciatemi morire" in scene six. Among the tragic motifs, such as the fallacious counselor with his specious reasoning—"non è fallo, signore," he tells Teseo, "sprezzar quelle promesse e quella fede / che tra lascivi ardori / incauto amante a bella donna diede" ("it's not a fault to break those promises and that faith which an incautious lover gave to a beautiful woman in the midst of lustful ardors" [358–361])—or the messenger who wonders how the sun can bear to see these deeds (679–681) or the chorus's musings on false hopes (682–683), we find the motif of underworld gloom. But the motif is employed far differently in Rinuccini than in Seneca: In Rinuccini, the motif pertains to the false hopes of the chorus, aroused when the noise of horns and drums announce the arrival of a hero. Hoping that it is Teseo, the chorus recalls such past heroes as Orfeo and Alceste. The reference to Orfeo brings to the poet's mind the familiar features of the descent:

> Su l'orride paludi
> de l'Acheronte oscuro,
> sentier penoso e duro,
> per mostri orrendi e crudi,
> fermò vedovo amante
> l'innamorate piante.
>   Non le tre fauci immense,
> formidabil latrato,
> non di Caron turbato
> l'orride luci accense
> da la sì dubbia impresa
> arrestâr l'alma accesa.

(910–921)

The widowed lover stayed his enamored steps on the awful swamp of dark Acheron, a harsh, painful path because of the horrendous and cruel monsters. Not the three immense jaws, the formidable barking, not the awful flaming eyes of angry Charon could hinder his aroused soul from so dubious a deed.

The reference to Charon, influencing Marino's later lyric treatment of Orpheus, is based on neither Ovid nor Virgil's account of Orpheus's descent. In the classical sources, the boatman is encountered only on Orpheus's second attempt to enter Hades, and in both authors, pictorial description is lacking. Rinuccini, recalling perhaps both the *Aeneid* and the *Commedia*, depicts a boatman who is both angry (*turbato*) and fearsome. As in Dante, the poet uses "eyes of flame" to emphasize Charon's fierceness. The use of *luci*, a poetic word for *occhi*, which recalls by antithesis lyric references to the light that burns in the eyes of beautiful maidens, is especially appropriate in Charon's case. That these are not *luci celesti* is however, rendered amply clear by the adjectives *horrid* and *inflamed* that modify the noun.

Striggio. Alessandro Striggio, librettist for the *Orfeo* put to music by Claudio Monteverdi, follows in general form the *Euridice* of Rinuccini, although the work as a whole ends in the loss of the poet's beloved. Also, unlike Rinuccini's use of *La Tragedia* to deliver the prologue, Striggio employs *La Musica*; the change is significant. Both Peri and Caccini, as members of the Florentine Camerata, based their music on Greek drama, thought to be delivered with a monodic recitative based on declamation rather than singing. Monteverdi, instead, to quote Marrone, "creò il vero melodramma col 'recitativo drammatico' e con le arie, elevando il dramma ad effetti inauditi di commozione e facendo partecipare l'orchestra all'azione" ("created true melodrama by means both of dramatic recitative and of arias, elevating drama to unheard of effects of emotion and making the orchestra participate in the action" ["Il mito di Orfeo," p. 152]). Rather than subordinating music to text, Monteverdi employs all the means available to him, combining the old polyphonic style with the new single-voice technique and using all the instrumental effects known at the time in order to emphasize the dramatic elements of the work itself.[14]

Once again, to return to the development of the *favola* we find Orfeo resolving to go to the underworld in act 2:

> N'andrò sicuro a' più profondi abissi,
> E, internerito il cor del Re de l'ombre,
> Meco trarrotti a riveder le stelle.
>
> (250–252)[15]

> I will go down to the deepest abysses,
> I will soften the heart of the king of shadows,
> and I will bring thee once more to see the starlight.

The Dantesque reminiscence, incidentally, is only one of many to come. Act 3 presents the descent, which is developed in greater detail than in Rinuccini. Guided by Speranza, Orfeo arrives "A questi regni tenebrosi e mesti, / Dove raggio di sol giamai non giunse," hoping "Di riveder quelle beate luci / Che sole a gli occhi miei portano il giorno" ("into this principality of shadows, / where

the rays of the sun can find no entrance [hoping] to see once more those blessed
rays of sunshine, / which only to my eyes bring back the morning" [317–324]).
Following this baroque play of light and darkness, Speranza describes the scene:

> Ecco l'artra palude, ecco il nocchiero
> Che trae gli spirti ignudi a l'altra sponda,
> Dov' ha Pluton de l'ombre il vasto impero.
> Oltra quel nero stagno, oltra quel fiume,
> In quei campi di pianto e di dolore,
> Destin crudele ogni tuo ben t'asconde.
>
> (325–330)

> See, here lie seething quagmires,
> see here the ferryman
> who beareth naked spirits to yonder shore,
> where Pluto sways the gloomy realm of shadows
> Beyond this slimy lake, this stagnant river,
> lie the dark fields of sighing and of weeping,
> where fate most cruel all thy desire concealeth.

The range of descriptive detail (*atra palude, nero stagno, quel fiume*) recalls
Dante's *variatio*, and the emphasis on nude spirits brings to mind those before
Charon's boat in *Inferno* 3. To render yet more obvious his tribute to the Florentine poet, Striggio has Speranza cite the verse "lasciate ogni speranza, voi
ch'entrate" ("all hope abandon ye who enter here" [337]). Unable to enter the
lower realm itself, Speranza leaves Orfeo, who laments being abandoned. The
following speech is Charon's:

> O tu ch'innanzi morte a queste rive
>   Temerario ten' vieni, arresta i passi;
>   Solcar quest'onde ad uom mortal non dassi
> Nè può coi morti albergo aver chi vive.
> Che? vuio forse, nemico al mio signore,
>   Cerbero trar da le Tartaree porte?
>   O rapir brami sua cara consorte,
>   D'impudico desire acceso il core?
> Pon freno al folle ardir, ch'entr'al mio legno
>   Non accorrò più mai corporea salma,
>   Sì de gli antichi oltraggi ancor ne l'alma
>   Serbo acerba memoria e giusto sdegno.
>
> (350–361)

> O thou who before thy time to these shores comest,
> most audacious of men, nor stay'st thy footsteps,
> these gloomy waters no mortal man may traverse,
> nor with the dead consort him he who liveth.
> What? Perchance thou an enemy doest come now,

Cerberus to snatch from Tartarean portals?
Or wouldst thou steal from my lord his beloved spouse,
thou whose heart beareth flames of lewd desire?
Restrain thy foolish boldness my bark to enter,
accustomed never mortal's weight to carry
since outrages of yore, which on my soul weigh
heavy, in bitter remembrance, and righteous anger.

Structurally, the boatman's speech is based on the *Aeneid*, but Striggio has enriched it with reminiscences of Dante and later poets. Since the classical sources of the Orpheus myth avoid a lengthy Charon scene, later poets who wish to develop the crossing motif most often avail themselves of epic features.

Orfeo's response to the boatman is both original and ingenious. Addressing Charon as "possente spirto e formidabil nume" (362), Orfeo says, "non viv'io, no, che poi di vita è priva / Mia cara sposa, il cor non è più meco, / E senza cor com' esser può ch'io viva?" ("thou powerful spirit, of Gods most dreadful form / . . . / I live no more, whose breath of life is taken, / my bride beloved; my heart no more dwells in me, / and without heart, say, how can I be living?" [365–367]). The baroque witticism continues when Orfeo says he has passed through *l'aer cieco* not to *l'inferno* but to *il paradiso*, for wherever so much beauty is there it is heaven (368–370). Claiming to be the first mortal to descend, Orfeo breaks off to address the eyes of his beloved and then returns to Charon:

> O de le luci mie luci serene,
>> S'un vostro sguardo può tornarmi in vita,
>> Ahi, chi niega il conforto a le mie pene?
> Sol tu, nobile Dio, puoi darmi aita,
>> Nè temer dèi, che sopra un'aurea cetra
>> Sol di corde soavi armo le dita
>> Contra cui rigid' alma invan s'impetra.

(374–380)

> O glorious lustrous eyes, eyes of my lov'd one,
> a single glance from you my life restoreth:
> Ah, who would deny me solace for my sorrow?
> Thou only, noble God, hast power to aid me;
> And nothing fear from my golden zither;
> Only with strings honey sweet arm I my fingers,
> 'gainst which e'en strongest spirit in vain opposeth.

In his attempt to placate the boatman, Orfeo apostrophizes him as a noble god, an unusual phrase despite the Virgilian precedent. It is not unusual that Orfeo claim to be the first descender, since Rinuccini also described the underworld as never before seen by *alcun mortale* (432). However, by following Virgil's confrontation scene in *Aeneid* 6 and Ovid's scene between Orpheus and Pluto in the *Metamorphoses*, where reference is made to previous descents, Striggio falls into a slight contradiction. That is, he first has Charon refer indirectly to the evil aims of previous descenders ("do you wish to drag off Cerberus or carry away Pluto's consort?") as well as to his intention to carry no more bodies across because of the insults he has suffered and then soon after has Orfeo claim he is the first mortal to descend. Poliziano avoids the contradiction by not claiming Orfeo's precedence. Minos, in fact, clearly refers to previous unspecified descenders. In presenting Orfeo as the first descender, Rinuccini wisely avoids referring to any other descents.

Despite Orfeo's plea for mercy, Charon, though touched, remains adamant:

> Ben solletica alquanto
> Dilettandomi il core,
> Sconsolato cantore,
> Il tuo pianto e 'l tuo canto.
> Ma lunge, ah lunge, sia da questo petto
> Pietà, di mio valor non degno affetto.
>
> (381–386)

> Strains of surpassing sweetness!
> Thou delightest my spirit,
> O thou grief-stricken singer,
> with thy songs and lamenting;
> But far, oh far lies pity from my bosom,
> for pity with my valour ill accordeth.

At this, the unfortunate lover begins a song that by its power puts Charon to sleep; as Orfeo informs us,

> Ei dorme, e la mia cetra
> Se pietà non impetra
> Ne l'indurato core, almeno il sonno
> Fuggir al mio cantar gli occhi non ponno.
>
> (399–402)

> He sleepeth, and thus my zither
> though his hard heart to soften
> with pity nought availing,
> at least brings slumber.
> His eyes cannot escape the charm of my singing.

Apparently entering the boat by himself—"Tempo è ben d'approdar su l'altra sponda" ("Then courage, e'er tis too late / No delay, I must haste to yonder shore" [404])—unless Charon has fallen asleep there, Orfeo leaves the scene, and the chorus of spirits launches into a song of praise for man's deeds.

Having detailed the scene of confrontation at the river, Striggio does not feel compelled to bring in Charon as one of the interlocutors in the underworld proper. Instead, in act 4, Proserpina has already convinced Plutone to release Euridice, although not without the restriction that the lover not look behind him. Deviating from Rinuccini's version, then, Striggio depicts Orfeo as turning around not only out of love but also mistrust of Plutone. Perhaps, he thinks, Euridice is not following, the gods of Avernus having kept her in envy of his happiness. When the descender loses his beloved, a spirit orders her back to hell:

> Torna a l'ombre di morte,
> Infelice Euridice,
> Nè più sperar di riveder le stelle,
> Ch'omai fia sordo a prieghi altrui l'Inferrno.
>
> (538–541)

> Turn again to death's shadows,
> Eurydice ill-fated.
> No longer hope to see again the starlight.
> For deaf from henceforth is Hades to thy pleadings.

Despite Orfeo's attempts to follow her, he cannot overcome the power of the infernal spirits. As the Chorus of Spirits says in closing the act,

> Orfeo vinse l'Inferno e vinto poi
> Fu dagli affetti suoi.
> Degno d'eterna gloria
> Fia sol colui ch'avrà di sè vittoria.
>
> (558–561)

> Behold how Orpheus conquer'd Hades with magic lyre,
> yet conquer'd was by his desire.
> He only aye is glorious,
> Who's o'er himself victorious.

The moralistic tone, typical of Counter-Reformation times, continues in act 5, which finds Orfeo after an echo scene conversing with Apollo about the fleetingness of human existence and the eternity of life in heaven.

Mattei. The final operatic work of interest to us is the *Morte di Orfeo* of Alessandro Mattei (A 53). Put to music by Stefano Landi in 1619 in Rome, this five-act work is subtitled a *tragicomedia pastorale.* Caronte, who makes his appearance in act 5, figures among a large cast of characters including Teti, the river Ebro, Aurora, a Fate, three Euretti, Mercurio, Apolline, Bacco, Giove, Orfeo's mother Calliope, Fosforo, shepherds, messengers, choruses of shepherds, satyrs, maenads, gods and a priestess of Bacco as well, of course, as Orfeo and Euridice themselves. Avoiding the traditonal emphasis on Orpheus's descent as a mortal, Mattei presents the musician's infernal voyage following his murder by enraged Menadi.

The dead poet's soul opens act 5 with a song addressed to the spirits of Avernus, asking

> Or m'accogliete in seno
> Di quel bel lido ameno,
> Ove tra mirti ed amorose fronde
> Euridice confonde—in dolce quiete
> I suoi sospir col muto suon di Lete.
>
> (661–665)

Accept me now in the bosom of that beautiful shore so pleasant, where among myrtles and loving leafs Eurydice mingles her sighs in sweet stillness with the mute sound of Lethe.

The following speech is Charon's:

> Qual'ombra sento in questi
> Spechi d'averno rimbombar soave?
> Altri lugubri e mesti
> Scendon qua giù, che di lasciar gli è grave
> Il ciel; questi gioisce.
> Or di', chi sei,
> Ombra, che canti al suon di tanti omei?
>
> (675–681)

What shade do I hear in these antrums of Avernus resound so softly? Others, lugubrious and sad, descend down here, others to whom it is grievous to leave the sky; this one rejoices. Now say, who are you, shade, who sings to the sound of so many dear me's?

The boatman accosts the descender, aroused not as Virgil's boatman by seeing an armed man but by the unusual sound of joy. Orfeo's response is a delightful twist, given the great familiarity with his descent as a living person:

> Non riconosci Orfeo,
> Caronte? Ecco ch'arrivo,
> Nuda ombra, al comun porto;
> Ove già scesi vivo,
> Or, rotta la prigion, vi giungo morto.
>
> (682–686)

Don't you recognize Orpheus, Charon? Behold I arrive, a nude shade, at the common gate; where once I descended alive, now, broken the prison cell, I reach you dead.

Having identified the boatman by name, Orfeo asks for passage to the other bank and directions to find Euridice. Charon, however, is cruel and obstinate:

Ancor vaneggi, ancora,
  Fredda ombra, porti al sen foco amoroso?
  Euridice dimora
  In luogo impenetrabile e nascoso.
  Getta pur tra quest'ombre ogni tua speme,
  Vedovo abitator di fredde arene!

(691–696)

Still you rave, still, cold shade, do you bring in your breast amorous fire? Eurydice dwells in a place hidden and impenetrable. Cast aside among these shades all your hope, widowed inhabitant of cold sand!

Struck by this "sì crude risposte" ("so cruel response" [698]), Orfeo pleads again for passage, so that he may soon see on the horizon "Il sol, vivendo, morto, / Al mio morir, risorto" ("the sun, living, dead, at my dying, arisen anew" [701–702]). Charon, however, is adamant, denying passage for traditional reasons:

Va' pur errando vagabondo intorno,
  Anima disperata, ad altro lido;
  Non v'ha varco per te, nè albergo fido,
  Finchè il lacero e sparso
  Corpo, unito non sia sepolto et arso.

(703–707)

By all means go wandering around vagabond, soul without hope, to another shore, there is no passage for you, nor faithful dwelling, until your torn and scattered body, gathered together, is burned and buried.

In the second scene, Mercurio arrives, wondering why Ordeo is trying to cross to hell when he is destined to live in heaven. The musician claims he would rather suffer in hell with Euridice then live in heaven with her. With this statement, the play takes a turn indicative of Counter-Reformation morality. Mercurio, claiming that Euridice has lost all remembrance of the world as well as her love for Orfeo, tells Charon to draw his boat to the shore, so that Mercurio may seek Euridice in Elysium. Charon obeys the god, but remains hostile to the dead spirit:

Ma tu non t'accostar, alma perversa;
  Va' pur girando altrove e lassa il canto
  Et apprendi formar, misera, il pianto.
  E se pur anco hai di cantar desio,
  Le pause canterai del remo mio.

(735–739)

But you, don't you approach, perverse soul; go along wandering elsewhere and forget your singing and learn, wretch, to form tears. And if still you desire to sing, you will sing the pauses of my oar.

Following a brief four-line lament by Orfeo, Mercurio announces their return with Euridice. As Orfeo notes, she is no longer beautiful nor does she recognize her beloved. Mercurio, she says, "chi è quel folle, / Che nel gelo di morte arde d'amore?" ("who is that madman, who in the chill of death burns with love?" [749–750]). When Orfeo protests his love for her, she treats him with indifference and finally departs.

Mercurio next offers Orfeo the water of Lethe, at which Charon breaks into a lengthy song, encouraging the dead soul to drink and find peace. Coming from the mouth of the cruel boatman, the words are unexpectedly lyrical, reminding us of the dithyrambic chorus in Poliziano. The following is a representative stanza with refrain:

> Beva, beva questo liquore,
>   Chi piagato si sente il cuor.
>   Beva, beva chi vuol dal petto
>   Trar le noie e sentir diletto.
> Non più affanni,
>   Non più morte,
>   Non più sorte;
>   Privo di doglia,
>   Pien di piacere,
>   Venga, chi ha sete a bere.

(785 ff.)

Drink, drink this liqueur, he who feels his heart wounded. Drink, drink, he who wishes to draw worries from his breast and feel delight. No more troubles, no more death, no more fate; empty of grief, full of pleasure, come, he who is thirsty to drink.

Freed of his grief, his love, and his anger, Orfeo rises to heaven with Mercurio. The final speech of the scene offers a glimpse of a comical boatman, blustering threats and complaining:

> Tante volte all'inferno e torni e parti,
>   Alma di cantar vaga,
>   Et in cantar un'ostinata maga.
> Or pàrtiti una volta, e non tornare
>   Nè a veder, nè a cantare;
>   Chè, se tu torni, certo ti prometto,
>   Per l'anima d'Aletto,
>   Cacciarti in un cantone;
>   Fatto immobile, batto col bastone.

(800–808)

So many times you come and go from hell, oh soul desirous of singing, and in singing an obstinate charmer. Now leave once and for all, and do not return, neither to see nor to sing; because, if you return, I promise you for sure, by the soul of Alecto, to chase you into a corner; once you're immobile to beat you with a club.

The play concludes with a final scene where the Chorus of Shepherds praises Orfeo, now eternally alive in heaven, and Giove offers him divinity. The boatman's role, though confined to the final act, has surprising scope. The diversity of attitudes, ranging from watchful belligerance and wonderment to the scornful and threatening, from lyric sweetness to comic blusterings, attests the originality of the portrayal while pointing out at the same time the inconsistencies that occasionally develop in works coming late in a long tradition. Developing the familiar tale in an unexpected manner, Mattei's *Morte di Orfeo* is pleasingly fresh.[16]

On the whole in works of melodrama, Charon is singularly fortunate. He is not only referred to by others but appears himself on stage in a singing role. Following the small part given the ferryman by Rinuccini, both Striggio and Mattei seize the opportunity for dramatic conflict offered by the figure. In Striggio, the boatman's role is based in part on the more developed action sequence of epic. Charon is overcome, of course, not by the golden bough nor physical force nor divine will but by the fantastic power of music. The necessity of conquering a recalcitrant boatman provides an excellent occasion for melodic virtuosity. Finally in Mattei, the ferryman is carried to his greatest extension as an operatic character. His role transcends the traditional bonds placed on the figure. In fact, in offering a purifying drink to Orpheus, Charon participates along with Mercury in the deification of the dead musician.

v. Conclusion

To conclude the discussion of Charon's representation in drama, it must be admitted that most often his role is relatively small and insignificant. It is difficult to speak of structural units save in all but a few works. When Charon is present, the influence is more likely to be from classical epic, mythological narrative, or dialogue rather than drama. The Senecan prologue where the soul of a dead person rises from Acheron to set the scene is one of the few truly dramatic sources for the figure (see A 41). Aside from the unusual and somewhat irregular comedy of Pellippari (A 42), which belongs in large part to the allegorical tradition and mythological drama, erudite forms of both comedy and tragedy seem to avoid extended portrayals of the ferryman and rarely include even minor references to him by name. Charon is occasionally present in the so-called irregular forms, especially in the early mythological *favole, intermedi*, and later mythological plays set to music. In these works, often based on the famous myths of descent—those of Orpheus and Psyche, for example—the sources employed are again most often more lyrical than epic (Ovid's *Metamorphoses*, Virgil's *Georgics*) or narrative (Apuleius's *Golden Ass*). References to the ferryman are often elegiac in tone. Where

Dante or classical epic has entered the picture, the boatman is seen as both wary and cruel, with his physical appearance patterned on Virgil. If Charon is occasionally a comic figure, blustering threats, as in the late work of Mattei (1619), the reminiscence seems to be of the Italian mock-heroic poets, who were especially popular during the early years of the Seicento, rather than Lucian or Aristophanes. As a final observation, perhaps the most noteworthy aspect of Charon is that he manages not only to survive in dramatic works but to acquire new and intriguing representations.

Notes

1. Underworld motifs are not lacking, however, with one of the popular ones being the harrowing of hell. Where this theme is found, for example, in *La discesa di Gesú all'inferno*, many devils are referred to by name, but none is called Charon. The more common names are Lucifero, Satanasse, Belzabutte, Asmodeo, Astaroth, Aliabutte, Calcabrino, and so forth. Interestingly, among the many demons, most merely numbered, in *La Rappresentazione del dì del giudizio* by Feo Belcari and Antonio Araldo, there appears the character Minos, *demonio*. Another popular theme related to life after death in sacred works is the *Contrasto del povero col ricco*, where Lucifer and his demons are described. The *Detto dell'Inferno*, a dialogue between a *vivo* and a *morto*, is an excellent example, offering a voyage to hell that occasionally seems to have classical reminiscences but in reality is based on Christian tradition. The punishments, for example, according to Vincenzo De Bartholomaeis (*Origini della poesia drammatica italiana*, pp. 296 ff.), are patterned on those of the *Visio Sancti Pauli*. For more on the appearance of Satan and his devils in these works, see Alessandro D'Ancona, ''Personaggi divini e diabolici nelle Sacre Rappresentazioni,'' vol. 2, pp. 1–13. Later sacred drama presents us with another topos, that of the infernal council, but again Charon seems to be lacking. G. B. Andreini, for example, names his demons Lucifero, Melecano, Arfarat, Lurcone, Ruspican, Maltea, Dulciato, Guliar, and so forth. For a bibliographical orientation to the *sacre rappresentazioni* in general, see the article by Luigi De Vendittis in the *Dizionario critico della letteratura italiana*, ed. Vittore Branca, s.v.

2. See, to list just one example of several, Pier Jacopo Martello's *Femia sentenziato* (1724).

3. Again, many later works of the Seicento, Settecento, and Ottocento contain representations of Charon, especially the *melodrammi*, which are often based on the myths of Psyche, Orpheus, Alcestis, and the like. Among the many examples with Charon, let me list the following works: G. B. Fusconi's *L'Amore innamorato* (1642); Francesco Buti's *Orfeo* (1647), represented in Paris with music by Luigi Rossi; Diamante Gabrielli's *Psiche* (1649); Francesco Melosio's *Orione (1653)*; Savaro di Mileto's *Psiche deificata* (1668); G. B. Lulli's *Alceste*, librettist Philippe Quinault (1647); Paolo Rolli's *Orfeo* (1743); Ranieri de' Calzabigi's *Alceste* (1768); and Ettore Romagnoli's *Sisifo* (1914).

4. My source is the edition of Giosuè Carducci, *Le Stanze, l'Orfeo e le Rime* (Florence: Barbèra, 1863).

5. Rather than imitating Virgil's *Aeneid*, however, Poliziano most likely recalls Ovid's *Metamorphoses* 10. 17–23.

6. Soon after the representation of the *Favola di Orfeo*, Poliziano's work spawned a series of imitations. Among the plays that attempted to develop the brief tale is the five-act *Orphei tragoedia*, possibly written by Antonio Tebaldeo. While dividing the work into a prologue and five acts, the poet has not greatly expanded the content. In fact, while Pliziano wrote 600 verses, the five-act play has only 434, although the author introduced a chorus of dryads and the satyr Mnesillo. When Orpheus pleads his case in hell, there is no Minos to suggest caution; rather, Proserpina is immediately touched by his plea. When Orpheus considers returning a second time for his lost Eurydice, he is hindered not by Charon or simply by an unnamed Furia but Tesifone herself. The play, incidentally, is contained in Carducci's editon of Poliziano's works. Another anonymous *Representazione de Orfeo e de Euridice*, referred to by Isidoro Del Lungo (*Florentia: Uomini e cose del Quattrocento*, p. 348), amplifies the mythological characters, going so far as to include the centaurs.

7. Luigi Marrone, "Il mito di Orfeo nella drammatica italiana," cites several parallels with both works, some however seeming to be fortuitous. He compares, for example, Charon's words in the anonymous play (3, 109–111) cited in note 6 to those of Dante's Charon (*Inf.* 3. 91–92), passages actually quite dissimilar.

8. While I have not been able to find a copy of Galeotto Del Carretto's *Noze de Psyche et Cupidine* (1502), I might mention that his work serves as a stepping stone to the *intermedi* of the last half of the sixteenth century. A comedy written in varied meter, the play follows with great fidelity the tale of Cupid and Psyche as related by Apuleius. Along with allegorical, mythological, and human characters appear such creatures from the Apuleian fable as ants, an eagle, and the Tower. Most likely, then, Charon figures in the play, either as a character or in a reference. Like the later *intermedi*, which develop this familiar story with Charon as a character, the comedy has a happy ending, with Jove consenting to the marriage of Cupid and Psyche. I have relied on the description of Del Carretto's work found in Enrico Furno, "Il dramma allegorico nelle origini del teatro italiano," pp. 62–64.

9. The well-known lament of Anton Francesco Grazzini, il Lasca, in the prologue to his comedy *La Strega* deserves to be cited: "Già si solevano fare gl'intermedi che servissero alla commedia, ma ora si fanno le commedie che servono agl'intermedi." The same lament reappears in his madrigal "La Commedia che si duol degli Intermezzi." I quote Grazzini from Angelo Solerti, *Gli albori del melodramma*, vol. 1, p. 9.

10. Adolfo Bonilla y San Martín, *El mito de Psyquis: Un cuento de niños, una tradición simbólica y un estudio sobre el problema fundamental de la filosofía*, p. 75.

11. The importance of these *intermedi* extends beyond spectacular scenic effects. Solerti claims that it is from them that "si suol datare il primo passo del melodramma, anche per la considerazione che il terzo di essi divenne poi il primo quadro della *Dafne*" (A 46; p. 18).

12. For a discussion of melodramma and the Camerata dei Bardi, see Umberto Renda and Piero Operti, *Dizionario storico della letteratura italiana*, s.v. *melodramma* as well as Angelo Solerti, *Le origini del melodramma* and *Gli albori del melodramma*, vol. 3, pp. 3–153.

13. This episode, set in Avernus, offered, as Marrone notes, the opportunity for "un grande sfoggio d'apparati e di meccanisimi, che, senza dubbio, non riuscì inferiore, nè meno splendido, che undici anni prima, quando il Bardi e il Buondelmonti l'avevano adoperata per uno degl'intermezzi della *Pellegrina* di Girolamo Bargigli [*sic*] recitata in Firenze il 2 marzo 1589" (Marrone, "Il mito di Orfeo nella drammatica italiana," p. 148). The reference, of course, is to the *intermedi* discussed in note 11. The correct date is actually May 2, 1589.

14. See Anna Amalie Abert, "L'Orfeo by Claudio Monteverdi" in Claudio Monteverdi, *L'Orfeo, favola in musica, parole di Alessandro Striggio* (Archiv Produktion: Musikhistorisches Studio der Deutschen Grammophon Gesellschaft, n.d.), no page numeration. The translations from Striggio's *Orfeo* are those of R. L. Stuart in *L'Orfeo, favola in musica di Claudio Monteverdi, parole di Alessandro Striggio* (Archive Production, n.d.).

15. My source, with slight modifications, is listed first in A 50.

16. I might note that the idea of developing a second descent of Orpheus had been used earlier by Gabriello Chiabrera in a "Favoletta da rappresentarsi cantando," entitled *Il pianto d'Orfeo*, performed in 1608. Composed of only 258 verses with three characters (Orfeo, Calliope, and Plutone) and a Coro di Pastori, the work has as its setting the forests of Taenarus at the mouth of hell. For an edition of the work, see Solerti, *Gli albori del melodramma*, vol. 3, pp. 89–100.The motif itself, of course, can be traced to the classical world, specifically to Seneca, who depicts Hercules' second descent, now as a dead soul, in *Hercules Oetaeus* 1550–1556.

11

Lyric and Related Poetic Forms

We cannot hope to account for all references to Charon in a genre with as much scope as lyric poetry. The lyric production of the Cinquecento alone is immense, and Charon can be found in all periods, including the modern, in both major and minor authors.[1] Isolated linguistic features in the description of Charon and the underworld crossing in Dante also appear in many later poets. Two examples are Poliziano's reference to Polifemo's *lanose gote* in the *Stanze per la giostra* (1. 116) and Campanella's use of *morta gora* for the swamp of ignorance in his political poem "Al carcere." Quite often in the briefer poetic forms, Charon simply becomes a rhetorical figure and thus lacks descriptive detail. He is referred to, however, in conjunction with epic, tragic, mythological, satirical, and religious themes, and I will briefly mention a few examples of each. I will also deal with the lengthier nonlyric poems on mythological subjects in this chapter.[2]

i. Epic Motifs

Petrarch. Francesco Petrarca, in referring to the lofty topics of epic poetry, alludes briefly to Charon in the first eclogue of his *Bucolicum Carmen*. Entitled "Parthenias" (A 54),[3] the ecolgue consists of a poetic contest between Silvius, an interlocutor representing the poet himself, and Monicus, the poet's brother Gherado. As is typical of Petrarch's psychology, the conflict contrasts the epic poetry of Homer and Virgil (Parthenias) to the sacred works of David. Silvius praises his pagan sources, noting that they sang of Rome and Troy and the three great brothers, Jove, Neptune, and Pluto. In describing Pluto, Silvius speaks of the god's companions:

> torva latus servat coniunx, aterque paludis
> navita tartaree piceas redit itque per undas,
> tergeminusque canis latrat; tum dura severis
> pensa trahunt manibus fixa sub lege sorores;
> quinetiam stygias eterna nocte tenebras
> anguicomasque simul Furias templumque forumque,
> tum silvas et rura canunt atque arma virosque,
> et totum altisonis illustrant versibus orbem.

(83–90)

And by his side [stands] his grim consort, while back and
    forth over the pitchy
Ooze of the stream of the marshes of Tartarus wends the dark
    boatman.
Hark to the three-headed hound a-baying, mark there the
    sisters
Spinning as the law bids them, the harsh threads with fingers
    relentless.
Aye, and they sing of the shades of the Styx and of eternal
    darkness;
Snake-headed furies they tell of and likewise of temple and
    forum;
Meadows and groves they describe and celebrate arms and
    great heroes.
So they light up the whole world with their lofty verses'
    effulgence.

Attracted by the Greek and Latin poets' lengthy portrayal of the underworld, Petrarch, in the person of Silvius, describes the more famous inhabitants of Hades, among them Charon, the *ater . . . navita* on the pitchy waves of the Tartarean swamp. Monicus's response is to note that David sang of the one and only God "quem turba deorum / victa tremit" ("whom the gods He defeated / Reverence" [91–92]).

Poliziano. While Petrarch refers to Charon as he appears in Latin epic, Angelo Poliziano, or an unknown Medicean poet, depicts the boatman in Dantesque terms (A 57).[4] In the second of two *capitoli*, "In morte del Magnifico Lorenzo de' Medici," the poet praises Piero de' Medici, who succeeded his father in the signory. Addressing the city of Florence, he asks for "pace, fede, alma concordia e iustizia" (14), continuing:

> Superbia in fuga al centro precipizia,
>   Del baratro infernal d'ira e di sdegno;
>   Discordia, invidia, a casa di malizia;
> Tutte scacciate nel tartareo regno,
>   Figliole della notte, ove Acheronte
>   Discorre il vecchio sempre d'ira pregno.

(16–21)

Let pride in flight rush headlong to the center of the infernal abyss of anger and disdain; discord, envy, to the house of wickedness; dispel all to the tartarean realm, daughters of night, where over Acheron rushes the old man always full of anger.

The request, worded in Dantesque language, has the vibrancy of a Savonarolian sermon. The vices listed—pride, anger, scorn, discord, envy, malice, all daughters of Night—belong more rightly in hell not on earth. Having mentioned the Tartarean realm, the poet characterizes it with an incidental but descriptive note. It is here that Charon hastens back and forth over the Acheron. The boatman himself is appropriately portrayed in Dantesque terms as old and heavy—literally, pregnant—with anger.[5]

Both poets describe the ferryman as a typical aspect of the underworld. But while Petrarch describes Charon in terms characteristic of classical epic, the Medicean poet depicts him with Dantesque features. As in the *intermedi*, Charon in lyric may serve as either a representative figure of the Hades of secular heroic poetry or a symbol of the hell of Christian epic.

ii. Tragic or Elegiac Motifs

Petrarch. The identification of Charon with the moment of death is a common theme in much lyric poetry; the gloomy ferryman appears in Petrarch's *Canzoniere* (A 54) in this context. In a sonnet addressed to a friend, Petrarch asks the recipient to accept three gifts, all suited to divert the individual from thoughts of love to thoughts of the brevity of life. In the final tercet, Petrarch turns from his friend to himself:

> Me riponete ove 'l piacer si serba,
> tal ch'i' non tema del nocchier di Stige:
> se la preghiera mia non è superba.

Put me away where pleasure is preserved, such that I not fear the ferryman of Styx, if my prayer is not too proud.

Asking his friend to hold the poet in his heart, Petrarch says that thus he will not fear the ferryman of Styx himself. In effect, the reference is to death, visualized through the boatman who ferries all to the beyond. This reference to Charon, however, is merely a verbal phrase with no life of its own. The paleness of the reference evokes no horror nor any reason why we should fear the ferryman. As a periphrastic figure drawn from the world of classical mythology, Charon raises the imagery to a level of educated refinement.

Poliziano. Like Petrarch, Angelo Poliziano employs the image of Charon's crossing in lyric in order to elevate the poetic tone from the common to the loftier. In an elegy addressed to the Benivieni family, the poet uses the boatman to symbolize the tragic fate that would have overtaken many were it not for the doctor Antonio Benivieni, whose abilities are praised:

> Nam quoniam stygiam facile est tibi pellere mortem,
>   Qual facile invidiae frangere colla potes?
> Felix cui liceat fati pervertere legem,
>   Quem propter cymba stet leviore Charon,

Stamina qui valeas invita nectere Parca
Atque animas vacua restituisse colo.

(A 57; 7–12)

Since it is easy for you to drive away Stygian death, can you easily break the necks of envy? Happy is he to whom it is permitted to subvert the law of fate, because of which Charon stands in a lighter boat, who has the power to weave the threads, though fate is unconquered, and to restore souls, though the distaff is empty.

Charon's boat enriches the poem through illustration, adding color and imagery to the poetic texture.[6] The vision of Charon's boat riding higher on the waves because of the lack of dead souls is very effective.

Serafino Aquilano. The crossing in Charon's boat may not only stand for a tragic event to be avoided but also a desired end to a life of torment. While not referring to Charon by name, a sonnet of Serafino Aquilano expresses, through the imagery of the underworld crossing, the poet's desire for peace and death (see A 59). As such, this sonnet is an early example of the *disperata*, a poetic form common near the end of the fifteenth century and beginning of the sixteenth, in which the poet gives vent to his despair, usually in a series of imprecations and invectives. In Serafino's poem, where the last two lines read: "Però vorria uscire di tanti guai, / Passare in su la bara d'Acheronte" ("for this reason I would like to get out of so many troubles, to cross over in the boat of Acheron" [A 59]),[7] the crossing by way of Charon's boat is a symbol of not only death but leaving behind one's earthly cares.

Cavassico. A more violent *disperata* written by the notary Bartolomeo Cavassico (ca. 1480–1555), presents Charon himself. The poet begins his lament with the following forceful lines:

O diavol, vienme a tuor e non star pi,
Chiama Caron e famme davrir l'us,
Po' che la crudelaza vuol cussì

(A 61; p. 14)

Oh devil, come get me and delay no longer; call Charon and kill me off, since the merciless girl wants it thus.

In his despair, the poet asks the devil not only to carry him away but also to call Charon and "to make me open (*davrir = aprire*) the exit (*l'us = l'uscio*)," since his cruel beloved wishes him to die. The force of the allusion to Charon is that he seems to be a death-demon who will possibly aid in killing the poet. Perhaps Cavassico was familiar with the popular Byzantine or Etruscan figuration where rather than being a boatman, Charon represents violent death.

Charun with his hammer, from Bomarzo. Staatliche Museum, Berlin. Photo Marburg, courtesy of the Art Reference Bureau.

Battista. As a final example of Charon's connection with lugubrious themes, let me point to a sonnet by Giuseppe Battista (1610–1675), entitled "Miserie d'uom vecchio" (A 69). This sonnet describing one of the ages of man is uniformly pessimistic. But despite its dark tones, the description of man in his old age is expressed through a variety of baroque contrasts and metaphors, which tend to undermine the seriousness of the poem. Man, for example, having reached the winter of his life, finds his face furrowed with sunken creases and hoary frost ("di cave rughe e di canute brine . . . arato") and his hair sown ("seminato il crine") by the icy hand of the winged old man. Soon after, we read of the alpine snows of his frozen heart ("dell'agghiacciato cor le nevi alpine" [7]). In the midst of this figurative language, which continues in the last three lines of the poem, the reference to Charon stands out for its simplicity:

Sempre il nocchier di Stige orrido e tetro
tien per lui tragittar spalmato il legno,
e figurano i fabri il suo ferètro.

(9–11)

The pilot of Styx, horrid and dark, keeps his bark always tightly pitched to ferry him across, and the craftsmen measure out his coffin.

Charon is not only dark and gloomy but ever ready, waiting impatiently for this victim of Time, the *vecchio alato*.

iii. Mythological and Amorous Motifs

Boccaccio. In lyric poetry dealing with mythological subjects, Charon appears most prominently in the descents of such lovers as Orpheus and Psyche. An early example of the boatman's connection to Orpheus, for example, is provided by Giovanni Boccaccio. In a sonnet based on the theme of the poet's inability to praise his beloved adequately, Boccaccio evokes a variety of mythological exempla:

Quel dolce canto col qual già Orfeo
Cerbero vinse e il nocchier d'Acheronte,
o quel con ch' Anfion dal duro monte
tirò li sassi al bel muro dirceo;
    o qual d'intorn'al fonte pegaseo
cantar più bel, color che già la fronte
s'ornar d'alloro, con le Muse conte
uomo lodando, o forse alcuno deo:
    sarebbe scarso a commendar costei,
    le cui bellezze assai più che mortali
ed i costumi e le parole sono.
    Ed io presumo in versi diseguali
di disegnarle in canto senza suono!
Vedete se son folli i pensier miei!

(A 56)

That sweet song with which Orpheus once conquered Cerberus and the helmsman of Acheron, or that with which Amphion drew the rocks from the hard mount to the beautiful Dircean walls; or like the more beautiful singing around the Pegasean fount, of those whose foreheads are already crowned with laurel, with the esteemed Muses praising man, or perhaps some god: all would be insufficient to praise her, whose beauties, habits, and words are much more than mortal. And I presume in unequal verses to sketch her in a song without sound! See if my thoughts are not mad!

Each exemplum presents a myth in which a poet overcame a difficult task through the beauty and power of his singing. Orpheus's obstacles, of course, were Cerberus and Charon, the latter here called the ferryman of Acheron, while Amphion's were the rocks of the hard mountain. But even these poets and previous masters of the panegyrical fall far short of the virtuosity needed to describe the poet's beloved, presumably Fiammetta, the inspiration of many of Boccaccio's lyrics.

Despite the fact that Boccaccio's *Rime* have been seen in large part as literary exercises, artificially elaborate and technically refined, with an overabundance of mythological *richiami*,[8] the poet's allusion to Charon is aesthetically pleasing. The poem comes across, I believe, with effectiveness, largely because of the movement from the traditional and impersonal mythological exempla to the ingenuous and self-deprecating analysis of the poet's own efforts. Sandwiched between the canto of the poets of classical fable and the *versi diseguali* with their "canto senza suono" of the modern poet, the *bellezze* of *costei* are, in effect, neglected. The sonnet's theme that her beauty is beyond human expression is exemplified by the poem itself. Even Boccaccio's final asseveration is an observation devoted not to the marvels of his beloved but his own mad thoughts.

Niccolò da Correggio. Niccolò da Correggio, who mentioned Charon in his dramatic *Fabula de Cefalo*, touches on the figure in a mythological poem in octaves, the *Fabula de Psiche*, dedicated in 1491 to Isabella d'Este, as well as in his *Rime* and *Silva* (A 58). The portrayal found in *Psiche* offers no original notes, following the Apuleian account in general outline. The Tower informs Psyche of her voyage:

> Giungerai al fiume che non corre troppo,
> e lì ritroverà' un vecchio canuto,
> che passa a precio e' morti a cui la toca:
> un de' denari il ti torrà di boca.

(oct. 153)

You will reach a river which doesn't flow too much, and there you will find an old white-haired man, who transports for a fee the dead whose turn it is; he'll take one of the coins from your mouth.

On her return, the Tower says,

> po' al squalido nochier canuto e mesto
> darai l'altro dinar, che nulla resti.

157

Then you will give the other coin, such that you have none left, to the squalid helmsman, white-haired and sad.

Compared to Apuleius, who offers little descriptive detail, Correggio is somewhat more pictorial, borrowing, it seems, from the Virgilian portrait.

In his *Rime*, the poet refers to the underworld crossing without specifically mentioning Charon,[9] but the boatman has a major role in the *Silva*. When the soul of a dead lover descends to the underworld, Charon denies it passage with a novel and poetically delightful excuse:

> Soglio portar in questa cimba al passo,
> o anima affogata, tutti i morti,
> ma te non portarò già al regno basso
> perchè più foco ne l'Inferno porti.
> Ferma pur tu su quella ripa il passo,
> chè i dannati non vo' che tu conforti,
> chè se vedesseno el tuo intenso ardore,
> mitigaresti in parte il suo dolore.

(oct. 13, p. 102)

I am accustomed to offer passage in this boat, O oppressed soul, to all the dead, but you for sure I will not carry to the lower realm because you are bringing more fire into hell. Just hold your step on that bank; I don't want you to give comfort to the damned. If they saw your intense ardor, it would lessen in part their pain.

The extent of the lover's passion is masterfully emphasized. The *amante*'s crestfallen answer is in part an exclamation of marvel and woe:

> O sorte extrema, che 'l foco ch'io porto
> mi debba far ancor d'Inferno privo!

(oct. 14)

O harsh fate, that the fire that I bear should keep me out of hell!

Charon, however, is unyielding:

> Volta, te dico, pur in là quel viso,
> ché 'l lago passan già i suspiri ardenti,
> e ben che 'l corpo sia da te diviso,
> qua giù non s'usa dar simil tormenti.
> Di là da questa Stige è il Campo Eliso
> dove locati son tutti i contenti:
> se i toi suspiri passasseno in quel loco,
> l'accenderesti d'amoroso foco.

(oct. 15)

Turn your face, I tell you, in that direction, because already your burning sighs are crossing the lake, and though your body is now torn from you, down here it's not usual to assign such torments. On the other side of the Styx are the Elysian Fields, where all the happy ones are sent. If your sighs were to cross to that place, you would ignite it with amorous fire.

The metaphorical fire of love assumes a physical reality in Correggio! Even the ardent sighs are torments, with their fire a hazard as well to the fields of Elysium. The artistic use of classical myth for lyric purposes is exemplified in this poem.

Udine. Ercole Udine, who also deals with the myth of *Psiche* in the late Cinquecento (A 65), is more expansive than Correggio. In Canto 7 of his poem, preceded in the 1601 editon by an illustration of Psiche's labors that includes the ferryman Charon, Udine details the crossing of the underworld river with several touches missing in the classical source. In octave 35, the Tower informs Psiche of the *auaro passaggier* and what she must do to succeed in her task. When the poet narrates the actual descent, he enriches the description of Charon, drawing on other classical portrayals:

> Giunge al fiume Acheronte al cui traggetto
> Stassi Caronte squallido nocchiero;
> Ardor di foco, d'ira, e di dispetto
> Vibra da gli occhi, e'l guardo cieco, e fiero,
> Ispida, e folta barba tutto il petto
> Gli copre, e da un sol manto rotto, e nero
> Sù gli homeri annodato è ricoperto;
> A lei sen vien, c'ha l'oro à lui già offerto.
>
> (44)

She arrives at the river Acheron, where for the ferrying stands Charon the squalid helmsman; from his eyes and his fierce blind stare throbs an ardor of fire, anger, and spite; a thick bristly beard hides all his chest, and he is covered by only a black tattered cloak knotted over his shoulders. He comes to her since she has already offered him the gold.

The description is in large part Virgilian, but the influence of Dante's fierce demon can be detected in verses 3 and 4. The use of the adjective *cieco*, here applied to Charon's *guardo*, seems unusual until we recall Dante's use of the word for so many aspects of hell.[10] Later, incidentally, Lope de Vega also describes Charon's eyes similarly in the verse: "brotando llamas de los ojos ciegos" (*La Circe* 3. 113).

A baroque conceit describes Psiche entering the boat for the crossing:

> Ne la Cimba se n'entra oscura, e lorda
> Con l'oro che rinchiuso anco tenea
> Trà le vermiglie labbra, e parea à punto
> Oro che fosse à bei rubin congiunto.
>
> (46)

She climbs into the boat, dark and filthy, with the gold which she still kept between her bright red lips, and it seemed in fact as if it were gold set with beautiful rubies.

And Charon's avarice is again mentioned:

> L'auaro passaggiero a l'hor le toglie
> D'ambo i denari l'un for de la bocca,
> E tosto il legno da la ripa scioglie,
> E tosto il passa, e l'altra sponda tocca.

(47)

Then the stingy ferryman takes from her of both coins the one in her mouth, and soon he frees the bark from the bank, and soon he ferries it across and touches the other shore.

On her return, Psiche avails herself of Proserpina's gift:

> Parte la bella donna, e seco porta
> Il richiesto liquor nel uaso chiuso;
> Di Dite passa la tremenda porta,
> E tien col Can già desto il primiero uso;
> Giunge à la gran Palude, et ella accorta
> Che'l passaggier sta ne la cimba chiuso,
> Il chiama, e col mostrarli il don l'aletta;
> Ei se ne uiene, e la ripassa in fretta.

(54)

The beautiful woman leaves and takes with her the requested liqueur in the closed vessel. She passes through the tremendous door of Dis and holds to the earlier pattern with the dog, already awake; she reaches the great swamp, and, seeing that the ferryman is enclosed in his boat, she calls him and, by showing him the gift, attracts him. He comes to her and ferries her back in haste.

Along with an original description of the wiles Psiche employs to gain the return passage, Udine also offers the novel vision of the ferryman enclosed in his boat, possibly at rest. Entranced by the gift, Charon hastily complies with Psiche's request.

Marino. In the early seventeenth century, Giovanni Battista Marino wrote several *Idilli favolosi*, two of which contain allusions to Charon. Published as part of *La sampogna* (Paris, 1620), the idylls in question treat the familiar stories of Orpheus and Proserpina. In his *Orfeo*, a polymetric poem based on both Virgil and Ovid, with reminiscences of such Italian poets as Dante, Poliziano, and Sannazaro, Marino describes the descent to hell as follows:

> Discese à le più cupe
> Del globo de la terra vltima parti.
> E per placar de l'implacabil Dite
> La superbia crudele,

> Non abhorrì d'errar viuo tra' morti;
> E la negra palude,
> Doue il vecchio Caron tragitta l'alme,
> Passò senza spauento, e corse, e vide
> De la patria de l'ombre,
> E de l'impero tristo
> Le sedi oscure, e le dolenti case;
> Et hebbe ardir cantando
> Di raccontar con lagrimose note
> De l'amorose sue dure fortune
> L'historia miserabile, e pietosa
> A l'anime spietate.
>
> (A 67; 142–157)

He descended to the darkest and furtherest parts of the globe of the earth. And to placate the cruel pride of implacable Dis, he did not abhor to wander alive among the dead; and the black swamp, where old Charon ferries the souls, he crossed without fear and ran to see the dark centers and sorrowful homes of the wicked empire and the country of the shades; and he dared to tell in song with tearful notes the history of his harsh amorous fortunes, miserable and pitiful, to the souls without pity.

The following lines, once again devoted to the ferryman, recall verses 916–921 in Rinuccini's *Arianna*:

> Nè gli vietò la barca
> Il pallido Nocchiero,
> Nè gli contese il passo
> Il can da le tre gole.
>
> (158–161)

Nor did the pale helmsman deny him the boat, nor did the dog with three throats contest his passage.

Rather than an angry Charon as in Rinuccini, however, we find a pale boatman—the adjective *pallido* is possibly a reminiscence of Rinuccini's "rive pallide e meste" in *Euridice* 431 but unusual for the dark ferryman (cf., however, Statius, *Thebaid* 8. 18).

When Orfeo attempts to return for Euridice a second time, he finds his passage blocked:

> E ben tentò di rientrar piangendo,
> E pregando sotterra,
> Ma inuan, peròche starsi
> Vide à guardia del varco
> Con fauci aperte il mostruoso Cane.
> Nè più su la riuiera di Cocito

Troua l'vsato lelgno, anzi rimira
Presso le torbid'onde
Del pigro stagno il Passaggero antico,
Che lo sgrida, e discaccia.

(488–497)

And he tried hard, crying and begging, to go back again underground, but in vain, because he saw the monstrous Dog standing guard over the passage with open jaws. No longer does he find the usual boat on the shore of Cocytus, instead he stares near the turbid waves of the lazy pool at the ancient ferryman, who chides him and chases him away.

The river is specified here as Cocytus in place of the more common Acheron or Styx. The descripton is faithful to the *Aneid* where Virgil pictures first the Acheron and then a turbid whirlpool that flows into Cocytus, a river with *stagna alta* (*Aen*. 6. 295–297; 323).[11] Rather than a Fury, we find the ancient ferryman, who shouts and chases off the descender.

In contrast to this traditional representation of Charon, Marino offers an original depiction in the idyll *Proserpina*, based in general on the *De raptu Proserpinae* of Claudian. When the maiden is made a queen in hell, Pluto exclaims that now the torments will cease, since with her there hell will be like heaven. In anticipation of the marriage ceremony, all hell rejoices:

Rompon de l'aria mesta
I silentij lugubri
Di canzon disusate allegri accenti.
Velato il crin canuto
Di palustri ghirlande
Il vecchio passaggier de l'onde nere,
De l'onde, che quel dì corsero latte
Moue cantando à lenta voga il remo.

(1128–1135)

Happy accents of unaccustomed songs break the lugubrious silences of the sad air. With his gray hair covered with fenland garlands, the old ferryman of the black waves, of the waves which that day ran milk, moves singing with slow strokes his oar.

The portrait of Charon, reminiscent of singing ferrymen in poets from Boiardo to the writers of melodrama, is carried a step further with the vivid detail of his hair garlanded with marsh flowers. If anything represents the inversion of hell, it is this idyllic and festive boatman along with the oxymoronic *onde nere*, now become waves of milk.

Bruni. Another type of mythological poem in which Charon is referred to is the Ovidian epistle. In his *Epistole eroiche* (1627), Antonio Bruni (1593–1635) deals with a variety of mythological, fictional, and historical figures, offering us letters from Erminia to Tancredi, Caterina d'Aragona to Arrigo VIII Re d'Inghilterra, Fiordispina to Bradamante, Turno to Lavinia, Tancredi to Clorinda, Olimpia to Bireno, Armida to Rinaldo, Nausicaa to Ulisse, Diana to Venere, Giove to Semele, Seneca to Nerone, Gismonda to Tancredi Principe di Salerno, and from many other interesting heroines and heroes of literature to their counterparts.

Euridice, for example, writes from the realm of death using a quill from one of the eagles tormenting Tityus and ink from the waves of Cocytus! Wandering among the "horrori / Del pallido Acheronte" (A 68; p. 206), she asks her spouse to rescue her. Although she mentions Cerberus and other *fidi custodi* as well as the *onde morte* of "Flegetonte e Cocito" (p. 209), she does not refer to the boatman himself. In another epistle, however, in which Amore writes to Psiche, foretelling her trials, including the necessity of descending to the underworld (Libro 2, Epistola 4), reference is made to the ferryman. Amore describes the difficult downward path, adding:

> Ne la soglia v'hà Cerbero feroce,
> Che latra, e vibra ogn'hor trisulca lingua;
> E par folgor la lingua, e tuon la voce.
>
> (p. 313)

On the threshold there is fierce Cerberus, who barks and shakes continually his trifid tongue; and his tongue seems lightening and thunder his voice.

Amore claims that even though he is "a solcar l'onde infernal non vso" ("not used to plowing the infernal waves"), he will guide her across the rivers:

> Varcherò teco anch'io l'onde infernali,
> Et oprerò, fatto d'Arcier Nocchiero,
> Per vela il velo, e per timon gli strali.
>
> (p. 313)

I, too, will cross with you the infernal waves, and will work, made steersman from an archer, for a sail the veil, and for a rudder the arrows.

We are reminded of Marc'Antonio Epicuro's *Cecaria*, where Love is described as a Charon figure, guiding a boat whose sail is torment, whose oars are thoughts, and whose winds are sighs. Here, the ship's implements are not allegorical, merely unusual. The thematic significance of Epicuro's image gives way to the playfulness of the Seicento poet, who treats themes lightly and wittily. A more obvious example of his approach, which is not so overtly whimsical, is his explanation of the origin of Euridice's quill.

iv. Satirical Motifs

Grazzini. Turning to works of a more comic nature, Charon is found in the *rime giocose* of both Francesco Berni and Anton Francesco Grazzini, Il Lasca. Grazzini, for example, a fervent admirer and imitator of Berni, does not employ the boat-man as a symbol of passing from life to death but as a representation of the demons of hell. Appropriately, Charon is mentioned in a poem "In lode delle Rime di M. Francesco Berni." A "maestro e padre del burlesco stile," Berni

> seppe in quello sì ben dire e fare,
> Insieme colla penna e col cervello,
> Che 'nvidiar si può ben, non già imitare.
> Non sia chi mi ragioni di Burchiello,
> Che saría proprio, come comparare
> Caron dimonio all'angel Gabriello.

(A 64)

A master and father of the burlesque style, Berni . . . knew how to speak and do so well in that style, both with his pen and with his brain, that one can well envy but hardly imitate him. Don't let anyone speak to me of Burchiello, since that would be like comparing the demon Charon to the angel Gabriel.

Desiring to contrast the excellence of his master with the earlier work of Burchi-ello (1404–1449), Grazzini finds the ultimate opposition—the angel Gabriel and the demon Charon. The impossibility of comparing the two emphasizes with wit the author's contention.

Lazzarelli. As a final example of Charon in humorous lyric, let me turn to a satiri-cal sonnet by Gianfrancesco Lazzarelli (1621–1693) in his *Cicceide*, a collection of over 400 poems attacking an acquaintance under the name of Don Ciccio (A 70). Almost every poem includes as its highlight an indecorous word beginning with *c*, the more common being *culo* and *coglioni*. The sonnet in which Charon is referred to, "Il passo di Lete," is unusual because it presents the boatman as a speaking character:

> Don Ciccio, allor che morte invida, e fera,
> Gli ebbe fatta provar l'ultima eclisse,
> Pregò Caronte, affin che su la nera
> Barca il guado letèo gli consentisse;
>   Ma con la man, da l'alta poppa, ov'era
> Ritto al governo, ei gli accennò che gisse
> Pur oltre a guazzo, e in placida maniera,
> Quando a lui fu vicin, così gli disse:
>   —E' privilegio a' pari tuoi concesso
> Il poter senza imbarco, e pagamento
> Avere a l'altro margine l'accesso;
>   Mentre un tondo Culo, gonfio di vento
> Galleggiando leggier, può da sè stesso
> Andar di là dal fiume a salvamento.

(A 70; sonnet 282)

Don Ciccio, after envious and cruel death had made him experience the ulti-mate eclipse, begged Charon to allow him to cross the Lethean ford in the black boat; but with his hand, from the lofty stern, where he was upright at the steering, he beckoned to him to come closer to the pool, and in a placid manner, when he was close to him, he spoke to him as follows: "It is a privilege conceded to your equals to be able to have access to the other side without embarcation and payment; as long as a round ass, full of wind and floating lightly, can safely make it to the other side of the river by itself."

Charon's reason for refusing passage in his boat is assuredly original! His placid manner is indicative of moral superiority, as is his ironic reference to Don Ciccio's privilege. Even after death, the amply vituperated fellow is not spared sarcastic remarks.

v. Religious Motifs

Ariosto. The variety of motifs with which Charon is connected includes, of course, the religious: Dante's poem assured the boatman's survival in the Christian scheme. Ludovico Ariosto, for example, refers to Charon in a poem of repentance. The psychological perspicuity of the poet informs the initial quatrains:

> Come creder debbo io che tu in ciel oda
> Signor benigno, i miei non caldi prieghi,
> se, gridando la lingua che mi sleghi,
> tu vedi quanto il cor nel laccio goda?
>   Tu che 'l vero conosci, me ne snoda,
> e non mirar ch'ogni mio senso il nieghi;
> ma prima il fa che, di me carco, pieghi
> Caron' il legno alla dannata proda.

$$(A\ 62)$$

How shall I believe that you hear in heaven, benign Lord, my lukewarm prayers, if, with my tongue shouting that you free me, you see how the heart enjoys the snare? O You who know the truth, unbind me from the snare and do not heed how every one of my senses denies it; but do it before Charon turns his bark, laden with me, to the dreadful shore.

Hoping that God listens to his tongue despite the pleasure his senses continue to feel in the nets of love, the poet is concerned lest he die before being delivered from his error. The fear of hell, from which only God, he says in the tercets, can save him, is embodied in Charon, who is visualized as turning his boat laden with the poet toward the far side of the river where the damned dwell. The sonnet is marked by its poetic beauty, the sincerity with which the theme is developed, and its psychological penetration. That Ariosto feels free to employ Charon illustrates the extent to which classical mythology was absorbed into the life of the Cinquecento poets and the thematics of sacred poetry.

Cammelli. A related use of Charon to signify damnation is found in a sonnet by Antonio Cammelli where the influence of Dante's underworld is more evident. Rather then being characterized by a tone of repentance as in Ariosto, Cammelli's sonnet pertains to the homiletic. The initial situation is a hypocritical confession:

> Una donna ne va tutta contrita,
> di cor no, a confessar, ma de apparenzia;
> che chi vedessi ben sua conscienzia,
> la troveria de mille error fornita.

> (A 60; p. 32)

A woman goes to confess, altogether contrite, not in the heart, no, but in appearance; because he who would look well into her conscience would find it endowed with a thousand errors.

As a result, says the poet, she will find herself in hell:

> Caron ha già per lei il legno al passo,
> ringe Minos e Cerber latra e grida,
> sta con la bocca aperta Satanasso;
> Neron crudel l'aspetta seco e Mida,
> et a la mensa sua l'avaro Crasso,
> così l'inferno e chi l'inferno guida.

Charon already has his ship ready for her at the crossing; Minos snarls and Cerberus barks and howls; Satan stands with open mouth; Cruel Nero waits for her to join him, and Midas, and miserly Crassus at his table, thus hell and he who hell controls.

Unsatisfied with this admonition, the poet adds a final coda: "A tal va chi si fida / in crudeltade al mondo, in avarizia, / chè in Dio non è pietà senza justizia" ("to such goes anyone who trusts in cruelty in the world, in avarice, because in God there is no mercy without justice").

vi. Conclusion

As with classical lyric, we must conclude that most references to the boatman are brief and only occasionally evocative. In many poets, the *nocchiero di Stige* becomes an abstract concept, representing death or the passage from life to death. In religious works, Charon becomes a symbol representing hell itself or damnation. When the ferryman is referred to as a person, it is often in a mythological poem treating a descent. Even in these instances, Charon rarely acts, being merely referred to as an obstacle either overcome or unsurmounted. When he is described, Charon is usually seen as simply old. Occasionally, an emotion or attitude is instilled in him, such as anger, avarice, or sadness. Concerning his features, the more common references are to his Virgilian squalor or his darkness, although now and then an extended epic portrait is found, such as in Ercole Udine. Among the notable representations is Marino's depiction of a ferryman with garlands of flowers in his hair, an image based on Claudian. Equally intriguing is Lazzarelli's calm and ironic ferryman, who addresses Don Ciccio in two tercets of a satirical sonnet. In the final accounting, it is impossible as in classical lyric to talk of structural units in a descent theme. Even the most extended narrative and mythological poems rarely seem to develop the figure of Charon or the descent as a major episode. Lacking the leisure of epic, these poems are less inclined to digressive description, concentrating instead on more lyrical motifs, such as the emotions of love, grief, and despair, emotions that in shorter lyric also bring to the page the figure of the boatman.

Notes

1. To mention one reference to Charon outside the confines of this study, which regarding lyric ends with Lazzarelli (1621–1693), let me quote a sonnet of Onofrio Minzoni (1734–1817), probably the most vivid of the shorter works dealing with Charon. The sonnet, in a sequence of two, follows an encounter between Rodomonte and Mandricardo in hell:

> Caròn, che dalla barca ferrugigna
> vede frattanto l'implacabile zuffa,
> gli occhi d'una feral luce sanguigna
> tosto raccende, e i sopraccigli arruffa.
>   Il cagnesco dentame ora digrigna,
> or ne' mustacchi arroncigliati sbuffa:
> amarissimamente alfin sogghigna,
> e le due combattenti ombre rabbuffa:
>   Seguite, anime forti, anime eccelse,
> l'ire degne di voi; ma vi rammenti
> ch'ambe da' corpi un sol Ruggier vi svelse.
>   Che bel vedere inabissar lo sguardo,
> e, smorti al suono di sì pochi accenti,
> ammutir Rodomonte e Mandricardo!

Lirici del Settecento, ed. Bruno Maier (Milano: Ricciardi, 1959), p. 1175.

2. In a more general study, the mythological poem as a type would deserve a place all its own, with a wide range of subtypes pertaining to other genres. However, due to the scarcity of examples, it seems best to treat poetic types with a certain degree of flexibility when discussing Charon, that is, to deal with the lyric genre on the basis of its complexity and richness rather than purity. Were the examples more numerous, we could deal separately with *poesia amorosa, giocosa, sacra, morale, satirica, mitologica, elegiaca, patriottica* or *civile, epigrafica* and so forth.

3. I have employed Thomas G. Bergin's translation of the eclogue, "Petrarch's *Bucolicum Carmen I: Parthenias*" in *Petrarch to Pirandello*, ed. Julius A. Molinaro.

4. The authenticity of the poem to be discussed has been questioned. Giosue Carducci quotes a previous editor, Silvestri, who excluded the poems from Poliziano's literary canon on the grounds that "'a giudizio degl'intelligenti, sono così meschini e vituperati, che sarebbe far grande ingiuria al Poliziano il tenerli per cosa sua.'" See *Le Stanze, l'Orfeo e le Rime*, ed. Carducci, p. 382. Carducci himself agrees, assigning the poems to "un aderente e un favorito di casa Medici."

5. The Dantesque language of these verses, extending from the list of vices to *baratro*, to *casa* (cf. *Inf*. 8. 120 where hell, specifically the city of Dite, is referred to as "le dolente case"), to *centro* (cf. *Inf*. 16. 63 where the depths of hell are at the center of the earth), and to *discorre* in the sense of *trascorrere* (see *Par*. 15. 14 and 29. 21), also embraces the use of the adjective *pregno* (cf. *Purg*. 5. 118;

22. 76–77; *Par.* 10. 68 *and 22.* 112–113). In Dante's representation, Charon is truly "saturated" with anger.

6. In her analysis of the poem, Ida Maïer claims that Poliziano's expression of his sentiments loses all spontaneity when "s'embarrasse d'un lourd bagage mythologique" (A 57; p. 146). She refers specifically to the lines just quoted.

7. Precedents for the *disperata* in Italian literature date as far back as Cecco Angiolieri's "S'i' fosse foco, arderei 'l mondo."

8. See Natalino Sapegno, *Storia letteraria d'Italia: Il Trecento*, pp. 282–283.

9. In sonnet 77, for example, the poet says, "Io vo in abisso / e per Stige passar spalmo la barca" (A 58; p. 145, 13–14). Elsewhere, we read of Hercules crossing: "Ercul sulcò già la palude inferna / e il tricipite Cerbaro provollo" (A 58; p. 254).

10. I refer, for example, to expressions such as the *cieco mondo* in *Inf.* 4. 13, the *cieco / carcere* in *Inf.* 10. 58–59, the *cieco fiume* of hell mentioned in *Purg.* 1. 40, and the *cieca cupidigia* in *Inf.* 12. 49.

11. Interestingly, in a medieval paraphrase of Martianus Capella's *Satyra de nuptiis Philologiae et Mercurii*, dating from the late twelfth century, the story of Orpheus and Eurydice is developed at great length and contains a Charon on the Cocytus. Part of the episode reads as follows:

> Turbidus est fluctus piceoque colore reductus,
> Sulphure fetet humus uolitatque per aera fumus,
> Cum, mercede data, nauli causaque relata,
> Nauta Karon, uetitum properans transferre Cocytum,
> Ancipiti prora transponit ad ulteriora.
> Territus absque mora tria Cerberus extulit ora
> Et quasi frustratus cumulat ringendo latratus.

(474–480)

I quote from the article by André Boutemy, "Une version médiévale inconnue de la légende d'Orphée," p. 59. Martianus himself refers to the "snaky hands" of Charon in *De nuptiis* 2. 140 ff.

12

Prose Forms

i. Commentators of Dante, Mythographers, and Iconographers

Among the first to deal with Charon in prose works are the commentators of Dante. Following in the tradition of Servius and the medieval allegorizers, commentators develop their explanations and moralizations of the Charon episode with great vitality.[1] In fact, in their eagerness to find a hidden meaning in Dante, the commentators most often leave the literal sense far behind, thereby suffocating the poetic qualities of Dante's representation with their own elaborate, exegetical comments.[2] The variety of symbolic and etymological interpretations of both Charon and Acheron is symptomatic of not only the medieval transformation of classical mythology but the Renaissance desire to reconcile pagan beliefs with Christian theology. Inspired by their desire to find significance in pagan myth, few commentators seem to consider whether or not Dante actually developed Charon's portrayal or the episode at the river with allegorical intentions. As an example of the early commentators' method, let me briefly cite a few interpretations of the Acheron, a river almost always connected with Charon for reasons of shared etymology and structural contiguity.

Etymologically, the most common meaning ascribed to the Acheron is, to use Guido da Pisa's words (A 71; p. 46), lacking joy (*sine gaudio*).[3] The allegorical significance is more varied: Jacopo Della Lana, for example, explains that the Acheron is the first river of hell, because allegorically, it represents "la dilettazione carnale, la quale è principio a tutti i vizzi" ("carnal delight, which is the beginning of all vices" [A 73; p. 132]). Boccaccio, with greater fidelity to the physical aspects of a river, interprets it as "la labile e flùssa condizione delle cose disiderate e la miseria di questo mondo" ("the transient and flux-like condition of desired objects and the misery of this world" [A 76]). Benvenuto da Imola, on the other hand, reverts to a vaguer significance of worldly concupiscence (A 77; p. 125), an idea repeated by Alessandro Vellutello (A 83; p. 22^r) and others (e.g., A 78; p. 24). Finally, Francesco da Buti expounds on the river as "l'ostinazione alla quale viene il peccatore, poi che è morto nel peccato" ("the obstinance to which the sinner comes, when he is dead in sin" [A 79, p. 102]), an interpretation that Cristoforo Landino varies to "deliberatione nel peccare" ("deliberation in sinning" [A 82; p. 30^v]).

222

Francesco da Buti. The symbolical import of the crossing itself receives greater emphasis: Not only is Charon's name interpreted both etymologically and allegorically but so also is every aspect of his being[4] as well his ship[5] and oar.[6] Francesco da Buti's *Commento* (ca. 1385–1395) is a good example of attempts to enucleate a hidden meaning in Dante's exposition. After summarizing in one page the *sentenzia litterale* (A 79; p. 95), Buti devotes the following twelve to the *allegoria*. Having discussed all four infernal rivers, he passes to Charon, who represents "lo disordinato amore" ("disorderly love" [p. 101])[7] and is called old because this evil love began with the fall of the angels who became enamored with their own loftiness. Buti goes on to allegorize Charon's flaming eyes as *desideri insaziabili* (insatiable desires [p. 101]), much as did Benvenuto da Imola (A 77; p. 127), while the ship is interpreted as "la colpa della congregazione, e collegazione de' sette peccati mortali" ("the fault of the gathering and joining together the seven deadly sins" [p. 100]). Even the boatman's gestures to the souls are interpreted allegorically:

> Lo cenno del dimonio, quanto a quelli del mondo, è la suggestione e il conforto e l'incitamento al peccato; ma quanto a quelli dell'inferno è lo rappresentamento del peccato commesso.

> The beckoning of the devil, as regards those of the world, is the suggestion, the encouragement, and the inciting to sin, but as regards those of hell, it is the representation of the sin committed. (P. 103)

Finally, the oar itself is

> la complacenzia delle cose mondane: imperò che con questo remo, l'amor disordinato fa andare li peccatori in su la nave de' vizi e de' peccati: e quanto a quelli dell'inferno si dee intendere che sia la coscienzia: imperò che noi doviamo credere che, come l'anime escono de' corpi, elle se ne vanno là ove la coscienzia loro le giudica.

> the enjoyment of world goods, because with this oar disorderly love forces the sinner into the ship of vice and sin, and, as regards those of hell, one must understand that it represents conscience, because we must believe that, once the souls leave the body, they go there where their conscience judges them. (P. 103)

Buti's most original comment is that Dante was transported across the river not by Charon but by an angel. While most previous commentators had interpreted the crossing in abstract terms, none had stipulated a physical means. Rather than continuing to list at length the commentators' elucidations, many of which are quite ingenious, let me examine the discourse of some of the more outstanding mythographers. While Boccaccio is perhaps the most famous, the works of Salutati and Conti are equally thorough and scholarly.

*Boccaccio.*Giovanni Boccaccio deals with Charon in his imposing *De genealogia deorum gentilium*, published for the first time in 1472 but widely known in manscript throughout the Quattrocento. Like other medieval poets and commentators, Boccaccio is not chary of reading meanings into myths, myths that he lists without attempting to clarify their variations or contradictions. Borrowing his method from such predecessors as Fulgentius, Boccaccio strives to find an edifying lesson in all aspects of the tales. His interpretations, consequently, cover a variety of levels, ranging from literal to moral, symbolic, and allegorical.

Charon, treated in Book 1, chapter 33, is described as the ninth son of Herebus, who himself was the ninth son of Demogorgon (1. 14). Identifying Charon as the *Acherontis nauta*, Boccaccio cites Crisippo as the source for the boatman's descent from Herebus and Nox. Following a quotation from Virgil's description of Charon, Boccaccio mentions what he claims is Servius's general explanation (but which, in reality, comes from Fulgentius) that "Charon, quem Servius devolvit in Cronon, tempus est" ("Charon, whose name Servius traces back to Cronus, is time" [A 88; 1. 62]) and then continues with the medival interpretation of the myth's features. Herebus, Charon's father, is taken as the inner counsel of the divine mind, from which time and all other things are created, while Night is Charon's mother, because before time was created, there was only darkness.[8] Charon is found in the underworld because the gods have no need of time. That he ferries bodies across the Acheron signifies that once we are born, time carries us to the far bank—that is, to death. Typically, the Acheron is interpreted as without joy in order to remind us, Boccaccio adds, that life is frail and full of misery. Two final Virgilian features—Charon's old age and his sordid garments—are given a symbolic import. Charon is old, yet robust, signifying that time does not lose its force because of years; it can do today what it did when first created. Finally, the boatman's clothes are squalid in order to demonstrate that terrestrial things are vile.

Despite the wide variety of interpretations extracted from the deeds of other mythological figures by Boccaccio and the varied meanings sought and found in the boatman by other early commentators of Dante, Boccaccio is content in the *De genealogia* with this one basic allegory. The hidden meaning, as with that elaborated for other mythical figures, has a Christian inspiration. Aware that poetic fable in itself was subject to much criticism as false and unworthy, the poet, like his friend Petrarch, believed that "nempe poeticis inest veritas figmentis, tenuissimis rimulis adeunda" ("truth to be sure is contained in poetic fictions, to be approached by the thinnest fissures").[9] The poet's duty, then, is not to correct or disprove pagan stories but to unveil the moral lesson hidden in them.

The medieval allegorical method perpetuated by Boccaccio does not, in general, give way in the early Renaissance to a study of myth in and for itself as modern manuals on the period might lead us to assume. The more popular treatises, in fact, continue to encumber classical myths with allegorical meanings. The extensive moralizations of an early humanist, such as Salutati, however, do tend in the Cinquecento to become mere appendages, added, it seems, for self-protection against religious zealots. The description of Charon in Salutati and Conti provides an example of the subtle changes that take place in mythological treatises.

Salutati. Coluccio Salutati's *De laboribus Herculis* is an early humanistic treatise written around 1383–1391. In dealing with Hercules' last labor, the author discusses at length the significance of the encounter with Charon. The episode intrigues Salutati to such an extent that he follows his lengthy exegesis, based on Seneca's *Hercules furens*, with a chapter devoted exclusively to Aeneas's confrontation with Charon.

In his treatment of Hercules' descent, Salutati quotes both his illustrious predecessor Boccaccio and the earlier Virigilian commentary by Servius. Following four lines devoted to these sources, he elaborates his own allegorical interpretation in over two hundred lines. Every detail of Seneca's description, as well as Virgil's, is given a hidden meaning. As one example among many, the Virgilian line "ratem conto subigit velisque ministrat," which is cited in relation to Seneca's verse, "Regit ipse longo portitor conto ratem," is embellished in part as follows:

> Et contus quidem nichil aliud est quam electio qua liberum arbitrium [sc. Charon] se determinat et ad id quod elegit impellit et dirigit voluntatem vel quasi scrutatorium quoddam examinato quod agendum sit eligit et voluntatem in sua libertate determinat. Hoc igitur Charon navim subigit, hoc est subtus agit, id est movet et ducit. Quod si ad voluntatem referas, que semper libertatis arbitrio moveatur, adeo congruit quod vis possit intellectus aliud cogitare. Nam quod Maro subdit, "velisque ministrat", ad celi respicit influentiam, quam per vela diximus importari. . . . Liberum quidem arbitrium navim, hoc est voluntatem, ministrat velis, id est dispositioni celestium preparat, quoniam quod illa vult libens eligit nisi ratio se opponat. (A 87; p. 556)

And indeed the oar is nothing other than the choice by which free will [*i.e.,* Charon] determines itself and impels itself toward what it has chosen and directs the will—or, like some investigatory body, having examined what needs to be done, it chooses and determines the will in its freedom. With this, then, Charon directs the boat; that is, he drives it from beneath; that is, he propels it and guides it. But, if you refer to the will which is always moved by the choice of freedom, it is even more appropriate, because the force of intellect could consider something else. For what Virgil adds "he tends the sails" refers back to the influence of heaven which we have already noted was signified by sails. . . . Indeed free will controls the ship, that is, the will, by means of sails; that is, free will prepares the will for the disposition of the heavens, because what it wishes it chooses willingly unless reason opposes itself.

Essentially, classical myth is a pretext for Salutati to display his philosophical learning and his ability to develop penetrating expositon. It is as a philosopher, in fact, rather than a mythographer that Salutati turns to the classical fables.

Conti. Natale Conti's *Mythologiae* (A 94), published not long after the scholarly treatise of L. G. Giraldi (A 93), is likewise a work of learning in which references to and quotations from the ancients predominate over exegetical demands. Seznec's comment that "Conti's mythological exegesis offers no innovation, and marks no advance"[10] is in error at least in some respects, for the mythographer explicates the myth of Charon and the crossing with originality. Furthermore, Conti's attention to classical sources is noteworthy. Regarding Charon, his philosophical exploration of the *sapientia veterum* is based on not merely Virgil or Seneca but quotations from Hesiod, Pausanias, Greek lyric, Lucian, Callimachus, Aristophanes, and others, all quoted in the original and then translated. When tracing details of the Charon myth, Conti includes classical references to infernal rivers, the obol, descenders who encountered the boatman, and so forth (A 94; p. 61^v).

Unlike Giraldi, who restrains himself regarding allegorical elaboration, Conti professes to be a philosopher, and consequently, following his scholarly comments, he offers his own detailed allegorical exegesis of the fable. While the method is that of his predecessors and the initial impetus possibly comes from Silvestris (see note 1), Conti's explication is developed with originality. In this, he illustrates his desire to surpass previous mythographers.[11] He elaborates in part on the crossing and other features of the myth as follows:

> Charon Erebi & Noctis filius dicitur, qui animas trans Acherontem, & Stygem, & Cocytum ac Phlegethontem traiicit, quoniam ex illa hominum mente, quae prius erat confusa, peccatorumque tenebris inuoluta, ac minime examinata conscientia, prius illi motus, qui superius nominati sunt per illa flumina exoriuntur: deinde vbi innocentiae opinio, aut innocentiae proxima deliberatio in posterum integritatis seruandae, surrexit; quae per praeteritorum scelerum poenitentiam comparatur, cum piget summi Dei voluntatem, per auaritiam, crudelitatem, impietatemve offendisse, tum spes de bonitate Dei exurgit, atque inde laetitia, quae nos tras ea turbulenta flumina traiicit: & Charon appellatur. Haec ad seueros iudices intrepidos nos deducit, haec in grauissimis periculis nos consolatur & adiuuat, haec pro viatico est quocunque accedamus. Quare siquis recte consideret, inueniet antiquos omnes animorum motus illos, qui sub mortis tempus in homine nascerentur, sub his fluuiorum figmentis fuisse complexos. Nam cum senex sit Charon, quid aliud significat, quam rectum consilium, & quae ex illo concepto prouenit, laetitiam? aut quae alia laetitia in morituro homine excitabitur, quam illa quae nascitur ex opinione innocentiae, aut è spe veniae? Illa vero quae ad obolos, naulumque portitoris attinent, ego ridicula esse conseo, & pro simplicium muliercularum opinionibus inuenta, & tanquam ad inuentae fabulae probabilitatem excogitata à sapientibus. . . . (A 94; pp. 61^v–62^r)

Charon, who ferries the souls across Acheron, Styx, Cocytus, and Phlegethon, is said to be the son of Erebus and Night. For those emotions, which the rivers produce, arise first out of that mind of men which first was confused and wrapped up in the darkness of sins, with an unexamined conscience. Later

Portitor has horrendus aquas , & flumina seruat
Terribili squallore Charon, cui plurima mento
Canities inculta iacet, stant lumina flamma .
Sordidus ex humeris nodo dependet amictus .

Hic erga omnes implacidus esse dicebatur,
quos traiciebat, neque Reges ac principes ciui-
tatum à reliqua multitudine putabat differre,
cùm omnes vno ordine nudos, & omnibus bo-
nis spoliatos cerneret vt testantur ea carmina :

κάτθαν᾽ ὁ μῶς ὅτ᾽ ἄτυμβος ἀνὴρ , ὅς τ᾽ ἔλλαχε
τύμβου.

ἐν δ᾽ ἰῇ τιμῇ ἦρος, κρείων τ᾽ Ἀγαμέμνων .
Θερσίτα δ᾽ ἴσος δ᾽ ἔτιδος παῖς ἢ ὑπόμοιο .
Πάντες εἰσὶν ὁμῶς νεκύων ἀμενηνὰ κάρηνα.
Γυμνοίτε ξηροίτε, κατ᾽ ἀσφοδελὸν λειμῶνα.

Mortuus est æquè tumuli qui haud cepit honorem,
Quiq; fuit nactus pragrandis pondera saxi.
Non Iro magis est Agamemnon clarus : & ipsi
Thersita similis Thetidis pulcherrima proles.
Hi pariter nudi atq; inopes per regna vagantur
Vmbrarum, apta suis referentes pręmia factis.

Testatur Lucianus in dialogo de luctu , mo-
ris id fuisse apud antiquos, vt obolum numisma
per exiguū in os singulis mortuis includerēt, φ
naulū esse Charōtis arbitrabātur, cū ita scribat:
ὥσε ἐπειδάντις ἀποθάνῃ τῶν οἰκείων πρῶτα
μὲν φέροντες ὀβολόν, ἐς τὸ σέμακατέ θηκαν
ἀυτῷ μισθὸν τῷ πορθμεῖ τῆς ναυτιλίας γενη-
σόμενον. Quare cum quis è domesticis obierit pri

mum quidem obolum illi in os depositum naulum
portitoris fore arbitrantur. Is autem nummulus
Danace à Grecis dicebatur, sicuti testatur Callimachus his carminibus in Hecale:

τὸν ἕνεκα καὶ νέκυες προθμήιον, ὅτι φέρονται,
μῶνοι ἐπιστολίων ὅτι μὴ θυμιασέμεν αὐτοῖς
ἀλλὰ κενοῖς σωμάτεσσι νεὼς ἀχερυσιὸς ἴταν
Βάθρον, ᾗ δανάκης ἐπιθεύεται ὅτις ἀπιών .
Idcirco nulli naulum portare feruntur
Vrbe ex hac vita functi: nisi sacra feramus
Nos & suffitus. adeunt Acherusia templa
Ore illi vacuo: danace non indiget vllus.

Aristophanes autem in Rhanis duos obolos
postea naulum eiusdem fuisse, scripsit in his
versibus:

ἐν πλοιαρίω τυννετοῖος᾽ ἀνὴρ γέρων
Ναύτης διάξ ει δὺ ὀβολὼ μισθὸν λαβὼν.

Mercede capta nauta te senex vehet
Binis obolis in naue parua protinus .

Neque tamen ea parua mercede semper con-
tentus fuit, sed aliquando ab Atheniensium Im-
peratoribus, ne illi æquari multitudini cogeren-
tur, auctum est Charonti stipendium, & vsq; ad
triobolum peruentum est. Tanta fuit antiquo-
rum nonnullorum dementia, vt inferos etiam
auaritia & numorum desiderio vexari arbi-
trati sint dicitur nonnullos Charon viuos ad inferos traiecisse:nā Hercules, Vlysses, Orpheus,
AEneas, Theseusque eo descendisse memoran-
tur,

Charon, in Natale Conti, *Mythologiae* (1616). By permission of the Department of Special
Collections, Joseph Regenstein Library, The University of Chicago.

when a general impression of innocence has arisen, or the deliberation to maintain integrity in the future (which is the nearest thing to that innocence attained through penance for past sins when one repents for having offended the will of the greatest God by avarice, cruelty, and impiety), then hope springs up out of the goodness of God and thence joy which ferries us across those turbulent rivers and Charon is its name. This conducts us unafraid before strict judges; this consoles and helps us in the gravest dangers; this serves as a viaticum wherever we may go. And so, if one considers rightly, he will find that the ancients have included under these figures of rivers all those emotions of souls which arise in man near the time of death. For, since Charon is old, what else does it mean except right counsel and the thing which comes forth from that concept—joy? Or, what other joy will be stirred up in a dying man than that which is born from the general impression of innocence or from the hope of pardon? But, as regards those things which pertain to the obols, the ferryman's fare, I consider them to be ridiculous and invented in accordance with the opinions of simple little women and, as it were, thought out by wise men for the verisimilitude of an invented story. . . .

The unusual interpretation of Charon's task is intriguing. When the boatman serves in a Christian scheme, he is no longer a medieval demon: As the joy that bears the soul through waves of trouble, upholding it in danger, Charon assumes a new and startling moral significance. The scoffing reference to the idea of an obol needed for passage, I might add, reinforces Conti's desire to be original and discerning.

Cartari. Before leaving the mythographers let us look at one of the iconographical works of the time, Vincenzo Cartari's *Imagini dei Dei degli antichi* (1556). Cartari, who follows in the steps of the mythographers, represents an attempt to popularize classical mythology by making it clear to all. In his discussion of Charon, Cartari quotes Dante and translates into Italian the traditional mythographic sources, namely, Virgil, Seneca, Servius, and Boccaccio as well as Pausanias's comments on Polygnotus. Cartari's allegorical exegesis is taken from Boccaccio, although Cartari closes his exposition with general comments that bring to mind some of Dante's commentators. Having referred, for example, to Charon's sordid outfit, representing as in Boccaccio the vile things of this life, Cartari adds:

Ma questa frale spoglia del corpo mortale, che habbiamo intorno, cosi ci cuopre il lume della ragione, che quasi ciechi ne andiamo per l'Inferno di questo mondo, scorti dal senso solamente, & da mille disordinati appetiti. (1647 ed., p. 164, as cited in A 95)

But this frail garment of our mortal body, which we have about us, conceals the light of reason from us; we, almost blind, go about through the hell of this world, led only by our senses and by a thousand uncontrolled appetites.

While Cartari lacks the originality and erudition of his predecessors, his work achieved a greater popularity than most scholarly treatises on myth. By acknowl-

Charon, in Vincenzo Cartari, *Imagini dei Dei degli'Antichi* (1603). By permission of the
Department of Special Collections, Joseph Regenstein Library, The University of Chicago.

edging his sources and borrowings, translating everything into Italian, and providing detailed inconographic descriptions, he fulfills his aim of providing pictorial subjects and promoting a better understanding of the writers of antiquity.

ii. Dialogues

The introduction of Lucian into Italy has been ascribed to the Sicilian Giovanni Aurispa (1376–1459), who brought over two hundred Greek manuscripts to Venice in 1423.[12] More likely, however, Lucian arrived in Italy late in the fourteenth century. Natale Caccia claims that a version of *Charon* entitled *Contemplanti* was produced by un unknown scholar under Chrysoloras in Florence and transcribed by Tebaldo della Casa as early as 1403. By 1417, Guarino had already translated three of Lucian's dialogues.[13] Although the original Greek text of the Lucianic corpus was not published until 1494–1496 by Constantine Lascaris, the second-century Syrian was widely read, translated, and imitated throughout the Quattrocento (see, for example, A 97, 99, 100). An early example of his influence is provided by Leon Battista Alberti's *Momus*, a treatise written in Latin before 1450. Imitating the initial situation of Lucian's *Charon, or The Inspectors*, Alberti develops in narrative form a brief dialogue of the dead (see Bibliography, Primary Sources, Part two, A 98).

Pontano. Another early dialogue of greater influence is Giovanni Pontano's *Charon*, first published in 1491, although possibly written as early as 1467. The Lucianic situation is employed by the poet as a pretext for a sarcastic condemnation of, among other evil men, priggish grammarians and avaricious churchmen. The dialogue opens with Aeacus and Minos, who are concerned with the disastrous events taking place on earth. Since they are on vacation, they decide to visit the banks of Acheron, hoping that a descending soul may bring news of what is taking place among the living.

Charon is introduced in the second vignette as a boatman engrossed in speculation concerning the vanity of human hopes. The model, of course, is Lucian's philosophic ferryman. When Charon speaks of a tyrant's deluded hopes, Aeacus marvels at the boatman's learning. Charon explains that he has often listened to educated men during his hours of leisure, though at times also having had to endure pseudointellectuals. With this note, Pontano takes the opportunity to satirize the use of etymologies, so common among the allegorizers of myth. A sophist, says Charon, claimed that the boatman will die some day. When Charon protested that he is not mortal, the sophist replied: "Charo . . . es, omnis autem caro morti est obnoxia, morieris igitur" ("you are Flesh, and all flesh is subject to death; therefore you will die" [A 101; p. 5]). A more humorous mocking of this practice is offered by another fool: "Remus, inquit, Romuli frater fuit; plures istic remos habes, plures ergo fratres tecum sunt Romuli" ("Remus, he said, was Romulus's brother; you have quite a few oars [*remos*] here, therefore quite a few brothers of Romulus are with you" [A 101; p. 5]). Pontano satirizes not only the sophists' recourse to distorted etymology but also their use of false syllogisms.

Turning to a tyrant who has been left alone on the banks of the Acheron outside of Hades, Minos explains to Charon that the man is so litigious he would have upset even the spirits of the dead. The tyrant's punishment is an example of Dantesque *contrappasso*: Because he devoured others, he is transformed periodically into a frog and eaten by a snake. "Quam iure, quam merito!" exclaims the boatman (A 101; p. 7). Minos continues to relate the evil deeds of living; they not only despise the just, but they have forgotten the truth taught by the poets concerning the underworld. As evidence, Pontano joins the pagan and the Christian: Among those who have been harmed by men are Socrates and Christ; both suffered because they taught the truth. Interestingly, while those on earth hated Christ, "a nobis vero et turbis his," says Minos, "quibus esset incognitus, ubi primum visus, statim cultusque et adoratus fuerit"! ("But, when first seen, he was at once venerated and adored by us and by these crowds to whom he was unkonwn" [A 101; p. 7]). Blaming the body for much of man's evil, Minos tells Charon that the boatman is blessed to have never had a body.

In the following episodes, Charon ferries Mercury and a variety of dead souls across the river, and Pontano offers educative and exemplary advice to his readers. Among those criticized for their deeds are usurers, priests who make love to women, doctors who kill people, priests who are corrupt and avaricious, tyrants, gluttonous priests, and academicians. The satire on priests is a motif repeated often; their vices are mentioned in episodes 4, 6, 8, and 10. One of the last groups of souls to arrive, for example, contains a whore and her friend, a cardinal. Another soul, that of a girl, tells how she lost her virginity to a priest, deceived by the trick of supposedly marrying Christ. The scene is narrated with Boccacian vivacity.

Another noteworthy episode, one satirizing pedants, is especially effective, where Pontano mocks the overpreciseness of grammarians, who are concerned with the most minute and meaningless details. Among the facts that Pedanus would like Mercury to take back to his disciples is that Acestes "lived a hundred twenty-four years, eleven months, twenty-nine days, three hours, two minutes, and half a second" (A 101; p. 33); Palamedes invented the letter ψ from a mark on his forehead (p. 34); Aeneas put neither the left nor the right foot on land first but was set down by his boatman with both feet touching the gound at once; Horace abstained from drinking and praised wine only because his father was a great drinker; and so forth. The burlesque scene, which continues at greater length, thoroughly mocks the foolishness of overblown erudition.

Charon speaks as a philosopher on a variety of subjects throughout the dialogue. Among the topics discussed are, for example, honest as compared to dishonest pleasure, the superiority of an active live to one of ease, free will, fortune, superstition, the failure of virtue to descend to one's offspring, and so forth. Concluding the work is the discourse of one wise man, who speaks of man's distance from God. His message is that through virtue, the middle term, one rises to God and attains true happiness, free from turmoil and earthly passions.

The success of Pontano's dialogues extends throughout the Cinquecento.[14] Among those influenced by the Neapolitan humanist is Desiderius Erasmus. While outside the direct scope of this study, his *Colloquies* contain a dialogue of interest, entitled *Charon* (A 103);[15] both the subject matter, a criticism of war, and the mythological framework owe more to Lucian, however, than to Pontano. Charon is seen searching for a new boat, because his dilapidated ferry has sunk under the weight of the souls. With an Aristophanic touch, Erasmus describes the souls as swimming among the frogs, while Charon himself is dripping wet.

Niccolò Franco. In Italy, two of the more original vernacular dialogues employing Charon belong to Niccolò Franco (A 104). Published in 1539 in the author's *Dialoghi piacevoli*, the two works recall both Pontano's criticism of pedants and Lucian's technique of examining souls awaiting embarcation. In both instances, Franco manifests his originality with interesting situations and humorous dialogue.

The dialogue concerning Borgio pedante begins with the pedant lamenting that though eighty years old, he was not able to live another month, during which time he could have straightened out his earthly affairs. To vent his frustration, he talks of his life on earth and lists all the literary works that he was in the middle of teaching. Charon's comment is that Borgio will not be missed: So many pedants descend to hell that there must be great competition for positions on earth.

Borgio asks for time, "Solamente quanto possa pensare dieci parole, e non più, ch'io intendo dire dinanzi a Plutone . . ." ("just enough to think of ten words, no more, which I intend to say to Pluto" [A 104; p. 42ʳ]). His ten words are more like ten pages, however. To gain Charon's favor, the pedant refers to their old age:

> Fa che questa gratia non si conceda nè a Borgio, nè a pedanti, ma all'età canuta. Sei uecchio tu ancora, e dei sapere quanto sieno grandi gli stimoli della ritrosia, che ci tiene. (P. 42ᵛ)

> Grant this favor not to Borgio, nor to pedants, but to hoary old age. You, too, are old and ought to know how great are the pressures of our shyness, which holds us back.

Having been granted his request to prepare what he now says are four words, Borgio launches into a discussion on the art of oratory. But though he quotes Cicero and lists the rhetorical ornaments needed, he is unable to pronounce his words well because of his lack of teeth. Throughout the pedant's discourse, Franco inserts humorous notes, such as the following sexual wordplay:

> Ecci poi la Contentione: La Esclamatione, la Interrogatione, il Discorso, et il colore, che si chiama Membro, il qual sempre mi piacque, e del quale è forza ch'io me serua nell'oratione in tutti i modi. (P. 43ᵛ)

Then there is disputation: esclamation, interrogation, discourse, and color, which is called a member, which always pleased me, and which of necessity I make use of in orating, in all the ways possible.

When Charon begs him to stop, Borgio asks for a moment more and continues for several more pages. As an example of his rhetoric, he sums up the awe he feels in hell with a sixteen-line sentence, where he notes, in part, the

grandissimi, e correnti fiumi, et a nominargli terribili, come è Cocito, Periflege-tonte, e la palude Acherusia, che posta alle frontiere, è il primo ricetto a tutti coloro, che vengono inanti, le cui onde sono di tanta profondità, e larghezza, che non si possono uarcare a noto, senza la barca di Caronte, huomo cortese, di canuta, e tremenda presenza. (p. 46ʳ)

extremely large and flowing rivers, terrible to name, like Cocytus, Periphlege-thon, and the Acherusian swamp, which, set at the border, is the first gathering place for those who come along, and whose waves are so deep and of such width that it is impossible to cross them swimming, without the boat of Cha-ron, a courteous man of hoary and tremendous presence.

When Charon again asks him to stop this chatter and the vain attempt at flat-tery, Borgio replies: "Non mi interrompere Caronte, perche hora mi trouo tutto acceso nella vehementia dell'orare" ("don't interrupt me Charon, because now I find myself all afire in the vehemence of orating"). As a result, long passages follow where the pedant displays all the devices of rhetoric at his command. The excellence with which this is done leads the reader to feel at times that Franco himself enjoys the pedant's verbiage. The poet's pleasure in spinning words renders the criticism not acerbic but subtle. The final note of satire occurs when Borgio, having finished his peroration, asks for time to make up a *memoriale* (p. 48ᵛ), a list of things to do. Charon mocks this affectation by telling Borgio that in hell he will soon have no memory to worry about.

The second dialogue offers a greater variety of targets for the poet's satire. The situation is again embarcation, with the problem being that none of the souls has the obol required for passage. After complaining of "le fatiche che fo da cane, da questa riua all'altra, così di festa, come di lauoro, così di giorno, come di notte" ("the toils which I undergo like a dog, from this bank to the other, on holidays just as on work days, by day just as by night" [p. 68ʳ]) and listening to Mercury's excuses for himself and Atropos ("who does not choose men as one chooses melons! "), Charon interrogates the souls, who, in turn, offer their own excuses for lacking a fare. In doing so, the souls paint a picture of various vices, ranging from those of a prostitute, who sold herself as a virgin seven times but died poor with syphilis; to those of a tyrant, who died by poison, losing all his possessions but "orgoglio con l'alterezza" ("pride with haughtiness" [p. 70ʳ]); to those of a merchant, who asks Charon for credit (with predictable word plays on *Caronte* and *creditori*); to those, finally, of a pedant and a braggart soldier. Regarding two final groups, ten poets and thirty philosophers, Mercury says that they have no fare because poetry and philosophy never had a cent. With this, Charon concludes the dialogue by adding, "Horsu entrate in barca voi tutte anime, et il conto, che nella riua non hauete fatto con Caronte, farete nell'inferno con Radamanto" ("come on, all you souls, get in the boat, and the bill which you didn't settle on the bank with Charon you can settle in hell with Rhadamanthys" [p. 74ʳ]).

Influenced by Lucian and Erasmian thought,[16] Franco develops his satire in imaginative prose destined for a broad audience. Characterized by his vibrant and expressive use of modern Florentine as well as his originial and witty touches, Franco satirizes the vices of his time with great effectiveness. In the case of the pedant Borgio, the author does so with especial enjoyment and subtlety. Franco's command of the rhetorical excesses he mocks is thorough enough to captivate and entice the reader. Entranced by the mellifluous sounds of Borgio's oration, the reader is led to a greater awareness of the pernicious effect of language if meaning and relevance are lacking.

iii. Narrative

Armannino. The representation of Charon in vernacular prose narrative is contemporary with the earliest poetic treatments of the descent myth in Italian. References to the boatman are found in works similar to medieval compendia, where an attempt was made to compress all knowledge. An excellent Italian example is the *Fiorita* by Armannino Giudice, composed in 1325.[17] The work, a vast collection of historical deeds, begins with the creation of the world, covers the events of Troy and Thebes, and traces the heroic feats of Aeneas and the Romans. Aeneas's descent, for example, provides an opportunity for the poet to describe the torments of the damned "per conducere i peccatori a pentersi e confermare li giusti a ben fare" ("in order to lead sinners to repentance and to strengthen the just in doing good" [p. 11]). While Armannino mentions Dante several times throughout the *Fiorita*, the fundamental features of the descent episode in Book 24 are taken directly from Virgil.[18] Evidence of medieval and Dantesque influence can be found, however, in the actual depiction of Charon and the crossing. For example, Aeneas and the Sibyl, arriving at a dark river, see a crowd of souls standing stiff like birds in winter swamps and shouting "guai, guai," much as Dante's Charon does. The boat, in the Virgilian mold, is not wooden but sewn like a basket and guided by a black devil ("uno diavolo nero") called Caronte. When Aeneas asks the Sibyl why the souls are anxious to cross the river, she respond with the original note that these are righteous spirits ("li giusti ispiriti") who are waiting to go to paradise. Before going, however, they must cleanse themselves anew, since they did not complete their purgation in purgatory. The Sibyl continues at length, delivering a discourse on various methods of purgation.

When the Sibyl accosts Charon, he both questions and threatens the descenders: " 'Chi siete voi, corpora viventi, che così andate sicuri per li nostri terreni, dove non sono corpi? Se voi entrerete in quella nave, voi anderete al profondo del fiume' " ("Who are you, living bodies, who go so surely through our lands, where there are no bodies? If you enter that ship, you will go to the bottom of the river"). In the Sibyl's response, in which she asks Charon to lend them the boat, she refers to the fact that the souls who are transported by Charon go to Elysium. Charon, of course, refuses her request, and Aeneas is constrained to show him the golden bough (A 106; D'Ancona-Bacci, pp. 494–495).

On the whole, Armannino's narrative, especially when no sermon is being delivered, is sparse; he sticks to the bare outline of the Virgilian story, cutting what he considers to be superfluous dialogue and description. Regarding earlier depictions, whereas in Dante Charon cries "guai" in order to threaten the souls, in Armannino, the spirits themselves use the word as a lament. Charon is not characterized by his age but by being a black devil, a note not found in Dante but typical of medieval demons. The reference to the boat is also novel, because the poet translates the Virgilian adjective *sutilis* as *tessuta come canestro*. Armannino's most striking innovation, however, is his reference to the spirits as souls undergoing purgation in preparation for paradise. The author's moralistic intentions become evident in the Sibyl's explanation, which is, at the same time, a brief sermon. As for the actual confrontation with Charon, the Sibyl is the first to speak, beginning instantly with an authoritative command. In response, we first see Charon's *mal volto* and then hear his lengthy and descriptive question. The boatman's threat is almost emotionless: If they enter the boat, they will sink straight to the bottom. The Sibyl, unconcerned, responds with equally plebian and ineffective discourse. Finally, as in the *Aeneid*, the golden bough is employed and passage obtained.

Armannino's narrative stands out in contrast to Virgil's poetic treatment of the descent in two fundamental ways. First, the medival author is concerned more with the punishments of the penitent and the moralistic superstructure than with the underlying action. Secondly, this diverse attitude is reflected in the rapid summary of elements necessary to the narrative flow. A good example is provided by the final sentence: "Vedendo Caronte lo ramo usato, lo quale già altre volte veduto avea, li ricolse nella nave." In Virgil, the display of the golden bough is a moment of awe, and the poem allows a moment of inactivity during which Charon's emotional response—from loss of anger to marvel—is registered. Virgil also depicts the subsequent physical activity in more expansive terms and Charon is seen with pictorial completeness: He draws his boat near the shore, routs out the load of souls he had just embarked, takes in Aeneas, and begins the difficult voyage. In contrast in the *Fiorita*, Armannino depicts the bough not as a "venerabile donum / . . . longo post tempore visum" (*Aen.* 6. 408–409) but as "the accustomed bough, which Charon had already seen at other times." The boatman is denied any emotional reaction; rather than lingering on the scene while his nautical maneuvers are described, Charon simply accepts the two descenders and disappears.

Caviceo. As a second example of narrative, let me mention the *Libro del peregrino* by Jacopo Caviceo, probably written in the last twenty years of the Quattrocento but not printed until 1508 (A 111). Characterized by the intense passion of the Peregrino who narrates his story in the first person, the *romanzo* is the story of a grieving lover. Caviceo, influenced by Boccaccio, develops his story with a variety of stylistic features, ranging from lengthy hypotactic sentences that flow with sonorous rhythms to brief incisive questions and rapid exclamations. Thematically, the work contains features reminiscent of many of Boccaccio's minor works.

When the Peregrino decides to descend into hell in order to learn the whereabouts of his beloved Ginevera, he falls asleep and finds himself at the banks of a dark, rapid, and deep river. He describes the boatman in Apuleian terms, but the ferry itself takes on the symbolical overtones familiar from Petrarch and some of the Dantesque commentators:

> Ivi gli era un vecchio squallido et avaro, qual con sottil cimba, aspettava il portatorio de chi all'altra riva volea commeare. Stupido fatto, mirai quella barca, qual mi parse la vera tristizia, li remi erano lagrime et affanni: li trastri sospir continui: la prora, penitenza sempiterna: la parte posterior, dannazione. Quivi circonfusa gli era una inestimabil turba. . . . (A 111; p. 435)

> There was a squalid and avaricious old man there, who was waiting with his small boat to ferry over anyone who wanted to go to the other bank. Astonished, I gazed at that boat, which seemed to me to be true sadness. The oars were tears and sorrow; the rowers' benches continuous sighs; the prow, eternal repentance; the hind part, damnation. Here surrounding the boat was an innumerable crowd. . . .

Thrusting himself into the crowd, the Peregrino searches for Ginevera but fails to find her. At this, he decides to cross the river and seems to face no difficulty. In fact, he pays his fare and is about to enter the boat when his actions suddenly enrage the ferryman, who, incidentally, is never named; the passage reads as follows:

> Dato il naulo al crudel Nocchiero, lo pregai che la mal fida cimba al litto volesse firmare, acciò che agevolmente puotessi salire. Tutto turbato in vista, col remo l'acqua percosse, e scostando la barca dissemi: —Per te ora non fia il passo, qual quando serà, gravemente te anoglierà. Ritorna adrieto: qua giù non è fiamma che petto vivo abrusci—. (A 111; p. 435)

> Having given the fare to the cruel helmsman, I beseeched him to hold the treacherous boat to the shore so that I could get in easily. With his face all enraged, he struck the water with his oar and shoving the boat off said to me:

"For you now there is no passage, which when it comes will wear on you heavily. Go back now; down here there is no flame which burns a living breast."

But despite the boatman's reluctance, the virtue of the poet's guide is such that they are afforded passage.

During the crossing the Peregrino carries on a conversation with another *ombra*, who tells him that he will find only cruelty, ingratitude, and avarice beyond the river. In the following chapter, the Peregrino turns to his guide, the saintly Anselmo, asking why four shades on the boat continue to lament. Anselmo explains that until completely purged in Lethe, the souls retain the remnants of their corporeal memory. These four are unfortunate political leaders from different regions of Italy. With this, the Peregrino returns to the narration of his voyage: "Fatto il tragietto vidi un gran Can tricipite con formidabile e crudel latrato" ("Having been ferried across, I saw a great three-headed dog with a dreadfully cruel howling" [A 111; p. 437]). As in the case of the ferryman, the dog remains unnamed.

On the whole, Caviceo's *romanzo* is reminiscent of the descents found in allegorical-didactic poems in the Quattrocento. Following each scene, the guide Anselmo explains at length the greater significance of the event. At times entire chapters, such as 8, dealing with the soul, are devoted to philosophical or moral questions. When Caviceo does develop his narrative thread, however, he treats familiar classical features with some originality. In the encounter with the infernal boatman, for example, we find a typically irascible *nocchiero*, but the situation that excites him is unusual, as is his striking the water with his oar and shoving off the boat. Interestingly, as a work of narrative, the *Peregrino* seems to go back to Apuleius as well as other poetic descents. The influence of Dante, while well disguised, is possibly evident in the boatman's response to the Peregrino, reminiscent of *Inferno* 3. 92.

Doni. Turning to the mid-sixteenth century, let me mention as a final example of Charon in narrative the *Mondi infernali* of Anton Francesco Doni (A 115). A bizarre and imaginative work, the "Libro secondo dei Mondi, chiamati i sette inferni" contains a variety of prose types. The two passages dealing with an underworld ferryman, for example, are situated, one in an infernal vision with subsequent commentary, the other in epistolary form.

Doni's humor becomes especially evident when the author decides that he wants to go to hell himself in order to write well about the region. He has searched, he says, for Dante's *selva* without being able to find it—"onde ho per fermo che la selua che egli trouò, sia stata tagliata" ("from which I firmly hold that the woods which he found have been cut down"); we are reminded of Lucian's technique where poetic fiction is taken as fact. Unable to find Virgil's Sibyl nor Menippus's Negromante and unable to play the *ribecca* like Orfeo, the author finally falls asleep exhausted, realizing that "Dante dormendo come me, andò

anch'egli all'Inferno . . .'' (''Dante went to hell, he, too, sleeping like me''
[A 115; p. 238]). What follows is a series of visions, in the second of which we find
the ''inferno de gli scolari vitiosi'' (''hell of depraved scholars''). The depiction of
this first hell is an innovation. Narrated by the Disperato, the vision presents
a magnificent view of Lucifer, who is seen swallowing men. Through the devil's
transparent body, the Disperato sees in his stomach a lake of *infiniti tormenti*; his
description follows:

> Andaua una barca atorno atorno sopra le acque, et se aggiraua come fa un
> uccello che vuole pigliar del pesce, subito che egli lo uede si tuffa, et gli dà di
> piglio. Quando il Nocchieri haueua carica la sua barca, andaua in giro, et
> secondo che egli uedeua nella fronte dell'anime scritto il suo tormento, le get-
> taua giù, et quelle agrauate dal peccato come piombo cadeuano sopra nella
> pena determinata loro. (A 115; p. 249)

> A boat was going around and around over the water and it was roving like a
> bird which wishes to catch fish which, once it sees one, dives and catches it.
> When the helmsman had loaded his boat, he went about, and according to the
> torment which he saw written on the forehead of the souls, he threw them
> down, and they, weighed down by the sin, fell like lead to the place deter-
> mined for their punishment.

Following this vision, we read the dichiaratione of both the Dubbioso and the
Negligente. The first holds that Lucifer represents the world into whose torments
we fall. The second adds an allegorical interpretaton in relation to the infernal
boatman:

> Vogliono costoro che la barcha che solca il pelago fatto da quattro fiume, la sia
> tessuta d'anni, et che li Nocchieri di quella sia il Tempo, che l'empio d'anime,
> et quando gli piace le getta in mare, che significa il corpo uostro composto da
> quattro Elementi. (A 115; pp. 251–252)

> Some say that the boat which furrows the sea, formed by four rivers, is woven
> from years and that the ferryman who fills the boat with souls is Time. When
> he wishes to, he throws the souls into the sea, which represents our body
> formed from four elements.

The familiar feature of Charon as time, found in the commentaries, comes to life
in a new and startling fashion in Doni. This infernal ferryman does not merely
represent the passing of life from birth to death but almost a creative force. It is
he who casts the souls into their earthly bodies.

A more traditional representation of the boatman occurs in the depiction of the
third hell, where Charon is referred to by name and performs his traditional functions as underworld ferryman. The form of this section is a letter written by the
Pazzo to the Antico Barcaiuolo, il Sig. Caronte Nocchieri spauenteuole, posto nel
numero de gli Dei Infernali, temuto da tutte l'anime Meschine, et Dannate''

("ancient boatman, Mr. Charon, dreadful ferryman, numbered among the infernal gods, feared by all souls wretched and damned" [A 115; p. 291]). The letter is followed by both an allegorical explanation of the fiction employed and a letter from Charon himself in response.

The Pazzo's letter is a satirical description and warning of what the *pazzi*, who are descending into hell in ever greater numbers, will do to Charon. First of all, says the Pazzo, the *pazzi* will not have the fare:

> poi se s'infuriano ui peleranno la barba, ui getteranno a un bisogno di sù la poppa in acqua: e faranno altri bischenchi strani che non ue gli imaginereste mai, pazzi eh? pazzi in là? fate a mio senno non ue gli lasciate appressare quanto è lungo il vostro remo. (P. 291)

> Then if they get angry, they will pluck out your beard; they will throw you from the stern if needed into the water; and they will play other strange tricks which you would never imagine of them, madmen eh? madmen there? Do as I advise and don't let them get any closer than the length of your oar.

The letter contains as well the imagined responses of Charon to this rare friend, as the Pazzo likes to call himself:

> Messersi, mi direte ma damegli a conoscere, per che egli è pur tanti e tanti anni ch'io uogo et solco questa palude, ne mai ho conosciuto questi pazzi che tu di [.] M. Caronte uoi hauete ragione, et di tutto ui renderò buon conto. (P. 292)

> Yes sir, you'll say to me, but tell me, why is it that I have rowed and plowed this swamp for so many, many years and I've never met these madmen you talk about. Mr. Charon, you're right, and I'll give you a good explanation why.

The familiar tone of the letter, addressed to a feared infernal god, adds to the humor.

The Pazzo explains that while the wise have always died, the crazy have continued to live—"i pazzi non son mai morti, sempre son uiuuti, et uiuono anchora" ("the madmen have never died; they've always lived, and still do live" [p. 292]). As a consequence, there are hardly any wise men left, and the crazy ones will descend in a swarm some day. Before Charon's replies, the author presents an "allegoria dello Stracco Academico Pellegrino" (p. 294), in which he explains that he is not the first to employ a "fauoloso Nume Infernale, et una fintion poetica" ("fabled infernal deity and a poetic fiction") to represent man's condition. "Simil pazzie honeste" ("similar honest follies"), he says, are traditional. But what is not traditional, what is, in fact, original, is Doni's interpretation of Charon's symbolic import:

> Caronte in questo Inferno del mondo che passa il fiume de trauagli, de fastidij, et delle liti humane, è il giudice, che sù la barca; cioè su 'l seggio del suo tribunale giudica il quale uiene auertito dalla pazzia nostra, che sia ben cauto a conoscere gli huomini et le donne [pazzi]. . . . (P. 294)

In this hell of a world, Charon, who crosses the river of travail, of annoyances, and of human quarrels, is the judge, who holds court on his boat—that is, on the bench of his tribunal—and who is warned by our madness, so that he may be very careful to recognize mad men and women.

Charon is a judge, then, who is warned by humanity's insanity to be wary of crazy men and women.

Charon's response begins with a proverb: "Bastaua fare un cenno a chi son golpe uecchia, messer Pazzo carissimo, et dire i pazzi ci sono multiplicati" ("It's enough to give a hint to one who is an old fox, my dear Mr. Madman, and to say that the madmen have multiplied" [p. 308]). In fact, he says, they have already begun to arrive. In a description of his narrow escape, Charon lets it be known that he has wings:

> E mi conuenne fuggir dalla riua con la mia burchiella che mai piu m'è interuenuto; et s'io non haueua l'ali rimaneuo impaniato; onde i pazzi che uoi dite si son messi a girar corrondo intorno al fiume. (P. 308)

> And it was necessary for me to flee from the shore with my little boat, something I've never had to do before. And, if I hadn't had wings, I would have been snared. Seeing this, the madmen of whom you speak began running around about the river.

Claiming that this is a rare situation for hell (p. 309), Charon blusters that he did not flee in fear but because he is no longer so young as he used to be. With this note, Doni ends his representation of the boatman, seen as a somewhat pitiful old man who has lost his power. Throughout these episodes, we are reminded of the burlesque treatment of the infernal ferryman in the *Baldus* by Folengo. Doni manifests a similar farcical bent, mocking not only the *pazzi* of this world but also the minor gods of the other realm.

In speaking of prose narratives in general, I note the close relationship to other poetic modes of the fourteenth and fifteenth centuries. I refer specifically to the allegorical-didactic poems, whose features reappear often in the prose writers. While there are differences in degree between Armannino Giudice, Caviceo, and Doni, all three are concerned with moral truths. Armannino's method is more medieval in that his work is a compilation of classical sources interfused with moralistic episodes and accompanied by allegorical exposition. His aim is inherently didactic—that is, he desires to organize and clarify the knowledge of ancient poets, rendering their thoughts in the vernacular in order to reach a wider audience. Caviceo, on the contrary, aims for a more courtly audience and attains a higher level of stylistic sophistication. Though dealing with love thematics, he strives to integrate didactic passages into his narrative and also tends at times toward allegory. Doni captures the attention of his audience through the use of a more common Florentine vernacular, enlivened by bizarre situations and intriguing fantasies. He aims not only to entertain, however, but to instruct. As opposed to the religious overtones in Armannino, Doni's method is to employ satire, focus less on religious truths and more on what could be called an Erasmian life of moderation and sanity. In their use of Charon, all three writers assert not only their ties to tradition but also their individual artistic temperaments.

Notes

1. Servius (fourth century A.D.) is one of the first to treat Virgil with an allegorical approach, approximating that used by the Greeks in relation to Homer and Hesiod. While not consistently allegorical in his method, Servius tends to find philosophical and moral significance throughout the *Aeneid*, but especially in Book 6, in which Virgil, he believes, expressed his most profound truths. Regarding the Acheron, Servius writes: "Acheronta vult quasi de imo nasci Tartaro, huius aestuaria Stygem creare, de Styge autem nasci Cocyton. Et haec est mythologia: nam physiologia hoc habet, quia qui caret gaudio sine dubio tristis est" (*ad Aen.* 6. 295). Charon himself is interpreted κατα ἀντίφρασιν quasi ἀχαίρων (ibid. 299), while Cerberus becomes earth, the consumer of bodies. In discussing Charon's remark that Hercules subdued Cerberus, Servius both allegorizes the episode—"haec ratio est, quia omnes cupiditates et cunctua vitia terrena contempsit et domuit" (ibid. 395)—and adds a mythographic detail to the Charon myth, namely, that "lectum est et in Orpheo quod, quando Hercules ad inferos descendit, Charon territus eum statim suscepit: ob quam rem anno integro in compedibus fuit" (ibid. 392). All quotations are from the edition by Thilo and Hagen, vol. 2. On Servius's methods of interpretation, see J. W. Jones, Jr., "Allegorical Interpretation in Servius."

Two of the widely used allegorizers of Virgil are Fabius Planciades Fulgentius (ca. A.D. 467–532) and Bernard Silvestris (fl. ca. 1140). Fulgentius offers the first detailed allegorical interpretation of the *Aeneid* by a Christian. In his *Virgiliana continentia*, when Aeneas descends to Hades, representing the undertaking of philosophical studies, he is led by Charon, who is time ("Caron vero quasi ceron, id est tempus"), across the boiling tide of youth (the Acheron), and hears the dissensions of men (the barking of Cerberus), which are calmed by the honey of wisdom (the sop thrown to Cerberus). For Fulgentius's text, see Rudolf Helm, *Expositio Virgilianae Continentiae*, p. 98, and for a discussion of his method, see H. C. Coffin, "Allegorical Interpretation of Vergil with Special Reference to Fulgentius."

Although Silvestris provides only a brief allegorical summary of the first five books of the *Aeneid*, he expands his analysis in Book 6, explicating the text almost word by word. In interpreting Aeneas's descent to the lower realms, Silvestris interprets the *inferi* in the Neoplatonic manner as referring to this earth, the lowest part of the universe. The concept is familiar to the Neoplatonists of the Italian Renaissance and was expressed by many ancient and medieval commentators before Silvestris, including Servius and Macrobius (fifth century A.D.). The latter writer's *In somnium Scipionis*, one of the most important sources of Platonism in the Latin West in the Middle Ages, also deals with the lower realm and the infernal rivers but without mentioning Charon. See Macrobius, *Commentary on the Dream of Scipio*, Book 1, chap. 10. Silvestris, who interprets the Acheron as *sine gaudio* and the passage to its banks as the descent into sadness caused by vice, expounds on the noun *portitor* as follows: "Predictas aquas Carrone duce oportet meare quia luctum et tristiciam relictis viciorum voluptatibus ductu temporis utile est transire. . . . Dictur autem Carron quasi cronon, tempus" (*ad Aen.* 6. 298). Silvestris also allegorizes Charon's ship and its oars (see ibid. 302). Charon's significance is alluded to a second time in Silvestris's comment on *Aen.* 6. 415–416: "Caron TANDEM post longum spatium eos TRANS FLUVIUM EXPONIT dum trans molestias laboriose vite in quietam vitam eos sistit." I quote from Julian W. Jones and Elizabeth F. Jones, *The Commentary on the First Six Books of the Aeneid of Vergil Commonly Attributed to Bernardus Silvestris*.

2. Some commentators, of course, remain faithful to the literal interpretation, often, for example, comparing Dante's portrayal of Charon to Virgil's. Among those to do so are the Ottimo commentary (A 74), Bernardino Daniello (A 85), and Ludovico Castelvetro (A 86).

3. Cf. the anonymous Marciano commentary (A 72; p. 13), the Ottimo (A 74; p. 31), Pietro di Dante (A 75; p. 70), Benvenuto da Imola (A 77; p. 123), Francesco da Buti (A 79; p. 97), the Anonymous Florentine (A 80; p. 75), Stefano Talice da Ricaldone (A 81; p. 47), Cristoforo Landino (A 82; p. 30ᵛ), and Giovan Battista Gelli (A 84; p. 261). This interpretation, of course, derives from Servius's commentary by way of Silvestris's.

4. See, for example, Guido da Pisa (A 71; p. 13), Anonymous Marciano (A 72; p. 13), Jacopo Della Lana (A 73; p. 133), Pietro di Dante (A 75; p. 70), Giovanni Boccaccio (A 76; p. 261), Benvenuto (A 77; p. 125), Buti (A 79; p. 100), Anonymous Florentine (A 80; pp. 75 ff.), Stefano Talice (A 81; pp.

47 ff.), Landino (A 82; p. 31ʳ), Alessandro Vellutello (A 83; p. 22ʳ), and Gelli (A 84; pp. 261–262) as well as, to mention just Charon's eyes, Benvenuto (A 77; p. 127), Buti (A 79; p. 101), Anonymous Florentine (A 80; p. 79), and Gelli (A 84; p. 264).

5. See, for example, Benvenuto (A 77; p. 125), Buti (A 79; p. 100), and Gelli (A 84; p. 262).

6. Pietro di Dante (A 75; p. 71), Boccaccio (A 76; p. 262), Buti (A 79; p. 103), Anonymous Florentine (A 80; pp. 79–80), Stefano Talice (A 81; p. 49), and Vellutello (A 83; p. 22ʳ).

7. Earlier, both Jacopo Della Lana (A 73) and Guido da Pisa (A 71) represent Charon as the flesh or carnal desire. The impulse for this interpretation, of course, derives from the supposed relationship between *Charon* and the Latin noun *caro*. The earliest anonymous commentary (A 72) interprets the boatman in the general sense of *l'antico peccato*, which Vellutello varies to *uitio* (A 83).

8. "Herebus autem hic pro intrinseco divine mentis consilio intelligendus est, a quo tempus et cetera omnia creata sunt, et sic Herebus Caronis pater. Nox autem illi ob id mater data est, quia ante creatum tempus nulla fuit sensibilis lux, et ideo in tenebris factum est, et ex tenebris productum videtur."

9. Francesco Petrarca, *Secretum* 2 in *Prose* a cura di Enrico Carrara (Milano: Ricciardi, 1955), p. 104.

10. Jean Seznec, *The Survival of the Pagan Gods: The Mythological Tradition and Its Place in Renaissance Humanism and Art*, p. 249. Seznec claims that Conti's feigned ignorance of the earlier work of Giraldi is due to his "excessive vanity" (p. 233). Regarding Charon, however, Conti does not rely on his predecessor. Giraldi, as Seznec notes, concentrates on names, epithets, and etymologies (p. 233); this is especially evident in his treatment of Charon. Giraldi writes of Charon, "dictus per antiphrasin, quasi Acharon," cites the etymologies of "Phurnutus" as "non satis," and adds: "Portitor Charon dictus, à Grecis Porthmeus, vt in nostris Nauigijs ostendimus. . . . Nauita etiam nuncupatus" (See A 93; p. 207).

11. Seznec, who stresses the lack of an original system in both Giraldi and Conti, notes Conti's scorn for his predecessors, who supposedly were unable to penetrate the deeper meaning of the myths. Given this attitude, Conti steers clear of traditional allegories connected to Charon. That his ideas were of influence, by the way, is evident in the *Philosophia secreta* (1585) of Juan Pèrez de Moya, who quotes both Boccaccio and Conti without acknowledgment, however, describing not only a Charonte (synonymous with time) on the river Acheronte (7. 1) but also a Caròn on the Flegeton, the latter moralized as *alegría* because "nos sirve de viático y provisión donde quiera que vamos" (7. 6). I quote from the edition with introduction by Eduardo Gómez de Baquero (Madrid: Compañía iberoamericana de publicaciónes, 1928), vol. 2, pp. 308–309 and 317–318.

12. Remigio Sabbadini, *Le scoperte dei codici latini e greci ne' secoli XIV e XV*, vol. 1, p. 49, and Francis G. Allinson, *Lucian: Satirist and Artist*, p. 140.

13. Natale Caccia, *Note su la fortuna di Luciano nel Rinascimento, le versioni e i dialoghi satirici di Erasmo de Rotterdam e di Ulrich Hutten*, p. 8.

14. Editions appeared in 1501, 1514, 1518–1519, 1538–1540, 1556, and 1579. From this latter date until 1874, however, the *Charon* dialogue was not reprinted. See G. Pontano, *I dialoghi*, ed. Carmelo Previtera (Florence, 1943), p. xxi.

15. The *Colloquia*, published without the author's consent in 1518, was reissued several times during Erasmus's life. The *Charon* dialogue was first added in an edition of 1529. See Caccia, *Note su la fortuna di Luciano nel Rinascimento*, p. 45, and Erasmus, *Ten Colloquies*, trans. Craig R. Thompson (New York: Bobbs-Merril, 1957), pp. xix–xx, xxiii.

16. See Paul F. Grendler, *Critics of the Italian World (1530–1560): Anton Francesco Doni, Nicolò Franco and Ortensio Lando*, p. 111 ff.

17. The significance of the title is expressed by the author himself at the beginning of the work: "[Q]uesto libro s'appella Fiorita e per più ragioni. Prima perchè raccoglie i fiori delle istorie e quella recita: seconda perchè in esse apaiono i colori delle materie per verità di tempi e di luoghi, terzia perchè . . . dimostri vari colori e figure poetiche. . . ." I quote from G. Mazzatinti, "La *Fiorita* di Armannino Giudice," p. 10. As regards the *Fiorita*, all future page references unless otherwise noted refer to this article.

18. Mazzatinti notes that Armannino, who begins his recitation of Aeneas's deeds in Book 22, employs as sources both Virgil and the *Roman d'Eneas* attributed to Benoît de Sainte-Maure (pp. 25–26). Armannino's description of hell, in general, has traits drawn from not only classical sources but Dante and other earlier medieval visions (see pp. 32–33).

Conclusion

Quite often, studies dealing with the history of a theme, dominant motif, or literary figure, simply end with no general conclusion. Such a procedure could indeed be justified in this case, since summarizing all the observations made in this history of the figure of Charon would mean repeating in good part what has already been said. Still, having labored through so many varied depictions and sometimes disparate analyses, the reader hopes to find a synthesis however brief.

Among the questions that might be asked is why has the figure of the underworld boatman been so attractive to so many different authors despite their often divergent aims and the dissimilar genres in which they are working? Clearly, like the moment of birth, crossing to the beyond, a nexus between this life and the hereafter, is at the center of human concerns. The crossing by way of Charon's boat becomes the visual and emblematic representation of death itself, for the ferrying signals the finality of that passage. The fear of, and fascination for, the transitional moment come to life in the boatman himself. Even in those authors not concerned with a full-bodied epic or dramatic portrayal, Charon remains a significant figure if only in speech—a metaphor, the visual referent for an intangible phenomenon. A reference to Charon's name, his boat, or his function intensifies the gloominess and horror of the moment, its inexorable finality.

The crossing itself, however visualized, is an event of universal consequence shared by all who have gone before as it will be shared by all who follow. The reference to Charon thus portends our common fate, establishing as well a connection between our remotest ancestors, who might have believed in the ferryman's reality, and us and our offspring, who accept his poetic vitality even while denying the existence of the gods.

Charon's longevity as a poetic figure can also be attributed in part to the basic human enchantment with obstacles and hindrances. As a liminal or threshold figure, Charon helps define the boundaries between worlds, between light above and darkness below, the known and the unknown, the living and the dead. As indicated by the many myths and fables where prohibition is a central theme (witness the biblical story of Adam and Eve and the pagan tale of Orpheus), humankind is captivated by the concept of limits and divine boundaries. Charon enforces the interdictions of the gods. When the gods do set conditions (Hades to Orpheus, Jehovah to Adam and Eve), such figures as Charon and the guardian angels appear in order to defend their realms against those guilty of transgression.

Given the parallel between heavenly and underworldly tasks in these stories, we understand the easy conversion of Charon from a pagan divinity to a fallen angel in certain writers of the Counter-Reformation.

Charon also has his attractions as a narrative tool, functioning stylistically to create the tension essential to any extended literary form, whether myth, fable, epic, narrative, or drama. In epic, Charon as guardian is an obstacle to be overcome and the crossing a focal point of heroic conflict. In fables, the ferryman is often a force of prohibition, keeping some out (Orpheus), allowing others in (Psyche). In dialogues, Charon's role ranges from a foil for the wit of others (e.g., Menippus) to a philosopher of the human condition. Whatever Charon's role, dramatic features are intrinsic to his character and function. An encounter with Charon is a moment of tension, of heightened awareness, and the encounter forces us to recognize human limits and our common mortality. For the dead, the crossing is to everlasting exile; for the living, it is a passage to knowledge of greater things. For both, the juncture is one where humanity comes in contact (and often conflict) with underworld divinity or as some authors have it, with demonry. Quite simply then, the crossing, to borrow Thomas Green's description of the descent from heaven, becomes a "crucial nexus of the narrative," a moment representing "the intersection of time and the timeless" (p. 7); the crossing points to the afterlife, of paramount concern to humans, and does so through tension.

In presenting this historical view of Charon's development and transmission and studying the intertextual transferences of the crossing's basic structural features and Charon's essence as well as the ever-varying local texture of the myth, reference has been made to a host of minor works that by merit of past critical judgment or present neglect have rarely been deemed worthy of much attention. My purpose in analyzing their Charon episodes has not been to suggest that all these works deserve more attention. While this is sometimes the case, I have been moved, rather, by a desire for thoroughness, a desire, I believe, that has critical validity in an historical work. Admittedly, the attempt to be exhaustive, wisely eschewed by most, is undeniably futile (even within limits) and quite often merely exhausting both to the reader and researcher. Nevertheless, the attempt allows the reader to form opinions concerning the vitality and versatility of a given literary figure. And the reader with well-defined interests can read selectively, deriving perhaps some profit from individual analyses.

To justify the study of individual literary artifacts, Antonio Belloni, in his work on the imitators of Tasso in the seventeenth century, called to mind the words of Vittorio Imbriani, who noted that no literary event "ought to be neglected by one who wishes to reconstruct the past, because even that which has little or no value esthetically can acquire much if it serves, let us assume, to show us a connection within which that event [or others] would have evaded us" (*Epigoni*, p. viii). To this justification, I might add that even a minor literary work can contain a major treatment of a particular mythological topos and a depiction of interest to students of myth and the general reader. By the same token, a major author's presentation, if less committed, may be of only minimal interest.

The tremendous variety of situations, themes, and forms in which Charon is employed and the innovative portrayals of such a traditional figure are impressive. From the modern standpoint, the more intriguing representations are those where an author, faced with the conflict between the desire to imitate the familiar and the necessity of maintaining interest with the novel, is of such strong and distinctive artistic temperament that the ferryman cannot help but be transformed.

The requirements of genre are equally demanding. It is quite natural of course, for the boatman to be employed for different purposes in different literary forms; to mention the *intermedi*, as just one example, the boatman is almost always an element of spectacle or marvel. That is, he serves not only to help situate the scene in hell but, more importantly, to illustrate the technical abilities of the scenographer. A boat on stage—the actual representation of a ferrying—becomes an awe-inspiring event. To say that Charon is also an element of marvel in epic is to point out an essential difference between the two forms. In epic, the boatman strikes terror in the hearts of the descenders: He is an infernal deity in whose boat all must pass. Charon himself—his majestic or horrific appearance, anger, physical force—inspires awe and fear. In the *intermedi*, on the contrary, a scene of confrontation is rarely mentioned; we do not know if Charon had a speaking role. What does stand out is that he appeared with his boat; we hear the sound of water and chains and an actual ferrying is represented on stage.

Similar distinctions apply to other forms and subgenres. Obviously, Charon is usually more demonic in allegorical-didactic poems or Christian epic than in epic of classical imitation. In both forms, he is often a figure of cruelty and power. In the chivalric romance, Charon appears in fairy-tale situations, with varying features, while in mock-heroic works, he is burlesqued, appearing not as a powerful ferryman but a weak, pitiful old man. Ridiculing Charon's age, (apparently a poetic feature of great antiquity, since Virgil bothers to clarify it by stating that a god in old age is still robust), extends from a subgenre in epic, the mock-heroic, to a stock type in drama. As a *vecchio*, Charon assumes some of the traits of the old man in Renaissance comedy. In Della Porta's *Sorella*, for example, Gelasto can compare the old Pardo to "Caronte, spavento di cimiteri" (A 45). In both forms, a similar feature is exaggerated for similar purposes.

One of the innovative ways of portraying Charon is by borrowing features characteristic of the ferryman in another genre. In lyric, where the boatman is often reduced to a figure of speech, Charon comes to represent, in part, the more elegiac aspects of death. Crossing to the beyond by way of his ferry brings to mind the rapidity with which time passes and the inevitability of death. These lyric motifs, familiar in Petrarch's *Canzoniere*, come to life in his epic poem *Africa* with startling results. Integrating lyric and elegiac themes into the imagined descent of his heroine, Petrarch effectively transforms the epic features of the boatman. The resulting figure—an enamored Charon—is a highly original touch, uncharacteristic of epic portrayals. In fact, the strangeness of the depiction is possibly what led later poets, such as Folengo, to mock the idea. When we see Charon in Folengo's *Baldus*, the boatman's love and compassion have been transformed into lust.

I can affirm the significance of genre on the choice of units selected for development. While authorial idiosyncrasies result in transforming the local texture of each unit, the form employed exercises its own constraints. This is seen, for example, in the fact that epic focuses on the middle units of encounter in order to highlight heroic conflict. The exchange between boatman and descender is a moment of dramatic intensity where the forces of the hero come into conflict with underworld powers. The hero's victory is a sign of his divinely ordained mission. Once he has gained passage with Charon, the actual crossing is of minor significance. This contrasts with lyric, for example, where the crossing itself becomes the unit of thematic importance.

In prose forms, specifically the dialogue, the units of confrontation and crossing are all important. Since the dialogue form is often employed for didactic reasons, the units of confrontation do not result in an epic conflict but lengthy interrogation of the passengers. The poet's purposes are further facilitated by the crossing, which rather than having an elegiac significance as in lyric merely serves to extend the initial dialogue between boatman and descenders.

While varying in details, Charon's portrayal is fairly consistent along generic lines. The august and powerful figure of epic, the cruel or sullen boatman, is foreign, for example, to the moral dialogue. In the latter form, the ferryman is most often a compliant figure, who only occasionally gets enraged at the untoward behavior of his passengers. Perhaps because the ferryman is dealing with dead, and not living descenders, his power need not be emphasized. With the souls obviously at his command, he is able to act with the restraint befitting a philosopher of the human condition. Gruesome details and horrific features of Charon in tragedy are an example of generic traits that can be borrowed by only a few other forms, most notably epic of Christian intent. When Charon becomes a demon or a fallen angel, a representative of the malign forces of hell, the tragic and epic features of the boatman are often merged.

Charon's possibilities within each genre are thus well defined, although subject to modification by creative poets. The expansion of generic types in Italy results in distinctive portrayals, which, in effect, are sufficient to classify the works as a whole. The buffoonish character of Folengo's *Baldus* or Lalli's travesty of the *Aeneid* serves to clarify both authors' attitude toward tradition as well as the subgenre in which they are writing. Along the same line, the portrayal of a wise ferryman, a congenial if not benevolent sort, is an indication that we are dealing with prose dialogues of moral intent.

As each author has his specific aims and idiosyncrasies, and each genre its exigencies, so, too, each age seems, to a certain extent, to favor a different Charon or at least offer different possibilities for the figure outside the traditional range of attributes. In classical Greece and the Greco-Roman period, Charon is a transporter of the dead, sometimes a ferryman overburdened by the volume of war dead but always an underworld god. The Hellenistic period depicts in elegiac tones a mournful minister of Hades, sometimes viewed as considerate, ferrying his heavily laden boat over sorrowful Acheron. By Lucian's time, an age of prevailing skepticism, the boatman has become a philosophical moralist in a satirical description of underworld marvels. In the Middle Ages, Charon comes to life as a demon, a threatening force, whereas in the Renaissance, to mention just two aspects of the figure, he is connected to magic (Ariosto) and fairies (Bello). And finally, in the Counter-Reformation atmosphere of the late Renaissance and the religious works of the Seicento, the boatman is transformed into a fallen angel with wings.

This is not to deny that certain features and generic traits extend throughout all periods. As a comic figure, Charon ranges from the rigid boatman of Aristophanes to the satirical ferryman of Lucian to the caricatured guardian of Renaissance and baroque mock-epic. The comic traits of Charon, in fact, extend well beyond the limits of this study, as can be seen, for example, in later Italian opera and English farces of the nineteenth century. Consider such works as Frances Talfourd's *Alcestis, The Original Strong-Minded Woman* (1850), where Charon is a jolly old waterman, or Henry J. Byron's *Orpheus and Eurydice: or, The Young Gentleman Who Charmed the Rocks* (1863), where Charon, a singing boatman full of puns, is "an important character but not the He-row."

Given the significance of Charon and the crossing, it is no wonder that his name extends well beyond the limits of this study. In discussing sea routes to Sicily, a recent Michelin Green Guide to Italy lists a Caronte society with offices at Porto Molo di Levante in Reggio di Calabria.[1] References to the boatman appear in the most unexpected contexts; as two examples, allow me to cite a novel on the military-industrial complex and its control of the United States government. Entitled *Trevayne* and signed with the pseudonym Jonathan Ryder, the work offers the following mythological reference:

Yet now, as he [Trevayne] stared down at the Genessee notebooks piled beside the folded newspaper, he found himself strangely reluctant to plunge back into the work he'd set aside three days ago. He'd traveled to and from his River Styx. Like Charon, he'd carried the souls of the dead across the turbulent waters, and now he needed rest, peace. He had to get out of the lower world for a while.

And Genessee Industries was the lower world.[2]

And more recently, an astronomer, James Christy, who discovered a moon of Pluto, has proposed for it the name of Charon.[3]

But these are only a fraction of the numerous references in other literatures—French, Spanish, Portuguese, German, and English, for example—where Charon depictions can be found, not only in the present but in a continuous line dating from the Renaissance to the earliest vernacular works of the Middle Ages. And the same can be said for Italian works extending from the seventeeth century to the present. Allusion to the continuing vitality of Charon as a poetic figure underlines the impossibility of truly ending this type of study. Even in the periods for which I claim responsibility, new sources continue to be uncovered, ranging from works still in manuscript, such as Teo da Perugia's *Caccia*,[4] to published (if not always well-known) texts, such as the *sacra rappresentazione* of Santa Uliva, where Charon appears in the third *intermedio* devoted to the myth of Narcissus,[5] and the *Angelica innamorata* of Vincenzo Brusantini, who emphasizes the number dead in battle by noting that "Travagliato Caron tolse compagno / per soccorso a passar seco lo stagno" (25. 121).[6]

To conclude, then, I can only point out that humanity's limits and potentialities are perhaps nowhere more sharply defined than at the moment of crossing. If in the pantheon of gods Charon is a lesser figure, the descent myth itself, the crossing to the beyond, is central to our imagination. When poets have dealt with eschatological concerns—fate, death, and an afterlife existence—they have availed themselves countless times of no less a figure than the ferryman of Hades. The variety of literary representations of the boatman, extending over two millenia, offers incontestable proof of both the ever-vital nature of artistic creation and the durability of myth. Truly, the creatures of myth, unlike those of us who must cross in Charon's boat, will never die.

Notes

1. Michelin Green Guide to Italy, English 8th ed. (Norwich: Jarrold and Sons, 1974), p. 254.

2. Jonathan Ryder, *Trevayne* (London: Weidenfeld and Nicolson, 1974), p. 314.

3. See Malcolm Browne, "Pluto moon discovery hints there's more," *Chicago Tribune*, 9 July 1978, sec. 1, p. 3.

4. A critical edition of the *Caccia* is being prepared by Dennis Dutschke, to whom I am indebted for this reference.

5. Valeria Laube has brought my attention to the reference in this anonymous work, which can be found in Emilio Faccioli's edition of *Il teatro italiano*, vol. 1.

6. Venezia: Francesco Marcolini, 1550, 1553 (2d ed.). Also published in vol. 3 of the Parnasso Italiano (Venezia, 1837).

Bibliography

Primary Sources: Part 1

The following works are cited in Part 1, dealing with classical Greek and Latin poets, and early Latin medieval sources referred to in the notes to Part 2. I should add that not all the works listed here contain references to Charon himself. Some merely refer to the Acheron or other related aspects of the descent and crossing.

All Loeb Classical Library volumes are published as follows: Cambridge, Mass.: Harvard University Press and London: Heinemann.

Acts of Thomas (138–139). In *The Acts of Thomas*. Introduction, text, and commentary by A. F. J. Klijn. Leiden: Brill, 1962.

Aemilianus (9. 218). In *The Greek Anthology: Hellenistic Epigrams*, edited A. S. F. Gow and D. L. Page. Cambridge: Cambridge University Press, 1965.

Aeschylus. *Aeschylus*. Translated by Herbert Weir Smyth. Loeb Library, 1963.

―――――. "Agamemnon." In *The Complete Greek Tragedies*, edited by David Grene and Richmond Lattimore. New York: Random House, Modern Library, n.d.

Agathias Scholasticus (7. 568). In *The Greek Anthology*. Translated by W. R. Paton. Loeb Library, 1953.

Alcaeus. In *Greek Lyric Poetry from Alcman to Simonides*, by C. M. Bowra. 2d ed. Oxford: Clarendon, 1962, pp. 161–162.

Alcaeus of Messene (11. 12). In *The Greek Anthology*. Translated by W. R. Paton. Loeb Library, 1953.

Ambrose. *De bono mortis* (8. 33). In *Corpus scriptorum ecclesiasticorum latinorum*, vol. 32. 1. Leipzig: Hoelder-Pichler-Tempsky, 1926, p. 731.

Ammianus (11. 209). In *The Greek Anthology*. Translated by W. R. Paton. Loeb Library, 1953.

Anacreon. Fragment 38. In *Early Greek Monody*. Translated by J. M. Kirkwood. Ithaca: Cornell University Press, 1974, p. 173.

―――――. In *Greek Lyric Poetry from Alcman to Simonides*, by C. M. Bowra. 2d ed. Oxford: Clarendon, 1962, pp. 161–162.

Andronicus (7. 181). In *The Greek Anthology*. Translated by W. R. Paton. Loeb Library, 1953.

Anonymous (7. 63). In *The Greek Anthology*. Translated by W. R. Paton. Loeb Library, 1953.

Anonymous (7. 482). In *The Greek Anthology*. Translated by W. R. Paton. Loeb Library, 1953.

Anonymous. Medieval paraphrase of Martianus Capella's *Satyra de nuptiis Philologiae et Mercurii* (474–480). See André Boutemy. "Une version médiévale inconnue de la légende d'Orphée." In *Hommages à Joseph Bidez et à Franz Cumont*. Brussels: Latomus, 1949, p. 591.

Antipater of Sidon (7. 464). In *The Greek Anthology*. Translated by W. R. Paton. Loeb Library, 1953.

Antipater of Thessalonica (7. 530). In *The Greek Anthology*. Translated by W. R. Paton. Loeb Library, 1953.

Antiphanes (11. 168). In *The Greek Anthology*. Translated by W. R. Paton. Loeb Library, 1953.

_____. Stobaeus. *Anthology* 4. 53. 3 ff. In *Comicorum atticorum fragmenta*, vol. 2, edited by Theodorus Kock. Leipzig: Teubner, 1880–1888, p. 86.

_____. In *The Fragments of Attic Comedy after Meineke, Bergk, and Kock*, edited by J. M. Edmonds. Leiden: Brill, 1959.

Antiphilus (7. 635, 9. 242). In *The Greek Anthology: Hellenistic Epigrams*, edited by A. S. F. Gow and D. L. Page. Cambridge: Cambridge University Press, 1965.

Antoninus Liberalis. *Les métamorphoses*. Edited by Manolis Papathomopoulos. Paris: Les Belles Lettres, 1968.

Anyte (7. 486). In *The Greek Anthology*. Translated by W. R. Paton. Loeb Library, 1953.

Apollodorus. *The Library*. Translated by Sir James George Frazer. Loeb Library, 1939.

Apuleius. *The Golden Ass*. Translated by W. Adlington. Revised by S. Gaselee. Loeb Library, 1958.

Archias (7. 68). In *The Greek Anthology*. Translated by W. R. Paton. Loeb Library, 1953.

Archilochus. Fragment 104D and 112D. In *Greek Lyric Poetry from Alcman to Simonides*, by C. M. Bowra. 2d ed. Oxford: Clarendon, 1962.

Aristides. *Oratio* 49. 4. In *Asclepius: A Collection and Interpretation of the Testimonies*, by Emma J. and Ludwig Edelstein. Baltimore: Johns Hopkins Press, 1945.

Aristophanes. *Aristophanes*. Translated by Benjamin Bickley Rogers. Loeb Library, 1946.

_____. *The Frogs*, edited by W. B. Stanford. 2d ed. 1963. Reprint with alterations Edinburgh: MacMillan, 1971.

_____. *Plays* II. Translated by Patric Dickinson. Oxford: Oxford University Press, 1970.

Artemidorus. *Oneirocritica* 1. 4. In *The Interpretation of Dreams*. Translated by Robert J. White. Park Ridge, N.J.: Noyes Press, 1975.

Asius of Samos. in *Early Greek Elegy*, edited by T. Hudson-Williams. London: Milford, 1926, p. 44.

Avienus. *Aratea* 208–211. Edited by Alfredus Breysig. Leipzig: Teubner, 1882, p. 10.

Bacchylides. *Ode* 5. 63–67. In *Lyra Graeca: Being the Remains of all the Greek Lyric Poets from Eumelus to Timotheus excepting Pindar*, vol. 3, edited by J. M. Edmonds. New York: G. P. Putnam's Sons, 1922, pp. 148–149.

Bernard Silvestris of Tours. *The Commentary on the First Six Books of the Aeneid of Vergil Commonly Attributed to Bernardus Silvestris*. Edited by Julian Ward Jones and Elizabeth Frances Jones. Lincoln: University of Nebraska Press, 1977.

Bianor (?) (7. 671). In *The Greek Anthology*. Translated by W. R. Paton. Loeb Library, 1953.

Bion. "Lament for Adonis" 1. 45–55. In *The Greek Bucolic Poets*, edited by J. M. Edmonds. Loeb Library, 1970.

Callimachus. Fragments 191, 278, and 628. In *Callimachus: Aetia-Iambi-Lyric Poems.* Translated by C. A. Trypanis. Loeb Library, 1958, p. 203.

Cicero. *De divinatione* 1. 79. In *De senectute, De amicitia, De divinatione.* Translated by William Armistead Falconer. Loeb Library, 1953.

————. *De natura deorum* 3. 43–44. In *De natura deorum, academica.* Translated by H. Rackham. Loeb Library, 1951.

Claudian. *Claudian.* Translated by Maurice Platnauer. Loeb Library, 1922.

Consolatio ad Liviam (357–358). P. Ovidius Naso. *Opera, e textu Burmanni; cum notis Bentleii hactenus ineditis, necnon Harlesii, Gieriggi, Burmanni, Lemairii, et aliorum selectissimis,* vol. 5. Oxford: Talboys et Wheeler, 1826, pp. 417–445.

Cornutus. *De natura deorum.* Edited by Fridericus Osannus. Gottingae: Libraria Dieterichiana, 1844, chap. 35, p. 213.

————. In *Theologiae graecae compendium,* edited by Carolus Lang. Leipzig: Teubner, 1881, p. 74.

Culex (216). In *Aeneid VII–XII; The Minor Poems.* Volume 2 of *Virgil.* Translated by H. Rushton Fairclough. Loeb Library, 1969.

Diodorus Grammaticus (7. 700). In *The Greek Anthology.* Translated by W. R. Paton. Loeb Library, 1953.

Diodorus Siculus. *Bibliotheke* 1. 92, 96. 5–7. In *Diodorus of Sicily,* vol. 1. Translated by C. H. Oldfather. Loeb Library, 1946.

Diogenes Laertius. "Pythagoras." *Lives of Eminent Philosophers* (8. 21). Translated by R. D. Hicks. Loeb Library, 1950.

Elegiae in Mecenatem. In *Minor Latin Poets,* edited by J. W. Duff. Loeb Library, 1934.

Epictetus. *The Discourses as Reported by Arrian* (3. 13–15). Translated by W. A. Oldfather. Loeb Library, 1952.

Epigrams and *Inscriptions.* In *Themes in Greek and Latin Epitaphs,* by Richmond Lattimore. Urbana: University of Illinois Press, 1942, pp. 75, 87, 287, and 316.

————. In *Epigrammata: Greek Inscriptions in Verse from the Beginnings to the Persian Wars,* edited by Paul Friedländer and Herbert B. Hoffleit. Berkeley and Los Angeles: University of California Press, 1948, p. 89.

————. In *Corpus inscriptionum graecarum,* edited by Ioannes Franzius. Berlin: Academiae Litterarum Regiae Borussicae, 1853 and 1877, volume 3, no. 6203.16, no. 6239.8, and vol. 4, no. 8138.

————. In *Epigrammata graeca ex lapidibus conlecta,* edited by Georgius Kaibel. Berlin: G. Reimer, 1878, no. 302.3, no. 566.8, no. 646.3, and no. 647.16.

Erycius (7. 377). In *The Greek Anthology.* Translated by W. R. Paton. Loeb Library, 1953.

Euripides. *The Complete Greek Tragedies.* Edited by David Grene and Richmond Lattimore. New York: Random House, Modern Library, n.d.

————. *Euripides.* Translated by Arthur S. Way. Loeb Library, 1947.

Eustathius. *Eustathii commentarii ad Homeri Odysseam.* Tomus I–II. Hildesheim and New York: Georg Olms, 1970, p. 391.

Fulgentius, Fabius Planciades. *Expositio Virgilianae continentiae.* Edited by Rudolf Helm. Leipzig: Teubner, 1898, p. 98.

————. *Mitologiarum libri iii.* In *Auctores mythographi latini,* edited by A. van Staveren. Leiden: Luchtmans, 1742, p. 756.

Glossaria duo. Edited by Henricus Stephanus (Henri Estienne). 1573 ed. Col. 150, p. g. ii^v, s.v. *Orcus*.

Gunzo of Novara. *Oratio*. In *Patrologia latina*, vol. 136, col. 1302*B*. Edited by J. P. Migne. Paris: Garnier Fratres, 1881.

Heraclitus. *Héraclite. Allégorie d'Homère*, chap. 70. 8. Translated by Félix Buffière. Paris: Les Belles Lettres, 1962.

Hermesianax of Colophon. *Leontion*. In *The Deipnosophists*, by Athenaeus (13. 597 ff.). Translated by Charles Burton Gulick. Loeb Library, 1950.

Hesiod. *The Homeric Hymns and Homerica*. Translated by Hugh G. Evelyn-White, 1914. Reprint Loeb Library, 1970.

Hesychius. *Hesychii Alexandrini lexicon*. Edited by Ioannes Albertus and Mauricius Schmidt. Jena: Frederici Maukii, 1862.

Homer. *The Iliad*. Translated by A. T. Murray. Loeb Library, 1967.

_____ . *The Iliad of Homer*. Translated by Richmond Lattimore. Chicago: University of Chicago Press, 1951.

_____ . *The Odyssey*. Translated by Robert Fitzgerald. Garden City, New York: Doubleday, Anchor Books, 1963.

_____ . *The Odyssey*. Translated by A. T. Murray. Loeb Library, 1966.

_____ . *The Odyssey*. Translated by E. V. Rieu. Baltimore: Penguin Books, 1946.

Honestus. In *The Greek Anthology* (7. 66). Translated by W. R. Paton. Loeb Library, 1953.

Horace. *The Odes, Epodes and Carmen Saeculare*. Edited by Clifford Herschel Moore. New York: American Book Co., 1902.

_____ . *The Odes and Epodes*. Translated by C. E. Bennett. Loeb Library, 1927.

Iamblichus. *On the Mysteries of the Egyptians, Chaldeans, and Assyrians*. Translated by Thomas Taylor. 2d ed. London: Dobell, Reeves and Turner, 1895, p. 205.

Isidore. *Origines* 8. 11. 42–43 and 14. 9. 2. In *Etymologiarum libri 20*. Edited by F. V. Otto. In *Corpus grammaticorum latinorum veterum*, vol. 3. Leipzig: Teubner, 1833.

_____ . Isidori Hispalensis Episcopi. *Etymologiarum sive originum libri xx*. Edited by W. M. Lindsay. Oxford: Clarendon, 1911.

Josephus. *Josephus*. Translated by H. St. J. Thackeray, et al. 8 vols. Loeb Library, 1930.

Julian the Apostate. *Oration* 7: "To the Cynic Heracleios." In *The Works of the Emperor Julian*, vol. 2. Translated by Wilmer Cave Wright. Loeb Library, 1953, p. 129.

Julian, Perfect of Egypt (7. 600, 603). In *The Greek Antholgy*. Translated by W. R. Paton. Loeb Library, 1953.

Juvenal. In *Juvenal and Persius*. Translated by G. G. Ramsay. Loeb Library, 1960.

Leonidas of Tarentum. In *The Greek Anthology: Hellenistic Epigrams*, edited by A. S. F. Gow and D. L. Page. Cambridge: Cambridge University Press, 1965.

_____ . *The Greek Anthology* (7. 67). Translated by W. R. Paton. Loeb Library, 1953.

Licymnius. In *Greek Melic Poets*, by Herbert Weir Smyth. London: MacMillan, 1900, pp. 135, 459.

Lucan. *Pharsalia*. Edited by C. E. Haskins. London: Bell, 1887.

_____ . *Lucan*. Translated by J. D. Duff. Loeb Library, 1928, 1951 reprint.

Lucian. *Lucian*. Translated by A. M. Harmon (vols. 1–6) and M. D. MacLeod (vols. 7–8). Loeb Library, 1963–1967.

_____ . *Satirical Sketches*. Translated by Paul Turner. London: Penguin, 1961.

_____ . *Selected Satires of Lucian*. Translated by Lionel Casson. Garden City: Doubleday, 1962. New York: Norton, 1968.

_____ . *The Works of Lucian of Samosata*. 4 vols. Translated by H. W. and F. G. Fowler. Oxford: Clarendon, 1905.

Lucillius (11. 133, 171). In *The Greek Anthology*. Translated by W. R. Paton. Loeb Library, 1953.

_____ . In "The Humor of the Greek Anthology," by Joseph William Hewitt. *Classical Journal* 17 (1921): 72.

Lucretius. *De rerum natura* (1. 115 ff.; 3. 37, 978–1023). Translated by H. D. Rouse. Loeb Library, 1924.

Macrobius. *Commentary on the Dream of Scipio* (1. 10). Translated by William Harris Stahl. New York: Columbia University Press, 1952.

Martianus Capella. *De nuptiis Philologiae et Mercurii* (2. 142–143). Edited by Adolfus Dick. Leipzig: Teubner, 1925, p. 62.

Melanippides. *Persephone*. In *Greek Melic Poets*, by Herbert Weir Smyth. London: MacMillan, 1900, pp. 453–454.

Mimnermus of Colophon. Fragment 2. In *Early Greek Elegy. The Elegiac Fragments of Callinus, Archilochus, Mimnermus, Trytaeus, Solon, Xenophanes, and Others*, edited by T. Hudson-Williams. London: Milford, 1926, pp. 44–45.

_____ . In *A Short History of Greek Literature from Homer to Julian*, by Wilmer C. Wright. New York: American Book Co., 1907, p. 77.

Minyas. In *Epicorum Graecorum fragmenta*, vol. 1, edited by Godofredus Kinkel. Leipziz: Teubner, 1877, pp. 215–216.

Mnasalcas (7. 488). In *The Greek Anthology*. Translated by W. R. Paton. Loeb Library, 1953.

Moschus (?). "Lament for Bion" (1. 13–14). In *The Greek Bucolic Poets*, edited by J. M. Edmonds. Loeb Library, 1970.

Nonnos. *Dionysiaca* (4. 151–155). Translated by W. H. D. Rouse. Loeb Library, 1940.

Origenes. *Contra haereses* (4. 32). In *Asclepius: A Collection and Interpretation of the Testimonies*, by Emma J. and Ludwig Edelstein. Baltimore: Johns Hopkins Press, 1945.

Ovid. *Metamorphoses: Books 6–10*. Edited by William S. Anderson. Norman: University of Oklahoma Press, 1972.

_____ . *Metamorphoses*. Translated by Rolfe Humphries. Bloomington: Indiana University Press, 1963.

Paulinus of Nola. *Carmina* 21. 477. In *Corpus scriptorum ecclesiasticorum Latinorum*, vol. 30. Leipzig: Hoelder-Pichler-Tempsky, 1926, p. 324.

Pausanias. *Description of Greece* (1. 17. 5; 3. 25. 4–6; 8. 18. 1–3; 10. 28). Translated by W. H. S. Jones. New York: G. P. Putnam's Sons, 1918.

Petronius. *Satyricon* 121. In *Petronius*, translated by Michael Heseltine. Loeb Library, 1951.

Philostratus. *The Life of Apollonius of Tyana* (4. 16). Translated by F. C. Conybeare. Loeb Library, 1948.

Pindar. *The Odes of Pindar Including the Principle Fragments*. Translated by Sir John Sandys. Loeb Library, 1968.

_____ . *The Odes of Pindar*. Translated by Richmond Lattimore. Chicago: University of Chicago Press, 1947, Phoenix Books, 1966.

Plato. *Republic* (3. 386A–387D; 10. 614A–621C). *Gorgias* (523A–526D). *Phaedo* (107D–108C, 111D–114D). In *Plato*, translated by Harold North Fowler. Loeb Library, 1923.

Plautus. *Captivi* (5. 4. 1). In *Plautus*, vol. 1, translated by Paul Nixon. Loeb Library, 1950.

Pliny. *Historia naturalis* (2. 95, 208). In *Natural History*, vol. 1, translated by H. Rackham. Loeb Library, 1949, p. 338.

Plutarch. "Anthony (15)." In *Plutarch's Lives*, vol. 9. Translated by Bernaelotte Perrin. Loeb Library, 1920.

————. *De genio Socratis* (590A ff.). *De sera numinis vindicta* (563E–564A). In *Plutarch's Moralia*, vol. 7. Translated by Phillip H. De Lacy and Benedict Einarson. Loeb Library, 1949.

————. *Life of Solon*. In *Elegy and Iambus: Being the Remains of all the Greek Elegiac and Iambic Poets from Callinus to Crates excepting the Choliambic Writers with the Anacreontea*, vol. 1, edited by J. M. Edmonds. New York: G. P. Putnam's Sons, 1931, p. 319.

Pollux (5. 47). Fragment of Aeschylus. In *Tragicorum graecorum fragmenta*, no. 245, edited by Augustus Nauck. 2d ed. Leipzig: Teubner, 1889.

Procopius. *History of the Wars* (8. 20. 48–58). In *Procopius*, vol. 5. Translated by H. B. Dewing. Loeb Library, 1928.

Propertius. *Elegiarum liber II*. Translated by H. E. Butler. Loeb Library, 1952.

Prudentius. *Hamartigenia* 501–503. *Contra orationem Symmachi libri duo* 1. 386–387. In *Corpus scriptorum ecclesiasticorum latinorum*, vol. 61. Leipzig: Hoelder-Pichler-Tempsky, 1926.

Quintus of Smyrna. *The War at Troy: What Homer Didn't Tell* (6. 131). Translated by Frederick M. Combellack. Norman: University of Oklahoma Press, 1968.

Sappho. Fragments 31, 94, and 95. In *Sappho and Alcaeus: An Introduction to the Study of Ancient Lesbian Poetry*, by D. L. Page. Oxford: Clarendon, 1955, 1959.

————. In *Poetarum lesbiorum fragmenta*, edited by Edgar Lobel and Denys Page. Oxford: Clarendon, 1955.

Seneca, Lucius Annaeus. *Tragedies*. Translated by Frank Justus Miller. Loeb Library, 1968.

Servius. *Servii grammatici qui feruntur in Vergilii carmina commentarii*, vol. 2. Edited by G. Thilo and H. Hagen. Leipzig: Teubner, 1884.

Silius Italicus. *Punica*. Translated by J. D. Duff. Loeb Library, 1933.

Simias (7. 203). In *The Greek Anthology*, translated by W. R. Paton. Loeb Library, 1953.

Solon. In *Elegy and Iambus: Being the Remains of all the Greek Elegiac and Iambic Poets from Callinus to Crates excepting the Choliambic Writers with the Anacreontea*, vol. 1, edited by J. M. Edmonds. New York: G. P. Putnam's Sons, 1931, p. 139.

Statius. *Statius*. Translated by J. H. Mozley. Loeb Library, 1928.

Strabo. *The Geography of Strabo*. Translated by Horace Leonard Jones. Loeb Library, 1949.

Suidae Lexicon (s.v. Χάρων ὁ Θάνατος). Edited by Immanuelis Bekkeri. Berlin: G. Reimer, 1854, p. 1120.

Theocritus. In *The Greek Bucolic Poets*, edited by J. M. Edmonds. Loeb Library, 1970.

————. *Theocritus*. Edited by A. S. F. Gow. Cambridge: Cambridge University Press, 1952.

Theodoridas (7. 732). In *The Greek Anthology*, translated by W. R. Paton. Loeb Library, 1953.

Theognis. In *Elegy and Iambus: Being the Remains of all the Greek Elegiac and Iambic Poets from Callinus to Crates excepting the Choliambic Writers with the Anacreontea*, edited by J. M. Edmonds. New York: G. P. Putnam's Sons, 1931, vol. 1, p. 315, vol. 3, p. 365.

Tibullus. In *Catullus, Tibullus and Pervigilium Veneris*, translated by J. P. Postgate. New York: MacMillan, 1912.

Timocles. *Heroes*. In *The Fragments of Attic Comedy after Meineke, Bergk, and Kock*, vol. 2, edited by J. M. Edmonds. Leiden: Brill, 1959, p. 613.

Timocreon of Rhodes. In *Lyra Graeca: Being the Remains of all the Greek Lyric Poets from Eumelus to Timotheus excepting Pindar*, vol. 2, edited by J. M. Edmonds. New York: G. P. Putnam's Sons, 1922, p. 427.

Timotheus of Miletus. *Niobè*. In *Lyra Graeca: Being the Remains of all the Greek Lyric Poets from Eumelus to Timotheus excepting Pindar*, vol. 3, edited by J. M. Edmonds. New York: G. P. Putnam's Sons, 1922, pp. 326–327.

Valerius Flaccus. *Argonautica*. Translated by J. H. Mozley. Loeb Library, 1934.

Virgil. *Virgil*. Translated by H. Rushton Fairclough. Loeb Library, 1974 reprint.

————. *Virgil's Works*. Translated by J. W. MacKail. New York: Random House, Modern Library, 1950.

————. *The Works of Virgil*. Edited by John Conington and Henry Nettleship. Vol. 1, *Eclogues and Georgics*. Revised by F. Haverfield. Hildesheim: Georg Olms, 1963.

Visio Tnugdali. Edited by Oscar Schade. Halis Saxonum: Libraria Orphanotrophei, 1869, pp. 6–7.

————. *Visio Tnugdali*. Edited by Albrecht Wagner. Erlangen: Deichert, 1882, pp. 17. 8, 35. 18, 61. 60 ff.

Zonas of Sardis (7. 365). In *The Greek Anthology*, translated by W. R. Paton. Loeb Library, 1953.

Primary Sources: Part 2

I have organized the following chronological catalog in four main categories: epic forms, dramatic forms, lyric forms, and prose forms. To clarify the varied nature of the prose works, I have further subdivided them into four sections: (1) commentators on Dante, (2) mythographers and iconographers, (3) dialogues, and (4) miscellaneous prose forms, a section containing philosophical, moral, and artistic treatises, lengthy narratives, short stories, humorous anecdotes, and prose satires. Entries without comment are those treated at length in the text.

Epic Forms

A 1. Dante Alighieri. *Inferno* 3. 82–118. In *La Commedia secondo l'antica vulgata*, edited by G. Petrocchi. Florence: Società Dantesca, 1966. Translations by Charles S. Singleton. Dante Alighieri. *The Divine Comedy. Inferno* and *Purgatorio*. Princeton: Princeton University Press, Bollingen Series 80, 1970, 1973.

A 2. Albertino Mussato. "Somnium." In *Una visione dell'oltretomba contemporanea alla Dantesca*, by Antonio Belloni. Rome: Pacinotti, 1921.

Early Trecento Latin vision in hexameters. The descent is situated in a Virgilian pattern with evidence of Senecan influence. Charon is both squalid as in Virgil and horrid as in Seneca. Mussato adds gruesome details to Charon's depiction, such as a masticated toad and snake-entangled beard, wet with bloody vomit. The boatman is further described with reference to his bloody eyes, hairy body, unkempt hair, dirty cap, snorting nostrils, and phlegm-coated lips. The poet himself descends in the form of a bird and escapes Charon by flying over his threatening oar. From Belloni's Italian translation, it appears that there are some analogies with Dante's poem. The forcefulness of Dante's depiction is challenged by a flurry of descriptive detail in Mussato. In Virgilian fashion, Charon is introduced before his appearance and the subsequent "and here he comes" is anticlimactic. In Virgil, these two moments are effectively separated by the Palinurus episode. Mussato's portrait, however, though lacking the focus of Dante's depiction, comes across with visual intensity, especially regarding the original details.

A 3. Francesco Petrarca. *Africa* 5. 643–674. In *Rime, Trionfi e poesie latine*, edited by Guido Martellotti. Milan: Ricciardi, 1951. Translations by Thomas G. Bergin and Alice S. Wilson. *Petrarch's* Africa. New Haven and London: Yale University Press, 1977.

A 4. Giovanni Boccaccio. *Teseida* 2. 31, 47, 65; 9. 41, 101; 12. 10; *Chiose* 31. 5. In *Opere minori in volgare*, vol. 2, edited by Mario Marti. Milan: Rizzoli, 1970.
A mixture of epic and romance in twelve books of octaves written around 1340. The *Teseida* does not mention Charon by name but refers often to crossing Acheron. In the *Chiose*, the poet notes that burial is prerequisite to passage.

A 5. *La Discesa di Ugo d'Alvernia allo inferno secondo il codice franco-italiano della Nazionale di Torino*. Edited by Rodolfo Renier. Bologna: Romagnoli, 1883. See also the fragments in A. Graf. "Di un poema inedito di Carlo Martello e di Ugo d'Alvernia." *Giornale di filologia romanza 1* (Rome, 1878): 92–110.

A 6. Federico Frezzi. *Il Quadriregio* 2. 7. 28–160. Edited by Enrico Filippini. Bari: Laterza, 1914.

A 7. Orazio Romano. *Porcaria* 1. 146–162. In *Vergilio nel Rinascimento italiano da Dante a Torquato Tasso*, by Vladimiro Zabughin. Bologna: Zanichelli, 1921, vol. 1, pp. 293–296.
Mid-Quattrocento epic in Latin hexameters. The descent follows the Virgilian pattern with some Dantesque features. Porcari is interrogated by Charon and responds along the same lines as the Virgilian Sibyl. The incidents during the passage recall those in Dante's crossing with Phlegyas in *Inferno* 8.

A 8. Matteo Palmieri. *Città di vita* 2. 3–4. In *Libro del poema chiamato Città di vita composto da Matteo Palmieri Florentino*, edited by Margaret Rooke. In *Smith College Studies in Modern Languages 8–9* (1926–1927): 1–241, 1–260.
Didactic poem in terza rima, written from 1455 to 1465. Palmieri follows the Virgilian descent pattern, integrating Dantesque features into his depiction of Charon. The boatman, a "vecchio crudele e gran demonio antico," is further characterized as an anthropophagic demon, reminiscent of the devouring monster Acharon in the twelfth-century *Vision of Tundal*. The poet describes Charon's physical features with Virgilian detail and methodically explains, in three tercets of doctrinal elucidation (25–27), the ferryman's duties. Palmieri also employs Petrarchan images, comparing the number of the souls to the people in Rome during jubilee or Jerusalem before Titus conquered it. The Sibyl, in her explanation of the scene, responds with an involved disquisition, reflecting in part Platonic beliefs, on the nature of the soul (tercets 39–50). In simplest terms, the soul weighted down by the sins of the body descends to cross Charon's boat, while those who remain free of carnal pleasures and other evils fly with their lightness to Elysium. Rather than a force of obstruction, Charon is an all too eager servant, readily consenting to transport the descenders. During the crossing, the poet describes the effect of his body on the boat ("la

nave sotto il peso cigolava / pescando più nella palude assai / per modo del condurmi dubitava''), employing the verb *pescando* as a refreshing variation of Dante's *segando* and Frezzi's *solcando*. The verb *cigolava*, chosen to translate Virgil's *gemuit* (*Aen.* 6. 413) is also effective and reminiscent of Dante's use of the verb in referring to a burning branch (*Inf.* 13. 42) and a squeaky scale (*Inf.* 23. 102).

A 9. Luigi Pulci. *Morgante* 2. 38–39, 26. 89–90, 27. 277–278. Edited by Franca Ageno. Milan: Ricciardi, 1955.

A 10. Matteo Maria Boiardo. *Orlando innamorato* 3. 1. 8. Edited by Aldo Scaglione. Turin: Unione Tipografico-editrice Torinese, 1951.

A 11. Francesco Bello, Cieco da Ferrara. *Libro d'arme e d'amore nomato Mambriano* 1. 33, 4. 41. Edited by Giuseppe Rua. Turin: Unione Tipografico-editrice Torinese, 1926.

A 12. Ludovico Ariosto. *Orlando furioso* 36. 65; 42. 8. In *Opere*, edited by Giuliano Innamorati. Bologna: Zanichelli, 1967. For related features, see 2. 5, 10. 43–44, 34. 5, 35. 30, 36. 65, 40. 54, 45. 17, and 46. 140. *Cinque canti* 1. 91, 4.36. In *Opere minori*, edited by Cesare Segre. Milan: Ricciardi, 1954. Translations of the *Furioso* by Barbara Reynolds. *Orlando furioso* (*The Frenzy of Orlando*): *A Romantic Epic by Ludovico Ariosto*. Middlesex: Penguin Books, 1977. And William Stewart Rose. *Orlando furioso*. Edited by Stewart A. Baker and A. Bartlett Giamatti. Indianapolis and New York: Bobbs-Merrill, 1968.

A 13. Teofilo Folengo. *Baldus* 24. 492–750. In *Il Baldo*, by Merlin Cocai (pseudonym). With an Italian translation by Giuseppe Tonna. Edited by Giampaolo Dossena. Milan: Feltrinelli, 1958.

A 14. Giacomo Bona. *Praeludium, in treis distinctum libros, trium gratiarum nominibus appellatos, atque Herculis labores et gesta in Christi figuram mystice ac pulcherrime eodem carmine continentes*. In *Virgilio nel Rinascimento italiano*, as cited in A 7, vol. 2, pp. 187–188.

Latin heroic poem in hexameters, first published in 1526. The author narrates the descent of Hercules-Christ to the underworld. Charon, a medieval demon, is conquered, in Virgilian fashion, with a *ramus aureus*.

A 15. Antonio Legname. *Astolfo innamorato, libro d'arme, e d'amor* 1. 15, 8. 18–51. Lucca: Salvatore e Gian Domenico Marescandoli, n.d.

A 16. Pietro Aretino. *Marfisa* 1. 45–106. In *Storia dei generi letterari italiani: Il poema cavalleresco*, by Francesco Fòffano. Milan: Vallardi, n.d., p. 133.

Chivalric romance in octaves, first published in 1535. When the soul of Herculean Rodomonte ''su la ripa Letea gridando è giunto,'' Charon refuses to ferry him. A fight breaks out, during which Rodomonte jumps into Charon's boat, grabs the demon by his beard, and mistreats him. As a result of the conflict, both figures fall ''nel fiume negro del perpetuo oblio,'' where Charon is forced to scream for help from Pluto.

A 17. Lodovico Dolce. *Achille ed Enea* 39. 8–30. Venice: Giolito, 1572.

Epic poem of fifty-five canti in octaves, published posthumously in 1572. Dolce joins a translation of Homer's *Iliad* to one of the *Aeneid*, remaining faithful to his Virgilian source for the descent. The only evidence of Dante's portrayal is found in Charon's response to Aeneas, which is perhaps more violent than in Virgil: ''Tutto di sdegno, e di furor s'accende, / E con aspre parole lo riprende'' (oct. 24). In the allegory preceding the episode, Dolce speaks of Charon as follows: ''Per Caronte, che vedendo il ramo portogli dalla Sibilla traggetta lietamente Enea, si manifesta, che le cose celesti son temute, et riverite fin nell'inferno, ilche dovrebbe esser' essempio à noi mortali di obedir' i divini precetti'' (p. 387).

A 18. Torquato Tasso. *Gerusalemme liberata* 18. 87 and *Gerusalemme conquistata* 23. 50. Edited by Luigi Bonfigli. Bari: Laterza, 1930, 1934. See also *Lib.* 1. 53, 4. 63, 18. 145.

Christian epic in octaves, published in 1581. Virgilian and Dantesque phrases used to describe Charon reappear in Tasso in other situations. See, for example, *Lib.* 1. 53: "Mostra in fresco vigor chiome canute," reminiscent of Charon's green old age in Virgil, and *Con.* 18. 145: "le lanose gote," recalling Dante's Charon. The actual reference to Charon is contained in a simile. The evil magician Ismeno is described between two of his followers: "E torvo e nero e squallido e barbuto / Fra due Furie parea Caronte o Pluto" (*Lib.* 18. 87). Three of the four adjectives depict his physical appearance: black, squalid, and bearded, the latter two terms Virgilian. The first adjective describes his surly manner or grim appearance in general.

A 19. Curzio Gonzaga. *Fidamante* 22. In *Gli epigoni della Gerusaleme liberata*, by Antonio Belloni. Padua: Draghi, 1893, pp. 54–60.

A mixture of epic and romance in octaves, first published in 1582. Gonzaga offers much Counter-Reformation moralization in his treatment of the descent theme, which follows Virgilian lines with a Dantesque Charon.

A 20. Ascanio Grandi. *Il Tancredi, poema heroico* 4. 13. Lecce: Borgognone, 1632.

Heroic poem in octaves combining epic and romance, first published in 1582. Charon appears when an infernal council is called by Plutone. In his fear, "tenne immoto / Caronte il remo." Charon, referred to in passing as a fixed feature of the underworld, lacks physical description.

A 21. Luigi Tansillo. *Le lacrime di San Pietro, poema sacro* 7. 81. Venice: Piacentini, 1738.

Sacred poem in octaves and fifteen canti, published posthumously in 1585. Mythology is adapted to a Christian scheme. St. Peter, for example, dreams of descending to hell, where the evil "nocchier di Stige" awaits him. Charon is depicted with an oar in his hand calling the saint to his boat.

A 22. Erasmo da Valvasone. *Angeleida* 3. 11. Venice: Sommasco, 1590.

A 23. Giovanni Ambrogio Biffi. *La Risorgente Roma, impresa del grande Costantino, allhor che trassela dal tirannico giogo di Massentino* 6. 1–4. Milan: Como, 1611.

Epic poem in octaves, published in 1611. Biffi combines Dantesque and Virgilian features in describing the descent of Proserpina. The souls, for example, having lost all hope "di riveder il giorno," are spurred by *divin terror* to desire "l'horrida conca / Del rigido Nocchier di morte ingombre" (oct. 1). Recalling in content Virgil's *rauca fluenta* (*Aen.* 6. 327), Biffi describes the scene at the river as:

> D'aspra armonia d'horror per le tenebre
> S'odono strepitar rochi concenti,
> Sbriga la barca allhor, pompa funebre,
> Il livido Caron da gli occhi ardenti.
> De l'ampia incolta barba, onde stenebre
> Il sì canuto aspetto, i crin pendenti
> Infino al cinto ei terge, e via più sodo
> Del lordo manto al cor ristringe il nodo.
>   Così colto il rigor del tetro aspetto,
> Fa le ruvide mani al remo pronte,
> E co' la cimba rende, atroce ricetto,
> L'infera Imperatrice oltra Acheronte.

(6. 3–4)

Though lacking great originality, Biffi successfully combines his sources and adds a few of his own details, such as the rough hands, to the description. As characteristic of so many imitators who transpose adjectives employed by Virgil and Dante from object to person and vice versa, the poet passes the attribute of the *vada livida* (*Aen.* 6. 320) and the *livida palude* (*Inf.* 3. 98) to Charon himself.

A 24. Francesco Bracciolini. *Croce racquistata* 11. In *Epigoni*, as cited in A 19, pp. 9 ff.

Historical epic in octaves, first published in 1605; complete edition 1611. The pagan warrior Sarbasso disdains to cross the Acheron in Charon's boat and dives into the water in order to swim across. An angry Charon calls for other demons to aid him. Not having seen the original, I am unable to say how Charon is depicted.

A 25. Napoleone or Capoleone Ghelfucci. *Il rosario della Madonna, poema heroico* 24. 33, 52. Venice: Polo, 1616.

A 26. Tomaso Stigliani. *Mondo nuovo* 2. 82. Rome: Mascardi, 1628.

Epic in octaves, published in 1617. Dealing with Columbus's discovery of America, Stigliani mentions Charon as part of the geographical setting in a long description of the infernal regions. The episode is initiated when a *mago* descends to hell for a council with Lucifer. Charon, referred to as a "vecchio demonio, che con remo, e barca / A guisa di nocchier gli spiriti varca," is found on the Acheron, the only infernal river without a bridge.

A 27. Francesco Bracciolini. *Lo scherno degli dei, poema piacevole* 11. 19, 44, 57. Bologna: Longhi, 1686.

A 28. Girolamo Gabrielli. *Lo stato della chiesa liberato*. In *Epigoni*, as cited in A 19, pp. 448–456.

Christian epic in octaves with many romance elements, published in 1620. Giustino's descent, guided by the Sibyl, is modeled on both Virgil and Dante. Giustino, golden bough in hand, passes by both the typical Virgilian monsters and a group of unbaptized souls. Arriving at the Acheron, he encounters Charon, who opposes his progress with fierceness. The Sibyl responds to Charon's questions with a Dantesque reference to divine will, and the two descenders pass on to the seven main circles of hell. I am unable to say if Charon is depicted at length, since I have not seen the original work.

A 29. Alessandro Tassoni. *Secchia rapita* 7. 39. Nizza: Società Tipografica, 1785.

Mock-heroic poem in octaves, written by 1615 but not published until 1622. In lines reminiscent of Lucan's portrayal, Charon is referred to as a tired ferryman. Interestingly, Charon, like the souls in Dante, curses his own fate.

A 30. Camillo Pancetti. *Venetia libera, poema heroico* 22. 59–60. Venice: Muschio, 1622.

A 31. Giovanni Battista Marino. *Adone* 12. 153–155, 13. 61. Florence: Salani, 1932. See also 12. 13, 21, 22–27.

A 32. Giambattista Lalli. *Eneide travestita*. Florence: Ricci, 1822, pp. 75, 80–81.

A 33. Carlo Torre. *I numi guerrieri* 5. 47. Venice: Giunti, 1640.

Mock-heroic poem in octaves, first published in 1640. Two warriors fill Charon's boat by killing great numbers of the enemy. The ferryman himself is referred to without description.

A 34. Bartolomeo Bocchini. *Le pazzie de' Savi, overo Il Lambertaccio* 5. 20. Bologna: Zenero, 1653.

A *poema tragicoeroicomico* in octaves, published in 1641. Charon appears in an infernal council. Having broken his oar over an unwilling soul's back, he threatens to quit if not provided with a new oar. Unlike Lucian's resourceful sailor who buys supplies from Hermes, this Charon is a frustrated and petulant figure. Even his outfit, incidentally, has been stolen from a passenger.

A 35. Carlo De' Dottori. *L'asino* 1. 19. Venice: Leni, 1652.

Mock-heroic poem in octaves, published in 1652 under the pseudonym Iroldo Crotta. Charon, who is referred to rather than described, will have so many dead to ferry that he will build a bridge over the Acheron. Elsewhere, Dottori transfers Virgil's adjective for Charon to the river Acheron: a soul descends "su la squallida riua d'Acheronte" (7. 55).

Dramatic Forms

A 36. *Rappresentazione di Santa Uliva*, 601–608. In *Il teatro italiano*. Vol. 1, *Dalle origini al Quattrocento*, edited by Emilio Faccioli. Turin: Einaudi, 1975.
Sacred drama in octaves. In the third intermezzo, Narcissus, about to die, feels his blood freeze, adding "e già comincio l'inferno a vedere, / sento il vecchio infernal che già s'è mosso / per passar l'onde nubilose e nere" (604–606).

A 37. *Favola di Orfeo e di Aristeo* 3. 109–111. Edited by G. Mazzoni, who published it as a *festa drammatica del sec. XV*. Florence: Alfani e Venturi, 1906. I refer to the play as described by Luigi Marrone. "Il mito di Orfeo nella drammatica italiana." *Studi di letteratura italiana 12* (Naples, 1922): 138–145.

A 38. Niccolò da Correggio. *Fabula di Cefalo*, 174–181, 218–221. In *Opere: Cefalo— Psiche—Silva—Rime*, edited by Antonia Tissoni Benvenuti. Bari: Laterza, 1969.

A 39. Pier Antonio Caracciolo. *Lo imagico*. In *Studi di storia letteraria napoletana*, by Francesco Torraca. Livorno: Vigo, 1884, pp. 429–444.

A 40. Marc'Antonio Epicuro. *La cecaria*. In *I drammi e le poesie italiane e latine*, edited by Alfredo Parenti. Bari: Laterza, 1942.

A 41. Angelo Leonico. *Il soldato*. In *Il teatro tragico italiano: Storia e testi*, by Federico Doglio. Bologna: Guanda, 1960.
Metric tragedy published in 1550 and based on a contemporary episode occuring in Padova. An *Ombra* delivers the prologue in Senecan fashion. He is prohibited from crossing the Acheron until he reveals his infamy and clarifies the situation on earth. Charon, unmentioned by name, is an arbiter of morality, denying passage to those who conceal a falsehood damaging to others.

A 42. Bernardino Pellippari. *Italia consolata*. In "Una commedia politica del sec. XVI," by Roberto Bergadani. *Giornale storico della letteratura italiana 104* (1934): 64–80. Compare Vittorio di Tocco. *Ideali d'indipendenza in Italia durante la preponderanza spagnuola*. Messina: Principato, 1926, pp. 2–3. Also cited in Leone Allacci. *Drammaturgia*. Edited by Francesco Bernardelli. Turin: Bottega di Erasmo, 1961, p. 476.
A comedy composed of four acts of unrhymed hendecasyllables represented in Vercelli in 1562. Charon and other mythological figures appear along with symbolic, allegorical, and historical characters. In act 3, Charon discusses war with Cloto and a dead soldier. The boatman, astounded at the evil deeds committed by soldiers, tells the mercenary that all the money he has accumulated will help him in the eternal fires of hell. The author was influenced by Lucian or later Renaissance imitators.

A 43. Giovan Battista Cini. *Intermedi* on myth of Cupid and Psyche, represented in 1565 with Francesco D'Ambra's *Cofanaria*. Giorgio Vasari. "Descrizione dell'apparato per le nozze di Francesco de' Medici e di Giovanna d'Austria." In *Vite de' più eccellenti pittori, scultori e architettori*, vol. 8. Milan: Club Del Libro, 1966, pp. 134–142. Compare the description of Anton Francesco Grazzini, Il Lasca, accompanying the text of *La Cofanaria*. Florence: n.p., 1750.

A 44. Leone De Sommi Hebreo. *Intermedi*. In *La favola di Amore e Psiche nella letteratura e nell'arte italiana con appendice di cose inedite*, by Ugo de Maria. Bologna: Zanichelli, 1899, pp. 282 ff.

A 45. Giambattista Della Porta. *La sorella*. In *Le commedie*, vol. 1, edited by Vincenzo Spampanato. Bari: Laterza, 1910.
A *commedia grave* in prose, most likely written in the 1850s. The reference to Charon is in a humorous context—a glutton mocking a stock figure, the *vecchio*. The parasite Gulone calls the Vecchio Pardo an old Charon, "spavento di cimiteri" (act 4, scene 7).

A 46. Giovanni de' Bardi di Vernio. *Intermedio:* "Comparsa di demoni celesti e infernali." In *Gli albori del melodramma*, vol. 2, by Angelo Solerti. Milan: Sandron, 1904, pp. 19–42.

A 47. *Intermedi: Favola delle nozze di Mercurio et Filologia*. In "Gli 'intermezzi' del 'Pastor fido,'" by Achille Neri. *Giornale storico della letteratura italiana* 11 (1888): 405 ff.

A 48. Camillo Schiafenati. *Intermedio*. In "Precedenti del melodramma," by Angelo Solerti. *Rivista musicale italiana* 10 (1903): 207–233.

A 49. Ottavio Rinuccini. *Euridice*. In *Teatro del Seicento*, edited by Luigi Fassò. Milan: Ricciardi, 1961.

A 50. Alessandro Striggio. *Orfeo*. In *Gli albori del melodramma*, vol. 3, by Angelo Solerti. Milan: Sandron, 1904. The work is also found in Andrea Della Corte. *Drammi per musica dal Rinuccini allo Zeno*, vol. 1. Turin: Unione tipografico-editrice torinese, 1958.

A 51. Guidubaldo Bonarelli. *Filli di Sciro*. In *Teatro del Seicento,* edited by Luigi Fassò. Milan: Ricciardi, 1961.

A pastoral play with various meters, represented in 1607. Celia, thinking herself dead, imagines an old shepherd to be Charon.

A 52. Ottavio Rinuccini. *Arianna*. In *Teatro del Seicento*, edited by Luigi Fassò. Milan: Ricciardi, 1961.

A 53. Alessandro Mattei. *Morte di Orfeo*. In *Gli albori del melodramma*, vol. 3, by Angelo Solerti. Milan: Sandron, 1904.

Lyric Forms

The following is a representative list of the forms and motifs of lyric with which Charon is likely to be connected.

A 54. Francesco Petrarca. *Bucolicum Carmen*: "Eclogue I." In *Rime, Trionfi e poesie latine*, edited by Guido Martellotti. Milan: Ricciardi, 1951. Translation by Thomas G. Bergin. "Petrarch's *Bucolicum Carmen I: Parthenias*." In *Petrarch to Pirandello: Studies in Italian Literature in Honor of Beatrice Corrigan*, edited by Julius A. Molinaro. Toronto: University of Toronto Press, 1973.

———. *Canzoniere* 58, "La guancia che fu già piangendo stanca." In *Rime, Trionfi e poesie latine*, as cited in A 54, with the Rime edited by Ferdinando Neri.

A 55. "Dialogo tra un Amante e Caronte." In *Vocabulario di cinque mila vocabuli toschi non men oscuri che utili e necessarii del Furioso, Boccaccio, Petrarcha, Dante, novamente dechiarati e raccolti da Fabricio Luna per alfabeta ad utilita di chi legge, scrive e favella. Opra nova et aurea*. Naples: Giovanni Sultzbach Alemanno, 1536.
Strambotto. The poem reads as follows:

> A. Charon! Charon! —C. Chi è st'importun che grida?
> A. Gli è un amante fidel. che cerca il passo.
> C. Chi è stato sto crudel, quest'homicida,
> Che talmente t'ha morto? —A. Amore, ahi lasso!
> C. Non varco amanti. Hor cercati altra guida.
> A. Al tuo dispetto. converrà ch'io passo;
> C'ho tanti strali al cor, tant'acque a i lumi,
> Ch'io mi faro la barca, i remi e fiumi.

A 56. Giovanni Boccaccio. *Rime*: Sonnet 8, "Quel dolce canto col qual già Orfeo." In *Opere minori in volgare*, vol. 4, edited by Mario Marti. Milan: Rizzoli, 1972, pp. 57–58.

A 57. Angelo Poliziano. "Elegy 6." In *Ange Politien: La formation d'un poète humaniste* (*1469–1480*), by Ida Maïer. Geneva: Librairie Droz, 1966, p. 146.

————. *Capitolo*: "In morte del Magnifico Lorenzo de' Medici." In *Le Stanze, l'Orfeo e le Rimi di messer Angelo Ambrogini Poliziano*, edited by G. Carducci. Florence: Barbèra, 1863, p. 382.

A 58. Niccolò da Correggio. *Fabula de Psiche*. In *Opere*, edited by Antonia Tissoni Benvenuti. Bari: Laterza, 1969.

————. *Silva*, octave 13–15. In *Opere*, as cited.

A 59. Serafino Aquilano. Sonnet: "Lasciame in pace ò dispietato Amore." In *Opere dello elegantissimo poeta Serafino Aquilano, quasi tutta di nuovo riformata*, sonnet 100. Venice: Bartolomeo detto l'Imperador, 1544.

A60. Antonio Cammelli. Sonnet: "Una donna ne va tutta contrita." In *I sonetti del Pistoia giusta l'apografo trivulziano*, sonnet 32, edited by Rodolfo Renier. Turin: Loescher, 1888.

A 61. Bartolomeo Cavassico. "Disperata Villanesca." In *Rime*, vol. 2, p. 14, edited by Carlo Salvioni. Scelta di curiosità letterarie inedite o rare dal secolo xiii al xvii diretta da G. Carducci, vols. 246–247. Bologna: Romagnoli Dall'Acqua, 1893–1894.

A 62. Ludovico Ariosto. Sonnet 23: "Come creder debbo io che tu in ciel oda." In *Opere minori*, edited by Cesare Segre. Milan: Ricciardi, 1954, p. 141.

A 63. Francesco Berni. *Rime burlesche* 2. 254. Source unfound.

A 64. Anton Francesco Grazzini, Il Lasca. Sonnet 119: "In lode delle Rime di M. Francesco Berni." In *Rime*. Florence: Moücke, 1741, p. 71.

A 65. Ercole Udine. *Psiche* 7. 44–54. 2d ed. Venice: Ciotti, 1601.

A 66. Francesco Guarino. *L'Inferno d'Amore* 12. 1–3. Naples: Roncagliolo, 1612.
Moralistic poem, modeled on Petrarch's *Trionfi*, in thirteen canti in terza rima, published in 1612. The crowds that flock about the poet and his guide remind him of those gathered for passage in Charon's boat.

A 67. Giovanni Battista Marino. *Idillii favolosi: Orfeo, Proserpina*. In *La sampogna*. Venice: Brigonci, 1664. Some punctuation is based on the *Idillii favolosi*, edited by Gustavo Balsamo-Crivelli. Turin: Unione tipografico-editrice Torinese, 1923.

A 68. Antonio Bruni. *Epistole heroiche, poesie del Bruni, libri due* 2. 4. Rome: Mascardi, 1647.

A 69. Giuseppe Battista. "Miserie d'uom vecchio." In *Marino e i Marinisti*, edited by Giuseppe Guido Ferrero. Milan: Ricciardi, 1954, p. 1012.

A 70. Gianfrancesco Lazzarelli. Sonnet 282: "Il passo di Lete." In *Cicceide*. Rome: Sommaruga, 1885.

Prose Forms

Commentators on Dante

A 71. Guido da Pisa. *Declaratio super Comediam Dantis*. Edited by Francesco Mazzoni. Florence: Società Dantesca Italiana, 1970.
Latin glosses of 1324. The Acheron is interpreted as *sine gaudio* (3. 25), while Charon "tenet figuram carnis, quia omnis caro descendit ad inferos in quantum in morte redit in terram . . . ; vel in quantum opera carnis, quibus anima trahitur ad peccatum, ad penas trahitur sempiternas." His name is derived from Latin *caro* and Greek *on*, thus signifying *caro tota* or *omnis caro* (3. 35).

A 72. *Le antiche chiose anonime all'inferno di Dante secondo il testo Marciano* (*Ital. CL. IX, Cod. 179*). Edited by Giuseppe Avalle. Città di Castello: Lapi, 1900.
Commentary written ca. 1321–1337. Regarding *Inf. 3*. 82, the commentator says: "E questo uecchio significa ell'antico pecchato, la naue significa la volontà, a cchui noi ci lassi-amo menare a pecchare" (p. 13). On *Inf. 3*. 94, he writes: "Caron si è la dilettacione e la volontà de' vicij carnali. . . . Esso Caron passa tucte queste anime con ispauento e con tris-titia, sì come con prontezza e con dilecto trapassano dal bene al male" (pp. 13–14).

A 73. Jacopo Della Lana. *Comedia di Dante Degli Allagherii col commento di Jacopo Della Lana, Bolognese*. Edited by Luciano Scarabelli. Bologna: Tip. Regia, 1866.
Commentary written ca. 1323–1328. Charon is "la voluntade carnale," and he refuses to transport Dante almost as if the poet "non era vizioso di dilettazione carnale" (3. 70, pp. 132–133).

A 74. Variously attributed to Andrea Lancia. *L'Ottimo Commento della Divina Comme-dia, testo inedito d'un contemporaneo di Dante citato dagli Accademici della Crusca.* Pisa: Capurro, 1827.
Commentary written ca. 1334. The Acheron is interpreted as "senza salute, o senza leti-zia" (3. 82). Charon refuses Dante because the descender is still alive.

A 75. Pietro di Dante. *Super Dantis ipsius genitoris comoediam commentarium*. Edited by Vincentio Nannucci. Florence: Piatti, 1845.
Latin commentary written ca. 1340–1341. The Acheron, meaning *sine gaudio*, represents "concupiscentia, quae caput est aliorum vitiorum" (p. 69). Charon is a ferryman, "qui figuratur pro tempore. Nam dicitur *Charon* quasi *Cronus*, idest tempus . . ." (p. 70).

A 76. Giovanni Boccaccio. *Il comento alla Divina Commedia e gli altri scritti intorno a Dante*. Edited by Domenico Guerri. Bari: Laterza, 1918. Or *Esposizioni sopra la Co-media di Dante*. Edited by Giorgio Padoan. Verona: Mondadori, 1965.
Lectures delivered in Florence from 1373–1374. The author establishes three hells—in our hearts or on earth, in limbo, and below the ground as a place of punishment. Charon is situated in the first hell! "E per Acheronte sentono la labile e flussa condizione delle cose disiderate e la miseria di questo mondo; e per Carone intendono il tempo, il quale per vari spazi le nostre volontà e le nostre speranze d'un termine trasporta in un altro: e voglion dire che, secondo i vari tempi, varie cose che muovono gli appetiti essere al cuore trasportate" (Accessus, 49 ff.; Padoan, p. 11).

A 77. Benvenuto da Imola. *Comentum super Dantis Aldigherij Comoediam*. Edited by Jacobo Philippo Lacaita. Florence: Barbèra, 1887.
Very learned Latin commentary ca. 1373–1380. Benvenuto, who influenced Landino among others, cites many classical authors. Benvenuto locates the entrance to hell in Cam-pania near Cumae. The Acheron is given the etymology "sine salute, ab *a*, quod est *sine*, et *chere*, quod est *salve*" (p. 123). Allegorically, the river represents worldly concupiscence. Charon stands for time "quasi *Cronon*, idest tempus"; his ship is human life, weak and unstable. Dante does not cross by means of Charon's boat but with his mind: "*più lieve legno conven che te porti*, scilicet mens tua, quae est levissima, nam Dantes intravit menta-liter, non corporaliter in Infernum" (p. 127). The flames of Charon's eyes represent concu-piscence or anger or the fact that the fires of time consume all things (pp. 127–28). For Cha-ron, some understand "death." Benvenuto also notes that Dante "Appellat Charonem demonem quem Virgilius vocat Deum" (p. 129).

A 78. *Chiose sopra Dante. Testo inedito ora per la prima volta pubblicato*. Florence: Piatti, 1846.
Commentary written in Italian ca. 1375. The author employs Benvenuto da Imola and confuses Acheron and Charon; see p. 25.

A 79. Francesco da Buti. *Commento sopra la Divina Comedia di Dante Allighieri*, vol. 1. Edited by Crescentino Giannini. Pisa: Nistri, 1858, pp. 94–107.

A 80.   *Commento alla Divina Commedia d'Anonimo Fiorentino del secolo XIV*. Edited by Pietro Fanfani. Bologna: Romagnoli, 1866, pp. 71–84.

Commentary written ca. 1400. Identifying Charon with a historical king of Molossía, the author claims that the boatman represents "l'età degli uomini e 'l nostro vivere" (p. 75). All aspects of the crossing are allegorized, including Charon's oar (p. 80).

A 81.   Stefano Talice da Ricaldone. *La Commedia di Dante Alighieri col commento inedito di Stefano Talice da Ricaldone*. Edited by Vincenzo Promis and Carlo Negroni. 2d ed. Milan: Hoepli, 1888.

Latin commentary of 1474. The author refers to Charon as "Acheron . . . quod est tempus (quo) omnes moriuntur. Sed per Acherontem intelligitur mors, ut dicit Virgilius; quia est squalida, et ducit nos ad finem" (vol. 1, p. 47). Charon is also allegorized as pleasure (p. 49). Dante crosses the Acheron in sleep: "Unde transivit infernum per abstractionem mentis" (p. 53).

A 82.   Cristoforo Landino. *Comedia del divino poeta Danthe Alighieri, con la dotta et leggiadra spositione di Cristoforo Landino*. Venice: Giolitto da Trino, 1536.

Commentary of 1480. Landino refers to the ancients and their allegories, beginning with Plato and the concept of hell being the body. Following the traditional reference to Acheron as *priuatione di gaudio*, Landino adds a second interpretation: Acheron "ha figura di deliberatione nel peccare. Et per questo Seneca lo discriue correre veloce et non sanza strepito. . . . Et perche questa deliberatione (è) vn transito di volonta: il quale ne porta l'animo al peccare: pero fingono che in questo sia Charone . . ." (p. 30ᵛ). He notes other interpretations of Charon as *la morte* and as *il disordinato appetito* (p. 31ʳ). Landino prefers, however, the sense of *libero arbitrio* and quotes Salutati at length without acknowledgment. Landino further claims that an angel, representing divine grace, transports Dante across the river.

A 83.   Alessandro Vellutello. *Dante con l'espositione di C. Landino, et di Alessandro Vellutello, sopra la sua comedia dell'Inferno, del Purgatorio, et del Paradiso*. Edited by Francesco Sansovino Fiorentino. Venice: Sessa, 1564.

Commentary of 1544. The author notes previous interpretations of Charon as time, death, and free will. He presents the boat as "l'humana fragilità condotta da Charon, cioè, dal uitio, Che batte col remo qualunque s'adagia, cioè, il quale molesta con lo stimolo delle tentationi ciascun che tarda a uolerlo seguire" (p. 22ʳ).

A 84.   Giovan Battista Gelli. "Lettura seconda sopra lo Inferno." In *Commento edito e inedito sopra la Divina Commedia*, edited by Carlo Negroni. Florence: Bocca, 1887.

Lectures delivered at the Accademia Fiorentina from 1541–1563, with regularity after 1553. In *lezione settima* Gelli cites Virgil as Dante's model, notes Diodorus Siculus's euhemeristic explanation of Charon's origin, and refers to various allegorizations of the figure as *il tempo*, *la consuetudine*, and *il libero arbitrio* (pp. 261–262). He analyzes Dante's episode in its entirety, holding that Charon or Virgil carried Dante in his sleep to the boat for passage ("Lezione ottava," p. 274).

A 85.   Bernardino Daniello. *Dante con l'espositione di M. Bernardino Daniello da Lucca*. Venice: Pietro da Fino, 1568.

Commentary written before 1560. Daniello refers to Virgil often and compares the embarcation scene to the souls arriving in purgatory. Dante crosses not by way of Charon's boat but aided by divine grace.

A 86.   Ludovico Castelvetro. *Sposizione di Ludovico Castelvetro a XXIX canti dell'Inferno dantesco*. Edited by Giovanni Franciosi. Modena, 1886.

Commentary written in 1567. Castelvetro believes that Dante crosses by way of Charon's boat. Castelvetro compares Virgil's portrayal of Charon to Dante's.

A 87.   Galileo Galilei. *Studi sulla Divina Commedia di Galileo Galilei, Vincenzo Borghini ed altri*. Edited by Ottavio Gigli. Florence: Le Monnier, 1855.

Treatise written in 1588. In the "lezioni di G. G. intorno la figura, sito, e grandezza dell'Inferno di Dante Alighieri," Charon is mentioned as he appears in Dante. In his similar dialogue, Antonio Manetti does not refer to the boatman.

Mythographers and Iconographers

A 88. Giovanni Boccaccio. *De genealogia deorum gentilium.* Edited by V. Romano. Bari: Laterza, 1951. Also translated in the Cinquecento by Giuseppe Betussi. Venice: Lorenzini, 1564.

As well as in the discussion in Book 1, chap. 33, Boccaccio asks in Book 14 why it should be evil to listen to poets, if painters, within churches, are allowed to paint pictures of Cerberus guarding the gates of Pluto and of Charon on the Acheron.

A 89. Coluccio Salutati. *De laboribus Herculis,* Book 4, treatise 2, chaps. 7–8. Edited by B. L. Ullman. Zurich: Thesauri Mundi, 1951.

A 90. Niccolò Perotti. *Cornucopiae, siue linguae latinae commentarij diligentissime recogniti: atque ex archetypo emendati.* Venice: Aldus, 1527.

Latin glossary written before 1480 (Perotti's death). The compiler discusses the infernal rivers (cols. 574–576), quotes Seneca and Servius, and notes that "Graeci enim Χαιρὸν laetum dicunt. Praeterea acheronta alium inferorum amnem commemorant dictum ab α priuattiua particula, et χαίρων, quod significat gaudens, quasi sine gaudio" (col. 574, 35–37).

A 91. Cristoforo Landino. *Interpretationes in P. Vergilium.* In *Vergilii P. Maronis opera cum tribus commentariis Servii, Donati, et Christophori L.* Venetiis: Liga Boaria, 1483.

Allegorical-philosophical interpretation of the *Aeneid,* pub. in 1483. Charon represents free will.

A 92. Andrea Alciati. *Emblema* 154: "De morte, et amore." In *Diverse imprese accomodate a diuerse moralità.* Lyon: Rovillio, 1551.

Emblem book, published in 1531 in an illustrated edition. This emblem was accompanied by a Latin poem by Guicciardini, which was translated with a reference to Charon in some instances. See *Emblemi di Andrea Alciati dal latino nel vulgare italiano ridotto* (Padua: Tozzi, 1626), Emblem 155. Since Love and Death have changed weapons, "Ecco ama il Vecchio . . . / . . . il Vecchio, c'hora essere in barca / Di Charonte deurebbe in Acheronte" (p. 229).

A 93. Lilio Gregorio Giraldi. *De deis gentium, varia et multiplex historia.* In *Operum quae extant ominum . . . Tomi duo.* Basel: Guarinum, 1580.

Mythological compendium, first published in 1548. Giraldi identifies Charon as a god of the underworld, "dictus per antiphrasin, quasi Acharon" (p. 207). He quotes *Aeneid* 6, cites Juvenal, and refers to the myth of Hercules' descent found "in Orpheo" (i.e., as referred to by Servius).

————. *De Sepulchris et vario sepelendi ritu.* In *Operum* cited.

Treatise. Giraldi traces the myth of Charon and the obol to Egyptian burial rites (p. 653).

A 94. Natale Conti. *Mythologiae, sive explicationum fabularum libri decem.* Venice: Comin da Trino, 1568.

There is an illustration of Charon in the 1616 editions (Verona: Petrum Antonium Berno and Padua: Tozzi).

A 95. Vincenzo Cartari. *Le Imagini con la spositione de i dei de gli antichi.* Venice: Marcolini, 1556.

Emblem book and artist's manual, first published in 1556 with no illustrations. Cartari refers to Virgil's description of Aeneas's descent but calls Charon a demon "con occhi di bragia" (p. lix^r). Relevant passages in Virgil and Seneca are translated into Italian, and Boccaccio's allegorization is discussed. For two illustrations of Charon rowing his boat, see the 1603 edition (Padua: Tozzi), p. 281 and the 1647 edition (Venice: Tomasini), p. 164.

A 96. Giovanni Fabrini. *L'Opere di Virgilio Mantovano commentate in lingua volgare toscana, da Giovanni Fabrini da Figline*. Venice: Heredi di Marchiò Sessa, 1604.
Commentary published as early as 1576. Influenced by Landino, Fabrini interprets Charon as *libero arbitrio*, as *l'anima*, and as *gratia*. He allegorizes all aspects of Charon, including his appearance, his boat, and the crossing (pp. 159^v–160^r).

Dialogues

A 97. Rinuccio of Arezzo. *Charon sive contemplantes*. See "De Rinucio Aretino graecarum literarum interprete," by D. P. Lockwood. In *Harvard Studies in Classical Philology* 24 (1913): 51–109. Compare "The First Edition of Lucian of Samosata," by E. P. Goldschmidt. In *Journal of the Warburg and Courtauld Institutes* 14 (1951): 7–20.
Translation of Lucian's dialogue ca. 1441–1442.

A 98. Leon Battista Alberti. *Momus o del principe*. Edited by Giuseppe Martini. Bologna: Zanichelli, 1942. For a brief discussion of the work, see Christopher Robinson, *Lucian and His Influence in Europe*, (Chapel Hill: University of North Carolina Press, 1979) pp. 92–94.
Lucianic and mythological narrative in dialogue form written in Latin before 1450. Charon visits the earth despite having been counseled against it by the dead souls who know how terrible life can be. A dead philosopher Gelasto, lacking an obol, agrees to guide Charon in return for free passage across the Acheron. On their voyage to the earth they discuss a variety of philosophical questions, and Charon relates an allegorical creation myth. The two also speak of the theater, which Charon ridicules. When they run into pirates on returning to Hades by sea, Charon flees to a swamp where he hides in the mud.

A 99. Maffeo Vegio of Lodi. *Palinurus*. See Goldschmidt, as cited in A 97, and Christopher Robinson, A 98; pp. 84–85. This dialogue was also published as *De felicitate et miseria* in the *Opera* of Vegio that appeared in Lodi in 1613.
Lucianic dialogue, printed in the first edition of Lucian (in Latin) published in Rome, 1470 (first Greek edition, Florence, 1496). Charon and Palinurus discuss the miseries of all estates on earth.

A 100. Christophorus Persona. *Tyrannus, seu trajectus*. See Goldschmidt, as cited in A 97. Quattrocento translation of Lucian's dialogue. Persona lived from 1416–1486.

A 101. Giovanni Pontano. *Charon*. In *I dialoghi*, edited by Carmelo Previtera. Florence: Sansoni, 1943.

A 102. Antonio Cammelli. *Dialogo Lucianeo*. In *I sonetti faceti di Antonio Cammelli*, edited by Erasmo Percopo. Naples: Jovene 1908.
Lucianic dialogue written before 1502. The interlocutors are Charon, Archidrommo, Spirito del Pistoia, and Pluto. Charon marvels that the author (Spirito del Pistoia) has descended into the underworld alone. The spirit, who like Menippus lacks a fare, in response, satirizes the folly of other men whom he avoids. Among those mocked are astrologers and alchemists. Charon philosophizes at length near the end of the dialogue. Pontanian reminiscences appear throughout.

A 103. Desiderius Erasmus. *Colloquia*: "Charon." In *Erasmi omnia opera*. Basel: J. Froben et N. Episcopius, 1540.
Lucianic dialogue in Latin, first published in 1529. The Dutch humanist applies Lucian's satire to current ethics and ecclesiastical practices. Charon's boat, old and rotten, has just sunk, leaving the boatman wet and the souls swimming like frogs. A new ship is needed, but all the wood of the Elysian forests has been used to burn heretics.

A 104. Niccolò Franco. *Dialoghi piacevoli*. Venice: Giunti, 1541.

A 105. "Canzone: Dialogo tra Caronte e un Gesuita." Vicenza: Biblioteca Bertoliana 23 (1, 3, 31) fol. 141, as cited in G. Mazzatinti. *Inventari dei manoscritti delle biblioteche d'Italia*.

Unseen dialogue of uncertain date, possibly of the Seicento (?). The work begins "Caronte. Chi è che chiama?"

Miscellaneous Prose Forms: Treaties, Narratives, Short
Stories, Anecdotes, and Satires

A 106. Armannino Giudice. *Fiorita*. In *Manuale della letteratura italiana*, vol. 1, by Alessandro D'Ancona and Orazio Bacci. Florence: Barbèra, 1925, pp. 494–495. See also "La fiorita di Armannino Giudice," by G. Mazzatinti. *Giornale di filologia romanza* 3 (1880): 1–55.

A 107. Andrea Da Barberino. *Storia di Ugone d'Alvernia volgarizzato nel sec. XIV da Andrea Da Barberino*. Scelta di curiosità letterarie inedite o rare dal secolo xiii al xvii, vol. 190. Bologna: Romagnoli, 1882. Compare A 5.

Trecento narrative. Book 4 begins with the note: "Ora qui comincia il libro quarto d'Ugone, quando entrò nello 'nferno; e prima in versi trinari. Ed è composizione di Giovanni Vincenzio isterliano di detto Ugo" (vol. 2, p. 83). Accompanied by Enea and San Guglielmo, Ugo sees "uno vecchio tutto canuto, e aveva gli occhi di fuoco" (p. 98).

A 108. Lorenzo Valla. *De voluptate* 2. 38. *Il piacere*. Translated into Italian and edited by Vincenzo Grillo. Naples: Pironti, 1948.

Treatise in the form of a dialogue, published in 1431. Valla employs Lucretius's words in order to say that there is no heaven nor hell, no Cerberus nor Charon.

A 109. Lodovico Carbone. *Facezie di Lodovico Carbone Ferrarese*. Edited by Abd-El-Kader Salza. Livorno: Giusti, 1900, pp. 35–36.

Humorous anecdote, compiled ca. 1466–1471. This collection of short stories and jests contained originally 130 *facezie* of which 108 are extant; no. 44 reads: "Fo una usanza apresso gli antichi, che quando uno moriva, gli metevano in bocha uno quatrino per pagare il nolo de la nave a Charone nuchiero de la Stygia palude, la qual bisognava passare cadauna anima, secondo il credere loro. Uno philosopho morendo non si ricordò di questo quatrino; e venendo al passagio e dimandandogli Charone il quatrino, rispose: Gli philosophi non si curano di queste cosse. Disse Charone: Non sapevi tu l'usanza? Ben sa', ch'io la sapeva, disse il philosopho; ma volivi tu, ch'io stesse per un quatrin di morire?"

A 110. Pandolfo Collenuccio. *Apologo intitolato specchio d'Esopo*. In *Operette morali, poesie latine e volgari*, edited by Alfredo Saviotti. Bari: Laterza, 1929.

Treatise in dialogue form, written in italian after 1497 and before the death of Collenuccio in 1504. Luciano says that he is unable to interpret a response by Esopo despite the fact that "ho veduto assai del mondo e insino con Caronte, infernal dio, ho già avuto commercio" (p. 98).

A 111. Iacopo Caviceo. *Libro del peregrino*. In *Opere di Iacopo Sannazaro . . . e di Iacopo Caviceo*, edited by Enrico Carrara. Turin: Unione tipografico-editrice Torinese, 1952.

A 112. Leone Ebreo. *Dialogi di amore, composti per Leone Medico, di natione hebreo, et dipoi fatto christiano*. Venice: Aldus, 1541.

Philosophical dialogues, published posthumously in 1535. In Dialogue 2 (p. 34^v) Philone refers to his death as that time when Charonte will bear Philone across the river of oblivion. On p. 67^v, we read that Charonte is a son of Erebus. He is allegorized as "l'obliuione, che seguita alla corruttione, e perdita dell'acquistato."

A 113. Agnolo Firenzuola. *L'asino d'oro di Lucio Apuleio volgarizzato da Agnolo Firenzuola*. Milan: Doelli, 1863.

Translation of Apuleius's prose narrative, first published in 1550. In the Psyche myth, Firenzuola elaborates on Charon's avarice and the necessity of paying for passage (Libro 6, p. 139).

A 114. Giorgio Vasari. *Vite de' più eccellenti pittori scultori ed architettori*. 2d ed. 1568. In *Cinquecento minore*, edited by R. Scrivano. Bologna: Zanichelli, 1966.

Art-historical biographical treatise, first published in 1550; 2d ed. enlarged in 1568. In discussing Michelangelo's life and work, Vasari speaks of the *Last Judgment* and the *terribilità* of the figures therein. Michelangelo's great labors are evident in all parts, "come chiaramente ancora nella barca di Caronte di dimostra, il quale con attitudine disperata l'anime tirate dai diavoli giù nella barca batte col remo, ad imitazione di quello che espresse il suo famigliarissimo Dante. . . ."

A 115. Anton Francesco Doni. *Libro secondo dei Mondi del Doni, chiamati i sette inferni*. In *Mondi celesti, terrestri, et infernali, de gli Academici Pellegrini composti da M. Anton Francesco Doni Fiorentino*. Vicenza: Heredi di Perin Libar, 1597.

A 116. Benvenuto Cellini. *Vita* 1. 84–85. Edited by Ettore Camesasca. Milan: Rizzoli, 1954.

Autobiography, composed between 1558–1566. Cellini, ill with a bad fever, imagines that *un vecchio terribile* comes to drag him by force "in una sua barca grandissima." A bystander, Mattio Franzesi, comments that Cellini has read Dante. The artist describes how the old man takes him by the arm and drags him to the *spaventata barca* into which he is thrown. Thought dead, Cellini wakes up, and his friends arrive to see "il miracolo de il resuscitato morto" (1. 84). In another dream soon after, Cellini sees the old man ready to bind him with ropes, but the terrifying *vecchio* is driven off with an ax by Cellini's companion Felice.

A 117. Giordano Bruno. *La cena delle ceneri* and *De la causa, principio et uno:* "Proemiale epistola." In *Dialoghi italiani: "Dialoghi metafisici" e "dialoghi morali" nuovamente ristampati con note da G. Gentile*, edited by G. Aquilecchia. 3d ed. Florence: Sansoni, 1958.

Moral dialogues, pub. in London in 1584–1585. In the *Cena*, Bruno relates a night trip across London in which he sees a ferryman like Charon. Quoting Virgil, he combines pagan (Charon) and biblical (the ark of Noah) images. In the *Causa*, Bruno notes that fear of the terrors of death and avaricious Charon are vain and poison the sweetness of life.

A 118. Giambattista Basile. *Lo cunto de li cunti* 5. 5. In *Trattatisti e narratori del Seicento*, edited by Ezio Raimondi. Milan: Ricciardi, 1960.

Short story in Neapolitan dialect, first published posthumously in 1634–1636. Charon appears in an image where an evil woman is cast into a fire. She will make cinders to warm (the water to wash) Charon's breeches—"Tanto la strascinavano a fare cennerale pe lo scaudatiello de le brache de Caronte."

Secondary Sources

Albizzati, Carlo. "Qualche nota su demoni etruschi." *Dessertazioni della Pontificia Accademia Romana di Archeologia*, 2d ser. 15 (1921): 233–268.

Allacci, Leone. *Drammaturgia*. Edited by Francesco Bernardelli. Turin: Bottega di Erasmo, 1961.

Allen, Don Cameron. *Mysteriously Meant; the Rediscovery of Pagan Symbolism and Allegorical Interpretation in the Renaissance*. Baltimore: Johns Hopkins Press, 1970.

Allen, James Turney. *The Greek Theater of the Fifth Century Before Christ.* Berkeley and Los Angeles: University of California Press, 1920

Allen, T. W. *Homer: The Origins and the Transmission.* Oxford: Clarendon, 1924.

Allinson, Francis G. *Lucian: Satirist and Artist.* Boston: Jones, 1926.

Ambrosch, Iulius Athanasius. *De Charonte etrusco commentatio antiquaria.* Vratislava: Aderholz, 1837.

Arrowsmith, William. "Introduction to Heracles." In *The Complete Greek Tragedies*, vol. 5, edited by David Grene and Richmond Lattimore. New York: Random House, Modern Library, n.d.

Austin, R. C. "*Aeneid* VI, 384–476." *Proceedings of the Virgil Society* 8 (1968–1969): 51–60.

Bailey, Cyril. *Religion in Virgil.* Oxford: Clarendon, 1935.

Baldello, Pio. "Caronte." In *Dizionario letterario Bompiani delle opere e dei personaggi di tutti i tempi e di tutte le letterature*, vol. 3. Milan: Bompiani, 1947, pp. 153–154.

Baldwin, Barry. *Studies in Lucian.* Toronto: Hakkert, 1973.

Banti, Luisa. "Il culto dei morti nella Roma antichissima." *Studi italiani di filologia classica* 7 (1929): 171–198.

————. *Etruscan Cities and Their Culture.* Translated by Erika Bizzarri. London: Batsford, 1973.

Bàrberi Squarotti, Giorgio. "L'inferno del 'Baldus.'" In *Cultura letteraria e tradizione popolare in Teofilo Folengo: Atti del Convegno di studi promosso dall'Accademia Virgiliana e dal Comitato Mantova-Padania*, edited by E. Bonora and M. Chiesa. Milan: Feltrinelli, 1979, pp. 153–185.

Barlow, Shirley A. *The Imagery of Euripides: A Study in the Dramatic Use of Pictorial Language.* London: Methuen, 1971.

Barrett, Anthony A. "The Topography of the Gnat's Descent." *Classical Journal* 65 (1970): 255–257.

Beazley, J. D. *Attic Red-Figure Vase-Painters.* 3 vols. 2d ed. Oxford: Clarendon, 1963.

Becker, Ernest J. *A Contribution to the Comparative Study of the Medieval Visions of Heaven and Hell.* Baltimore: Murphy, 1899.

Bellinger, Alfred R. *Lucian's Dramatic Technique.* New Haven: Yale University Press, 1928.

Belloni, Antonio. *Gli epigoni della Gerusalemme liberata.* Padua: Draghi, 1893.

————. *Storia dei generi letterari italiani: Il poema epico e mitologico.* Milan: Vallardi, n.d.

————. *Una visione dell'oltretomba contemporanea alla dantesca.* Pistoia: Pacinotti, 1921.

Bergadani, Roberto. "Una commedia politica del sec. XVI." *Giornale storico della letteratura italiana* 104 (1934): 64–80.

Bertana, Emilio. *Storia dei generi letterari italiani: La tragedia.* Milan: Vallardi, n.d.

Biagi, Guido. *La "Divina Comedia" nella figurazione artistica e nel secolare commento.* Turin: Union Tipografico-editrice torinese, 1921.

Bieber, Margarete. *The History of the Greek and Roman Theater.* Princeton: Princeton University Press, 1939. 2d ed. enlarged 1961.

Bigi, Emilio. "L'episodio di Caronte nel 'Baldus' e il metodo del Folengo." In *Studi in memoria di Luigi Russo.* Pisa: Nistri-Lischi, 1974, pp. 32–49.

Binet, Benjamin. *Traité historique des dieux et des démons du paganisme.* Delft: Andre Voorstad, 1969.

Blanc, L. G. *Saggio di una interpretazione filologica di parecchi passi oscuri e controversi della Divina Commedia.* Trieste: Coen, 1865.

Boas, G. *Essays in Primitivism and Related Ideas in the Middle Ages.* Baltimore: Johns Hopkins Press, 1948.

Bompaire, Jacques. *Lucien écrivain: Imitation et création.* Paris: De Boccard, 1958.

Bonilla y San Martín, Adolfo. *El mito de Psyquis: Un cuento de niños, una tradición simbólica y un estudio sobre el problema fundamental de la filosofia.* Barcelona: Henrich, 1908.

Bonnet, Hans. "jenseitsfährmann." In *Reallexikon der ägyptischen Religionsgeschichte.* Berlin: De Gruyter, 1952.

Born, L. K. "Ovid and Allegory." *Speculum* 9 (1943): 362–379.

Borza, Horatiu. "Le mythe de l'obole à Charon et le symbolisme actuel de la monnaie dans le cercueil." *Orbis: Bulletin International de Documentation Linguistique* 4 (1955): 134–148.

Bosanquet, R. C. "Some Early Funeral Lecythoi." *Journal of Hellenic Studies* 19 (1890): 169–184.

Boswell, C. S. *An Irish Precursor of Dante: A Study on the Vision of Heaven and Hell ascribed to the Eighth-Century Irish Saint Adamnán, with Translations of the Irish Text.* London: Nutt, 1908.

Boulanger, André. *Orphée, rapports de l'orphisme et du christianisme.* Paris: Rieder, 1925.

Boutemy, André. "Une version médiévale inconnue de la légende d'Orphée." In *Homages à Joseph Bidez et à Franz Cumont.* Brussels: Latomus, n.d. but 1949, pp. 43–70.

Bowra, C. M. "Earlier Lyric and Elegiac Poetry." In *New Chapters in the History of Greek Literature,* edited by J. U. Powell. 3d ser. Oxford: Clarendon, 1933, pp. 1–67.

————. *Greek Lyric Poetry from Alcman to Simonides.* 2d ed. Oxford: Clarendon, 1962.

————. "Orpheus and Eurydice." *Classical Quarterly* 2 (1952): 113–126.

————. *Pindar.* Oxford: Clarendon, 1964.

————. *Tradition and Design in the Iliad.* 1930. Reprint Oxford: Clarendon, 1963.

Branca, Vittore, ed. *Dizionario critico della letteratura italiana.* Turin: Union tipografico-editrice torinese, 1974.

Brandon, S. G. F. *The Judgment of the Dead: An Historical and Comparative Study of the Idea of a "Post-Mortem" Judgment in the Major Religions.* London: Weidenfeld and Nicolson, 1967.

————. *Man and His Destiny in the Great Religions: An Historical and Comparative Study Containing the Wilde Lectures in Natural and Comparative Religion Delivered in the University of Oxford, 1954–1957.* Manchester: Manchester University Press, 1962.

Brown, Robert J. *The Myth of Kirke: Including the Visit of Odysseus to the Shades. An Homerik Study.* London: Longmans, Green and Co., 1883.

————. *Semitic Influence in Hellenic Mythology.* London: Williams and Norgate, 1898.

Brunel, Pierre. *L'évocation des morts et la descente aux Enfers: Homère—Virgile—Dante —Claudel.* Paris: Société d'édition d'enseignement supérieur, 1974.

Buck, August. *Der Orpheus-Mythos in der Italianischen Renaissance.* Krefeld: Scherpe, 1961.

Buonomo, Salvatore. *Il passaggio dell'Acheronte: Contributo all'esegesi dantesca.* Naples: Pironti, 1950.

Butler, H. E. *The Sixth Book of the Aeneid with Introduction and Notes.* Oxford: Blackwell, 1920.

Cabañas, Pablo. *El mito de Orfeo en la literatura española.* Madrid: Consejo Superior de Investigaciones Científicas, Instituto Miguel de Cervantes de Filología Hispánica, 1948.

Caccia, Natale. *Luciano nel quattrocento in Italia: le rappresentazioni e le figurazioni.* Florence: Tip. Galileiana, 1907.

_____ . *Note su la fortuna di Luciano nel Rinascimento, le versioni e i dialoghi satirici di Erasmo de Rotterdam e di Ulrico Hutten.* Milan: C. Signorelli, 1914.

Camps, W. A. "The Role of the Sixth Book in the *Aeneid.*" *Proceedings of the Virgil Society* 7 (1967–1968): 22–30.

Cartault, Augustin. *L'art de Virgile dans l'Énéide.* Paris: Presses Universitaires de France, 1926.

Cary, A. L. M. "The Appearance of Charon in the *Frogs.*" *Classical Review* 51 (1937): 52–53.

Caster, Marcel. *Lucien et la pensée religieuse de son temps.* Paris: Les Belles Lettres, 1937.

Cavallari, Elisabeth. *La fortuna di Dante nel Trecento.* Florence: F. Perrella, 1921.

Chaintraine, Pierre. *Dictionnaire étymologique de la langue grecque: Histoire des mots.* Paris: Klincksieck, 1968.

Chiappelli, A. *Il Canto III dell'Inferno letto da Alessandro Chiappelli nella "Casa di Dante" in Roma.* Florence: Sansoni, n.d. but 1914.

Christiansen, Reidar. *The Dead and the Living.* Oslo: Studia Norvegica, 1946.

Coffey, Michael. "Seneca, Tragedies 1922–1955." *Lustrum* 2 (1957): 113–186.

Coffin, H. C. "Allegorical Interpretation of Vergil with Special Reference to Fulgentius." *The Classical Weekly* 15, no. 5 (1921): 33–35.

Collignon, Maxime. "Essai sur les monuments grecs et romains relatifs au mythe de Psyché." *Bibliothèque des écoles françaises d'Athènes et de Rome* 2 (Paris: Thorin, 1877): 285–443.

Collins, Stanley Tate. *The Interpretation of Vergil with Special Reference to Macrobius.* Oxford: Blackwell's, 1909.

Comparetti, D. *Virgilio nel medioevo.* Livorno: Francesco Vigo, 1872.

Conington, John, and Nettleship, Henry. *The Works of Virgil with a commentary.* Vol. 1, *Eclogues and Georgics.* Revised by F. Haverfield. Hildesheim: Georg Olms, 1963.

Conway, Robert Seymour. *The Etruscan Influence on Roman Religion.* Manchester: Manchester University Press, 1932.

_____ . "The Growth of the Underworld." In *New Studies of a Great Inheritance.* London: Murray, 1921.

_____ . *The Structure of the Sixth Book of the Aeneid.* Cambridge: Cambridge University Press, 1913. Also in *Essays and Studies Presented to William Ridgeway,* edited by E. C. Quiggin. Freeport, New York: Books for Libraries Press, 1913, 1966 reprint, pp. 1–26.

_____ . *The Vergilian Age: Vergil as a Student of Homer.* Cambridge, Mass.: Harvard University Press, 1931.

Cook, Arthur Bernard. *Zeus: A Study in Ancient Religion*, vol. 2. Cambridge: Cambridge University Press, 1914, p. 641.

Cooke, J. D. "Euhemerism: a Medieval Interpretation of Classical Paganism." *Speculum* 2 (1927): 396–410.

Cordié, Carlo. "Quadriregio." In *Dizionario letterario Bompiani: Opere,* vol. 6. Milan: Bompiani, 1957.

Cornford, Francis MacDonald. *Greek Religious Thought from Homer to the Age of Alexander.* New York: Dutton, 1923.

————. *The Origin of Attic Comedy.* Cambridge: Cambridge University Press, 1934.

Couat, Auguste. *Alexandrian Poetry under the First Three Ptolemies, 324–222 B.C.* Translated by James Loeb. 1st ed. in French 1882. London: Heinemann, 1931.

Courcelle, Pierre. "Interpretations néo-platonisantes du livre VI de l'Enéide." In *Recherches sur la tradition platonicienne: Sept exposés.* Geneva: Fondation Hardt pour l'étude de l'antiquité classique, 1955, 1957.

————. *Les Lettres grecques en occident de Macrobe à Cassiodore.* Paris: De Boccard, 1943.

————. "Les pères de l'église devant les enfers virgiliens." *Archives d'historie doctrinale et littéraire du Moyen-Age* 30 (1955): 5–74.

Croiset, Maurice. *Essai sur la vie et les oeuvres de Lucien.* Paris: Hachette, 1882.

Crusius, G. C. *A Complete Greek and English Lexicon for the Poems of Homer, and the Homeridae.* Translated by Henry Smith. Revised by Thomas K. Arnold. 1st ed. in German 1835. London: Rivingtons, 1868.

Cumont, Franz. *After Life in Roman Paganism.* 1922. Reprint New York: Dover, 1959.

————. "Lucrèce et le symbolisme pythagoricien des enfers." *Revue de Philologie* 44 (1920): 229–240.

————. *Recherches sur le symbolisme funéraire des Romains.* Paris: Geuthner, 1942.

Curtius, Ernst Robert. *European Literature and the Latin Middle Ages.* Translated by Willard R. Trask. 1st ed. in German 1948. Reprint. New York: Pantheon Books, 1948. 1st ed., *Europäische Literatur und lateinisches Mittelalter.* Berne: A. Francke AG Verlag, 1948. New York: Harper and Row, Harper Torchbooks, 1963.

Dale, Amy M., ed. *Alcestis.* Oxford: Clarendon, 1954.

————. *The Lyric Meters of Greek Drama.* 2d ed. Cambridge: Cambridge University Press, 1968.

Dana, H. W. L. Medieval Visions of the Other World." Ph.D. diss. Harvard University, 1910.

D'Ancona, Alessandro. "Personaggi divini e diabolici nelle Sacre Rappresentazioni." In *Origini del teatro in Italia: Studi sulle sacre rappresentazioni,* vol. 2. Florence: Le Monnier, 1877, pp. 1–13.

————. *I precursori di Dante.* 1874. Reprint Florence: Sansoni, 1916.

Daremberg, Charles, and Saglio, Edmund. Dictionnaire des antiquités grecques et romains, vol. 1. Paris: Hachette, 1887.

Davison, J. A. *From Archilochus to Pindar.* London: MacMillan, 1968.

De Bartholomaeis, Vincenzo. *Origini della poesia drammatica italiana.* 2d ed. Turin: Società Editrice Internazionale, 1952.

Decharme, P. *Mythologie de la Grèce antique.* 3d ed. Paris: Garnier Frères, n.d. (1912).

Della Corte, Andrea. *Drammi per musica dal Rinuccini allo Zeno*. Turin: Union tipografico-editrice torinese, 1958.

Del Lungo, Isidoro, *Florentia: Uomini e cose del Quattrocento*. Florence: Barbèra, 1897.

Del Noce, G. "L'ironia di Caronte." In *Giornale Dantesco*, diretto da G. L. Passerini, 2 (Venice, 1895): 1–18.

De Maria, Ugo. *Dell' "Asino d'oro" di Apuleio e di varie sue imitazioni nella nostra letteratura*. Rome: Pistolesi, 1901.

_____. *La favola di Amore e Psiche nella letteratura e nell'arte italiana con appendice di cose inedite*. Bologna: Zanichelli, 1899.

De Ruyt, Franz. *Charun: Démon étrusque de la mort*. Rome: Institut Historique Belge, 1934.

_____. "Le Thanatos d'Euripide et le Charun étrusque." *L'Antiquité Classique* 1 (1932): 70–73.

Didron, Adolphe Napoleon. *Christian Iconography: The History of Christian Art in the Middle Ages*. Translated by E. J. Millington. 1886. Reprint New York: Ungar, 1965.

Dieterich, Albrecht. *Nekyia: Beiträge zur Erklärung der neuentdeckten Petrusapokalypse*. Leipzig: Teubner, 1893.

Dod, Marcus. *Forerunners of Dante: An Account of Some of the More Important Visions of the Unseen World, from the Earliest Times*. Edinburgh: Clark, 1903.

Doglio, Federico. *Il teatro tragico italiano: Storia e testi del teatro tragico in Italia*. Bologna: Guanda, 1960.

Doppioni, Lino. *Virgilio nell'arte e nel pensiero di Seneca*. Florence: Tip. Fiorenza, 1939.

Dover, K. J. *Aristophanic Comedy*. Berkeley and Los Angeles: University of California Press, 1972.

Dräseke, Johannes, "Byzantinische Hadesfahrten." *Neue Jahrbücher für das klassische Altertum* 15 (1912): 343–366.

Ducati, P. "Osservazioni di demonologia etrusca." *Rendiconti dei Lincei, Scienze morali* 24 (1916): 515–550.

Duckworth, George E. *The Complete Roman Drama*. New York: Random House, 1942.

Duhn, Friedrich K. von. "Charondarstellungen." *Archäologische Zeitung* 43 (1885): 12–24.

Durkheim, Emile. *The Elementary Forms of the Religious Life*. Translated by Joseph Ward Swain. 1915. Reprint New York: The Free Press, 1968.

Ebeling, E. "Eine Beschreibung der Unterwelt in sumerischer Sprache." *Orientalia* 18 (1949): 285–287.

Edelstein, Ludwig, and Edelstein, Emma J. *Asclepius: A Collection and Interpretation of the Testimonies*. Baltimore: Johns Hopkins Press, 1945.

Egilsrud, Johan S. *Les "Dialogues des morts" dans les littératures française, allemande et anglaise (1644–1789)*. Paris: L'Entente linotypiste, 1934.

Ehrenberg, Victor. *The People of Aristophanes: A Sociology of Old Attic Comedy*. 1943. Reprint London: Methuen, 1974.

Ellis, Hilda R. *The Road to Hel: A Study of the Conception of the Dead in Old Norse Literature*. Cambridge: Cambridge University Press, 1943.

Else, Gerald F. *The Origin and Early Form of Greek Tragedy*. 1965. Reprint New York: Norton, 1972.

Engels, Joseph. *Études sur l'Ovide Moralisé*. Groningen: Wolters, 1945.

Faccioli, Emilio. *Il teatro italiano*. Vol. 1, *Dalle origini al Quattrocento*. Turin: Einaudi, 1975.

Farnell, Lewis R. *Greece and Babylon: A Comparative Sketch of Mesopotamia, Anatolia and Hellenic Religions*. Edinburgh: Clark, 1911.

Feldman, Burton, and Richardson, Robert D. *The Rise of Modern Mythology 1680–1860*. Bloomington: Indiana University Press, 1975.

Félice, Philippe de. *L'autre monde, mythes et légends: Le purgatoire de Saint Patrice*. Paris: Champion, 1906.

Ferguson, John. *A Companion to Greek Tragedy*. Austin: University of Texas Press, 1972.

Ferrari, O. "Il mondo degli inferi in Claudiano." *Athenaeum* 4 (1916): 335–338 ff.

Flickinger, Roy C. *The Greek Theater and Its Drama*. 4th ed. Chicago: University of Chicago Press, 1936.

Fòffano, Francesco. *Storia dei generi letterari italiani: Il poema cavalleresco*. Milan: Vallardi, n.d.

Forrers, Robert. "Charon." In *Reallexikon der prähistorischen, klassischen und frühchristlichen Altertümer*. Stuttgart: Spemann, 1907.

Fox, William Sherwood. *The Mythology of all Races: Greek and Roman*. Edited by Louis Herbert Gray. Boston: Marshall Jones, 1916.

Fransoni, Domingo. "L'inferno di Virgilio e di Dante: confronto." In *Studi vari sulla Divina Commedia di Dante Alighieri*, con prefazione di Enrico Fani. Florence: Patronato, 1887.

Friedel, Victor Henri, and Meyer, Kuno. *La vision de Tondale: Textes français, anglo-normand et irlandais*. Paris, 1907.

Friedman, J. B. *Orpheus in the Middle Ages*. Cambridge, Mass.: Harvard University Press, 1970.

Frisk, Hjalmar. *Griechisches Etymologisches Wörterbuch*. Heidelberg: Carl Winter, 1970.

Frova, Arturo. *L'Arte Etrusca*. Milan: Garzanti, 1957.

_____. "La morte e l'oltretomba nell'arte etrusca." *Rinnovamento* 30 (1908): 95–131.

Funaioli, Gino. *Allegorie Virgiliane*. Naples: Perella, 1920.

_____. "Dante e il mondo antico." In *Medioevo e Rinascimento: Studi in onore di Bruno Nardi*, vol. 1. Florence: Sansoni, 1955, pp. 321–338.

_____. *Esegesi Virgiliana antica. Prolegomeni alla edizione del commento di Giunio Filargirio e di Tito Gallo*. Milan: Vita e Pensiero, 1930.

_____. *Lezioni di letteratura latina tenute da Gino Funaioli: L'oltretomba di Virgilio*. Rome: Castellani, 1948.

_____. *L'Oltretomba nell'Eneide di Virgilio: Saggio critico*. Palermo: Sandron, 1924.

_____. *Studi di letteratura antica: Spiriti e forme, figure e problemi delle letterature classiche*. Bologna: Zanichelli, 1946.

_____. *Vergilio nel medio evo*. Turin: Chiantire, 1932.

Furno, Enrico. "Il dramma allegorico nelle origini del teatro italiano." In *Studi di letteratura italiana diretti da Erasmo Pèrcopo* 11, 12 (1915, 1922): 276–432, 1–117.

Furtwängler, Adolf. "Charon, eine altattische Malerei." *Archiv für Religionswissenschaft* 8 (1904–1905): 191–202.

Galletier, E. *Étude sur la poésie funéraire romaine d'après les inscriptions*. Paris: Hachette, 1922.

Gayley, Charles Mills. *The Classic Myths in English Literature, based chiefly on Bullfinch's "Age of Fable."* Boston: Ginn, 1904.

Germain, Gabriel. *Homer*. Translated by Richard Howard. New York: Grove Press, 1960.

Ghisoni, Paul. *Eschatologie infernale*. Paris: Editions du Vieux Colombier, 1962.

Giglioli, Giulio Quirino. *L'arte etrusca*. Milan: Fratelli Treves, 1935.

_____ . *Storia delle religioni*. Vol. 1, *La religione degli etruschi*. Edited by Pietro Tacchi Venturi. 3d ed. Turin: Unione tipografico-editrice torinese, 1949.

_____ . "Le tombe etrusche." In *Meraviglie del Passato*. Part 1, *Monumenti dell'antichità*, edited by Fausto Franco and Ferdinando Reggiori, vol. 2. 2d ed. Milan: Mondadori, 1945, pp. 227–232.

Gimorri, Adriano. *Caron dimonio: Contributo all'interpretazione del III canto dell'Inferno*. Modena: Tip. Immacolata Concezione, 1921.

Glover, T. R. *Virgil*. 2d ed. London: Methuen, 1912.

Goldschmidt, E. P. "The first Edition of Lucian of Samosata." *Journal of the Warburg and Courtauld Institutes* 14 (1951): 7–20.

Gow, A. S. F. *Theocritus*. Edited with translation and commentary. Cambridge: Cambridge University Press, 1952.

Grant, Michael. *Myths of the Greeks and Romans*. Cleveland and New York: World Publishing Co., Meridian Books, 1965.

Graves, Robert. *The Golden Ass of Apuleius*. New York: Pocket Books, 1953.

_____ . *The Greek Myths*. 2 vols. 1955. Reprint Baltimore: Penguin Books, 1955.

Greene, Thomas M. *The Descent from Heaven: A Study in Epic Continuity*. 1963. Reprint New Haven: Yale University Press, 1975.

Greenwood, L. H. G. *Aspects of Euripidean Tragedy*. Cambridge: Cambridge University Press, 1953.

Grendler, Paul F. *Critics of the Italian World (1530–1560): Anton Francesco Doni, Nicolò Franco, and Ortensio Lando*. Madison: University of Wisconsin Press, 1969.

Grimal, Pierre. *Dictionnaire de la mythologie grecque et romaine*. 3d ed. Paris: Presses Universitaires De France, 1963.

Grinsell, L.V. "The Ferryman and His Fee: A Study in Ethnology, Archaeology, and Tradition." *Folklore: Being the Transactions of the Folk-Lore Society* 68 (1957): 257–269.

Grube, G. M. A. *The Drama of Euripides*. London: Methuen, 1941.

Guerber, H. A. *Myths of Greece and Rome*. New York: American Book Co., 1893.

Hadas, Moses. *A History of Greek Literature*. 1950. Reprint New York: Columbia University Press, 1962.

Haley, Herman Wadsworth. *The Alcestis of Euripides*. Boston: Ginn, 1898.

Hammond, M. "*Concilia deorum* from Homer through Milton." *Studies in Philology* 30 (1933): 1–16.

Harrison, Jane. *Prolegomena to the Study of Greek Religion*. 1903. Reprint New York: Meridian Books, 1960.

Hatzantonis, Emmanuel. "Variations of a Virgilian Theme in Dante and Lope de Vega." *Pacific Coast Philology* 6 (1971): 35–42.

Headlam, W. "Ghost-Raising, Magic, and the Underworld." *Classical Review* 16 (1902): 52–61.

Helm, Rudolf. *Lucian und Menipp.* Leipzig: Teubner, 1906.

Henry, James. *Aeneidea, or Critical, Exegetical, and Aesthetical Remarks on the Aeneis.* Dublin: Trustees of the Author, 1889.

Hermann, Alfred. "Charon." In *Reallexikon für Antike und Christentum*, vol. 2. Stuttgart: Hiersemann, 1954, pp. 1040–1061.

Herrick, Marvin T. *Italian Comedy in the Renaissance.* 1960. Reprint Urbana: University of Illinois Press, 1966.

————. *Italian Tragedy in the Renaissance.* Urbana: University of Illinois Press, 1965.

Herzog, Rudolf. "Charon und Kerberos." *Archiv für Religionswissenschaft* 10 (1907): 222–224.

Hesseling, D. C. "Le Charos byzantin." *Neophilologus* 16 (1931): 131–135.

————. *Charos, ein Beitrag zur Kenntnis des neugriechen Volksglaubens.* Leiden, 1897.

————. "Charos rediens." *Byzantinische Zeitschrift* 30 (1930): 186–191.

Hewitt, Joseph William. "The Humor of the Greek Anthology." *Classical Journal* 17 (1921): 66–76.

————. "A Second Century Voltaire." *Classical Journal* 20 (1924): 132–142.

Highet, Gilbert. *The Classical Tradition: Greek and Roman Influences on Western Literature.* Oxford: Clarendon, 1951.

Hodges, John C. "Two Otherworld Stories." *Modern Language Notes* 32 (1917): 280–284.

Hoorn, G. van. "Charon, Charu, Kerberos." *Mélanges Bijvanck. Nederlands Kunsthistorisch Jaarboek* (in honorem A. W. Bijvanck) 5 (1954): 141–150.

Hudson-Williams, T. *Early Greek Elegy: The Elegiac Fragments of Callinus, Archilochus, Mimnermus, Tyrtaeus, Solon, Xenophanes, and Others.* London: Milford, 1926.

Hughes, Thiry. "Homero y el perro de Hades (*Iliade* VIII, 368 y *Odisea* XI, 623)." *Emerita, Revista de Lingüística y Filología Clásica* 42 (1974): 103–108.

Hungur, Herbert. "Charon." In *Lexikon der Griechischen und Römischen Mythologie.* Vienna: Hollinek, 1959.

Jaconianni, Luca. *Il Caronte di Dante paragonato col Caronte di Virgilio e con quello di un altro autore moderno.* Florence: Arte della Stampa, 1888.

Jacquot, Jean, Ed. *Les fêtes de la Renaissance.* Vol. 2, *Fêtes et cérémonies au temps de Charles Quint*, plate 45, no. 1. Paris: Centre national de la recherche scientifique, 1960.

Jannaco, Carmine. *Storia letteraria d'Italia: Il Seicento.* 2d ed. Milan: Vallardi, 1966.

Jeremias, Alfred. *The Babylonian Conception of Heaven and Hell.* Translated by J. Hutchinson. London: Nutt, 1902.

Jevons, Frank Byron. *A History of Greek Literature.* New York: Charles Scribner's Sons, 1886.

Jones, J. W. Jr. "Allegorical Interpretation in Servius." *Classical Journal* 56 (1961): 217–226.

Jones, Julian Ward, and Jones, Elizabeth Frances. *The Commentary on the First Six Books of the Aeneid of Vergil Commonly Attributed to Bernardus Silvestris: A New Critical Edition.* Lincoln: University of Nebraska Press, 1977.

Jorio, Virginia. "L'autenticità della tragedia *Hercules Oetaeus* di Seneca." *Rivista Indo-Greco-Italica* 20 (1936): 1–59.

Keener, Frederick M. *English Dialogues of the Dead: A Critical History, An Anthology, and A Check List.* New York: Columbia University Press, 1973.

Kirk, G. S. *Myth: Its Meaning and Functions in Ancient and Other Cultures.* 1970. Reprint Berkeley and Los Angeles: University of California Press, 1974.

Kitto, H. D. F. *Form and Meaning in Drama: A Study of Six Greek Plays and of Hamlet.* 1956. Reprint New York: Barnes and Noble, 1959.

————. *Greek Tragedy: A Literary Study.* 1939. Reprint London: Methuen, 1961.

Knight, W. F. Jackson. *Elysion: On Ancient Greek and Roman Beliefs Concerning a Life After Death.* New York: Barnes and Noble, 1970.

————. *Roman Vergil.* 1944. Reprint Middlesex: Penguin, 1966.

Körte, Alfred. *Hellenistic Poetry.* Translated by Jacob Hammer and Moses Hadas. New York: Columbia University Press, 1929.

Kohler, Kaufmann. *Heaven and Hell in Comparative Religion with Special Reference to Dante's Divine Comedy.* New York: MacMillan, 1923.

Kretzmann, P. E. "A Few Notes on 'The Harrowing of Hell.'" *Modern Philology* 13 (1915): 49–51.

Krüger, Gustav. *Charon und Thanatos.* Berlin: Unger, 1866.

Kyriazopoulou, Panayota. "Le personnage de Charon de la Grèce ancienne à la Grèce moderne." Diss., Université de Paris, 1950.

Lang, Andrew. *Myth, Ritual and Religion.* 1887. Reprint London: Longmans, Green and Co., 1913.

Lattimore, Richmond. *The Poetry of Greek Tragedy.* Baltimore: Johns Hopkins Press, 1958.

————. *Story Patterns in Greek Tragedy.* Ann Arbor: University of Michigan Press, 1969.

————. *Themes in Greek and Latin Epitaphs.* Urbana: University of Illinois Press, 1942.

Laurie, Helen C. R. "A New Look at the Marvellous in *Eneas*, and Its Influence." *Romania* 91 (Paris, 1970): 48–74.

Lawson, John Cuthbert. *Modern Greek Folklore and Ancient Greek Religion: A Study in Survivals.* Cambridge: Cambridge University Press, 1910.

Lazar, Moshé. "L'enfer et les diables dans le théatre médiéval italien." In *Studi di filologia romanza offerti a Silvio Pellegrini.* Padua: Liviana, 1971.

Lee, M. Owen. "Orpheus and Eurydice." *Classica et Mediaevalia* 26 (1967): 402–412.

Le Roy, Alexander. *The Religion of the Primitives.* 1922. Reprint New York: Negro Universities Press, 1969.

Lever, Katherine. *The Art of Greek Comedy.* London: Methuen, 1956.

Linforth, Ivan M. *The Arts of Orpheus.* Berkeley and Los Angeles: University of California Press, 1941.

Lockwood, D. P. "De Rinucio Aretino graecarum literarum interprete." *Harvard Studies in Classical Philology* 24 (1913): 51–109.

Lucas, D. W. *The Greek Tragic Poets.* 2d ed. Aberdeen: Cohen and West, 1959.

Macchioro, Vittorio D. "La Catabasi Orfica." *Classical Philology* 23 (1928): 239–249.

MacCulloch, John Arnott. *Early Christian Visions of the Other-World.* Edinburgh: Clark, 1912.

_____ . *The Harrowing of Hell: A Comparative Study of an Early Christian Doctrine*. Edinburgh: Clark, 1930.

MacKail, J.W. *The Aeneid*. Edited with introduction and commentary. Oxford: Clarendon, 1930.

_____ . *Virgil's Works*. New York: Random House, Modern Library, 1950.

MacKay, L. A. "Three Levels of Meaning in *Aeneid* VI." *Transactions and Proceedings of the American Philological Association* 86 (1955): 180–189.

MacKenzie, Donald A. "Il viaggio dell'anima nel paradiso egizio." In *Meraviglie del Passato*. Part 1, *Monumenti dell'antichità*. Edited by F. Franco and F. Reggiori. 2d ed. Milan, 1954.

Maïer, Ida. *Ange Politien: La formation d'un poète humaniste* (1469–1480). Geneva: Librairie Droz, 1966.

Marrone, Luigi. "Il mito di Orfeo nella drammatica italiana." *Studi di letteratura italiana diretti da Erasmo Pèrcopo* 12 (1922): 119–259.

Maspero, G. *Bibliothèque egyptologique*. Vol. 1, *Études de mythologie et d'archéologie égyptiennes*. Paris: Leroux, 1893.

_____ . *Les inscriptions des pyramides de Saqqarah*. Paris: Libraire Émile Bouillon, 1894.

_____ . *Life in Ancient Egypt and Assyria*. New York and London: Appleton, 1914.

May, Esther Isopel, ed. *The "De Jerusalem Celesti" and the "De Babilonia Infernali" of Fra Giacomino da Verona*. Florence: Le Monnier, 1930.

Mazzatinti, G. "La *Fiorita* di Armannino Giudice." *Giornale di filologia romanza* 3, no. 6 (1880): 1–55.

Mazzoli, Giancarlo. *Seneca e la poesia*. Milan: Ceschina, 1970.

Mazzoni, Francesco. "Il Canto III dell'Inferno." In *Saggio di un nuovo commento alla Divina Commedia. Inferno: Canti I–III*. Florence: Sansoni, 1967, pp. 315–455.

Mazzoni, Guido. *Almae luces malae cruces: Studii danteschi*. Bologna: Zanichelli, 1941.

McCarthy, Barbara P. "Lucian and Menippus." *Yale Classical Studies* 4 (1934): 3–55.

McLeod, W. "The Wooden Horse and Charon's Barque: Inconsistency in Virgil's 'Vivid Particularization.' " *Phoenix* 24 (1970): 144–149.

Melzi, Robert C. *Castelvetro's Annotations to The Inferno: A New Perspective in Sixteenth-Century Criticism*. Hague: Mouton, 1966.

Meyer, Kuno, ed. and trans. *The Voyage of Bran Son of Febal to the Land of the Living . . . with an Essay upon the Irish Vision of the Happy Otherworld and the Celtic Doctrine of Rebirth by Alfred Nutt*. 2 vols. London: Grimm Library, 1895–1897.

Mézières, M. "De fluminibus inferorum." Diss., Université de Paris. 1853.

Michalopoulos, Andre. "The Classical Tradition." Translated by Benjamin Jowett. In *Greek and Byzantine Studies* 1 (July, 1958): 1–8.

Mitchell, T. *The Frogs of Aristophanes, with notes*. London: John Murray, 1839.

Monnier, Jean "La descente aux enfers: Étude de pensée religieuse, d'art et de littérature." Diss., Université de Paris, 1904.

Moore, Edward. *Studies in Dante. First Series: Scripture and Classical Authors in Dante*. Oxford: Clarendon, 1896.

Moore, Olin H. "The Infernal Council." *Modern Philology* 16 (1918): 169–193 and 19 (1921): 47–64.

Moravcsik, Gyula. "Il Caronte bizantino." *Studi bizantini e neoellenici* 3 (1931): 45–68.

Motto, Anna Lydia, and Clark, John R. "*Descensus Averno* in Seneca's Epistle 55." Classical Journal 68 (1972–1973): 193–198.

Murray, Gilbert. *Aristophanes: A Study*. New York: Russell and Russell, 1964.

Musumarra, Carmelo. *La poesia tragica italiana nel Rinascimento*. Florence: Olschki, 1972.

Mylonas, George E. "Homeric and Mycenaean Burial Customs." *American Journal of Archaeology* 52 (1948): 56–81.

Neri, Achille. "Gli 'intermezzi' del 'Pastor fido.'" *Giornale storico della letteratura italiana* 11 (1888): 405–415.

Neri, Ferdinando. *La tragedia italiana del Cinquecento*. Florence: Galletti e Cocci, 1904.

Nicosia, Paolo. "Batte col remo qualunque s'adagia. *Inf.* III, 111." In *Alla ricerca della coerenza: Saggi di esegèsi dantesca*. Florence: D'Anna, 1967, pp. 67–81.

————. "Il Caronte dantesco ovvero della frodolenza demoniaca (III, 82–99, 127–129)." In *Dieci saggi sull'Inferno dantesco*. Florence: D'Anna, 1969.

Nilsson, Martin P. *Homer and Mycenae*. London: Methuen, 1933.

————. *The Minoan-Mycenaean Religion and Its Survival in Greek Religion*. 2d ed. New York: Biblo and Tannen, 1971.

————. *The Mycenaean Origin of Greek Mythology*. Berkeley and Los Angeles: University of California Press, 1932.

Nogara, B. *Gli Etruschi e la loro civiltà*. Milan: Hoepli, 1933.

Norden, Eduard. *Aeneis Buch VI*. Leipzig: Teubner, 1934.

Norwood, Frances. "The Tripartite Eschatology of *Aeneid* 6." *Classical Philology* 49 (1954): 15–26.

Norword, Gilbert. *Essays on Euripidean Drama*. London: Cambridge: Cambridge University Press, 1954.

————. *Greek Comedy*. 1931. Reprint New York: Hill and Wang, 1963.

Olrik, Axel. *The Heroic Legends of Denmark*. Translated by L. M. Hollander. New York, 1919.

Os, Arnold B. van. *Religious Visions: The Development of the Eschatological Elements in Mediaeval English Religious Literature*. Amsterdam: H. J. Paris, 1932.

Osgood, Charles G. *Boccaccio on Poetry: Being the preface and the Fourteenth and Fifteenth Books of Boccaccio's Genealogia Deorum Gentilium*. New York: Liberal Arts Press, 1930.

Otis, Brooks. "Three Problems of *Aeneid* 6." *Transactions and Proceedings of the American Philological Association* 90 (1959): 165–179.

————. *Virgil: A Study in Civilized Poetry*. 1964. Reprint Oxford: Clarendon, 1967.

Owen, Douglas D. R. *The Vision of Hell: Infernal Journeys in Medieval French Literature*. 1970. Reprint New York: Barnes and Noble, 1971.

Oxford Classical Dictionary. 2d ed. Edited by N. G. L. Hammond and H. H. Scullard. 1970. Reprint Oxford: Clarendon, 1976.

Padoan, G. *Il Canto III dell'Inferno*. Florence: Le Monnier, 1967.

Page, Denys. *The Homeric Odyssey*. Oxford: Clarendon, 1955.

————. "Multiple Authorship in the *Iliad*." In *History and the Homeric Iliad*. Berkeley and Los Angeles: University of California Press, 1963.

————. *Sappho and Alcaeus: An Introduction to the Study of Ancient Lesbian Poetry*. 1955. Reprint Oxford: Clarendon, 1959.

Pallottino, Massimo. *Art of the Etruscans*. New York: Vanguard, 1955.

Palm, E. W. "A Classical Reference in *The Divina Commedia.*" *Italica* 22 (1945): 59–61.

Panofsky, Erwin. *Studies in Iconology: Humanistic Themes in the Art of the Renaissance.* New York: Oxford University Press, 1939, Harper and Row, 1967.

Parenti, G. "Caracciolo, Pietro Antonio." In *Dizionario biografico degli italiani,* vol. 19. Rome: Istituto della Enciclopedia Italiana, 1976, pp. 442–443.

Pascal, Carlo. *Le credenze d'oltretomba nelle opere letterarie dell'antichità classica.* Catania: Battiato, 1912.

_____. *Il mondo infernale nell'antica commedia attica.* Mantua: Mondovi, 1910.

Patch, Howard Rollin. *The Other World According to Descriptions in Medieval Literature.* Cambridge, Mass.: Harvard University Press, 1950.

Pavry, Jal Dastur Cursetju. *The Zoroastrian Doctrine of a Future Life: From Death to the Individual Judgment.* New York: Columbia University Press, 1926.

Pernety, Antonio-Giuseppe (Antoine-Joseph). *Le favole egizie e greche svelate e riportate ad un unico fondamento.* Translated by G. Catinella. 1st ed. in French, 1758. Bari: Laterza and Polo, 1936.

Pfiffig, Ambros Josef. *Religio Etrusca.* Graz: Akademische Druck-und Verlagsanstalt, 1975.

Pharr, Clyde. *Vergil's Aeneid, Books I–VI.* Lexington, Mass.: Heath, 1964.

Pickard-Cambridge, Sir Arthur. *Dithyramb, Tragedy and Comedy.* 2d ed. Revised by T. B. L. Webster. Oxford: Clarendon, 1968.

_____. *The Dramatic Festivals of Athens.* Revised by John Gould and D. M. Lewis. 2d ed. Oxford: Clarendon, 1968.

Platnauer, Maurice, ed. *Fifty Years (and Twelve) of Classical Scholarship: Being "Fifty Years of Classical Scholarship" Revised with Appendices.* Oxford: Blackwell, 1968.

Politis, Linos. "Venezia come centro della stampa e della diffusione della prima letteratura neoellenica." In *Venezia. Centro di mediazione tra oriente e occidente (Secoli XV–XVI). Aspetti e problemi.* Edited by H.-G. Beck, M. Manoussacas, and N. Agostino Pertusi. Florence: Olschki, 1977.

Pottier, Edmond. *Étude sur les lécythes blacs attiques à représentations funéraires.* Paris: Fontemoing, 1883.

Prato, Stanislao. *Caronte e la barca dei morti nell'Eneide, nella Divina Commedia e nella tradizione popolare neo-greca.* Florence: Olschki, 1895.

Propp, Vladimir. *Morphology of the Folktale.* Translated by Lawrence Scott. 2d ed. Revised and edited by Louis A. Wagner. Austin: University of Texas Press, 1968.

Putnam, Emily James. "Lucian the Sophist." *Classical Philology* 4 (1909): 162–177.

Putnam, Michael C. J. *The Poetry of the Aeneid.* Cambridge, Mass.: Harvard University Press, 1965.

Quinn, Kenneth. *Virgil's Aeneid: A Critical Description.* Ann Arbor: University of Michigan Press, 1968. 2d printing with corrections 1969.

Quint, David. "Epic Tradition and *Inferno* IX." *Dante Studies* 93 (1975): 201–207.

Raby, F. J. E. *A History of Christian-Latin Poetry: From the Beginnings to the Close of the Middle Ages.* Oxford: Clarendon, 1927.

_____. *A History of Secular Latin Poetry in the Middle Ages.* 2 vols. Oxford: Clarendon, 1934.

Radermacher, Ludwig. *Das Jenseits im Mythos der Hellenen.* Bonn: Marcus and Weber, 1903.

Regenbogen, Otto. "Schmerz und Tod in den Tragödien Senecas." In *Kleine Schriften.* Munich: Beck, 1961, pp. 409–462.

Renda, Umberto, and Operti, Piero. *Dizionario storico della letteratura italiana.* Nuova edizione sul testo originale di Vittorio Turri. 4th ed. Turin: Paravia, 1959.

Ricci, Corrado. *La Divina Commedia di Dante Alighieri nell'arte del Cinquecento.* Milan: Fratelli Treves, 1908.

Richmond, J. A. "Charon's Boat." *Classical Quarterly* 19 (1969): 388.

Ridgeway, William. *The Origin of Tragedy with Special Reference to the Greek Tragedians.* 1910. Reprint New York: Blom, 1966.

Riezler, Walter. *Weisgrundige attische Lekythen.* Munich: Bruckmann, 1914.

Robert, Carl. *Thanatos.* Berlin: Reimer, 1879.

_____ . "Zu Sophokles' Ixneytai." *Hermes* 47 (1912): 536–561.

Robinson, Christopher. *Lucian and His Influence in Europe.* Chapel Hill: University of North Carolina Press, 1979.

Rocco, Serafino. *Il mito di Caronte nell'arte e nella letteratura.* Turin: Clausen, 1897.

_____ . "Sull'origine del mito di Caronte." *Rivista di storia antica* 2 (1897): 73–81.

Rogers, Benjamin Bickley. *The Comedies of Aristophanes*, vol. 5. 2d ed. London: Bell, 1919.

Rohde, Erwin. *Psyche: The Cult of Souls and Belief in Immortality among the Greeks.* Translated by W. B. Hillis. 1925. Reprint New York: Harper and Row, 1966.

Ronconi, Alessandro. "Per Dante interprete dei poeti latini." *Studi danteschi* 41 (1964): 5–44.

Roscher, Wilhelm Heinrich. "Charon." In *Ausführliches Lexikon der Griechischen und Römischen Mythologie*, vol. 1. Leipzig: Teubner, 1884–1886, pp. 883–886.

Rose, H. J. *A Handbook of Greek Mythology.* 1928. Reprint London: Methuen, 1974.

Rosenmeyer, Thomas G. *The Masks of Tragedy: Essays on Six Greek Dramas.* Austin: University of Texas Press, 1963.

_____ . *The Green Cabinet: Theocritus and the European Pastoral Lyric.* Berkeley and Los Angeles: University of California Press, 1969.

Rossi, Salvatore. *Il tipo e l'ufficio del Charun etrusco.* Messina: D'Amico, 1900. Also in *Atti della R. Accademia Peloritana* 15 (1900–1901): 65–103.

Sabbadini, Remigio. *Le scoperte dei codici latini e greci ne' secoli XIV e XV.* 1914. Reprint Florence: Sansoni, 1967.

Saglio, E. "Charon (Χάρων)." In *Dictionnaire des antiquités grecques et romaines*, edited by Daremberg et Saglio, vol. 1, part 2. Paris: Librairie Hachette, 1887, pp. 1099–1101.

Sapegno, Natalino. *Il Canto III dell'Inferno.* Florence: Le Monnier, 1960.

_____ . *Storia letteraria d'Italia: Il Trecento.* 3d ed. Milan: Vallardi, 1966.

Sartori, P. "Die Totenmünze." *Archiv für Religionswissenschaft* 2 (1899): 205–225.

Savage, J. J. "The Medieval Tradition of Cerberus." *Traditio* 7 (1949–1951): 405–410.

Schmidt, B. "Charon." *Archiv für Religionswissenschaft* 25 (1927): 79–82.

Schmidt, Joël. "Charon." In *Dictionnaire de la mythologie grecque et romaine.* Paris: Librairie Larousse, 1965.

Schoell, Franck L. "Les mythologistes italiens de la Renaissance et la poésie élisabéthaine." *Revue de Littérature Comparée* 4 (1924): 1–25.

Schwartz, Jacques. *Biographie de Lucien de Samosate.* Brussels: Latomus, 1965.

Sebeok, Thomas A. *Myth: A Symposium*. Bloomington: Indiana University Press, 1968.

Segal, Charles P. "The Character and Cults of Dionysus and the Unity of the *Frogs.*" *Harvard Studies in Classical Philology* 65 (1961): 207–242.

_____. "Like Winds and Winged Dream: A Note on Virgil's Development." *Classical Journal* 69 (1973): 97–101.

Seymour, St. John D. *Irish Visions of the Other-World*. London: Society for Promoting Christian Knowledge, 1930.

Seznec, Jean. *The Survival of the Pagan Gods: The Mythological Tradition and Its Place in Renaissance Humanism and Art*. Translated by Barbara F. Sessions. 1st ed. in French 1940. New York: Pantheon Books, 1953.

Sibzehner-Vivanti, Giorgio. *Dizionario della Divina Commedia*. Edited by Michele Messina. 1st ed. Florence: Olschki, 1954. Reprint Milan: Feltrinelli, 1965.

Sirago, Vito. "Il testo di Virgilio nell'espressione di Dante." *Lettere Italiane* 2 (1950): 145–163.

Smyth, Herbert Weir. *Greek Melic Poets*. MacMillan, 1900.

Solerti, Angelo. *Gli albori del melodramma*. 3 vols. Milan: Sandron, 1904.

_____. *Le origini del melodramma*. Turin: Fratelli Bocca, 1903.

_____. "Precedenti del Melodramma." *Rivista musicale italiana* 10 (1903): 207–233.

Solmsen, Friedrich. "The Erinys in Aischylos' *Septem.*" *Transactions and Proceedings of the American Philological Association* 68 (1937): 197–211.

_____. *Hesiod and Aeschylus*. 1949. Reprint Ithaca: Cornell University Press, 1967.

_____. "The World of the Dead in Book 6 of the *Aeneid.*" *Classical Philology* 67 (1972): 31–41.

Spongano, Raffaele. *Nozioni ed esempi di metrica italiana*. Bologna: Pàtron, 1966.

Stanford, W. B., ed. *The Odyssey of Homer*. Vol. 1, *Books I–XII*. London: MacMillan, 1947.

_____. *The Ulysses Theme: A Study in the Adaptability of a Traditonal Hero*. 2d ed. Ann Arbor: University of Michigan Press, 1968.

Stella, Luigia Achillea. *Il poema di Ulisse*. Florence: La Nuova Italia, 1955.

Stuart, Donald Clive. "The Stage Setting of Hell and the Iconography of the Middle Ages." *Romanic Review* 4 (1913): 330–342.

Sullivan, F. A. "Charon, the Ferryman of the Dead." *Classical Journal* 46 (1950): 11–17.

Tackaberry, William Hamilton. *Lucian's Relation to Plato and the Post-Aristotelian Philosophers*. Toronto: University of Toronto Press, 1930.

Terpening, Ronnie H. "The Representation of Charon in the *Siglo de Oro:* Innovation in the Myth of Orpheus." *Kentucky Romance Quarterly* 22 (1975): 345–364.

Thomson, J. A. K. *Studies in the Odyssey*. Oxford: Clarendon, 1914.

Toffanin, Giuseppe. *Storia letteraria d'Italia: Il Cinquecento*. 7th ed. Milan: Vallardi, 1965.

Tollman, J. A. *A Study of the Sepulchral Inscriptions in Buecheler's "Carmina Epigraphica Latina.*" Chicago: Chicago University Press, 1910.

Tommaseo, Niccolò. *La Commedia di Dante Allighieri col comento di Niccolò Tommaseo*. Venice: Gondoliere, 1837.

Torraca, Francesco. *Studi di storia letteraria napoletana*. Livorno: Francesco Vigo, 1884.

Toynbee, Paget. *Dante Alighieri: His Life and Works*. Edited by Charles S. Singleton. 1900. Reprint New York: Harper and Row, 1965.

Turcan, R. "La catabase orphique du papyrus de Bologne." *Revue de l'Histoire des Religions* 150 (1956): 136–172.

Turner, Ralph V. "*Descendit ad Inferos*: Medieval Views on Christ's Descent into Hell and Savation of the Ancient Just." *Journal of the History of Ideas* 27 (1966): 173–194.

Tylor, Edward B. *Primitive Culture: Researches into the Development of Mythology, Philosphy, Religion, Language, Art, and Custom*. London: John Murray, 1920.

―――――. *Religion in Primitive Culture*. Introduction by Paul Radin. 1871. Reprint New York: Harper and Row, 1958.

―――――. *Researches into the Early History of Mankind and the Development of Civilization*. 2d ed. London: John Murray, 1870.

Valk, Van der. *Beiträge zur Nekyia*. Leiden: Kampen Kok, 1935.

Vazzana, Steno. *Il Canto III dell'Inferno*. Turin: Società Editrice Internationale, 1965.

Verrall, A. W. *Essays on Four Plays of Euripides*. Cambridge: Cambridge University Press, 1905.

―――――. *Euripides the Rationalist*. Cambridge: Cambridge University Press, 1895.

―――――. ed. *The Seven against Thebes of Aeschylus*. London: MacMillan, 1887.

Vickers, Brian. *Towards Greek Tragedy: Drama, Myth, Society*. London: Longman, 1973.

Vogel, E. *Biblioteca della musica vocale italiana di genere profano stampata dal 1500 al 1700*. Berlin: Aack, 1892.

Warden, John, ed. *Orpheus: The Metamorphoses of a Myth*. Toronto: University of Toronto Press, 1982.

Waser, Otto. "Charon." In *Real-Encyclopädie der classischen Altertumswissenschaft*, edited by Pauly-Wissowa-(Kroll), vol. 3. Stuttgart: Metzlerscher, 1898 ff, pp. 2176–2180.

―――――. *Charon, Charun, Charos. Mythologisch-archäologische Monographie*. Berlin: Weidmannsche Buchhandlung, 1898.

Webster, T. B. L. *Greek Theater Production*. London: Methuen, 1956.

―――――. *Hellenistic Poetry and Art*. London: Methuen, 1964.

Weinberg, Bernard. *A History of Literary Criticism in the Italian Renaissance*. Chicago: University of Chicago Press, 1961. Midway reprint 1974.

Weitzmann, Kurt. *Greek Mythology in Byzantine Art*. Princeton: Princeton University Press, 1951.

―――――. "The Survival of Mythological Representation in Early Christian and Byzantine Art." *Dumbarton Oaks Papers* 14 (1960): 43–68.

Whitman, Cedric H. *Aristophanes and the Comic Hero*. Cambridge, Mass.: Harvard University Press, 1964.

―――――. *Homer and the Heroic Tradition*. New York: Norton, 1958.

Whitmore, Charles Edward. *The Supernatural in Tragedy*. Cambridge, Mass.: Harvard University Press, 1915.

Wilkin, D. " 'Holà Charon!' " *Bibliothèque d'Humanisme et Renaissance* 42 (1980): 115–121.

Wilamowitz-Moellendorff, Ulrich von. "Charon und Charongroschen." *Hermes* 34 (1899): 227–230.

Williams, R. D. *The Aeneid of Virgil, Books 1–6*. London: MacMillan, 1972.

————. "The Sixth Book of the *Aeneid.*" Greece and Rome 2d ser. 11 (1964): 48–63.

————. "Virgil's underworld—the opening scenes (*Aen.* 6. 268–416)." *Proceedings of the Virgil Society* 10 (1970–1971): 1–7.

Willson, Elizabeth. *The Middle English Legends of Visits to the Other World and Their Relation to the Metrical Romances.* Chicago: University of Chicago Press, 1917.

Wind, Edgar. *Pagan Mysteries in the Renaissance.* Revised edition. Middlesex: Penguin, 1967.

Windekens, A. J. van. "Sur les noms de quelques figures divines ou mythiques grecques." *Beiträge zur Namenforschung* 9 (Heidelberg, 1958): 161–172.

Wright, Thomas. *Saint Patrick's Purgatory: An Essay on the Legends of Purgatory, Hell, and Paradise Current during the Middle Ages.* London: Russel Smith, 1844.

————. ed. *Saint Brandan: A Medieval Legend of the Sea, in English Verse and Prose.* London: Percy Society, 1842.

Wright, Wilmer C. *A Short History of Greek Literature from Homer to Julian.* New York: American Book Co., 1907.

Zabughin, Vladimiro. *Dante e l'iconografia d'oltretomba: arte bizantina, romanica, gotica.* Milan: Alfieri, 1929.

————. *L'oltretomba classico medievale dantesco nel Rinascimento. Parte prima: Italia, secoli XIV e XV.* Florence: Olschki, 1922.

————. *Vergilio nel rinascimento italiano da Dante a Torquato Tasso.* 2 vols. Bologna: Zanichelli, 1921–1923.

Zardo, A. *Il Canto III dell'Inferno letto da Antonio Zardo nella Sala di Dante in Orsanmichele.* Florence: Sansoni, 1901.

Index